CLASSICS
OF
SEMIOTICS

TOPICS IN CONTEMPORARY SEMIOTICS

Series Editors: Thomas A. Sebeok and Jean Umiker-Sebeok
Indiana University

CLASSICS
OF
SEMIOTICS

Edited by
Martin Krampen
Hochschule der Künste
Berlin, Federal Republic of Germany

Klaus Oehler
Universität Hamburg
Hamburg, Federal Republic of Germany

Roland Posner
Technische Universität Berlin
Berlin, Federal Republic of Germany

Thomas A. Sebeok
Indiana University
Bloomington, Indiana

Thure von Uexküll
Universität Ulm
Ulm, Federal Republic of Germany

PLENUM PRESS • NEW YORK AND LONDON

Library of Congress Cataloging in Publication Data

Welt als Zeichen. English
  Classics of semiotics.

  (Topics in contemporary semiotics)
  Translation of: Die Welt als Zeichen.
  Includes bibliographical references and index.
  1. Semiotics. I. Krampen, Martin, date. II. Title. III. Series.
  P99.W3813   1987   001.51   87-2283
  ISBN 0-306-42321-9

This volume is a translation of *Die Welt als Zeichen: Klassiker der modernen Semiotik,*
edited by Martin Krampen, Klaus Oehler, Roland Posner, and Thure von Uexküll, published
in 1981 by Wolf Jobst Siedler Verlag GmbH, Berlin. Chapters 5, 6, and 8 were originally
published in English, and it is the original versions of Chapters 5 and 6 and a revised
version of Chapter 8 that are reprinted herein, with permission of the copyright holders.

German edition © 1981 by Wolf Jobst Siedler Verlag GmbH, Berlin

© 1987 Plenum Press, New York
A Division of Plenum Publishing Corporation
233 Spring Street, New York, N.Y. 10013

All rights reserved

Printed in the United States of America

Contributors

EUGEN BAER, Department of Philosophy, Hobart and William Smith Colleges, Geneva, New York

UMBERTO ECO, Department of Semiotics, University of Bologna, Bologna, Italy

MARTIN KRAMPEN, Professor of Theory of Visual Communication, University of the Arts, Berlin, West Germany

KLAUS OEHLER, Department of Philosophy, University of Hamburg, Hamburg, West Germany

ROLAND POSNER, Department of Linguistics, Technical University of Berlin, Berlin, West Germany, and Netherlands Institute for Advanced Study in the Humanities and Social Sciences, Wassenaar, The Netherlands

THOMAS A. SEBEOK, Director of the Research Center for Language and Semiotic Studies, Indiana University, Bloomington, Indiana

JÜRGEN TRABANT, Department of Romance Languages, Free University of Berlin, Berlin, West Germany

THURE VON UEXKÜLL, Professor Emeritus of Internal Medicine and Psychosomatics, University of Ulm, Ulm West Germany

Foreword to the English Language Edition

The idea for this book grew out of discussions held by its four editors when they were preparing the first issue of the journal *Zeitschrift für Semiotik*, which appeared in 1979. The German edition of the book was then published in 1981, coedited by Krampen, Oehler, Posner, and Thure von Uexküll. The chapters by Oehler on Peirce, Posner on Morris, Krampen on Saussure, and Thure von Uexküll on Jakob von Uexküll were enlarged versions of articles that had appeared in *Zeitschrift für Semiotik* 1 (1979), while those by Eco on Jackobson and by Sebeok on Bühler had previously been published in English, as had also an early version of Baer on Sebeok.

The German edition was such a success that I decided to arrange for an English language edition; this book is the result. The chapters by Oehler, Posner, Krampen, Trabant, and Thure von Uexküll have been variously translated, either by the author himself or under his immediate supervision in Germany; the chapter by Baer has been translated by Felicia Kruse of Pennsylvania State University, with Professor Baer's approval; the two chapters which appeared originally in English are reprinted from their respective sources with minor emendations. The Preface has been reformulated by Posner, on the basis of a translation by Iris Smith (Indiana University) of the original German Preface. The German language glossary, which was rendered into English in Bloomington under my close supervision, incorporates extensive English citations restored from the respective first-hand sources, while the Index of Names has been adapted by me from the German version to conform to the text as printed here.

Because of the limited space provided by a volume of this kind, not all semioticians, even from among those who can justifiably be considered progenitors of this discipline, could be included. Indeed, there could well have been chapters on Barthes, Cassirer, Eco, Greimas, Thom—to name only a few of the moderns. Happily, I can assure the reader that plans are afoot to provide just such a complement to the contents of this book. Posner and I have already discussed further volumes, comparable in size, which would both expand contemporary scope and extent historical depth, thus transforming this book into the first of an eventual series.

THOMAS A. SEBEOK

Preface

This book is designed to usher the reader into the realm of semiotic studies. It analyzes the most important approaches to semiotics as they have developed over the last hundred years out of philosophy, linguistics, psychology, and biology.

As a science of sign processes, semiotics investigates all types of communication and information exchange among human beings, animals, plants, internal systems of organisms, and machines. Thus it encompasses most of the subject areas of the arts and the social sciences, as well as those of biology and medicine. Semiotic inquiry into the conditions, functions, and structures of sign processes is older than any one scientific discipline. As a result, it is able to make the underlying unity of these disciplines apparent once again without impairing their function as specializations.

Semiotics is, above all, research into the theoretical foundations of sign-oriented disciplines: that is, it is *General Semiotics*. Under the name of *Zeichenlehre*, it has been pursued in the German-speaking countries since the age of the Enlightenment. During the nineteenth century, the systematic inquiry into the functioning of signs was superseded by historical investigations into the origins of signs. This opposition was overcome in the first half of the twentieth century by American *Semiotic* as well as by various directions of European structuralism working in the tradition of *Semiology*. Present-day General Semiotics builds on all these developments.

Research into the theoretical foundations of the sign-oriented disciplines can reach its goal only by contrasting detailed analyses of as many types of sign processes as possible. This is done in *Comparative Semiotics*, which has set itself the task of studying the sign processes in all life systems on the basis of a uniform methodology and terminology. In this way, sign processes are made comparable also for practical purposes.

The optimization of sign use in practical situations is the task of *Applied Semiotics*. It explores and helps us to perform sign processes in different channels (person to person, person to animal, person to machine, organism to organism, within the organism, within the machine, etc.), in different modalities (the senses, nerves, enzymes), in different codes (e.g. the genetic code, the dances of bees, bird song, traffic signs, human sign languages), in various media (written texts, phonograph recordings, radio broadcasts, television), and in diverse genres of communication (commanding, narration, argumentation, flirting, etc.). The usefulness of semiotics in the production, reception, and analysis of cultural phenomena of all kinds has often been proven and is generally recognized. Semiotics is applied to sight and sound as well as to smell, taste, and touch in bodily communication and food-culture, industrial design and shaping of the environment; to acoustic (music) and visual communication (painting, graphics, design) as well as to multi-media sign processes (theater, cinema, opera, dance, and sports); to literary communication (the production, interpretation, and criticism of literature) as well as to sign processes in management, government, and legal institutions; to apparent sign activity as well as to its biological origin and historical development. The strengths of the semiotic approach are demonstrated particularly well in questions which go beyond the competence of the individual specialized disciplines.

When one attempts to define the *subject matter* of a discipline that is undergoing continual development, one runs the risk of drawing its limits too broadly or too narrowly, or of missing its essential features. If one leaves it undefined, one easily succumbs to the temptation of taking its subject matter for that which can be easily investigated by methods that are generally available. The history of semiotics is full of examples of both types. In order to withstand these temptations, semioticians must confront the abundance of sign processes and the wealth of possible avenues of inquiry, especially if they do not fit into the framework of widely held preconceptions. One way of doing this is to have classical semioticians—who often developed their sign conceptions without knowledge of each other—enter into a dialogue, and to analyze the favorite examples of each within the theoretical framework of the others. Such is the approach of this volume.

However, the dialogue about signs and sign conceptions must not be allowed to get stuck in one or another sort of eclecticism. Its sole value lies in the contribution it can make towards a comprehensive *semiotic theory*. For the time being, such a theory exists only in preliminary forms, and it is too early to refer to it as "the theory of signs" without qualification. In any case, using a theory as a doctrine which excuses avoiding discussion of its alternatives will never be justified. Critical examination of all contemporary approaches, including their historical background, is one of the prerequisites of theory-building. The present volume was written to provide a framework for an open discussion of some of the major options we have for a comprehensive theory of signs.

As scholars and scientists, semioticians themselves produce sign processes which can become the object of semiotic analysis. Both the *methods of investigation and of presentation* in semiotics must be scrutinized and developed further. In this venture, semioticians can draw on the tradition of the philosophy of science, which attempts to reconstruct concepts and schemata of the individual disciplines that have become unintelligible. This volume emphasizes the close connection between semiotics and the philosophy of science.

The *critical potential* of semiotics, however, is in no way limited to the realm of the sciences. It can also help to change behavior patterns in the arts, in the mass media, in public institutions, and in personal habits of communication that have lost their original function and have become irrational. This volume attempts to contribute to this process of cultural self-scrutiny.

The improvement of communication processes is usually not possible without interference in these processes. Insofar as such interference has to do with sign processes in animals and plants (zoosemiotics) and sign processes within lower-level organisms (endosemiotics) and machines, it can be justified if its goals are justified. However, when we are concerned with communication between people (as in anthroposemiotics), changes can only be justified if they are introduced with the consent of those involved. True consent is the result of a special type of sign process which is characterized by comprehensiveness with regard to its subject matter, by the self-determination of its participants, and by the lack of external constraints. The attempt to help people practice this type of sign process, which is known as *rational communication*, is one of the highest tasks of semiotics. We have kept it in mind while writing the present volume.

The reader may find it remarkable that individual scholars living in different times and places, and working in disciplines that are as different as philosophy, linguistics, psychology, and biology, found themselves united in striving towards the same goal: the development of a theory of signs which would demonstrate the underlying unity of all these disciplines. In acquainting oneself with the terminology used in the pursuit of that goal, one gets a sense of the divergent sources from which the semiotic tradition has sprung. It is only by recognizing these sources that the common goal of semiotics will be achieved. That is why we have included an extensive *glossary* in this book which can guide the reader in comparing the approaches described.

With the help of the glossary, readers can begin their perusal of the book from whatever chapter they please and read the chapters in the order that best suits their purposes. This virtue also makes the present volume suitable for use as a textbook for introductory courses in philosophy, linguistics, psychology, biology, and semiotics.

ROLAND POSNER

Contents

CHAPTER 1

An Outline of Peirce's Semiotics

KLAUS OEHLER

This chapter is divided into four parts. After an introduction, which shows Peirce's place in the history of semiotics, part 1 exhibits the different stations which Peirce passed in his foundation of semiotics. It starts with Peirce's Harvard Lectures, held in 1865, on "The Logic of Science" and ends with the correspondence between Peirce and Lady Welby which ran from 1903 to 1911. Part 2 analyses the foundations of Peirce's semiotics from a systematic point of view. Part 3 is concerned with the fundamental and universal role, which Peirce ascribes to "the most general science," that is, semiotics, and its significance for a new theory of knowledge constructed in semiotic terms. Part 4 discusses some aspects of Peirce's consensus theory in relation to possible pragmatic universals and goes some way towards answering the question of whether, and in what way, situative speech (in contrast to abstract "language") can be made the object of logical analysis.

Since Greek antiquity the term *Semiotics* has been used for "the theory of signs." Similarly, the majority of terms in use today in semiotic discourse can be traced back to Greek origins or to Latin translations of Greek expressions. The origins of the theory of signs reach back as far as the sixth century before Christ. Semiotic investigations can be found in the Presocratics, the Sophists, and Plato: discussions of the nature of language, of communication in general, of the relation of sign to signified, of the roles of speaker and listener, of the combinability and non-combinability of words, of the grounds for the possibility of false sentences, and so on. These investigations were continued by Aristotle, who developed within the framework of his logic and rhetoric what might be described as a first semiotic system including the concept of symbol. The most developed system of Semiotics in Antiquity is that of the Stoics, to whom we

---

KLAUS OEHLER • Department of Philosophy, University of Hamburg, Hamburg, West Germany.

owe the first formulation of a logic of propositions. But Epicurus and the Epi-
cureans also provided important contributions such as the empirical school of
medicine, founded in the third century B.C. by Philinos and Serapion, with its
theory of symptoms and analogical procedures. The concept of the sign under-
went an important extension in the Neoplatonic and Christian metaphysics of
late Antiquity, notably with Augustine. Then in the Middle Ages the Scholastics,
in their subtle investigations, continued research into semiotic problems. Next
our attention is drawn to the philosophy of the 17th- and 18th centuries, with
contributions to semiotics by philosophers such as Locke, Leibniz, Berkeley,
Hume, and Lambert.[1] The transition to Semiotics in its modern shape took place
in the course of the 19th century, first of all through Bolzano's *Wissenschaftslehre*
of 1837 and then, since 1867, primarily through the work of the American
logician, mathematician, scientist, and philosopher Charles Sanders Peirce. Today
Peirce (1839–1914) ranks as the chief founder of modern Semiotics. On the
basis of the foundations of Semiotics which he laid, the further development of
Semiotics as the science of signs has taken place. In the meantime it has become
a basic science of central importance, following the realization that behind logic
and linguistics there is still another foundation. This foundation is the sign *qua*
sign, without which no representation or communication in any form whatever
is possible.

1. STAGES IN THE FOUNDATION OF SEMIOTICS

The first published sketch of Peirce's Semiotics is found in the essay "On
a New List of Categories" which dates from 1867.[2] But he had already dealt
with the subject of semiotics in a series of lectures which he held at Harvard
University in 1865 under the title "The Logic of Science." The manuscripts
which have survived[3] of this series of lectures make it clear that Peirce's chief
objective at this stage was to redefine logic, and to reconstruct it as a theory of
signs. The concept of the sign which he first begins to develop here is already
essentially in the form which we find in his mature formulations, except for
terminological changes and refinements which were introduced later. It is here
that he introduces his central semiotic concepts giving them firm foundation in
the basic structure of his Semiotic. With remarkable self-confidence and control
he organizes the approaches which are to determine this analysis of the sign
(which he still calls "symbol"): that the symbol is a representation, that is, that
it stands for something, but also that it stands to something, namely to its
interpretant, and that the sign therefore contains information; that in addition the
concept of representation implies the distinction of various sorts of representation
from objects, at which point Peirce distinguishes sorts which effectively correspond to his later classification into Index, Icon and Symbol. In connection with
the concept of representation, further classifications occur to him including the

concept of the triad, which is central to his whole theory, here still in the form of "thing," "representation," and "form," where he understands "form" as the relation in which a representation stands. We can be absolutely certain, he remarks, that representations are all we can know; things and forms are only known through representations.

In the Lowell Lectures of 1866 on the subject of "The Logic of Science, or Induction and Hypothesis" Peirce continued the working out of his theory of signs. The manuscripts of these lectures[4] also make absolutely clear that from the beginning Peirce's thoughts on the concept of sign are directly related to his logical investigations and the development of his doctrine of categories. In particular, it was his investigations into relational logic which even at this early stage was already exerting a significant influence on his semiotic researches.[5] The reverse is also true. His elaboration of a logic of relations was greatly influenced by his thoughts on the subject of Semiotics.

We can see the first published sketch of his Semiotics in the essay "On a New List of Categories" as presenting the essence of these reflections undertaken in the preceeding two years. The expression "representations" is still used in the way that "sign" will be later on. Peirce substitutes for the tables of categories of Aristotle and Kant, with their ten and twelve categories respectively, a new list of three categories: Quality, Relation and Representations. With the help of these categories he distinguishes (1) three types of representation: similarities (which he later calls Icons), Indices, and Symbols, (2) with reference to the traditional classification, formal grammar, logic, and formal rhetoric, (3) types of symbols which are common to these three sciences: terms, propositions, and consequences, and (4) three sorts of consequences: deduction, hypothesis, and induction.

That Peirce was not content to build up logic as a theory of signs is shown by the series of three articles published in 1868–69, "Questions Concerning Certain Faculties Claimed for Man," "Some Consequences of Four Incapacities," and "Grounds of Validity of the Laws of Logic: Further Consequences of Four Incapacities."[6] In these three papers the tendency to make Semiotics the fundamental science, that is, the science of sciences, takes on a concrete character. The main thesis of this series of articles, that "all thought is in signs" embodies implicitly the claim of Semiotics to unversal applicability. Peirce tries to develop this claim consistently by developing in these papers the first of all semiotic epistemologies.

In 1877–78 Peirce published a series of six "Illustrations of the Logic of Science" of which the first two, "The Fixation of Belief" and "How to Make our Ideas Clear"[7] are the most famous. It was here that the foundation of Pierce's pragmatism was laid. One of the most incontrovertible findings of Peirce research is that Peirce's pragmatism also developed from the start under the influence of his theory of signs, and hence can be completely understood only from this perspective. The best evidence for this is Peirce's exposition of his pragmatism in the lectures[8] held in 1903 at Harvard University and the Lowell Institute.

The same holds for Peirce's logic of mathematics. In 1870 he published his "Description of a Notation for the Logic of Relatives,"[9] with discussions of various signs such as, for example, inclusion, equality, addition, and multiplication. The logic of relatives made it possible for him to extend the concept of Iconicity from the graphs to the algebraic formulations of the laws of logic. While the Iconicity of the Graphs was self-evident, that of the algebraic formulations of the laws of logic becomes clear only with the help of the logic of relatives. The final and most inclusive exposition which Peirce himself ever published of his theory of signs as well his theory of Graphs is in his "Prolegomena to an Apology for Pragmaticism" of 1906.[10] This essay is the third of a series which Peirce wrote about pragmatism. In the first of these, "What Pragmatism Is," which appeared in 1905,[11] he renamed his version of pragmatism in order to distinguish himself from other pragmatists, above all James and Schiller, and called it "Pragmaticism." In the second essay, which is called "Pragmaticism,"[12] also from 1905, he deals with his theory of Critical Common-Sensism, and his reception of Scholastic realism, as consequences of his pragmatism. He had already dealt with both theories much earlier in the '70s. What is new in the second of these essays is the Semiotics of vagueness, which is developed as part of his theory of Common-Sensism.

In 1903, Lady Victoria Welby published a book entitled "What is Meaning?" The same year also saw the appearance of a review in the magazine *The Nation*.[13] Its author was Peirce. There followed a correspondence[14] between the Englishwoman and Peirce about Semiotics, which contains some of the best expositions of his conception of Semiotics that Peirce ever gave. It was also the Englishwoman that provoked Peirce into making an important autobiographical confession. In a letter dating December 4th, 1908, she wrote to him: "You have always been kindly interested in the work to which my life is devoted." Peirce answered this in a letter on December 23rd: "But I smiled at your speaking of my having been 'kindly interested' in your work, as if it were a divergence—I should say a deviation, from my ordinary line of attention. Know that from the day when at the age of 12 or 13 I took up, in my elder brother's room a copy of Whately's 'Logic,' and asked him what Logic was, and getting some simple answer, flung myself on the floor and buried myself in it, it has never been in my power to study anything,—mathematics, ethics, metaphysics, gravitation, thermodynamics, optics, chemistry, comparitive anatomy, astronomy, psychology, phonetics, economics, the history of science, whist, men and women, wine, metrology, except as a study of semiotic."[15]

Richard Whately's *Elements of Logic*, which Peirce alludes to in his letter to Lady Welby, had been a standard textbook in English and American universities for several generations since its appearance in 1826, and was still used by Peirce as a student at Harvard. Whately's *Elements of Rhetoric* (1828) was also used as a textbook. Whately, and after him Peirce, continued a tradition whose main representatives had been Ockham, Bacon, Hobbes, Locke, Leibniz, Berkeley, and Condillac. As a principal result of the effect of this tradition, Peirce always emphasizes the logical character of his investigation of signs, and goes to great lengths to avoid psychologism. It was in this sense that Whately played a formative role in the development of Peirce's conception of logic, and it is probably true to say that both the fact and the methodology of Peirce's *Semiotics* must be traced back to his influence.

If it is now a more or less accepted fact that Peirce is the real founder of modern Semiotics and that without him Semiotics as it has developed since his time would be inconceivable, it remains the case that only a small number of his works are at present in print, while the majority will reach publication for the first time in the new edition of his papers which is presently in preparation. If we add to this the fact that material, both published and unpublished, documents an internal dialogue which occurred in Peirce's semiotic thinking over a period of half a century, it should be clear that, even taking unpublished material into account, an exposition of the fundamentals of Peirce's Semiotics faces special difficulties. To give a clear idea of the paradigm within which Peirce's Semiotics appeared to him in spite of these difficulties, I have decided to adopt the synoptic method of exposition. A thorough synopsis of Peirce's numerous semiotic sketches seems essential to the systematic investigation of his general theory of signs.

2. THE FOUNDATIONS OF PEIRCE'S SEMIOTICS

Peirce's reflections about what a sign is begin with something everybody knows: that a sign is something that stands for something else and is understood by someone, or has a meaning for someone. This common-sense definition of the sign has the appearance of being self-evident at first, but on further reflection ceases to look so simple. The three aspects or elements of the sign—(1) the sign itself, (2) the sign in relation to its object, (3) the sign in relation to its interpretant—stand in a special relationship to one another that is logically a three-place or triadic relation. The three aspects of the triad—the sign-aspect, the object-aspect, the interpretant-aspect—can each be divided into three further elements. The sign-aspect divides into (1) the Qualisign, (2) the Sinsign and (3) the Legisign, whereby the Qualisign characterizes the sensory quality of a sign, its intrinsic visible appearance (e.g. "green"), the Sinsign, by contrast, its individual reality (e.g., a particular road sign in a particular street), and the Legisign, the general type of a sign (e.g. the word "tree"). With regard to their connection to their objects, signs can be divided into (1) Icons, (2) Indices and (3) Symbols. An icon is a sign that shares a resemblance with its real or fictional object, e.g. a picture, a pattern, a diagram; an Index is a sign that relates to its object not as a copy but in some real way, as a pointer or marker, e.g. a signpost, a weathercock, an arrow or the symptom of a disease. A symbol is a sign that is determined by its object only in the sense that it is interpreted as being such, and is thus totally independent of similarity or physical connection to its object, e.g. a flag. And finally, with respect to its connections to its interpretant a sign can be called either (1) a Rhema, (2) a Dicent or (3) an Argument. This classification corresponds to the old classification into Term, Proposition and Argument, but is modified in such a way as to apply to signs in general. Any sign that is neither true nor false is a Rhema, e.g. individual words. A Dicent is a sign that is capable of being translated into a proposition. An Argument is a sign whose rational necessity must be acknowledged.

On the basis of this trichotomization of the sign triad, further classes of signs can be constructed by combination, which again, as ordered triads, each have an element relating to the sign-, object- and interpretant aspects.[16] The classification of the sign into triads and trichotomies is pursued rigorously and adhered to, and reveals itself also to be effective in the analysis of the main relationships into which the sign is divided. The two most important relationships are to the object and to the interpretant.

Three factors contribute to the functioning of a sign: the sign itself, its object, and its interpretant. The interpretant is that which a sign produces in an interpreter, in that it determines a feeling, an action, or a sign. This determination is the interpretant. There are various sorts of interpretants, just as there are various sorts of object. There is (1) the immediate object, that is the object as the sign itself represents it, whose existence thus depends on its representation in the sign, and there is (2) the dynamic object, that is the object itself, independent of any representation, but which nevertheless determines the sign, the sign as its representation. The immediate object is the object that is represented by the sign, while the dynamic object is the object that produces the sign. With regard to the interpretant a distinction must be made between (1) the immediate interpretant, that is the interpretant which manifests itself in the correct understanding of the sign, i.e. what is called the meaning of the sign, (2) the dynamic interpretant, that is, the actual effect of the sign, the reaction which a sign provokes, and (3) the final interpretant, that is, the effect that the sign would have in every awareness if circumstances were such that the sign could evince its full effect. In other words, the final interpretant is the interpretative result which every interpreter is destined to reach if the sign is scrutinized adequately. The immediate interpretant arises from the fact that every sign has its own specific form of interpretation before it has an interpretant. The dynamic interpretant is what is experienced in every act of interpretation and is different from every other act of interpretation. Thus the immediate interpretant is an abstraction consisting in a possibility, the dynamic interpretant is a singular actual event, the final interpretant is that interpretant to which the actual process of interpretation tends. The question of interpretation must always proceed from a precise analysis of the nature of the sign. The conceptual distinctions necessary for this are formulated in an explicit ontology of the sign, in which the sign's modes of existence are classified trichotometrically into ten main groups.

So far in our sketch of Pcirce's Semiotics, in which we have obviously not been able to reproduce every single aspect of the system, we have said nothing about the doctrine which constitutes the basis of his theory of signs, namely the doctrine of categories[17] in relation to his logic of relations. It is already apparent from the general definition of the sign as something that stands in a relation for something (the object) to something (the interpretant) that the sign is relational in character. In particular it is clear that the basic structure of the sign relation is triadic, whereby the correlata or relata are described by Peirce as a "First," a "Second," and a "Third." These terms, which Peirce borrows from his doctrine of categories, are used in an analogous fashion in his theory of signs. Formally the three categories "Firstness," "Secondness" and "Thirdness" are three classes of relation: monadic, dyadic, and triadic. In other words his universal categories of "Firstness," "Secondness," and "Thirdness" are defined as one-, two-, and three-place relations, as developed in his logic of relations.[18] It seems to have been Peirce's opinion that each of these classes is irreducible and all relations of a higher order are reducible to a combination of these three classes. Thus tetradic, pentadic, etc., relations can be analyzed into triadic relations; a triadic relations, however, cannot be reduced to a dyadic or monadic relation, but is irreducible.[19] For Peirce, this logical theory of relations had the status of a heuristic principle. A complete triadic relation is one in which no two of the three correlata are related to each other without the mediation of the third correlatum. Precisely the same is true in the sign relation: the sign connects the object and the interpretant, the interpretant connects sign and object, and the object connects sign and interpretant.

The sufficient condition for something to function as a sign is thus that it enters into the triadic relation, and so signifies something else, while this signification has a meaning which is understood by some further thing, an intelligence. This ability to be understood presupposes conventions which are also requisite for the repeatability of the sign, as well as its capacity to be taught or learned. In addition the existence of signs also presupposes that they always occur in connection with a material, perceivable vehicle, i.e., a sign is, as sign, bonded with its material form in order to be an object of sensory perception.

The concept of the sign as a three-place relation also throws light on another aspect of signification, namely the fact that a sign never exists alone, that is, without connection to other signs. For every sign must, as a matter of definition, be interpretable. This, however, presupposes the existence of at least one other sign. This further sign is similarly a sign only on condition that it is interpretable, and hence presupposes another sign. And so on ad infinitum. This argument might be called the semiotic proof of the interminability of every process of interpretation. From a practical point of view the theoretical interminability is unproblematical, since our everyday actions are governed by abbreviated procedures. In our daily interactions we communicate with one another by means of a limited number of explanations, contractions, gestures, demeanors, intonations, and so on. This attenuated exchange of signs in everyday communication is forced on us by the necessity of action. At any given time we interrupt the in principle infinite process of interpretation because we have to act. The action then testifies to the necessarily interrupted interpretation of a situation.

The triadic relationship between the sign elements implies a process—the so-called process of signification or "semiosis." In order for a sign to function as a sign it must produce a reaction, which in turn is only possible if the sign is mediated by a third element in such a way that for the receiver of the sign the sign really represents its object. This third element is the interpretant, that constituent of the sign which makes it into a conventional, interpretative social entity. In the Saussurian model signs express information which is communicated from a sender to a receiver. The Peircian model of triadic semiosis proves itself superior, in contrast, because it is also applicable to phenomena which do not involve a sender as such, e.g. natural phenomena, which we interpret as symptoms, like fever as a symptom of specific illnesses. This inclusion of symptoms into the class of semiotic processes means that natural phenomena can also be decoded as signs, and are thus correspondingly amenable to semiotic representation. The triadic definition of signs can also include within its scope the transmission of signals, as transmission is not some unmediated state existing between two poles, but rather, as we now know, a complicated process of selection which can only be explained by analogy to the process of interpretation.

3. THE IMPORTANCE AND GENERALITY OF PEIRCIAN SEMIOTICS

Whatever a future "History of Semiotics" will one day look like, it is certain that the historian of Semiotics will be obliged to divide the development of Semiotics into two eras, the one before Peirce, the other beginning with him. Nobody can doubt that Peirce's emergence marks the main caesura in the history of Semiotics. The reason for this goes back to the point he starts from, which is as fundamental as it is universal: the world consists not of two mutually exclusive sorts of things, signs and non-signs, or put otherwise, of one category of entities which are meaningful, and another of things which are not. For Peirce, there are no meaningless objects. All our objects are the objects of signification, and there is no such thing as a meaningless sign—an idea which is self-contradictory. This state of affairs is precisely what the triadic structure of the concept of the sign makes clear. And in the same way, the particular types of sign, e.g. Icon, Index, Symbol, are not mutually exclusive, but rather, individual aspects of the process of signification, of semiosis. Thus we name a sign only with respect to the aspect which dominates it at any given time, rather than in any absolute sense.

The series of articles dating from 1868–69 about four incapacities of man shows that from the beginning Semiotics was for Peirce more than a sub-category of logic. Here the theory of signs is brought to bear on traditional epistemological problems, and extended to Semiotics of knowledge, or a semiotic epistemology, which amounts at the same time to a theory of reality. The main proposal which is developed here is that all thinking is a thinking of signs: "all thought is in signs."[20] The implication of this is that we do not have the capacity for presuppositionless knowledge, of intuition, but rather all knowledge is determined by previous knowledge. We are incapable of conceiving the absolutely unknowable, and hence no such concept is at our disposal. Wherever thought occurs it is in the medium of words and signs: "If we seek the light of external facts, the only cases of thought which we can find are of thought in signs. Plainly no other thought can be evidenced by external facts. But we have seen that only by external facts can thought be known at all. The only thought, then, which can possibly be cognized is thought in signs. But thought which cannot be cognized does not exist. All thought, therefore, must necessarily be in signs."[21] Having started from this conception of the thought-sign it was only consistent to interpret the basic structure or thought, like the sign, as a three-place relation, and to show that the relationship between the thinking mind and the thought object cannot be adequately represented as a two-place relation. Starting from this premise Peirce develops his devastating criticisms of the rationalist and empiricist theories of experience.

His definition of an object accords entirely with his definition of the thought-sign. The latter definition explains what a thought-sign stands for. "The thought-sign stands for its object in the respect which it is thought; that is to say, this respect is the immediate object of consciousness in the thought, or, in other words, it is the thought itself, or at least what the thought is thought to be in the subsequent thought to which it is a sign."[22] In a manuscript which has not yet been published (MS 318, c. 1907) Peirce expands on his concept of the sign of an object in a way which makes particularly clear the difference—but also the special connection—between the immediate object and the real object. The immediate object of the sign is an *ens rationis* which is identical with the intention of the symbolizer or utterer, an idea or a representation. "It may be that there is no such thing or fact in existence, or in any other mode of reality." But: "If there be anything *real* (that is, anything whose characters are true of it independently of whether you or I, or any man, or any number of men think them as being characters of it, or not), that sufficiently corresponds with the immediate object (which, since it is an apprehension, is not real), then whether this be identifiable with the object strictly so-called or not, it ought to be called, and usually is called, the 'real object' of the sign."[23] In other words, immediate objects without real objects are possible, but not real objects without immediate objects. This connection with the immediate object is constitutive for the real object. In the framework of his definition of the sign-object this takes the following metaphorical form: "This *requaesitum* I term the object of the sign:— the immediate object, if it be the idea which the sign is built upon, the real object, if it be that real thing or circumstance upon which that idea is founded as bed-rock."[24] This means that since the immediate object is "subjective,"[25] an idea, the result of a "collateral observation, aided by imagination and thought,"[26] it would be logically inconsistent to start from the assumption that for a thinking being there could ever be a meaningless object, i.e. an object without significance. On the contrary, if one starts from the fundamental and universal premise of Peirce's Semiotics, that every thought is a sign, then it is difficult to say what is not a sign for a thinking being. It was this initial standpoint that led Peirce to call Semiotics "the most general science."[27] What makes it into a general science, and hence the fundamental science, is the general structure of the sign relation, which is thus the structure of our experience or of the objects of our experience. Given this premise there can be no such thing as "reality," independent of our thought. In other words: a reality which is incapable of being represented by signs cannot exist for human beings.

This semiotic epistemology has radical consequences for the traditional concept of mind. The problem of the origin of the unity of thinking, the basic question in the philosophy of mind from Descartes to German Idealism, and to answering which Kant's doctrine of the transcendental unity of apperception was directed (*Critique of Pure Reason*, B 132 ff.) is solved in a new and more convincing way in semiotic epistemology. At the end of his treatise "Some Consequences of Four Incapacities" Peirce asks what the reality of mind consists in.[28] The answer is: "Consciousness is sometimes used to signify the *I think*, or unity in thought; but the unity is nothing but consistency, or the recognition of it. Consistency belongs to every sign, so far as it is a sign; and therefore every sign, since it signifies primarily that it is a sign, signifies its own consistency."[29] But the consistency of the sign is nothing other than the intelligible essence of the object, or in Peirce's formulation: "Consistency is the intellectual character of a thing; that is, is its expressing something."[30] With this solution he also overcomes the difficulties which modern philosophy faced as a result of the question how the variety of the manifold in experience could be derived from the unity and identity of self-awareness. For Peirce this problem proves from the first illusory, because the requisite mediation of unity and diversity is carried out not by the individual self-awareness, but by the sign in the process of semiosis, and this process is by nature a social one which has its roots in a community. On this point it is important to know that Peirce reached his concept of signification as a result of a phenomenological analysis of the dialogue situation.[31] The distribution of roles between speaker and hearer, and the relations which hold between them, caused him to conceive thinking as a communicative process as well, as a conversation with oneself, and hence to attribute the structure of a dialogue to thought.

Towards the end of his life this tendency to conceive subjectivity inter-subjectively gets stronger. His semiotic epistemology transforms more and more into a formal Semiotic which he sees as identical with logic, but in such a way that logic is understood as Semiotics. *A System of Logic, Considered as Semeiotic* is the title of the unfinished work on which he labored during the last decade of his life. The goal which he had before him was a logic of communication, and he hoped that this work would acquire the significance in the twentieth century that John Stuart Mill's *System of Logic* (1843) had had in the nineteenth. More and more he was drawn by the idea of a cosmic rationality, within whose field of force thought is not only the function of a brain, but also manifests itself in all appearances of the material world. In the "Prolegomena to an Apology for Pragmaticism" (1906) we read: "Thought is not necessarily connected with a brain. It appears in the work of bees, of crystals, and throughout the purely physical world; and one can no more deny that it is really there, than that the colors, the shapes, etc., of objects are really there. Consistently adhere to that unwarrantable denial, and you will be driven to some form of idealistic nomi-nalism akin to Fichte's. Not only is thought in the organic world, but it develops there. But as there cannot be a General without Instances embodying it, so there cannot be thought without Signs."[32] Mind is conceived as a (propositional) function of the universe, whose values are the meanings of all signs; the effects of the signs are effectively interconnected: "Mind is a propositional function of the widest possible universe, such that its values are the meanings of all signs whose actual effects are in effective interconnection."[33] The leading position of Peircian Semiotics derives from this universality, which extends from a semiotic cosmology and noology to a semiotic epistemology and theory of interaction which direct practical consequences and empirical applicability. The empirical relevance of Peirce's theory of signs has now been recognized and evaluated by information theorists.[34] This and other developments suggest that the renaissance of interest in Peirce which we are today witnessing does indeed amount to a realization of some of Peirce's hopes regarding his influence on the 20th century, albeit probably not in the form he would have expected.

4.   SOME ASPECTS OF PEIRCE'S CONSENSUS THEORY

It is no longer possible to see the core of Kant's epistemology, the tran-scendental synthesis of apperception, as providing an adequate answer to the question of the intersubjective validity of knowledge. Kant's metaphysical pro-posal of a consciousness in general has had to make way to new attempts to explain the public validity of knowledge. Previously philosophers had held to the classical transcendental epistemology, simply adding language on to it as an extra ingredient, without calling into question Kant's concept of a consciousness in general as the "transcendental subject" of knowledge. Cassirer's "symbolic forms," for example, are still conceived within the framework of the traditional epistemology as the instruments of a thoroughly solipsistically conceived consciousness. In this respect Cassirer's "Philosophy of Symbolic Forms" is noticeably less advanced than positions that had been reached at a much earlier date— positions that had not only apparently, but in reality, liberated themselves from the solipsistic approach to epistemology by seeing and analyzing thought as a function that is essentially dependent on communication. This applies not so much to the early Wittgenstein or Carnap, from whose work the theme of subjectivity is missing, but to attempts that consciously rethought the question from a new standpoint.

It was Peirce who substituted, in place of Kant's transcendental synthesis of apperception, the semiotic synthesis of interpretation, which takes place in a real communicative world and tends approximately towards an ideal limit, the "final opinion," an ultimate consensus which he conceives as the essential constituent of an ideal community. The idea of the general consensus functions as a regulative principle controlling the actions of the community that are directed towards its realization. This "transformation" of the concept of transcendental subjectivity is not therefore a recent event,[35] but one that was effected by Peirce a hundred years ago. My aim in what follows is to discuss some aspects of Peirce's consensus theory in relation to possible pragmatic universals, and to go some way towards answering the question of whether, and in what way, situative speech (in contrast to abstract "language") can be made the object of logical analysis. Hence we are dealing with the question of the logic of pragmatic universals.

I take as my starting point the concept of the ideal communicative group. Peirce combined this concept with his theory of reality, which is based on the premise that the concept of an object tends to a finally valid form whose content is that which an ideal community of investigators would agree on if research were to continue indefinitely. He assumed that the infinite progression of knowledge converges on a true conception of reality. The crucial question that faces Peirce's consensus theory is about the best method for producing the consensus. In answering this question Peirce undertakes a large-scale attempt to justify scientific method, which was for him equivalent to a justification of induction and hypothesis. The ultimate purpose of scientific thinking he sees as lying in the unity of an insurpassable system of true sentences whose object is reality. Peirce considered this presupposition to be a matter of conviction rather than proof: one of the articles of faith of his metaphysics of consensus, which is fundamentally eschatalogical in character. It is dominated by the idea that the persistent and repeated use of the scientific method will inevitably lead to a final conclusion's being reached, to the "final opinion." The concept of the "final opinion" is the catalyst of an ideal process of reiterated application of the scientific method to the uncritical spectrum of opinions stemming from common sense.

The "final opinion" has the integral function of an ideal consensus only with respect to some future existing humanity. Its immediate function is to provide a practical application for the concept of ideal conditions which is so important in scientific thought. It is by way of these ideal conditions that the difference from the real conditions operative in the present situation become perceptible. Thus the ideal conditions can function as criteria in the selection of relevant objects of investigation, as well as in the simplification of planning and above all in the definition of theoretical and practical goals. Peirce clearly emphasized this aspect of his consensus theory. His concept of truth relates to the ideal conditions under which a proposition stands in relation to real objects. The concepts of truth and reality have for Peirce, *mutatis mutandis*, the function that Kant attributes to regulative ideas. Peirce's concept of the ideal community in which the final consensus, established by means of scientific method, governs action normatively, takes on the appearance of a regulative idea of scientific reason. It should also be mentioned that some of Peirce's utterances seem to allude to the historical realizability of this idea. It is the ideal of a body of scientific knowledge which is complete, and of a humanity organized in accordance with it.

There remains the question of what it is in this proposal that constitutes the intersubjective basis of communication, and whether Peirce's idea of an ideal community of knowers and reasoners actually is capable of providing such a basis. The problem is one of linguistic universals. Peirce was intensively occupied with the search for constants that make possible the translation of one natural language into another, and at the same time lead to a convergence of results in different natural languages. It led him to the grounding of a science, semiotics, for which the central problem is to investigate the universal mechanisms by which communication takes place. He sees linguistic universals not as facts that fall purely within the competence of linguistics, but as universal structures of thought that make communication possible.

Peirce has left us with many definitions of what a sign is. In general, a sign is something that stands for something in a relation to something. This definition makes clear the relational character of the sign. The sign relation is triadic, the three correlata or relata of which are described by Peirce as "First," "Second" and "Third." This terminology coordinates with Peirce's categorial scheme, from which it acquires its significance.

Peirce's thesis that the universal structure of communicative action is the triadic relation seems incontestable, and any attempt to transcend this structure in search of an even more generalized foundation is based on a reductive fallacy. Linguistic universals as they are sought and investigated by linguistics are as a matter of simple fact, subject to the logical constraints embodied in the category of Thirdness. Not only Peirce, with his insistence on the irreducibility of Thirdness, but also Wittgenstein contested such a reductionism.[36] Wittgenstein's chief argument against all forms of reductionism is to point to the infinite regress that they generate. This is the same argument that Peirce uses to attack Cartesian intuitionism.

These considerations yield consequences that are of relevance to the question of the "transformation" of transcendental philosophy discussed initially, in the sense of Apel's so-called "transcendental hermeneutic programme."[37] What this program has in mind is the replacement of the "transcendental synthesis of apperception" by the "transcendental synthesis of linguistically mediated interpretation." It is thus consistent for this program to pursue the search for general constants as universal conditions of linguistically mediated interpretation. The thesis I want to defend is that the logic of these universal conditions is the logic of the fundamentally three-place mediation of signification, and that this logic represents an absolute limit of the functional explicability of the universal conditions of possible communication, further simplification of which is impossible. Apel's transcendental hermeneutics or transcendental pragmatics seems, in spite of assurances to the contrary, not always to do justice to the essential triadicity of the sign-relation. The objections contained in Apel's program to the analytic logic of science, which criticize its failure to provide an account of subjectivity, and its reductionism towards a two-place logic, seem to apply as well to Apel's own program, when it—purportedly within a transcendental philosophical framework—has recourse to anthropological constants in the human situation and an allegedly inborn "universal linguistic competence," which is supposed to represent the possibility of a language instinct in man. One has little choice but to see these sorts of tactics as constituting reductionism under the guise of transcendental philosophy. It is a relapse to the temptation to reduce Thirdness to Secondness. Peirce took care to describe this as "Nominalism."

On this point it is probably worth reiterating the doubt as to whether the expression "transcendental" in Apel's program means anything but the factual conditions of knowledge.[38] This doubt cannot be eradicated by Apel's attempt to give plausibility to his concept of the "transcendental" with the aid of Peirce's regulative concept of an ideal community of knowers and reasoners—a concept that was developed in a totally different logical framework. In a critical sense, Peirce's concept has demonstrably nothing to do with what has since Kant been called transcendental investigation. What makes Peirce of such immanent contemporary interest is precisely the fact that the aprioristic core of Kant's critique of reason loses its systematic status for Peirce, in favor of a theory of the constitution of experience, that is relativized in more than one sense. There remains only the overall question of the constitution of experience. In the present situation there seems little point in referring to whatever happens to be thrown into this framework as "transcendental"—not least a universal pragmatism whose goal it is to analyze the universal presuppositions of argumentative discourse. The logical tool at its disposal is that of the triadic relational logic of signs, and this is the only logic that fits the purpose and character of a universal pragmatics.

A universal pragmatism of the type suggested by Habermas[39] aims to discover the general presuppositions of communication, whereby the communicative process representative for the socio-cultural stage of development is categorized in principle as a speech act. Habermas identifies and reconstructs for any speech act four universal claims that anyone involved in a communicative act inevitably makes, and the reasonableness of which he recognizes: comprehensability, truth, truthfulness, and correctness. The identification of these as essential features of the speaker–listener relationship seems plausible. They are also to be found in Antiquity at the center of a dispute, ranging across the centuries, between philosophy and rhetoric, and they also play an important role in the tradition of the Topics. The comprehensibility of the expression, the truth of the message, the truthfulness of the utterance and the correctness of speech in the sense of a conformity to generally recognized norms and values viewed as universal conditions are elements of a system of possible communication the structure of which is only describable in relational terms. These universal conditions dictate the criteria for the satisfaction of the three general pragmatic functions of representation, expression, and message, and these three functions can likewise only be analyzed logically in relational terms. Their structure is essentially triadic, which is to say that they satisfy the logical conditions of the Peircian concept of a sign, and hence that this structure is fundamental to every speech act. Beyond the universal pragmatic analyses as they occur in a theory of elementary propositions, intentional expressions, or in a theory of illocutionary acts, analysis must aim first of all at the logic of a universal pragmatics which will be constitutive in force for the individual parts of a universal pragmatics and ultimately for any theory of communication whatsoever. As we have seen, this logic will have to be triadic in nature. Habermas' proposals for a universal pragmatics seem to me to be compatible with refinements of this sort. Such refinements could amount to a structural simplification of his sketch of a universal pragmatics. At any rate it seems to me that the basic question of the universal conditions of possible communication can no longer be adequately posed without relational logic. The same holds of the problem of the intersubjectivity of meanings that are identical for at least two speakers.

The proposal that the sign-relation is fundamentally triadic is universally valid in the phenomenology of human behavior. It is equivalent to the claim that the triadicity of the sign relation is irreducible, and provides the basis of semiotics' universal validity.[40]

It also determines its character and function as a basic science, which is why Peirce described semiotics as "the most general science." This formulation appears in the unpublished manuscript 318 (dating from c. 1907), that has recently attracted much attention as one of the very clearest expositions of Peirce's theory of signs.[41] In this manuscript (MS 318, Prag 15–46) Peirce takes as his starting point the claim that every concept and every thought is a sign, and that the Greeks' use of the word "Logos" shows that they can only have conceived thought in this way. Anyone can convince himself on the basis of introspective self-observation that his reflection takes the form of dialogue, a conversation with himself, and that it is superfluous to add "that conversation is composed of signs" (Prag 14). Peirce could have substantiated this interpretation of thought as dialogue with a number of classical philosophical texts. But instead he undertakes an impressive phenomenological analysis of the basic communicative situation, thereby making it possible to make clear the irreducible triadic structure of the sign, that is, to make the concept of the sign, of the sign-object, and of the sign-interpretant derivable from a reconstruction of the basic dialogue situation. This is realized specifically in Peirce's search for "essential ingredients" (Prag 21) of the sign-utterer, sign-utterance, and sign-interpretant. We cannot here go into detail about the results that Peirce reaches. For our purposes it is enough to point out that Peirce succeeds in demonstrating the reciprocal dependence of the three terms of the sign. The producer of the sign communicates his message (whether acoustic, optical or haptic, etc.) about something to someone, the interpretant. But the producer does not merely transmit a message, he also has an intention in doing so. This intention relates to the interpretation of the utterance by the interpretant. Hence the intention of the producer of the sign is the criterion for the rightness or wrongness of its interpretation, with the result that the possibility of misinterpretation exists. Hence the interpretant's interest in the intentions of the speaker or utterer.

This definition of the relationship between the sign and its interpretation determines in advance what it is to be the object of a sign. Since the sign as sign has only one function—a pragmatic one—to be interpreted correctly, the objectivity of the object of the sign consists purely in the correct interpretation of the sign. The object of the sign is called by Peirce the "immediate object": it is the representation or concept on which the sign is based. The object in so far as it is that thing or state of affairs on which that representation or concept rests is called by Peirce the "real" object; as he specifies in the passage quoted earlier: "This *requaesitum* I term the object of the sign:—the immediate object, if it be the idea which the sign is built upon, the real object, if it be that real thing or circumstance upon which that idea is founded as on bed-rock." (Prag 33) The "immediate" object of the sign can depend on observation, but also on mere imagination; in either case it remains essentially dependent on subjectivity, and is described in this sense by Peirce as "subjective," "in the intention of its utterer," "some idea," "an apprehension." "It may be that there is no such thing or fact in existence, or in any other mode of reality; but we surely shall not deny to the common picture of a phenix or to a figure of naked truth in her well the name of a 'sign,' simply because the bird is a fiction and Truth an *ens rationis*." (Prag 41) The "real" object also remains dependent on subjectivity, namely the subjectivity of the "immediate object" of the sign. But it is not totally engulfed by this subjectivity, and amounts to something more: namely that aspect of the object, in so far as it is independent of subjectivity, that corresponds to something in the subjective "immediate object" of the sign. "If there be anything real (that is, anything whose characters are true of it independently of whether you or I, or any man, or any number of men think them as being characters of it, or not,) that sufficiently corresponds with the immediate object (which, since it is an apprehension, is not real) then whether this be identifiable with the object strictly so called or not, it ought to be called, and usually is called, the 'real object' of the sign." (Prag 41/42). Every sign has an "immediate object," but not every sign has a "real object," and every "real object" has an "immediate object," but not every "immediate object" has a "real object." The concept of an object that is developed here within the theory of signs stands in both cases in a relationship to the interpretant—though different in each case—is relative to the interpretant, and is, within the limits of this theory, unimaginable without the interpretant. Thus a sign mediates between the interpretant and its object in such a way that it on the one hand relates to the object, on the other to the interpretant, and thereby brings the interpretant into a relationship with the object. The consequent relationship between object and interpretant is the most basic form of triadic relation. Peirce can consequently represent the object and the interpretant as the two "correlative correlates" of the sign, thereby theoretically guaranteeing that object and interpretant correspond to one another.

Towards the end of this outline of his sign theory in MS 318, Peirce gives a definition of the sign that is of particular clarity, concentrating as it does only on essentials. It reads as follows: "I will say that a sign is anything of whatsoever mode of being, which mediates between an object and an interpretant; since it is both determined by the object relatively to the interpretant, and determines the interpretant in reference to the object, in such wise as to cause the interpretant to be determined by the object through the mediation of this sign." (Prag 44) This definition of the sign reduces semiotics, conceived as a logic of communicative action, to the most precise formulation conceivable, in terms of the universal triadic relational structure of the sign. The three terms of this relation (sign, object, interpretant; first term, second term, third term) describe the objectivity of the object—what makes it an object—and at the same time describe the logical structure of thought, speech, and action, in such a way that the isomorphism of these three elements of communicative behavior is made clear. The consequence of this, that there is nothing thinkable that does not manifest this relational structure, I consider to be an established semiotic fact, and I consider attempts to reduce Thirdness to Secondness to be impracticable. Semiotics as the logic of communicative behaviour (thinking, speaking, acting) is a theory of Thirdness, that is, of representation. This means that "thinking," "speaking," or "acting" within this theory means nothing other than the possibility of being represented in a way that agrees with the logical form of the original triadic relation. This solution is, measured against other attempts to find a logical foundation for the elements of communicative behavior, of considerably greater simplicity. The simplicity of the formal structure of this concept of sign also explains the universality of its validity for anything and everything that is connected with or can be connected to thought, conceived as an interpretative process. In this way the relational concept of sign succeeds in bringing unity not merely to science but to interpretative behavior as a whole.

NOTES

1. On the antecedents of modern Semiotics see E. Walther, *Allgemeine Zeichenlehre Stuttgart: Deutsche Verlagsanstalt*, (1975), p. 9 ff.; and R. Jakobson, *Coup d'Oeil sur le Développement de la Sémiotique*, (*-Studies in Semiotics* 3 [Bloomington, Ind.: Research Center for Language and Semiotic Studies, 1975]).
2. *Collected Papers of Charles Sanders Peirce*, (Cambridge, Mass.: Harvard University Press), vols. 1–6 edited by Ch. Hartshorne and P. Weiss, 1931–1935; vols. 7–8 edited by A. Burks, 1958. Citations are to volume and paragraph numbers. Thus the paper "On A New List of Categories" receives the citation: 1.545–567.
3. Mss 340–348. Unless stated otherwise, the citation of the manuscripts is in accordance with the numbering of the Charles S. Peirce papers in the Houghton Library of Harvard University.
4. Mss 351–359.
5. Cf. E. Michael, "Peirce's Early Study of the Logic of Relations 1865–67," *Transactions of the Charles S. Peirce Society*, 10 (1974), 63–76, E. Walther, "Erste Überlegungen zur Semiotik von C. S. Peirce in den Jahren 1860–1866," *Semiosis*, 1 (1976), pp. 35–41.
6. CP 5.213–357.
7. CP 5.358–410. On this cf. K. Oehler, Charles S. Peirce: *Über die Klarheit unserer Gedanken* (How to Make Our Ideas Clear). *Einleitung, Übersetzung, Kommentar* (Frankfurt: Klostermann Texte Philosophie, 1968). On the thesis that Peirce's pragmatism has its roots in his theory of signs see in particular John J. Fitzgerald, *Peirce's Theory of Signs as Foundation for Pragmatism*, (The Hague: Mouton, 1966), and Max H. Fisch, "Peirce's General Theory of Signs," *Sight, Sound, and Sense*, ed. Thomas A. Sebeok, Indiana University Press (1978), Bloomington Indiana,. pp. 134–159.
8. CP 5.14–212.
9. CP 3.45–149.
10. CP 4.530–572.
11. CP 5.411–437.
12. CP 5.438–463.
13. *The Nation*, 77 (1903), 308–09.
14. The complete correspondence is now available in the volume: *Semiotic and Significs. The Correspondence between Charles S. Peirce and Victoria Lady Welby*, ed. Charles S. Hardwick (Bloomington and London: Indiana University Press, 1977).
15. *Semiotic and Significs*, p. 85 ff.
16. On this point see *Semiotic and Significs*, Appendix B: "Irwin Lieb on Peirce's Classification of Signs," p. 160 ff. Also E. Walther, "Die Haupteinteilungen der Zeichen von C. S. Peirce," *Semiosis*, 3 (1976), pp. 32–41.
17. On the systematic relationship between Peirce's theories of signs and categories cf. D. Greenlee, *Peirce's Concept of Sign*, (The Hague: Mouton, 1973), as well as the subsequent controversy, in *Transactions of the Charles S. Peirce Society*, 10 (1974), p. 185 ff., and 12, no. 2 (1976),

"A Symposium on Douglas Greenlee's 'Peirce's Concept of Sign' " (with contributions by J. Ransdell, J. E. Brock, J. J. Fitzgerald, D. Greenlee), p. 97 ff; Gayle L. Ormiston, "Peirce's Categories: Structure of Semiotic," *Semiotica*, 19 (1977), 209–232; K. Oehler, "Peirce contra Aristotle. Two Forms of the Theory of Categories," *Proceedings of the C. S. Peirce Bicentennial International Congress Amsterdam* (Lubbock, Tex.: Texas Univ. Press, 1981), pp. 335–342.

18. On Peirce's logic of relations see the following: M. H. Fisch and A. Turquette, "Peirce's Triadic Logic," *Transactions of the Charles S. Peirce Society*, 2 (1966), 71–85; A. R. Turquette, "Peirce's Phi and Psi Operators for Triadic Logic," *TCSPS*, 3 (1967), 66–73; idem, "Peirce's Complete System of Triadic Logic, "*TCSPS*, 5 (1969), 199–210; D. E. Buzelli, "The Argument of Peirce's 'New List of Categories' " *TCSPS* 8 (1972), 63–89; E. Michael, "Peirce's Early Study of the Logic of Realtions 1865–1867," *TCSPS*, 10 (1974), 63–75; K. Oehler, "Peirce contra Aristotle," *Proceedings of the C. S. Peirce Bicentennial International Congress Amsterdam, 1976*, (Lubbock, Tex., 1981), pp. 335–340. H. M. Stiebing, Dreistelligkeit der Relationenlogik-Kommentierende Bemerkungen zu Peirce's 'The Logic of Relatives,' " *Semiosis, 3* (1976), 20–25; G. Günther, *Grundzüge einer neuen Theorie des Denkens in Hegels Logik*, [1933], 2. Mit einem neuen Vorwort erweiterte Auflage, (1978) pp. V–XV; H. G. Herzberger, "Peirce on Definability," *Pragmatism and Purpose: Essays Presented to Thomas A. Goudge*, ed. John G. Slater, Fred Wilson, and L. W. Sumner, (Toronto: University of Toronto Press, 1979).

19. A formal proof that a triadic relation (triad) cannot be defined using only dyadic or monadic relations (dyads or monads) and that it is sufficient for the definition of all 3 + n - ads is given by H. G. Herzberger in the study cited above (note 18).

20. CP 5.253.

21. CP 5.251.

22. CP 5.286.

23. Ms 318 (Prag 41/42).

24. Ms 318 (Prag 33).

25. Ms 318 (Prag 45).

26. Ms 318 (Prag 40).

27. Ms 318 (Prag 15).

28. CP 5.313.

29. CP 5.313.

30. CP 5.315.

31. See K. Oehler, "Zur Logik einer Universalpragmatik," *Semiosis*, 1 (1976), 14–23. J. Jay Zeman, "Peirce's Theory of Signs," *A Perfusion of Signs*, ed. T. A. Sebeok, (Bloomington and London: Indiana University Press, 1977), pp. 22–39. Idem, "The Esthetic Sign in Peirce's Semiotic," *Semiotica*, 19 (1977), 241–258. An important source for the comparison of the concepts of sign and symbol in Peirce and Cassirer is Rulon S. Wells, "Peirce's Notion of the Symbol," *Semiotica*, 19 (1977), 197–208.

32. CP 4.551.

33. CP 4.550 (footnote).

34. See Charles Pearson, "A Theory of Sign Structure," *Semiotic Scene*, 1 (1977), 1.

35. This false impression can arise, if the contributions by Apel are read without a sufficient knowledge of Peirce's work. Cf. under this aspect e.g. K.-O. Apel, *Transformation der Philosophie*, I and II, (Frankfurt a.M., 1973).

36. On this and other similarities between Peirce and Wittgenstein, see R. Rorty's essay "Pragmatism, Categories and Language" in: *Philosophical Review*, (1961), 197–223. On Peirce's epistemology and its relation to probability theory see *H. S. Thayer, Meaning and Action. A Critical History of Pragmatism*, (New York, 1968), p. 101 ff.

37. Cf. Apel's exposition of the "transcendental-hermeneutic" concept of language, in: *Handbuch Philosophischer Grundbegriffe III*, (Munich, 1974), 1383–1402.

38. The question is discussed in R. Bittner, "Transzendental," in: *Handbuch Philosophischer Grundbegriffe III*, (Munich, 1974), p. 1524 ff. See also H. Albert's fundamental critique: "Transzendentale Träumereien. Karl-Otto Apels Sprachspiele und sein hermeneutischer Gott", (Hamburg, 1975).
39. I refer here to J. Habermas' preliminary sketches for a universal pragmatism: J. Habermas, "Vorbereitende Bemerkungen zu einer Theorie der kommunikativen Kompetenz," in: J. Habermas, and N. Luhmann, *Theorie der Gesellschaft*, (Frankfurt a.M., 1971), pp. 101–141; and J. Habermas, "Was heisst Universalpragmatik?" in: *Sprachpragmatik und Philosophie*, ed. by K.-O. Apel, (Frankfurt a.M., 1976), pp. 174–272. See also J. Habermas, *Theorie des kommunikativen Handelns*, (Frankfurt a.M., 1981).
40. Cf. M. Bense, "Fundamentalität und Universalität der Semiotik," Paper 1 of the Institute for Philosophy and Theory of Science at the University of Stuttgart, 1975. Max Bense's proposals are developed on the basis of the contribution of the Stuttgart Institute to semiotic studies, in the development of the basic Peircian theory to a modern functionally operative theory. Cf. E. Walther, *Allgemeine Zeichentheorie. Einführung in die Grundlagen der Semiotik*, (Stuttgart, 1975), and M. Bense, *Semiotische Prozesse und Systeme*, (Baden-Baden, 1975).
41. See the evaluation and interpretation of MS 318 by J. M. Ransdell in *Transactions of the Charles S. Peirce Society*, 12 (1976), as well as my own assessment of it ibid., 10 (1974), 185 ff.

REFERENCES

Apel, K.-O. (1973). *Transformation der Philosophie, I, II*. Frankfurt a. M.: Suhrkamp.

Apel, K.-O. (1975), *Der Denkweg von Charles S. Peirce. Eine Einführung in den amerikanischen Pragmatismus*. Frankfurt a. M.: Suhrkamp.

Buzelli, D. E. (1972). "The Argument of Peirce's 'New List of Categories.' " *Transactions of the Charles S. Peirce Society*, 8:63–89.

Eisele, C. (1979). *Studies in the Scientific and Mathematical Philosophy of Charles S. Peirce. Essays*. Ed. R. M. Martin. The Hague, Paris and New York: Mouton.

Fisch, M. H., and Turquette, A. (1966). "Peirce's Triadic Logic." *Transactions of the Charles S. Peirce Society*, 2:71–85.

Fisch, M. H. (1978). "Peirce's General Theory of Signs." In: T. A. Sebeok, ed. *Sight, Sound and Sense*. Bloomington, Indiana University Press, pp. 31–70.

Fitzgerald, J. J. (1966). *Peirce's Theory of Signs as Foundation for Pragmatism*. The Hague: Mouton.

Freeman, E., ed. (1980). "The Relevance of Charles Peirce." *The Monist*, 63, no. 3.

Greenlee, D. (1973). *Peirce's Concept of Sign*. The Hague: Mouton.

Günther, G. (1983). *Grundzüge einer neuen Theorie des Denkens in Hegels Logik*. 2. Aufl. Leipzig: Meiner. Hamburg, 1978.

Hardwick, C. S., ed. (1977). *Semiotic and Significs. The Correspondence between Charles S. Peirce and Victoria Lady Welby*. Bloomington and London: Indiana University Press.

Henrich, D. (1967). *Fichtes ursprüngliche Einsicht*. Frankfurt a. M.

Henrich, D. (1976), Identität and Objektivität. Eine Untersuchung über Kants transzendentale Deduktion. Heidelberg (Sitzungsberichte der Heidelberger Akademie der Wissenshaften. Philosophisch-Historische Klasse. Erste Abteilung. Jahrgang 1976).

Herzberger, H. G. (1979). "Peirce on Definability." In: J. G. Slater, S. Wilson, K. W. Summer, eds. *Pragmatism and Purpose: Essays Presented to Thomas A. Goudge*.

Jakobson, R. (1975). *Coup d'oeil sur le développement de la sémiotique*. (Studies in Semiotics 3.) Bloomington, Ind.: Research Center for Language and Semiotic Studies.

Lieb, J. (1977). "On Peirce's Classification of Signs." In: C. S. Hardwick, ed. *Semiotic and Significs*. [Appendix B.] Bloomington and London: Indiana University Press, p. 160 ff.

Martens, E. (1975). *Texte der Philosophie des Pragmatismus: Peirce, James, Schiller, Dewey.* Stuttgart: Reclam.

Martens, E. (1981). "Pragmatismus." In: *Handwörterbuch der Wirtschaftswissenschaft* (HdWW), pp. 146–153.

Michael, E. (1974). "Peirce's Early Study of the Logic of Relations 1865–67." *Transactions of the Charles S. Peirce Society*, 10:63–75.

Oehler, K. (1976). "Zur Logik einer Universalpragmatik." *Semiosis*, 1:14–23.

Oehler, K. (1978). "A New Tool for Peirce Research." *Semiotica.*

Oehler, K. (1979). "Peirce's Foundation of a Semiotic Theory of Cognition. In: *Peirce Studies, I.* Lubbock: Texas Tech University Press: 67–76.

Oehler, K. (1981a). "Peirce contra Aristotle. Two Forms of the Theory of Categories." In: *Proceedings of the C. S. Peirce Bicentennial International Congress, Amsterdam 1976.*

Oehler, K. (1981b). "Ein in Vergessenheit geratener Zeichentheoretiker des Deutschen Idealismus." In: *Akten 2. Symposiums der Deutschen Gesellschaft für Semiotik.*

Oehler, K. (1981c). "Logic of Relations and Inference from Signs in Aristotle." *ars semeiotica*, 4.

Oehler, K. (1981d). "On the Reception of Pragmatism in Germany." *Transactions of the Charles S. Peirce Society*, 17, 3.

Ormiston, G. L. (1977). "Peirce's Categories: Structure of Semiotic." *Semiotica*, 19:202–232.

Pearson, C. (1977). "A Theory of Sign Structure," *Semiotic Scene* 1, No. 2:1–22.

Peirce, C. S. (1931–35). *Collected Papers*, vol. 1–6. Ed. C. Hartshorne and P. Weiss. Cambridge: Harvard University Press.

Peirce, C. S. (1958). *Collected Papers*, vol. 7–8. Ed. A. W. Burks. Cambridge: Harvard University Press.

Peirce, C. S. (1968). *Über die Klarheit unserer Gedanken.* Einleitung, Übersetzung und Kommentar von K. Oehler. Frankfurt a.M.: Vittorio Klostermann.

Peirce, C. S. (1967, 1970). *Schriften*, I, II. Übersetzt von G. Wartenberg. Mit einer Einführung hrsg. von K.-O. Apel. Frankfurt a.M.: Suhrkamp.

Peirce, C. S. (Ms). Manuscripts. Harvard University.

Peirce, C. S. (1976). *The New Elements of Mathematics*, vol. 1–4. Ed., C. Eisele, The Hague: Mouton.

Peirce, C. S. (1977a). *Complete Published Works Including Secondary Materials.* Microfiche Edition. Ed. K. Ketner, C. Kloesel, J. Ransdell und C. Hardwick. Greenwich, Conn.: Johnson.

Peirce, C. S. (1977b). *A Comprehensive Bibliography and Index of the Published Works with a Bibliography of Secondary Studies.* Ed. K. Ketner, C. Kloesel, J. Ransdell and C. Hardwick. Greenwich, Conn.: Johnson.

Stiebing, H. M. (1976). "Dreistelligkeit der Relationenlogik - Kommentierende Bemerkungen zu Peirces 'The Logic of Relatives.' " *Semiosis*, 3:20–25.

Tugendhat, E. (1976). *Vorlesungen zur Einführung in die sprachanalytische Philosophie.* Frankfurt a.M.

Turquette, A. R. (1967). "Peirce's phi and psi Operators for Triadic Logic." *Transactions of the Charles S. Peirce Society*, 3:66–73.

Turquette, A. R. (1969). "Peirce's Complete System of Triadic Logic." *Transactions of the Charles S. Peirce Society*, 5:199–210.

Walther, E. (1974). *Allgemeine Zeichenlehre.* Stuttgart: Deutsche Verlagsanstalt.

Walther, E. (1976a). "Erste Überlegungen zur Semiotik von C. S. Peirce in den Jahren 1860–1866." *Semiosis*, 1:35–41.

Walther, E. (1976b). "Die Haupteinteilungen der Zeichen von C. S. Peirce." *Semiosis*, 3:32–41.

Wells, R. S. (1977). "Peirce's Notion of the Symbol," *Semiotica*, 19:197–208.

Zeman, J. J. (1977a). "Peirce's Theory of Signs." In: T. A. Sebeok, ed., *A Perfusion of Signs.* Bloomington and London: Indiana University Press, pp. 22–39.

Zeman, J. J. (1977b). "The Esthetic Sign in Peirce's Semiotic." *Semiotica*, 19:241–258.

CHAPTER 2

Charles Morris and the Behavioral Foundations of Semiotics

ROLAND POSNER

1. INTELLECTUAL DEVELOPMENT AND SPECIALIZATION

Charles W. Morris[1] studied psychology at the University of Chicago in the early 1920s and originally planned on a career in psychiatry. He wanted to learn why and how human beings act so that he would later be able to help them. These goals went through his mind when he was sitting in a car one evening, waiting for his good friend, Bauhaus artist László Moholy-Nagy. Suddenly it became clear to Morris that human action is unthinkable without sign processes and evaluations. How could he become a good psychiatrist without acquiring a theoretical understanding of signs and values himself?

Morris altered his course of study and became one of George H. Mead's[2] most diligent students of philosophy at the University of Chicago. He completed his doctoral dissertation "Symbolism and Reality—A Study in the Nature of Mind" under Mead in 1925, and subsequently embarked on a career as professor, first teaching at Rice University and then returning to Chicago in the early 1930s. Later, he would serve as visiting professor at the New School for Social Research and at Harvard. All of Morris's lectures and publications reflect a remarkably consistent dedication to the topic he chose for lifetime research: signs and values.

Equally remarkable was the circumspection with which the young Morris approached his topic. The philosophy of pragmatism and the methodology of social behaviorism, with which he had become acquainted at the University of Chicago, did not seem sufficient to him, and so Morris looked beyond the United States to Europe and Asia. In the early thirties he visited the centers of European

ROLAND POSNER • Department of Linguistics, Technical University of Berlin, Berlin, West Germany and Netherlands Institute for Advanced Study in the Humanities and Social Sciences, Wassenaar, the Netherlands.

philosophy, became more intimately acquainted with the philosophy of science
and logic of the Vienna Circle, and in 1935 attended the first International
Congress for the Unity of Science in Paris. In 1948 and 1949 Morris traveled
to China and India to investigate their concepts of value, thus executing a project
upon which his sights had been set for some time.[3]

Morris's great talent for synthesizing material from disparate fields is
already obvious in his earliest publications. Attention is paid to the details of a
given question only insofar as an understanding of them will contribute to the
solution of more general problems. He analyzes the practical insights and theoretical conclusions of experts from all over the world, demonstrates their mutual
compatibility, and tries to build up a comprehensive conceptual framework in
which they can complement each other. This lifelong pursuit becomes particularly
apparent in his *programmatic essays* "Logical Positivism, Pragmatism and Scientific Empiricism" (1937) and "Foundations of the Theory of Signs" (1938); it
characterizes his *historical treatises* "Six Theories of Mind" (1932) and "The
Pragmatic Movement in American Philosophy" (1970); it motivates his writings
about a *rational world view*, such as "Paths of Life: Preface to a World Religion"
(1942) and "The Open Self" (1948a); and it is most convincingly realized in his
systematic works on sign theory "Signs, Language, and Behavior" (1946a), and
on value "Varieties of Human Value" (1956), the essence of which is—as its
title indicates—once again summarized in the late work "Signification and Significance" (1946).[4]

Initially Morris had set out to find answers to the questions which preoccupied him by examining individual disciplines and prominent directions of
thought. He found three philosophical movements, each particularly influential
in a given geographical area and strongly associated with certain individual
disciplines:

1. The North American tradition of pragmatism, oriented toward the social
   sciences and biology (and represented by C. S. Peirce, W. James,
   G. H. Mead, J. Dewey, and C. I. Lewis)
2. The Anglo-American tradition of empiricism, oriented toward the natural sciences (and represented by the British empiricists from the 17th
   to the 19th centuries and by American behaviorism)
3. The Central European tradition of logical positivism, oriented toward
   logic and mathematics (and represented by E. Mach, M. Schlick,
   L. Wittgenstein, R. Carnap, H. Reichenbach, and F. Waismann).

Morris was one of the first to recognize the similarities between these
philosophical movements and to state that their differences did not make them
contradictory.[5] The similarities between positivism and empiricism were manifest
in their common preference for intersubjective observation in securing the data.
Empiricism and pragmaticsm were connected by their emphasis on the social

and biological conditions of all knowledge. Pragmatism and positivism had a common objective in their attempt to clarify and solve philosophical problems through the analysis of meaning.[6]

All three movements rejected "a priori synthetic judgments" as a source of knowledge, and for that reason each movement considered itself "scientific" (cf. Morris, 1937:54). According to them, what makes knowledge different from empirical data, was to be found

- in the formal structure of the language employed (logical positivism),
- in the function-dependent substitution of signs for objects (behaviorist empiricism), and
- in the social conventions of communication (pragmatism),

and these were differences that could be empirically investigated in their own right (cf. Morris, 1937:28 and 50 ff).

Morris generalized these historically given approaches step by step in a series of treatises,[7] and in 1934 he drew his first systematic conclusion, noting that "symbols have three types of relation": to a person or persons, to objects, and to other symbols.[8] Three years later he also dispensed with historically given terminology, christening the disciplines which deal with these sign relations "pragmatics," "semantics," and "syntactics."[9] In this way, Morris set up a systematic relationship between three historical modes of thought, legitimizing each without rendering any of them superfluous. Morris called the science created through this synthesis "semiotic" (cf. Morris, 1937:4ff.).[10]

Thus, from the outset, semiotics was a Janus-like enterprise. On the one hand, it involved a loose connection between individual disciplines and directions of research, none of which required semiotics to continue existing; on the other, it claimed to provide both these and other research activities with a common goal which was justifiable independently of their historical development. This was also the reason why Morris subsequently became rather selective in the use of his own "magic formula," which defines semiotics as syntactics, semantics, and pragmatics and their interrelations: "Otto Neurath warned years ago that these terms would engender pseudo-problems; the course of events has proved in part the legitimacy of his fears. Yet these terms, if carefully introduced, serve to mark the scope and subdivisions of semiotic. [. . .] Nevertheless, in general it is more important to keep in mind the field of semiotic as a whole, and to bring to bear upon specific problems all that is relevant to their solution" (Morris, 1946a:217ff.). Note, however, that this critique does not imply a modification of either subject or method. On the contrary, Morris's basic assumptions and scientific ethos remained unchanged from the stormy '30s to the end of his life. They can best be summarized by the following quotation from his main work on semiotics:

[. . .] sign behavior, as formulated in the present account, lends itself to treatment within the categories of a general *theory of behavior*. Vague speculation on these matters is no longer necessary; the problems of sign-behavior have already reached the stage of *empirical* formulation and possible *experimental* resolution.[11]

From what "categories of a general theory of behavior" does Morris proceed?

2. PHASES OF AN ACTION

In the behavioral approach to semiotics—which is to be distinguished sharply from Watson-type behaviorist psychology—behavior is defined as any change taking place in an organism.[12] Thus an animal begins to behave at the moment of its creation and its behavior ceases only when it dies. There is no one who does not continually behave in one way or another.

An action can be delimited within the continuum of behavior by the fact that it has a beginning and an end. It can be structured with a view to reaching a goal. This goal is determined by an impulse.[13]

In order to understand the structure of an action, let us analyze the behavior of a person who is hungry and who yields to this impulse:

Phase 1: He examines his environment and reacts preferentially to external or internal perceptions connected with food (cf. Morris in Mead, 1938:ixf. and xxivf.). *Examples*: (a) He smells the delicate aroma of food from downstairs. (b) He sees a bakery van drive by. (c) He hears the factory siren announcing lunch time. (d) He feels for the sandwich he is not allowed to eat during the lecture.

Phase 2: The organism acts to realize the possibilities offered by these perceptions in order to get something to eat. *Examples*: (a) He follows the smell of food downstairs, finds a cafeteria there, puts a coin in a slot-machine, takes out a bowl of goulash soup, sits down with it at a table, picks up a spoon, and tastes the soup. (b) He looks to see at which shop the bakery van has stopped, goes there, and buys a piece of pastry. (c) He stops working, washes his hands, goes to the locker room, and takes a container of potato salad out of his bag. (d) He removes the rubber band and unwraps his sandwich.

Phase 3: He consumes the food so prepared, thus satisfying his hunger. *Examples*: (a) He brings spoonful after spoonful of the soup to his mouth, chews, and swallows until nothing is left in the bowl. (b) He bites into the piece of pastry and continues chewing until he has eaten it all. (c) He brings the potato salad to his mouth and eventually finishes it all. (d) He breaks off piece after piece of the sandwich, puts it in his mouth, chews, and gradually eats the whole thing.

The three phases of each action can be called *orientation, manipulation,* and *consummation*.[14] They are determined respectively by impulse-controlled perception, preparation of the impulse-satisfying object, and satisfaction or suppression of the impulse.

Impulse-controlled perception in the *orientation* phase takes place primarily with the aid of the so-called "distance senses" of sight, hearing, and smell. The object perceived is not in the immediate surroundings of the actor, but motivates him to go to it. The stimuli in the perception phase have the function of orientation: the properties of the impulse-satisfying object from which they arise serve as orientation properties for the actor (cf. Morris in Mead, 1938:xxvi).

The preparation of the object in the *manipulation* phase can involve widely differing types of activities. These may range from the simple arranging of an object that is already impulse-satisfying to the production of such an object according to the actor's conception. The manipulation of the object takes place primarily in the actor's immediate surroundings. It is also guided by perception, which in this case makes use not only of the distance senses but also of the contact senses of touch and taste. The stimuli received during the manipulation phase function primarily as manipulation stimuli and can be traced back to the manipulation properties of the impulse-satisfying object.

The elimination of the impulse in the *consummation* phase occurs either through its partial or total satisfaction or through the fact that another, competing impulse comes to the fore and assumes control of the behavior.[15] The perception stimuli connected with the satisfaction of the impulse primarily make use of the contact senses. They function as consummation stimuli and can be traced back to the consummation properties of the impulse-satisfying object.[16]

According to Mead, the origination of an individual's ability to act involves the reciprocal influence and development of all these factors. Actions, objects acted upon, and actors are mutually dependent and can become ever more complex within this configuration. The impulse to act is refined to need, interest, inclination, intention, desire, fancy, or caprice (cf. Tranöy, 1972/75:143ff.). The impulse-satisfying object need no longer be one physically concrete thing; there may be several objects involved which may, moreover, be abstract and general. The satisfaction of the impulse no longer takes place via the contact senses alone, but also via the distance senses or even through internal and external action which itself may be multi-phased. This course of development can go so far that all specifications given in the definitions of the phases of an action become invalid. Only the phase-specific functions of orientation, manipulation, and consummation remain. Thus in the later stages of his development, a small child's contact senses will be used as receptors of orientation stimuli and the distance senses as receptors of consummation stimuli. In this way, each manifest property of an object can become relevant for one action in the orientation phase, for another in the manipulation or consummation phase. It often happens that parts of the manipulation phase become ends in themselves and thus enter the consummation phase of the action.

These facts do not, however, invalidate the Meadian analysis of action, because their underlying *functional schema* remains untouched. Indeed, this schema also provides a suitable framework for localizing the onto- and phylogenesis of higher functional processes, and Mead employed it in his attempts to explain the development of communication and consciousness through the structure of action, in particular of social action.

Morris followed this approach and constructed his theory of signs on the basis of Mead's analysis of action.[17]

3. TYPES OF SIGNS

As implied by the functional characterization of action, the first two phases of an action serve the purpose of making the third phase possible. Orientation stimuli are relevant only to the degree that they show the actor how to find the manipulatory and consummatory properties of an impulse-satisfying object. Repeated experience in the satisfaction of similar impulses leads to increasing automatization in the actor's responses: given certain orientation stimuli, the organism is disposed for certain manipulation properties, and the manipulation stimuli dispose the organism for the enjoyment of the impulse-satisfying object. In the end, even orientation stimuli can direct an organism prepared by a certain impulse toward the consummatory properties of the corresponding impulse-satisfying object. In this way the visual or olfactory properties of a piece of cheese, for example, may become a sign for its gustatory properties. The existence of a sign relationship between the two kinds of properties is reflected in the disposition of the organism which sees or smells the cheese to enjoy its typical taste—given that the organism has a desire for it (i.e. that the impulse is present).[18]

With reference to Mead's functional characterization of action, we can therefore generalize the following:

- The role of a *sign* is played primarily by a stimulus which occurs in the orientation phase of an action and which is perceived via the distance senses.
- The *denotatum* of a sign is primarily an impulse-satisfying object which as such occurs in the consummation phase of the action. It is characterized by a number of consummation properties (called "designatum" in Morris, 1938, and "significatum" in Morris, 1946a and 1964), which are perceived via the contact senses.
- An *interpretant* is primarily the disposition of the actor to eliminate the impulse to act through consummation of the denotatum.[19]

Thus a *sign* is a preparatory stimulus that, in the absence of an impulse-satisfying object, causes in an organism a disposition to a sequence of responses of the same type that would be caused by the object itself.[20]

This characterization of signs so obviously refers to the onto- and phylogenetically primary situation of action that it may arouse doubt about its capacity to account for all the pre-theoretical uses of the word "sign" in the various possible contexts. However, as in the case of Mead's characterization of action, it is not the isolated specification of the factors involved that is relevant, but their functional relationship: "The uniqueness of sign-processes lies, in short, in the pattern of their constituents, and not in the constituents themselves" (Morris, 1946a:308). And open questions (e.g., whether or not functional processes within organisms or within inanimate information systems such as computers should be considered sign processes) can be treated through extrapolations on the basis of the approach given. Morris himself conceded that the above characterization may not delineate all the necessary conditions for something to be a sign, but he insisted that it presents sufficient conditions, i.e., that if the conditions laid down in it are met, one is indeed dealing with a sign (cf. Morris, 1946a:12f.).

Proceeding from the primary sign situation, we find that orientation stimuli are still very special signs:

- They are *modality-restricted* since they are not received by the organism that produces them.
- They are *impulse-related* since their denotatum and significatum are determined by the impulse of the recipient.
- They are *situation-contingent* since the disposition to act (interpretant) which they trigger in the recipient changes according to the situation in which they occur.
- They are *function-dependent* since they trigger a later phase of the recipient's action only within the impulse-oriented context of action, and they lose their role as signs when this context disappears.

In general, stimuli which cause a later phase of recipient behavior by indicating an impulse-satisfying object to the recipient are called *signals* (cf. Mead, 1934:190f.; and Morris 1946a:24f.). For the most part, signals function automatically, i.e., the recipients have no opportunity to consider the later phase of an action before it is triggered by the signal.

In signals there need not be any non-functional relationship between the object from which the signal stimulus originates and the object which satisfies the recipient's impulse. Identity of these two objects thus provides a special case in which the orientation stimulus refers the recipient to a consummation property of the same object. In situations in which the object is itself an organism, the early phase of an action of that organism may serve the recipient as an orientation property referring to a later phase of the same action as a consummation property of that organism (cf. Morris in Mead, 1934:xxf.). Making a fist refers the recipient to the blow that will follow, in which case the maker of the fist is (both the sender and) the denotatum and the blow is the significatum. Reaching out one's hand refers the recipient to the grasping of an object located in the direction of the hand, in which case the sender and the object are the denotata and the grasping of the object is the significatum of the initial hand movement. The movement perceived thus shows the recipient what the sender is going to do next and enables him to react preventively to an action which has yet to be completed.

In general, stimuli which cause a later phase of recipient action by indicating a later phase of sender action to the recipient are called *gestures*.[21]

If the opponent understands the making of the fist as a gesture indicating that he is going to be hit, then his reaction will be to move out of the way. As for the actor, if he understands the beginning of the opponent's movement as a gesture indicating that a countermove is being prepared, then he himself will either discontinue or redirect his blow. Such reciprocal influence provides support for Mead's claim that the early stages of a lengthy action may cause other more rapid actions that control its later stages (cf. Morris in Mead, 1934:xxi). Mead calls this type of interaction "a conversation of gestures" and regards it as a step toward "social action" (cf. Mead, 1934:44).

Gestures of this sort influence the behavior of the recipient, but they do not control that of the sender, since they are emitted without awareness of their sign function and without communicative intent. The recipient of such a gesture thus understands the sender better than the sender understands himself. For the sender, such a gesture has no signification and is thus "unintelligent" (cf. Mead, 1922:162). If he is to overcome this condition, the sender must himself acquire the ability to anticipate his own next move. This will come about when he changes his conception of the interaction.

In interaction with *insignificant* gestures, each participant regards the other's gesture as indicating that person's continuing action. His own gestures are experienced independently, if at all (cf. Mead, 1934:81f.).

This situation is changed only when it becomes possible to interpret the temporally adjacent behaviors of two different persons as phases of one and the same action: when a participant can view another participant's behavior as a

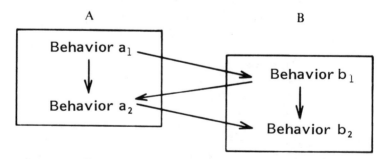

Figure 1. Gestural interaction with insignificant gestures.[22] B regards A's behavior a_1 as an earlier phase of A's behavior a_2, and A regards B's behavior b_1 as an earlier phase of B's behavior b_2. Although behaviors a_1 and b_1, as well as b_1 and a_2, and a_2 and b_2, are temporally adjacent, neither participant sees a relationship between them.

continuation of his own, he will pay more attention to his own behavior. He will vary it with respect to the way he wants his partner to react and will learn to anticipate these reactions on the basis of his own behavior. He will experience his behavior as an earlier phase of a social action of which a later phase will be performed by his partner. Thus it is the expected reaction that makes a gesture significant for its sender (cf. Mead, 1934:81f.; and Morris, 1946a:38f. and 43f.). A significant gesture is a gesture recognized as such by the sender himself: the sender takes over the role of a recipient of his own sign. We may call such a sender a *sign producer*.

In general, a stimulus is called a *significant gesture* if it not only causes a later phase of recipient action (= reaction) by referring the recipient to a later phase of sender action, but also causes a later phase of sender action by referring the sender to a later phase of recipient action (= reaction) (cf. Morris, 1946a:43ff.).

The significatum of a significant gesture for the recipient is its expected continuation by the sender; the significatum of a significant gesture for the sender is the expected reaction to it by the recipient. These mutually expected actions (significata) must be distinguished from the respective dispositions to act (interpretants). Otherwise, threatening or feinting through gestures in sports such as fencing, tennis, and soccer would be impossible. The purpose of a threat, after all, is generally to spare the sign producer the trouble of having to enact the behavior he is threatening to enact, and, although he may not in fact have the disposition to do so, he still has to assume that the person threatened will take the threat seriously, that is, will expect him to enact the threatened behavior under the given conditions. This is possible only when both participants have similar views on what an enactment of the threat by its sender would be like. A threat also loses its purpose if the person threatened does not know how he can cede to the threat. Thus, even when the person threatened does not have the

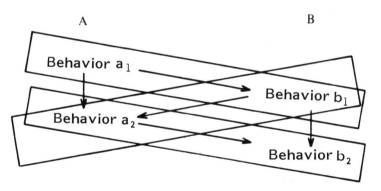

Figure 2. Gestural interaction with significant gestures.[23] A regards his behavior a_1 as an earlier phase of B's behavior b_1, and B regards his behavior b_1 as an earlier phase of A's behavior a_2, and so forth.

disposition to comply with the sender's wishes, he must assume that the sender expects him to, if he is to take the threat seriously. This, in turn, is possible only when both participants have similar views on what compliance with the threat by its recipient would be like. Interaction with significant gestures is thus improved as the significata of a gesture become more and more similar in scope and content for producer and recipient.[24]

So it is only a small step from the production of a significant gesture to the production of a comsignal in the Morrisian sense (cf. Morris, 1946:253f.). According to Morris, *comsignals* are signals which can be produced and received by the same organism and which have the same significatum for producer and recipient.[25] The reception of signs which have the same significatum for sign producer and recipient is called interpretation, and producers and recipients of such signs are both included under the term *interpreters*.

Comsignals are by definition modality-neutral and interpersonal since they are interpreted in the same way by all the participants in the sign process. However, they have the character of signals insofar as they are situation-contingent and function-dependent: their interpretation changes with the context, since the significatum in each case includes a later phase of the action the interpreter is involved in; and they lose their role as signs if the context of action is disrupted before completion.

Take the example of a driver who asks for directions to a certain public building and receives the answer "Turn right at the third intersection." The driver must retain the significatum of this instruction until the moment that he arrives at the third intersection, no matter what might happen in the traffic. He can achieve this by holding three fingers in the air or by quietly repeating the instruction while driving to the third intersection. Holding one's fingers in the air and repeating instructions to oneself are signs which the recipient uses to replace the original sign. For the driver, they constitute a new context of action which assists him in bridging the temporal gap between the context of reception and the execution of the instruction he has received.[26]

Morris calls signs with such capacities *symbols*. In general, a sign is called a symbol if it can be produced by each of its interpreters and if it can replace a signal with the same significatum in any given context of action (cf. Morris, 1946a:24ff., 33f., and 39f.).

The use of symbols is tied neither to specific contexts of action nor to specific signals; symbols are autonomous, i.e., independent of any particular situation or functional process (cf. Morris, 1946a:26f.). This explains why they are generally said to be arbitrary: neither aided nor restricted by a specific type of action context, the choice of the sign carrier is a matter of mere convention.

When a sign unites the properties of comsignal and symbol, Morris calls it a *comsymbol*. Comsymbols are not only independent of situation and function (as are symbols), they are also modality-neutral and interpersonal (as are comsignals). They are the signs with the greatest capacities and are to be found in all natural languages.[27]

If we look once again at the path of onto- and phylogenetic development (i) from contact to distance senses, (ii) from signal via insignificant gesture to significant gesture and comsignal, as well as (iii) from symbol to comsymbol, we can see that the instruments at the individual's and the community's disposal for dealing with the problems of life have become increasingly more powerful: Step by step they have broadened the *horizon* of the individual

(i) (a) from perception through the contact senses (b) to perception through the distance senses and (c) signaling through the distance senses;

(ii) (a) from the anticipation of objects and processes through signals (b) to their anticipation through gestures and (c) the anticipation of one's own actions through significant gestures;

(iii) (a) from the production of significata through comsignals (b) to the stabilization of significata through symbols and (c) to the construction of interpersonal networks of significata on the basis of comsymbols.

These instruments have multiplied the *potential of behavioral alternatives* (i) from one-sided ad-hoc adaptation to unmanipulated circumstances accessible through perceptions and signals (ii) to mutual ad-hoc adaptation to the behavior of interaction partners via gestures and (iii) to the formation of constant patterns of behavior with the help of the comsymbols used in a community.

Little by little, these instruments have enlarged and restructured the *environment* of the individual and of the community from the narrow immediate environment accessible via the contact senses (i) to the broader immediate environment accessible via the distance senses (ii) to the mediated impulse-dependent environment accessible via signals, and (iii) to the mediated impulse-independent environment accessible via comsymbols. This development has granted the individual a growing measure of freedom with respect to his environment, with respect to other individuals, and with respect to himself, a freedom which he may use in the refinement of his impulse to act (see above).

It is at this point that Morris introduces ethics, for if a person's freedom rests upon his ability to anticipate the consequences of his own behavior with the help of signs, the growing freedom is accompanied by increased responsibility for that behavior.[28] According to Morris, we fulfill this responsibility when our decisions take not only our own interests into account, but those of all parties involved.

4. DIMENSIONS OF SIGNIFICATION

In the course of our discussion of sign types, we used Mead's functional model of action as a basis, but abstracted more and more from it and eventually recognized instruments for signifying in any given phase of action that are themselves context-independent: comsymbols. In this section, we will turn to Morris's classification of the dimensions of signification ("modi significandi";

Morris, 1946a: "modes of signifying"; Morris, 1964: "dimensions of signification"), again building, like Morris, on the Meadian analysis of action.

A sign may play a role in each phase of an action. However, its function
can vary, depending upon the phase in which it occurs:

(a) In the *orientation* phase the actor's main concern is to gather information
on his surroundings and thus to discover possible ways of satisfying his particular
impulse to act. Signs that occur in the orientation phase serve mainly to help
the recipient to ascertain the properties of the situation with respect to finding
impulse-satisfying objects. Morris calls signs that indicate properties of a situation ascertainable in this way *designative* signs (cf. Morris, 1964:3ff.).

(b) In the *manipulation* phase the actor's main concern is to treat the
impulse-satisfying object in such a way that its satisfaction potential will be
improved. Signs that occur in the manipulation phase guide the recipient in his
behavior toward the object. Morris calls signs that thus indicate how the impulse-
satisfying object can be manipulated *prescriptive* signs.

(c) In the *consummation* phase the actor's main concern is to enjoy the
impulse-satisfying object with all those properties that fulfill his needs. Signs
that occur in the consummation phase influence the recipient's evaluation of
such properties. Morris calls signs that thus indicate the value of the impulse-
satisfying object *appraisive* signs.

According to Mead, action and object mutually determine each other (Mead,
1938: 10ff.). Thus, as was discussed in section 2, each phase of an action brings
to the fore a different type of properties of the impulse-satisfying object itself.
These properties are what the three sign types signify. However, we should not
be misled by the parallel formulation of the phenomena: the properties of orientation cause the actor to react in a different way from those of manipulation,
which in turn lead to different reactions from those of consummation. Correspondingly, designative signs signify orientation properties in a way which differs
from that in which prescriptive signs signify manipulation properties or appraisive
signs signify consummation properties. The difference between the dimensions
of signification manifest themselves in the interpretant (cf. Morris, 1964:6):

A recipient responds to a designative sign with the disposition to behave
vis-à-vis the denotatum as though it *possesses* the suggested properties. For
example, if it is stated that the banister has just been painted or that the goulash
is hot, then the recipient will focus on the corresponding experiences of touch
and taste.

A recipient responds to a prescriptive sign with the disposition to *manip-
ulate* the denotatum in the suggested way with regard to its satisfaction potential.
For example, if it is requested that one shake the orange juice before pouring it
or that one take the cheese out of the refrigerator half an hour before eating it,
the recipient will have the disposition to act accordingly if he is thirsty for orange
juice or hungry for cheese.

A recipient responds to an appraisive sign with the disposition to *evaluate*
the denotatum in the suggested way with regard to its satisfaction potential. For

example, if a child who normally listens to his mother is deliberating about whether to ignore the spinach on his plate and eat the pudding instead, his disposition to eat the spinach will be reinforced if the mother looks at the spinach, rubs her stomach in ostensive delight, and says "Mmm, good!"

Originally, any sign could be interpreted according to any of these dimensions of signification, depending only on the phase of action the interpreter was in. However, unequal distribution of signs over the different phases of action has led to a division of labor among the signs themselves such that certain signs are now more suited to the orientation phase, others to the manipulation phase, and still others to the consummation phase (cf. Morris, 1946a:62ff.; and 1964:4f.). Take, for example, a word like "deer" (in the sense of a wild animal), which today is designative, a word like "should," which today is usually prescriptive, and a word like "fine," which today is usually appraisive. The type of signification in these comsymbols has become o well established that wherever they appear, they are understood only as designators, or as prescriptors, or as appraisors, respectively.

Since the association with a specific dimension of signification has become fixed for each comsymbol, it is possible for it to occur outside its specific phase of action without another dimension of signification coming to the fore. For example, it can happen in the orientation phase that a car driver[29] (a) is not only informed about the traffic conditions, but also (b) encouraged to judge them in a certain way and (c) called upon to react by driving in a certain way.

Take the following text:

(1) (a) The main road to B is full of pot-holes.
     (b) It is terrible to drive on.
     (c) You should avoid it by taking the detour via C.

The utterance of (1) is complex, for it includes signs of the designative (a), appraisive (b), and prescriptive (c) types of signification. If (1a), (1b), and (1c) are uttered one after the other before the driver has carried out his intention to take the main road to B, they are capable of changing not only his orientation with regard to the two roads to B, but also his evaluation of their consummation properties and his disposition to drive in a certain way. The advantage of such a sign process for the driver is that he need not experience these things himself. For example, he need not drive halfway to B on the main road only to turn back because of the bad road conditions, for he can already anticipate, and thus avoid, such a course of events in the orientation phase.

However, utterance (1) is complex not only because it includes three partial utterances with different types of signification. Each of these partial utterances is itself a complex sign which is in turn made up of several comsymbols. For what reason are such highly differentiated signs necessary? Why do we not use a single undifferentiated sign for the task of (1a), (1b), and (1c), respectively? There are at least two answers to these questions (cf. Morris, 1946a:73ff.):

1. The situation that calls for action is complex. It includes a number of denoted objects: town B, town C, the main road from A to B, the detour from A via C to B, pot-holes.

2. There are features common both to this and to other situations that can best be grasped if each is expressed by the same sign in all situations of this type. The comsymbols "full (of something)" and "terrible" can also refer to objects other than roads; one can "drive on" or "avoid" roads other than the main road from A to B or the detour from A via C to B.

Morris calls signs that facilitate the identification of the denoted objects *identifiors* (1946:64ff., 75ff.). If for one and the same object specific orientation properties are to be ascertained, specific consummation properties evaluated, and specific manipulation properties recommended, it is natural to use the same identifior (I) and to couple it with the appropriate designator (D), appraisor (A), or prescriptor (P):

(1') (a') [The main road to B]$_I$
            [is full of pot-holes]$_D$
      (b') [The main road to B]$_I$
            [is terrible to drive on]$_A$
      (c') [The main road to B]$_I$
            [you should avoid by taking the detour via C]$_P$

Such complex expressions are called *ascriptors* (Morris, 1946a:73ff.); they all ascribe certain impulse-relevant properties to one object, in this case the main road to B. The minimal form of an ascriptor is:

$$I \begin{Bmatrix} D \\ A \\ P \end{Bmatrix}$$

Each constituent of an ascriptor can in turn be complex:

- The complex designator in (a') can be broken down into a designator "full" and an identifior "pot-holes," which are joined by the two formators "is" and "of".
- The complex appraisor in (b') can be broken down into an appraisor "terrible," a designator "drive on," and the two formators "is" and "to."
- The complex prescriptor in (c') can be broken down into a prescriptor "should," two identifiors "you" and "the detour via C," two designators "avoid" and "tak-," and the formators "by" and "-ing."
- Two of the identifiors are complex as well: "the main road to B" can be broken down into the identifiors "the" and "B," the designator "main

road," and the formator "to"; "the detour via C" can be broken down into the identifiors "the" and "C," the designator "detour," and the formator "via."[30]

Such an analysis of the sign complexes under (1′) raises the following questions: (a) Why is the expression "full of pot-holes" a designator, when it also contains identifiors and formators? (b) Why is the expression "is terrible to drive on" an appraisor, when it also contains designators and formators? (c) Why is the expression "you should avoid by taking the detour via C" a prescriptor, when it also contains designators, identifiors, and formators?

The answer to these questions is not simple; it brings us to the heart of the grammar of natural languages (cf. Morris, 1938:18f.; and 1946a:74f.). Morris, however, is concerned only with the *behavioral foundation* of grammar, and he indicates that we could not interpret complex ascriptors at all if we assigned the same relevance to the interpretants of all their constituents. For example, in the reception of (1c)

- we would not know whether we should have in mind primarily town B or town C,
- we would not know whether we should pay attention chiefly to the orientation properties of a certain main road or to those of a detour,
- we would not know how to adjust to the surroundings thus characterized, i.e., which, of all the properties mentioned, the utterance of the word form "should" is asking us to realize.

According to Morris, it is the formators that create order here:[31] The coupling of "should" with "avoid" and "tak-" with the insertion of "by" and "-ing" turns the orientation property of avoidance into a manipulative property. The coupling of "terrible" and "drive" with the insertion of the particle "to" turns the orientation property of driving into a consummation property with negative satisfaction value.

But even if we ascribe to the formators the task of connecting the constituent signs, we have not yet answered the question what distinguishes (1b) from:

(1) (b.1) The main road to B is *terrible* to drive on.
     (b.2) The main road to *B* is terrible to drive on.
     (b.3) The main road to B is terrible to *drive on*.

Such differences must be described by differentiating between *dominant* and *dominated* signs (cf. Morris, 1938:18f.; and 1946a:74f.). In (b.1) the appraisor "terrible" is dominant, and the whole expression thus becomes an appraisive ascriptor. In (b.2) the identifior "B" is dominant, and the whole expression thus becomes an identificative ascriptor.[32] In (b.3) the designator "drive" is dominant, and the whole expression thus becomes a designative ascriptor.

The question of which formators natural languages such as German employ to indicate dominance is answered in more detail in Posner (1972a; and 1972b; cf. also 1982:87ff.). The analysis given there shows that not only sentence-grammatical (ascriptor-internal) but also text-linguistic (ascriptor-external) contexts play a role. For example, we could have changed the ordering of text (1) in the following way:

(2) (a) The main road to B is full of pot-holes.
     (b) You should avoid it by taking the detour via C.
     (c) It is terrible to drive on.

or

(3) (a) The main road to B is terrible to drive on.
     (b) You should avoid it by taking the detour via C.
     (c) The main road to B is full of pot-holes.

As in sentence-grammar, a change of order can lead to a change in the semantic relations between the ascriptors involved: In (1), sentence (a) provides a reason for (b), and (b) a justification for the advice (c). In (2), sentence (a) provides a reason for (b), and (b) an affirmation of the valuation (c). In (3), sentence (a) provides a justification for (b), and (b) an affirmation of the statement (c).

But apart from the semantic relations, the dominance relations are also changed when the order in the texts is changed, as various studies have shown:[33] In standard situations, text (1) taken as a whole answers a question of the type "What should I do?" and is thus prescriptive. In standard situations, text (2) taken as a whole answers a question of the type "How good is the road?" and is thus appraisive. In standard situations, text (3) answers a question of the type "What kind of road is that?" and is thus designative. And this is the case even though the texts all consist of the same ascriptors (if we allow for the alteration of different types of identifiors).

Relying on sentence-grammar, we can reinforce this effect by utilizing syntactic subordination.[34] Instead of (1) we could say:

(4) You should avoid the main road to B, which is terrible to drive on since it is full of pot-holes, by taking the detour via C.

Instead of (2) we could say:

(5) The main road to B, which, on account of the many pot-holes, you really should avoid by taking the detour via C, is terrible to drive on.

Instead of (3) we could say:

(6)   The main road to B, which, because of the terrible driving conditions, you
      really should avoid by taking the detour via C, is full of pot-holes.

A semiotically based grammar should be capable of fully grasping the differences
in the recipient's behavior in the interpretation of all these sentences. Since the
publication of Morris's writings, many authors have recommended the construction of such a grammar (cf. Brown, 1974). But detailed work is only now
beginning.

5.   DIMENSIONS OF SIGN USE

Every sign has not only a significatum, but also an interpretant. The
significatum consists of those properties which an object must have in order to
be *denoted* by the sign. The interpretant consists of the behavioral disposition
with which the recipient must react in order to *understand* the sign.

In sign processes initiated by signals and insignificant gestures, the sender,
if any, and his intentions do not greatly affect the interpretation of the significatum. What counts is rather the recipient's context of action. For example, the
discovery of footprints may provide the recipient with clues as to what preventive
measures to take against their sender, independently of what that individual may
have been up to when leaving those imprints.

In sign processes involving comsymbols, the significatum is even independent of the recipient's context of action. Comsymbols change their significatum neither according to the phase of action the sender happens to be in while
emitting them nor according to the phase of action the recipient happens to be
in while receiving them. But the very fact that comsymbols have constant significata enables their senders to use them as instruments for their own goals
(Morris, 1946a:92f.). A politician who gives particularly impartial explanations
in order to prove himself a good politician in the eyes of an intellectual audience
is using designative signs to attain valuations. A traitorous officer who gives his
subordinates particularly clear directions in order to inform a spy present about
the situation is using prescriptive signs to make orientation possible. A court
poet who writes hymns of praise to his patron in order to move him to give
financial support is using appraisive signs to bring about action. All these goals
could have been pursued in more direct ways, but in these cases it would have
been less effective.

Morris (1946a:92f.) speaks of the *use* of a sign if an organism produces
it as a means to attain a certain objective. This objective usually is a change in
behavior on the part of the interpreter (cf. Morris, 1946a:95f.). Corresponding
to the phase of the interpreter's action that the sign producer has in mind, we

can again distinguish three dimensions in sign use (cf. Morris, 1946:95f.). The producer can use signs

(a) so that the interpreter will be informed about the orientation properties of the object identified (*informative* sign use),
(b) so that the interpreter will improve the manipulation properties of the object identified in a specific way (*incitive* sign use), and
(c) so that the interpreter will make a specific valuation of the consummation properties of the object identified (*valuative* sign use).

As shown above, it is not desirable in all situations to use signs whose dimension of signification brings the sign producer's objective immediately into focus. If this takes place, however, Morris (1946a:94f.) speaks of *primary sign use*. In primary sign use

• a designator is used informatively and answers a question of the type "What kind of object is this?" ("What kind?");
• a prescriptor is used incitively and answers a question of the type "What should I do?" ("What do do?");
• an appraisor is used valuatively and answers a question of the type "How good is the object?" ("How good?").

It is now interesting to ask what happens when someone uses a "what kind?" sign to answer a "what to do?" question, etc. In such cases Morris speaks of *secondary sign use*.[35] Secondary sign use involves processes of reinterpretation. They can be illustrated with reference to our traffic examples again:

Someone who wants to take the main road to B and asks "What kind of road is it?" receives the answer "It is terrible to drive on." Whether or not he adopts this valuation, he will conclude from the fact of its utterance that, in the opinion of the person he is talking with, the road poses obstacles to traffic. He will assume that this message was to be communicated to him. What is valid for this informative use of an appraisive ascriptor also holds true for the informative use of the prescriptive ascriptor in an answer of the type: "You should avoid the main road to B by taking the detour via C."

Someone who wants to take the main road to B and asks "How do I get there?" receives only the answer "The main road to B is full of pot-holes." Whether or not he considers this description true, he will conclude from the fact of its utterance that, in the opinion of the person he is talking with, he should avoid the main road. He will assume that this message was to be communicated to him. What is valid for this incitive use of a designative ascriptor also holds true for the incitive use of the appraisive ascriptor in an answer of the type: "The main road to B is terrible to drive on."

Or, someone who wants to take the main road to B and asks "How good is the main road to B?" receives only the answer "You should avoid it by taking the detour via C." Whether or not he follows this advice, he will conclude from the fact of its utterance that, in the opinion of the person he is talking with, the main road to B is bad. He will assume that this message was to be communicated to him. What is valid for this valuative use of a prescriptive ascriptor also holds true for the valuative use of the designative ascriptor in an answer of the type: "The main road to B is full of pot-holes."[36]

We must reckon with such inference processes even when the indirectly used signs are not simple ascriptors, but whole texts, or (disregarding the special media involved) discourses.[37] The most important question arising here is that of the advantages of secondary sign use over primary sign use. Morris answered this question by referring to the conclusions of *content analysis*. It was empirically proven in the 1940s that the interpreter's behavior depends not only on the purpose of the discourse but also on the dominant type of signification in its ascriptors. The use of a designative discourse for valuative purposes (Morris, 1946a:128ff.: "fictive discourse") has the effect of greater impartiality and is thus in many cases more effective than the use of an appraisive discourse for such purposes. The use of an appraisive discourse for incitive purposes (Morris, 1946a:138f.: "moral discourse") has the effect of being less obtrusive and is thus in many cases more persuasive than the use of a prescriptive discourse for such purposes. The use of a prescriptive discourse for informative purposes (Morris, 1946a:143f.: "technological discourse") has the effect of being less theoretical and is thus in many cases more convincing than the use of a designative discourse for such purposes. And so on.[38]

These conclusions can be further differentiated if we determine how the types of signification of a discourse's constituent signs vary in their percentage of distribution (cf. Morris, 1946a:74f. and 123f.). However, it is still an unsolved problem how and to what extent the distribution of types of signification in a text—analyzed independently of the grammatical structure—influences the recipient's behavior. What is clear, of course, is the fact that it would not suffice to simply take the percentages as they stand and to state, for example, that texts (1) through (6) are 70% designative, 15% prescriptive, and 15% appraisive (cf. Morris, 1946a:264f.).

In the double characterization of signs according to their dimensions of signification and their dimensions of use we have an efficient instrument for the classification of discourses. Notwithstanding the theoretical and methodological difficulties indicated, this instrument has remained irreplacable, especially in journalism and media research.[39]

The evaluation of a discourse with respect to its effect (Morris, 1946:96: "appropriateness") is to be clearly distinguished from evaluation with respect to its truth. According to Morris (1946a:105ff.), an ascriptor is true if it denotes something. And an ascriptor denotes something when the object denoted by the identifior is also denoted by the dominant designator, prescriptor, or appraisor, i.e., when the ascriptor corresponds to a real state of affairs. This correspondence theory of truth has much in common with the early position of Wittgenstein (1922) and with the positions of Tarski (1935) and Carnap (1947). In one decisive point, however, it goes further: Morris speaks not only of the truth of statements, but also of the truth of requests and evaluations. This again is a consequence of the behavioral approach to semiotics. If one projects the phases of an action onto the properties of the object in question, three types of properties appear with respect to the impulse to act: A given object exhibits specific orientation, manipulation, and consummation properties, and their existence provides the basis for the truth of utterances about that object:

A designative ascriptor is true if the object denoted by the identifior really possesses the orientation properties signified by the designator. "The main road to B is full of pot-holes" is true if the main road to B really is full of pot-holes.

A prescriptive ascriptor is true if the object denoted by the identifior possesses the manipulation properties signified by the prescriptor. This means that the method of handling prescribed for the impulse-satisfying object must actually increase the object's satisfaction potential with respect to the recipient's present impulse to act. Thus the sentence "Take the route via C to B" is true if taking the route via C to B conforms to the recipient's current interests.[40]

An appraisive ascriptor is true if the object denoted by the identifior possesses the consummation properties signified by the appraisor. This means that the satisfaction which the impulse-satisfying object would provide for the recipient must actually still his current impulse to act. Thus the sentence "Oh, what a wonderful road this is!" is true if the road really fulfills the recipient's current needs in the way indicated.

These examples show that by taking into account not only orientation properties, but also manipulation and consummation properties of the denoted object, the truth of the ascriptor is relativized to the recipient's current impulse to act. Although this solution is one to which not everyone would subscribe, it remains preferable to such popular alternatives as the interactionist or the performative approaches. The former declares a prescriptive ascriptor to be true if the act that it prescribes is actually carried out (cf. Lewis, 1969:149ff. and 188ff.). The latter declares every meaningful utterance to be true, since its communicative function can be explicated on the basis of sentences that are all either nonsensical or true (e.g., "I hereby advise you to take the detour via C to B"; cf. Lewis, 1970:56ff.). The advantage of a generalization of the concept of truth on Morrisian lines lies in the fact that it explains a language use that seems firmly fixed in the native speaker's intuition: Who has not reacted to advice of the type "You should take the detour via C to B!" with "That's right," and meant it literally! And who has not reacted to a valuation of the type "What a wonderful trip this is!" with "That's true!"

6. DIMENSIONS OF VALUE

Our actions reveal not only the signs we use, but our values as well, and for this reason Mead's model of action can also serve as a basis for depicting the Morrisian theory of value (cf. Morris, 1939a:131, footnote 1).

According to Morris and Mead, sign processes originally arose through the conditioning of the distance senses in the orientation phase of an action; valuations, on the other hand, are to be located in the consummation phase, from a developmental point of view. For the actor, the impulse-satisfying object itself is the primary value ("object value"; cf. Morris, 1939a:134, and 1964:20). The value properties of an object are to be considered the same as its consummation properties.[41] Since they cannot be determined independently of an action's purpose, values, too, are relative. The value of an object lies neither in the object alone nor in the interests of the actor alone, but rather in the object's capabilities to realize the actor's interest.

An object's value to an organism is demonstrated if the organism prefers that object to others in satisfying his impulse to act ("operative value"; cf. Morris, 1964:19). Initially the preference process occurs subconsciously, but with the emergence of signs it becomes a decision-making process which may eventually take place on a conscious level (see above pp. 27f. and 32f.).

In the course of development, orientation stimuli may be divorced from the impulse-satisfying object and become signs for its consummation properties; and in interpreting orientation stimuli, the actor may develop "conceived values" which anticipate the value properties of the object (Morris, 1964:21). It is with the help of his conceived values that an actor can transfer his choice of an impulse-satisfying object from the consummation phase to the orientation phase. The differentiation of object values, operative values, and conceived values is thus synchronized with the differentiation of denotata, interpretants, and significata in the development of signs, and it plays an equally important role in the control of behavior.

Like signs in the form of significata, values in the form of conceived values have become an instrument in all three phases of action. Here, too, a division of labor has emerged in that an efficient actor needs to realize different types of values in the different phases of an action. As in his analysis of signs, Morris utilizes this approach in introducing dimensions of value (1964:21f.):

(a) During orientation, the actor is most aware of environmental information. Assimilation of such information is greatest if the actor neither tries to dominate his environment nor allows it to dominate him. He cannot assimilate all information, but rather must be selective with regard to his current interest to act. Decisive for the actor in this phase is thus *detachment*.

(b) During manipulation, the actor aims to influence his environment. He must obtain or produce objects of his choice to satisfy his impulse to act. This is best achieved if the actor extends his sphere of influence to include such objects. What is decisive for the actor in this phase in thus *dominance*.

(c) During consummation, the actor seeks to be influenced by his environment. The impulse-satisfying object should unfold in its most effectual way. What is now decisive is no longer independence and control but rather acceptance and submission. Morris therefore calls the actor's attitude in this phase *dependence*.

These descriptions remain valid even for social actions in which several alternating actors cooperate in the pursuit of a common goal. A community that wants to construct a bridge (cf. Morris, 1964:23), for example, will ascertain its needs, choose a site, survey it, and then execute appropriate construction while placing value on certain consummation properties (such as good driving conditions, easy passage for ships, elegant form, and view from the bridge). In this case, detachment, dominance, and dependence are as necessary as in other actions, but they are required in different degrees from the various collaborators: information about the various possibilities of realizing the project is collected and given by the city planner and surveyors, the execution of the project is performed by the architect and construction engineers, and the enjoyment of the result is the affair of the residents.

Morris only arrived at the value dimensions of detachment, dominance, and dependence after detailed studies of cultural history. In his first essay about a rational world view, "Paths of Life" (1942), Morris designates these dimensions as Buddhistic, Promethean, and Dionysian and makes them the basis for a value profile of world religions.[43] Christianity, Buddhism, and Mohammedanism are compared with regard to the relative importance given to each dimension in their conceived values: Christianity is characterized, in order of decreasing importance, through detachment, dependence, and dominance, Mohammedanism through dependence, dominance, and detachment, and Buddhism through detachment, dominance, and dependence. Morris was later able to give operational descriptions for each dimension and to use these in an empirical comparison of cultures (cf. Morris, 1956:27ff.). He found that the values of individuals and groups in all human cultures around the world can be classified and differentiated on the basis of these dimensions. This result is equal in importance to the classification and differentiation of all sign processes on the basis of the dimensions of signification.

Even more interesting are the correlations found by Morris and Jones (1956), when they compared the value conceptions of individuals with the phases of social actions which these individuals were predominantly involved in because of their professions:

There are those whose activities are largely restricted to the orientation phase of social actions, e.g., the land surveyors in the bridge project. Detachment plays the greatest role in their conceived values, informative sign use is what they are accustomed to in sign behavior, and designative signs are preferred by them even when they find themselves in the manipulation or consummation phases of an action.[44]

Others, such as construction engineers, are chiefly concerned with environmental manipulation. Dominance plays the greatest role in their conceived values, incitive sign use is what they are accustomed to in sign behavior, and prescriptive signs are preferred by them even when they are involved in the orientation or consummation phase of an action.

Others, finally, are able to concentrate their lives on the consummation phase of social actions. Dependence is given the greatest importance in their conceived values, valuative sign use is what they are accustomed to in sign behavior, and appraisive signs are preferred by them even when they find themselves in the orientation or manipulation phases of an action.

Morris regarded the scientist (detached; informative; designative), the technologist (dominant; incitive; prescriptive), and the artist (dependent; valuative; appreciative) as prototypical realizations of these modes of living, and he analyzed their patterns of behavior and ways of problem-solving in more detail (cf. Morris, 1936b; and 1964: 22f., 26f.).

Taken separately, each of these modes of living may seem questionable and unjustified. However, they receive a purpose and a justification when one takes them as specialized contributions to the existence of a community as a whole, for each can be related to one of the three phases of social actions as outlined in Table 1. This table, which Morris presented in several versions in his last systematic publication (cf. Morris, 1964:8,22, and 27), summarizes a lifetime's search for an answer to the question: what signs and values are required in order for a human being to act?

The answer is not given in the form of prescriptive grammar or of normative ethics. It does not propagate particular values as do the material ethics of an Aristotle or of a Nicolai Hartmann, nor does it provide instructions of a Kantian kind concerning which actions to reject as immoral. Still, the actor is not left helpless, for the answer shows him what attitude he must take when he wants to satisfy an impulse. And it provides an explanation when the actor reflects upon his tendency toward a particular dimension of value. Indeed, Morris's answer helps the actor to organize his impulses to act in such a way as to avoid conflicts with his fellow human beings. Morrisian ethics is a situational ethics. For Morris, morality is the harmonization of each individual's interest with those of his society, and of each society's interests with those of all other societies.[45] And the responsibility of an individual and of a society for specific decisions required in a given situation cannot be abrogated by any higher court, be it human or superhuman.

As opposed to the "General Semantics" of Korzybski or Hayakawa, the Morrisian answer does not propagate specific sign actions, nor does it provide

Table 1

Phase of Action	Dimension of Signification	Dimension of Use	Dimension of Value
orientation	designative	informative	detached
manipulation	prescriptive	incitive	dominant
consummation	appraisive	valuative	dependent

absolute criteria for their rejection as the formalists of logical positivism did. Still, the actor is not left helpless, for the answer shows him how to express himself most effectively when he wants to satisfy an impulse. And it provides an explanation when the actor reflects upon his tendency toward a particular dimension of signification or sign use.

Morris carefully avoids the temptation to offer a definitive position or an absolute perspective. On the contrary, he constantly emphasizes that a multitude of positions and perspectives is possible. For Morris, everything is given only under particular perspectives. Invalidating the prejudices of those who like to condemn him as a "behaviorist neo-positivist," he has never tried to achieve objectivity through abstraction from the observer, but rather through multiplication of the number of his perspectives (cf. Morris, 1948a:129). His preferred point of view is neither the merely external perspective of the behaviorists nor the merely internal perspective of the introspectionists, but rather a combination of the two. In this way, Morris can do justice to subjective experience and intersubjective experience as well as to subjective experience of intersubjective experience, and include all such experiential data in the subject matter of his semiotic theory (cf. Morris, 1927:255ff.; 1938:45ff.; 1946a:228ff.; and 1964:29ff.).

For Morris, no all-encompassing perspective is possible, and for this reason it is necessary to construct the unity of the world by appropriately organizing the many possible perspectives. This is a genuinely semiotic approach. Morris introduced it in 1932 under the term "objective relativism" and maintained it until his death.[46] He was well aware that theoretical construction is a special type of scientific action, which itself implies a certain way of looking at things. To compensate, he wrote poems:[47] "Science deepens all our surfaces/ Yet it is but one surface of our depths."

NOTES

1. Morris was born on May 23, 1901 in Denver, Colorado. He died on January 15, 1979 in Gainesville, Florida.
2. Mead, one of the main representatives of philosophical pragmatism, studied at Harvard, Leipzig, and Berlin. He was professor of philosophy at the University of Chicago from 1894 until his death in 1931 and became well known in the twenties because of the originality of his lectures on social psychology.
3. The biographical information given here is based on a personal discussion with Morris which took place in the summer of 1975 in Gainesville, Florida.
4. Comprehensive information about the publications of Morris can be found in the monograph by Fiordo (1977), which, however, contains some chronological errors. More reliable is the unpublished Ph.D. dissertation by Eakins (1972). A collection of important essays about Morris was edited by Eschbach (1981).
5. Cf. Morris, 1929; 1934; 1935a; 1935b; 1935c; and 1936. Also see Morris, 1937:4.
6. Cf. Morris, 1937:56ff., where further similarities are discussed.

7. Cf. Morris, 1929; 1934; 1935a; 1935b; 1935c; and 1936. With the exception of Morris, 1929, all of these publications reappear in Morris, 1937. Also see Morris 1970.

8. Cf. Morris, 1936:135 = 1937:27f. Morris, 1948b discusses Dewey's criticism that this and similar formulations of his constitute an adoption and misinterpretation of the Peircean triad "sign/object/interpretant." This type of reproach is worth dealing with in more detail, since it has been taken up by Peirceans time and time again and was recently repeated in very strong terms by Rochberg-Halton and McMurtrey (1983). They mention several points of convergence between the approaches of Morris and Peirce and consider all the differences between them as errors committed by Morris in the explication of Peirce. The truth is that Morris never saw himself as an exegete of Peirce. Apart from his encyclopedic article of 1938, "Foundations of the Theory of Signs," where he introduced Peircean terms along with those of Mead, Husserl, Ogden and Richards, Carnap, Tarski, Reichenbach, and others in order to provide his readers with an encyclopedic orientation, Morris carefully constructed his own theory of signs. And saying that this was not Peirce's theory is like blaming Morris for having one at all. Equally ridiculous is Rochberg-Halton and McMurtrey's reproach that Morris suppressed "all explicit acknowledgement of Peirce's influence" (1983:152) in view of the fact that Peirce's name is mentioned in prominent places nine times in Morris, 1938 and sixteen times in Morris, 1946a—the number of occurrences being second only to those of Mead's name. Morris gladly referred to Peirce as soon as the first three double volumes of the latter's "Collected Papers" (Peirce, 1931–1935) had become available to him, and he devoted a whole subchapter of his 1946 book to "Charles Peirce on Signs" (1946a:287–291). In hindsight, he went so far as to say: "[. . .] in historical perspective, it seems to me that the position of 'Signs, Language, and Behavior,' though its orientation was not derived from Peirce, is in effect 'an attempt to carry out resolutely' his approach to semiotic" (1948b:124). But at the same time, he insisted: "[. . .] the position developed in 'Signs, Language, and Behavior' did not start from Peirce. George H. Mead first stimulated me to think about signs behaviorally. 'Signs, Language, and Behavior' is in many ways a further development of Mead's 'Mind, Self, and Society.' I never heard Mead in lecture or conversation refer to Peirce. Only later did I work earnestly at Peirce, Ogden and Richards, Russell, and Carnap, and still later at Tolman and Hull" (1948b:124). Morris, 1946a:290f. clearly states what distinguished Morris from Peirce: "Peirce's account of signs is embedded in the metaphysics of his categories (possibility, existence, and law are the basic terms in his classification of signs) and in the metaphysics of his view of mind." Thus the similarity between Morris's formulation in 1936:135 and the Peircean triad is a systematically based coincidence and a historical accident rather than a suppressed quotation.

9. Cf. Morris, 1937:4; and 1938:6ff. For the historical precursors of this division, cf. Morris, 1937:4, note 1; and Henne, 1975:92ff.: "Neue Sprachpragmatik und altes Trivium." Romeo (1981) quotes Sanctius (1587), who, in accounting for the creation of Man, wrote (I,1,ch.2): "Creavit Deus hominem rationis participem; cui, quia 'sociabilem' esse voluit, magno pro munere dedit 'sermonem.' Sermoni autem perficiendo 'tres opifices' adhibuit. Prima est 'grammatica,' quae ab oratione solaecismos et barbarismos expellit. Secunda 'dialectica,' quae in sermonis veritate versatur. Tertia 'rhetorica,' quae ornatum sermonis tantum exquirit." In the present essay little will be said of the three sign dimensions syntactics, semantics, and pragmatics. The Peircean sign classes icon, index, and symbol will not be discussed at all. These were prominent concepts in the account Morris gave of semiotics in 1938 and 1939; however, their prominence faded: they do not even appear in the subject index of Morris, 1964. Readers wishing to study these concepts in detail are referred to Morris, 1938 and 1939a. The relationship between syntactics, semantics, and pragmatics is discussed in detail on the Morrisian basis in Posner, 1986a.

10. Referring to syntactics, semantics, and pragmatics, Morris (1937:4) envisioned "semiotic" as "the general science which includes all of these and their interrelations." He chose the term "semiotic" in conformity with traditional English usage (cf. Sebeok in Morris, 1971:9f.). Over the past half century, however, many other terms have become current in this connection in

various parts of the world and in different areas of research, among them "semiotics," "semeiotic," "semiology," "semasiology," and "sematology." Because of the parallel with "syntactics," "semantics," and "pragmatics," "semiotics" has become the most widely used variant in the last two decades. It will therefore be consistently used instead of "semiotic" in the present essay.

11. Cf. Morris, 1946a:58f. (my italics). Similar statements can be found in Morris as early as 1935 and as late as 1964. In this context, the following empirical studies which Morris designed and executed himself should be mentioned: (a) the intracultural comparison of job type, character structure, and conceived values (cf. Morris, 1939b:409–423; and Morris and Jones, 1956:345–349); (b) the intercultural comparison of conceived values (cf. Morris and Jones, 1955:523–535; and Morris, 1956:31–34); (c) the correlation of two different dimensions of signification (as exemplified by "good" and "ought"; cf. Morris, 1956:164–176); (d) the correlation of dimensions of signification with dimensions of value (cf. Morris, 1956:144ff.; and Morris 1964:73ff.); (e) the correlation of Morris's dimensions of signification with Osgood's dimensions of meaning (cf. Morris, Osgood and Ware, 1961:62–73); (f) the measuring of attitudes toward works of art (cf. Morris, 1956:144ff.; and Morris and Sciadini 1966:144–149); (g) the comparison of the conceived values found in mentally healthy individuals with those found in the mentally ill (cf. Morris, Eiduson, and O'Donnovan, 1960:297–312). Morris, 1964:49ff. summarizes the methods and results of the above research.

12. Cf. Morris in the introduction to Mead's "Mind, Self, and Society" (Mead, 1934:xix). Morris called the investigation of behavior "behavioral studies" (1946a:v) or "behavioristics" (cf. 1938:5f.; and 1946a:2f.), which can be translated as "ethology" today (cf. Eibl-Eisesfeldt 1967:15ff.). For him, behavioristics as a discipline was neutral with regard to the question of which approach (behaviorist or other) should be taken in the study of behavior: " 'Behavioristics' is a more general term than 'behaviorism,' the latter being a particular theory about the behavior of organisms" (1946a:346f.). Morris was well aware of the fact that, in his time, behavioristics was "not sufficiently developed to account adequately for the more complex human actions, nor for the signs, which they utilize" (1946a:2f.). Therefore, he found it quite natural that there should be a number of different approaches to the study of behavior competing with each other within behavioristics: mentalist ones like that of Ogden and Richards (1923), who use introspection and refer to private consciousness and mental events in order to define sign processes (cf. Morris, 1946a: 294–298), and behaviorist ones like those of Watson, M. F. Meyer, Mead, Feigl, Tolman, Hull, and Skinner (cf. Morris, 1946a: 299–310). However, an adequate understanding of Morris's own approach to semiotics is impossible if one does not differentiate among the various behaviorist approaches. One has to distinguish between (a) the ontological behaviorism of Watson (1913; 1914; 1919) and Skinner (1938) that denied the existence of a mind and of specific mental events, and concluded that they cannot be legitimate subjects of scientific investigation, whether through introspection or other methods, (b) the methodological behaviorism of M. F. Meyer (1921) and Tolman (1932) that discards introspection as a method of research without committing itself to the existence or non-existence of private consciousness and mental events, (c) the logical behaviorism of Feigl (1934; also see Feigl, 1950, 1958) and Hull (1937, 1943) that thematized the results of introspection into individual and social consciousness and used mentalistic terms, but tried to explicate them within the theoretical framework of behavioral concepts.

The latter approach could focus either on the terms of mentalist psychology (psychological behaviorism) or on those of mentalist sociology (sociological behaviorism). G. H. Mead's "social behaviorism" (1922; 1932; 1934; 1938) is an early variant of sociological behaviorism. Logical behaviorism was influenced by Bridgman's operationalism (1927; 1936; 1938), which advocated the explication of all technical terms in science on the basis of the operations involved in their use, and by the logical positivism of the Vienna Circle.

Morris himself oscillated between the logical behaviorism of his 1938 "Foundations of the Theory of Signs" and the methodological behaviorism of his 1946 "Signs, Language, and Behavior." This is apparent in his utilization of the term "behavior" itself. While in 1938 he followed Mead's wide use of the term (see above), in 1946 behavior was restricted to muscle movement and gland activity, but by 1948 Morris had returned to the wider use of the term (cf. Morris, 1948b). Note also the difference between the term "response" (standing for muscle and gland activity caused by some stimulus) and "reaction" (standing for any given change in an organism occurring as a consequence of some stimulus). Very instructive in this respect is a comparison of Morris, 1946a:32f. with Morris, 1964:2,3,6,8,49 (cf. Eakins, 1972:348ff.).

In building the terminology of semiotics, Morris always tried to avoid the use of mentalist terms (cf. 1938:5f.; and 1946a:27f.), thinking that all mentalist terms may turn out to be explicable within a behavioral semiotics (1946a:30f.). But he never refused to acknowledge the possibility of self-observation (cf. Morris, 1946a:299f.) and even sought to account for private experience that is intrinsically personal (i.e., tied to a certain historically given individual) or intrinsically social (i.e., tied to a certain historically given community); cf. Morris, 1938:46ff. Only to a philosopher with such wide horizons could the project of semiotics make any sense at all.

13. Cf. Mead, 1938:3–25; and Shibutani, 1961:66. Also see Meltzer, Petras, and Reynolds, 1975:33f. An impulse can be regarded as "an innate drive (e.g., of playing, hunting, collecting, ranking) which is not associated with definite motor activities" (Eibl-Eibesfeldt, 1967:447). Morris distinguished between behavior, sign processes, and communication. Therefore, he would have subscribed to the thesis that it is impossible not to behave, but Watzlawick's claim about the "impossibility of not communicating" (Watzlawick, Beavin, and Jackson, 1967:45ff.) would have been unacceptable to him (cf. Morris, 1946a:32ff. and 117ff.).

14. In this context, Mead refers to Craig (1918), who was the first to distinguish the "rigid" "consummatory action" which satisfies drives from the variable appetence behavior with which an organism seeks out a stimulus situation (cf. Eibl-Eibesfeldt, 1967:20 and 57). However, Craig is more concerned with the difference between innate and acquired behavior than Mead and Morris; cf. Mead, 1938:3–25 and Morris in Mead, 1938:xxvf. Also see Morris in Mead, 1934:xxii.

15. Mead and Morris's description is surprisingly similar to that of the "functional circle" by Jacob von Uexküll (1937:34): "The relevant property is either objectively extinguished when the food to which it belongs is eaten, or it is subjectively extinguished when the appetite is ultimately appeased, in which case the sieve of the sense organs closes." Morris (in Mead, 1934:xxxii) here differentiates once again between an impulse satisfaction which in the long run strengthens an impulse of the corresponding type and one which leads to its disappearance.

16. An actor's behavior in any given phase can in turn be broken into actions with related subcategories.

17. Cf. Morris, 1946:42ff. More than a generation after Mead's death, when Morris himself was approaching the end of his academic career, he emphasized: "The contemporary British, and to a certain extent American, philosophers seem to be drawing upon Mead without having read him. Mead, I believe, will come to be seen as the pivotal figure in the development of an adequate behavioral psychology and philosophy." (Morris, 1964:31, note 19) All that Morris presents as basic to Mead's social psychology can also be regarded as basic to his own semiotics (cf. Fiordo, 1977:14).

18. On the semiotic relation between the contact and the distance senses, see Morris in Mead, 1938:xxvi ff. Also see Johnson, 1836; Gustafsson in Posner and Reinecke, 1977: 303; as well as Stokoe in Posner and Reinecke 1977:174f.

19. The difference between "significatum" and "interpretant" in Morris corresponds to two different uses of the term "interpretant" in Peirce; cf. Morris, 1948b:127.

20. Cf. Morris, 1938:31f.; 1946a:10f. and 353f.; and 1964:2f. Apel (1973:28–31) has given an elaborate account of the essential advances of the Morrisian characterization of signs vis-à-vis other approaches. However, much of Apel's criticism of Morris proves to be unjustified when compared with Morris's actual writings:

1. Concerning the unmaintainable view that Morris has reduced semiotics to "a theory of conditioning and stimulus replacement" (Apel, 1973:29), see Morris, 1946a:29f.

2. Concerning the demand that all languages (also those of scientific theory) be regarded as semiotic unities and that they be analyzed not only syntactically and semantically, but also pragmatically (Apel, 1973:18), see Morris, 1946a:217f., who emphasizes that there are no "purely syntactic" or "purely semantic" signs.

3. Concerning an alleged "new pragmatic turn" taken by Morris between 1938 and 1946, compare the section about pragmatics in Morris, 1938:29ff. with that in Morris, 1964:14f. and 44f.; the comparison shows that such a claim has no basis.

4. Concerning the distinction between the program of a "pragmatically integrated semiotics" and the "methodologically behaviorist approach" to its realization (Apel, 1973:25), which Morris made from the beginning, see Morris, 1938:5f. and 1946a:29ff.

5. Concerning the claim that Morris did not take into account the intentions of the sign producer (Apel, 1973:33), see the theory of sign use in Morris, 1946a:93ff. and 1964:14f. as well as the definition of "behavior" in the glossary of Morris, 1946a, where Morris explicitly states: "Behavior is therefore 'purposive'[. . .]."

6. Concerning the possibilities of legitimizing actions and requests to act (Apel, 1973:25,51, and 53), see Morris, 1964:41ff. on "the absolutist–relativist controversy."

7. Concerning the distinction between empirical and communicative experience (Apel, 1973:37 and 49) and the inclusion of communicative experience within semiotics, see Morris, 1946a:296f. and 299f. as well as 1964:29ff. An extended sign theory proceeding from the assumptions of Mead and Morris can demonstrate why Apel's dualistic opposition between empirical and communicative experience is itself misleading and how it originates: the error lies in his having singled out two types of sign behavior which in reality are tied to one another in a long chain of bio-social developmental stages.

21. Cf. Morris, 1946a:119ff. This definition does not cover the pre-theoretical usage of the English word "gesture" which conforms more to what is defined below as "significant gesture."

22. The arrows "...→---" and "---←..." are to be read as "... influences ---".

23. The behavior of two different persons represented within one and the same box constitutes two phases of the same action.

24. On the role of mutual expectation of sender and recipient in the sign process, see Lewis, 1969:52ff. and 152ff. Also see Jones and Gerard 1967.

25. It is not necessary that the interpretants be the same for the producer and the recipient of a comsignal, as is clearly shown in the analysis of prescripive comsignals; cf. Morris, 1946a:38f., 42f., and 346f.

26. Cf. Morris, 1946a:24f. Also see the discussion of Hull's concept of the "pure-stimulus act" in Morris, 1946a:305ff.

27. The analysis of language signs as comsymbols shows that Resnikov and others are wrong when they claim that Morris has misunderstood "the essence of the regularities in signal activity which Pavlov discovered" and overlooked the fact that speaking is "a signaling activity [. . .] of a higher order," "an activity of the second signaling system [. . .] which exhibits new, specific traits qualitatively different from those found in animal signaling" (Resnikov, 1977:229). Resnikov's misreading of Morris is due to his neglect of Morris' explicit warnings not to mistake the sign characterization discussed on page 28 for a definition (cf. Morris, 1946a:353f.).

28. Cf. Morris, 1927:261; 1940:583ff.; as well as 1946a:197 and 274f. The 1940 essay "The Mechanism of Freedom" contains interesting parallels to Mead's 1912 "The Mechanism of Social Consciousness" and is closely related to the systems-theory approach to ethics discussed in Germany in the 1970s (cf. Habermas and Luhmann, 1971 and Posner, 1974 = 1976).

29. Cf. Eakins, 1972:79. Morris, 1946a:5f. analyzes a similar example. In standard situations, someone who hears text (1) and who intends to take the main road to B will react to the utterance of (1a), (1b), and (1c) with the following dispositions to act: Because of (1a), he will prepare himself for difficult road conditions, i.e., if he takes the main road, he will be on the lookout for pot-holes and will either avoid them or drive over them at a reduced speed. Because of

(1b), his appreciation of the main road as the best means for getting to B will be reduced, and he will look for ways to avoid it. Because of (1c), he will watch for road signs to C, follow them, and then drive on to B. Text (1) can also be replaced by a road sign such as the following:

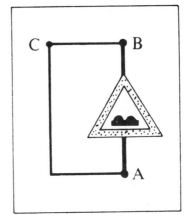

Figure 3

However, this sign signifies only in the designative dimension of signification and can convey neither the appraisive message of (1b) nor the prescriptive message of (1a).

30. If we compare the expressions in (1') with those in (1), we will conclude that the anaphoric sign "it" in (1b) and (1c) assumes the place of the identifior "the main road to B."

31. Cf. Morris, 1946a:85ff. The extended problematics of "formative ascriptors," a "formative dimension of signification," and a "systemic use of signs" are not further discussed here because Morris did not arrive at a conclusive position with regard to these concepts. Cf. Morris, 1946a:153ff.; and 1964:11ff.

32. Morris gives only marginal consideration to ascriptors of this kind; cf. Morris, 1946a:75f.

33. Cf. Hovland, 1957; Miller and Campbell, 1959; Wilson and Miller 1968; Teigeler 1968. Boehme-Dürr 1987 provides a summary.

34. Cf. Posner, 1972a:148ff.; and 1972b; as well as 1982:95ff. On the difference between a text and a complex sentence, see Posner, 1972a:166ff.

35. Cf. Morris, 1946a:94f. and 116. In this chapter Morris anticipates—in a theoretically well-founded and generalized way—what has been discussed with respect to natural languages under the label of "indirect speech acts"; cf. Searle, 1969; and 1975.

36. The reasoning required in the interpretation of secondary sign use is discussed in detail in Posner, 1982:21ff.

37. Cf. Morris, 1939:142ff.; and 1946a:123ff. "Discourse" in the Morrisian sense is not to be equated with "discourse" in the sense of Habermas (nonauthoritarian, argumentative, verbal dialogue; cf. Habermas 1962 = 1979); it includes other kinds of communication and other media as well. Cf. Posner, 1972c:10f.

38. On the criteria for judging the effect of informative, incitive, and appraisive sign use, see Morris, 1946a:94–105.

39. On content analysis, see Kaplan, 1943 and the response in Morris 1943. Also see Geller, Kaplan, and Lasswell, 1942 and Berelson, 1952. Bessler, 1970 provides a comprehensive account of the merits and limitations of this method of text analysis.

40. Restricting the analysis to the impulse to act which is operative at the time eliminates legitimation problems of the kind discussed in Apel, 1973:52ff.

41. This approach is reminiscent of the axiology of Thomas Aquinas, who equated the "highest being" with the "highest good" because for him being and being good are actually the same ("Ens et bonum convertuntur"). However, this formula is relativized by Mead and Morris both genetically and behaviorally: The equation of object and value is valid only for primary situations of action and depends on the given impulse to act. Being and being good may converge for person x in the context of an impulse to act y, but they need not when the person's preferences change because of a change of impulse.

42. These attitudes are defined formally with the help of system theory in Morris, 1964:20f. It is an interesting task to reconstruct aesthetics, and especially poetics, within the Morrisian framework. Morris has devoted attention to aesthetic sign processes throughout his life. With reference to Mead's analysis of action, Morris, 1964:79 regards aesthetic experience as a penetration of the consummatory stage of an action into stages earlier than the actual consummation. In this way, the whole action gains something of the consummatory quality. This is generally facilitated through three features of the work of art: 1. As in the special case of poetic texts, a work of art is characterized through valuative sign use (1946a:136ff.). 2. Although usually signifying in all dimensions of signification, a work of art tends to be dominated by appraisive signs signifying value properties (1946a:135ff.). 3. A work of art not only signifies values, but also embodies them since it is an iconic sign structure (1939a:137). This is a characterization of art in purely semiotic terms. Whatever truth there may be in it, it exemplifies two positions that Morris has always held: first, that every work of art is a sign and hence that aesthetics is part of semiotics; second, that it is possible to differentiate the aesthetic sign from other signs by the joint application of semiotical and axiological concepts. For an account of the debate about art between Morris and the new critics see W. Steiner, 1981. The relationship between the aesthetics of Morris and that of Mukařovský is discussed in P. Steiner, 1977. Also see Sebeok, 1981 and Posner, 1986b.

43. In the "popular science" book "The Open Self," Morris (1948:32ff.) relates the classification of value dimensions (in detachment, dominance, and dependence) to the taxonomy of temperaments (cerebrotony, somatotony, and viscerotony). He refers to Sheldon (1940), who attempts to locate the bases for the emergence of temperaments in the physical constitution of the ectomorph, mesomorph, and endomorph (cf. also the character analysis in Kretschmer, 1921). However, in 1956 and 1964 Morris deemphasizes these attempts at a biological and medical foundation for his theory of values, once again preferring the behavioral approach.

44. Sign habits such as these lead to secondary sign use.

45. Cf. Morris, 1927b: "The Total-Situation Theory of Ethics." This conception also has its precursor in the works of Mead. Morris, 1970:92 quotes from Mead, 1938: "The moral question is not one of setting up a right value over against a wrong value; it is a question of finding the possibility of acting so as to take into account as far as possible all the values involved." (1938:465) "We have no more right to neglect a real value than we have to neglect a fact in a scientific problem. In the solution of a problem we must take all relevant values into account." (1938:461)

46. Cf. Morris, 1932:205. The position of objective relativism can be traced back to Mead's "perspectivism" (cf. Mead, 1938:283) and Dewey's "objective subjectivism" (cf. Dewey, 1925:285). The term was introduced by Murphy (1927) in the essay "Objective Relativism in Dewey and Whitehead" (cf. Morris, 1970:139, note 30). While Murphy was later to distance himself from the term again ("What Happened to Objective Relativism?"; in Murphy, 1963), Morris maintained it and used it in characterizing not only his theory of values (cf. Morris, 1939a:135) but also his theory of signs: "I use no term to label my philosophical views. I am suspicious of such terms and their necessity. I would like 'objective relativism' perhaps best of all, but hesitate even on this" (letter of July 5, 1973 to Richard Fiordo; cf. Fiordo, 1977:14).

47. These are the closing lines of "Scientia" from the collection "Festival" (cf. Morris, 1966:5).

REFERENCES

Apel, K.-O. (1959). "Sprache und Wahrheit in der gegenwärtigen Situation der Philosophie. Eine Betrachtung anlässich der Vollendung der neopositivistischen Sprachphilosophie in der Semiotik von Charles Morris." *Philosophische Rundschau*, 7:161–184.

Apel, K.-O. (1973). "Charles Morris und das Programm einer pragmatisch integrierten Semiotik." Introduction to the German translation of Morris, 1946a: Charles W. Morris, *Zeichen, Sprache und Verhalten* (pp. 9–66). Düsseldorf: Schwann.

Apel, K.-O. (1980). *Towards a Transformation of Philosophy.* Translated from the German by D. Frisby and G. Adey. London: Routledge.

Ballard, E. G. (1953). "In Defense of Symbolic Aesthetics." *Journal of Aesthetics and Art Criticism*, 12:38–43.

Berelson, B. (1952). *Content Analysis in Communication Research.* Glencoe: Free Press.

Bessler, H. (1970). *Aussagenanalyse.* Bielefeld: Bertelsmann.

Black, M. (1949). "The Semiotic of Charles Morris." In: M. Black, *Language and Philosophy. Studies in Method* (pp. 167–185 and 253–254). Ithaca, N.Y.: Cornell University Press.

Boehme-Dürr, K. (1987). "Medienspezifische Präsentationsformen und ihre Wirkungen." *Zeitschrift für Semiotik*, 9.

Boring, E. G. (1929). *A History of Experimental Psychology.* 2nd ed. New York: Appleton-Century-Crofts, 1950.

Bridgman, P. W. (1927). *Logic of Modern Physics.* New York: Macmillan.

Bridgman, P. W. (1936). *The Nature of Physical Theory.* Princeton: Princeton University Press.

Bridgman, P. W. (1938). "Operational Analysis." *Philosophy of Science*, 5:114–131.

Brown, C. H. (1974). *Wittgensteinian Linguistics.* The Hague and Paris: Mouton.

Carnap, R. (1934). *Logische Syntax der Sprache.* Vienna and New York: Springer. 2nd edition. 1968. (English by A. Smeaton, *The Logical Syntax of Language.* London: Kegan Paul 1937.)

Carnap, R. (1947). *Meaning and Necessity—A Study in Semantics and Modal Logic.* Chicago: University of Chicago Press. 2nd ed. 1956.

Craig, M. (1918). "Appetites and Aversions as Constituents of Instincts." *Biological Bulletin* (Woods Hole), 34:91–107.

Dewey, J. (1925). *Experience and Nature.* Chicago: Open Court.

Dewey, J. (1946). "Peirce's Theory of Linguistic Signs, Thought, and Meaning." *Journal of Philosophy*, 43:85–95, 280.

Dutz, K. D. (1979). *Glossar der semiotischen Terminologie Charles W. Morris'. Zur Terminologie der Semiotik. 2.* Münster: MAkS.

Dutz, K. D. (1983). "Die Semiotiken des Charles W. Morris und ihre Rezeption." In: K. D. Dutz & H. J. Wulff, eds., *Kommunikation, Funktion und Zeichentheorie. Zur Terminologie der Semiotik. 3.* Münster: MAkS.

Eakins, B. W. (1972). *Charles Morris and the Study of Signification.* Ph.D.Diss.: University of Iowa.

Eibl-Eibesfeldt, I. (1967). *Grundriss der vergleichenden Verhaltensforschung.* München: Piper.

Eschbach, A. (1975). "Charles W. Morris' dreidimensionale Semiotik und die Texttheorie." In: A. Eschbach, ed., *Charles W. Morris: Zeichen, Wert, Ästhetik* (pp. 7–68). Frankfurt: Suhrkamp.

Eschbach, A. (Ed.) (1981). *Zeichen über Zeichen über Zeichen. 15 Studien über Charles W. Morris.* Tübingen: Narr.

Feigl, H. (1934). "Logical Analysis of the Psychophysical Problem." *Philosophy of Science*, 1:420ff.

Feigl, H. (1950). "Logical Reconstruction, Realism, and Pure Semiotic." *Philosophy of Science*, 17:35ff.

Feigl, H. (1958). The 'Mental' and the 'Physical'. In: H. Feigl, M. Scriven, & G. Maxwell, eds., *Minnesota Studies in the Philosophy of Science*, 2. Minneapolis, University of Minnesota Press, 370ff.

Fiordo, R. A. (1977). *Charles Morris and the Criticism of Discourse*. Bloomington, Ind.: Indiana University Press and Lisse, Netherlands: The Peter de Ridder Press.

Geller, A., Kaplan, D., & Lasswell, H. D. (1942). "An Experimental Comparison of Four Ways of Coding Editorial Content." *Journalism Quarterly*, 19.

Günther, A. F. (1968). "Der Zeichenbegriff bei K. Bühler und G. H. Mead." *IPK-Forschungsbericht*, 68(2):1–82. Bonn: Institut für Phonetik und Kommunikationswissenschaft.

Gustafsson, L. (1977). "Grammatik, Logik, Realität." In: Posner & Reinecke, 1977:295–306.

Habermas, J. (1962). *Strukturwandel der Öffentlichkeit—Untersuchungen zu einer Kategorie der bürgerlichen Gesellschaft*. Neuwied and Berlin: Luchterhand. (English translation: *Communication and the Evolution of Society*. London: Heinemann 1979.)

Habermas, J. & Luhmann, N. (1971). *Theorie der Gesellschaft oder Sozialtechnologie*. Frankfurt: Suhrkamp.

Henne, H. (1975). *Sprachpragmatik—Nachschrift einer Vorlesung*. Tübingen: Niemeyer.

Hovland, C. I., ed. (1957). *The Order of Presentation in Persuasion*. New Haven: Yale University Press.

Hull, C. L. (1937). "Mind, Mechanism, and Adaptive Behavior." *Psychological Review*, 44:1–32.

Hull, C. L. (1943). *Principles of Behavior*. New York: Appleton-Century.

Johnson, A. B. (1936). *A Treatise on Language*. New York: Harper. (New ed., D. Rynin, Berkeley: University of California Press 1959.)

Jones, E. E. & Gerard, H.B. (1967). *Foundations of Social Psychology*. New York: Wiley.

Kaplan, A. (1943). "Content Analysis and the Theory of Signs." *Philosophy of Science*, 10:230–247.

Klaus, G. & Segeth, W. (1962). "Semiotik und materialistische Abbildtheorie." *Deutsche Zeitschrift für Philosophie*, 10:1245–1260.

Kretschmer, E. (1921). *Körperbau und Charakter*. Berlin: Springer. (25th ed., 1967.)

Lewis, D. (1969). *Convention—A Philosophical Study*. Cambridge, Mass.: Harvard University Press.

Lewis, D. (1970). "General Semantics." *Synthese*, 22:18–67.

Lieb, H.-H. (1971). "On Subdividing Semiotic." In Y. Bar-Hillel, ed. (1971), *Pragmatics of Natural Languages* (pp. 94–119). Dordrecht: Reidel.

Mead, G. H. (1912). "The Mechanism of Social Consciousness." *Journal of Philosophy*, 9:401–406.

Mead, G. H. (1922). "A Behavioristic Account of the Significant Symbol." *Journal of Philosophy*, 19:157–163.

Mead, G. H. (1932). *The Philosophy of the Present*. Ed. w. introd., A. E. Murphy. La Salle, Ill.: Open Court.

Mead, G. H. (1934). *Mind, Self, and Society—From the Standpoint of a Social Behaviorist*. Ed. w. introd., C. W. Morris. Chicago and London: University of Chicago Press.

Mead, G. H. (1938). *The Philosophy of the Act*. Ed. w. introd., C. W. Morris in cooperation with J. M. Brewster, A. M. Dunham, & D. L. Miller. Chicago and London: University of Chicago Press.

Mead, G. H. (1956). *On Social Psychology—Selected Papers*. Ed. w. introd., A. Strauss. Chicago and London: University of Chicago Press.

Meltzer, B. N., Petras, J. W., & Reynolds, L. T. (1975). *Symbolic Interactionism—Genesis, Varieties, and Criticism*. London and Boston: Routledge and Kegan Paul.

Meyer, M. F. (1921). *The Psychology of the Other One*. Columbia, Mo.: The Missouri Book Company.

Miller, N. & Campbell, D. T. (1959). "Recency and Primacy in Persuasion as a Function of the Timing of Speeches and Measurements." *Journal of Abnormal and Social Psychology*, 59:1–9.

Morris, C. W. (1927a). "The Concept of the Symbol." *Journal of Philosophy*, 24:253–262 and 281–291.

Morris, C. W. (1927b). "The Total-Situation Theory of Ethics." *International Journal of Ethics*, 37:258–268.

Morris, C. W. (1929). "The Relation of Formal to Instrumental Logic." In: T. V. Smith & W. K. Wright, eds., *Essays in Philosophy. By Seventeen Doctors of Philosophy* (pp. 251–268). Chicago: Open Court.

Morris, C. W. (1932). *Six Theories of Mind.* Chicago: University of Chicago Press.

Morris, C. W. (1934). "Pragmatism and Metaphysics." *Philosophical Review,* 43:549–564.

Morris, C. W. (1935a). "Philosophy of Science and Science of Philosophy." *Philosophy of Science,* 2:271–286.

Morris, C. W. (1935b). "The Relation of Formal and Empirical Sciences within Scientific Empiricism." *Erkenntnis,* 5:6–14.

Morris, C. W. (1935c). "Semiotic and Scientific Empiricism." *Actes du Congrès International de Philosophie Scientifique 1935* (pp. 2–16). Paris: Hermann.

Morris, C. W. (1936). "The Concept of Meaning in Pragmatism and Logical Positivism." *Actes du Huitième Congrès International de Philosophie à Prague, 2–7 Septembre 1934* (pp. 130–138). Prague. (Reprint Nendeln, Liechtenstein: Kraus, 1968.)

Morris, C. W. (1937). *Logical Positivism, Pragmatism, and Scientific Empiricism.* Paris: Hermann. (= Morris, 1934, 1935a,b,c, 1936).

Morris, C. W. (1938). *Foundations of the Theory of Signs.* Chicago: University of Chicago Press.

Morris, C. W. (1939a). "Aesthetics and the Theory of Signs." *Erkenntnis. Journal of Unified Science,* 8:131–150.

Morris, C. W. (1939b). "Science, Art, and Technology." *Kenyon Review,* 1:409–423.

Morris, C. W. (1940). "The Mechanism of Freedom." In R. N. Anshen, ed., *Freedom—Its Meaning* (pp. 579–589). New York: Harcourt and Brace.

Morris, C. W. (1942). *Paths of Life: Preface to a World Religion.* New York: Harper.

Morris, C. W. (1943). "Comments on a Paper by A. Kaplan." *Philosophy of Science,* 10:247–249.

Morris, C. W. (1946a). *Signs, Language, and Behavior.* Englewood Cliffs: Prentice-Hall.

Morris, C. W. (1946b). "Answer to Dewey." *Journal of Philosophy,* 63:196 and 363f.

Morris, C. W. (1948a). *The Open Self.* New York: Prentice-Hall.

Morris, C. W. (1948b). "Signs about Signs about Signs." *Philosophy and Phenomenological Research,* 9:115–133.

Morris, C. W. (1956). *Varieties of Human Value.* Chicago: University of Chicago Press.

Morris, C. W. (1958). "Words without Meaning." *Contemporary Psychology,* 3:212–214. (= Review of B. F. Skinner, *Verbal Behavior*).

Morris, C. W. (1964). *Signification and Significance.* Cambridge, Mass.: The M.I.T. Press.

Morris, C. W. (1966). *Festival.* New York: Braziller.

Morris, C. W. (1970). *The Pragmatic Movement in American Philosophy.* New York: Braziller.

Morris, C. W. (1971). *Writings on the General Theory of Signs.* The Hague: Mouton. (Contains Morris, 1938, Morris, 1946a, and other essays, as well as the first chapter of Morris, 1964.)

Morris, C. W. & Jones, L. V. (1955). "Value Scales and Dimensions." *Journal of Abnormal and Social Psychology,* 51:523–535.

Morris, C. W. & Jones, L. V. (1956). "Relations of Temperament to Choice of Values." *Journal of Abnormal and Social Psychology,* 53:345–349.

Morris, C. W., Eiduson, B. B., & O'Donnovan, D. (1960). "Values of Psychiatric Patients." *Behavioral Science,* 5:297–312.

Morris, C. W., Osgood, C. E., & Ware, E. E. (1961). "Analysis of the Connotative Meanings of a Variety of Human Values as Expressed by American College Students." *Journal of Abnormal and Social Psychology,* 62:62–73.

Morris, C. W. & Hamilton, D. J. (1964). "Aesthetics, Signs, and Icons." *Philosophy and Phenomenological Research,* 25:356–364.

Morris, C. W. & Sciadini, F. (1966). "Paintings, Ways to Live, and Values." In G. Kepes, ed., *Sign, Image, Symbol* (pp. 144–149). New York: Braziller.

Müller, A. (1970). *Probleme der behavioristischen Semiotik.* Ph.D. Dissertation: University of Frankfurt.

Murphy, A. E. (1927). "Objective Relativism in Dewey and Whitehead." *Philosophical Review*, 36:121–144.

Murphy, A. E. (1963). *Reason and the Common Good*. Englewood Cliffs: Prentice-Hall.

Ogden, C. K. & Richards, I. A. (1923). *The Meaning of Meaning*. London: Kegan Paul.

Peirce, C. S. (1931–1935). *Collected Papers*, Vol. 1–6, ed. by C. Hartshorne & P. Weiss. Cambridge, Mass.: Harvard University Press.

Peirce, C. S. (1958). *Collected Papers*, Vol. 7 and 8, ed. by A. W. Burks. Cambridge, Mass.: Harvard University Press.

Pelc, Jerzy (1978). "A Guide to Morris." *Semiotica*, 23:377–379.

Posner, R. (1972a). *Theorie des Kommentierens—Eine Grundlagenstudie zur Semantik und Pragmatik*. Frankfurt: Athenäum. 2nd improved ed. Wiesbaden: Athenaion 1980.

Posner, R. (1972b). "Commenting: A Diagnostic Procedure for Semantico-Pragmatic Sentence Representation." *Poetics*, 5:67–88.

Posner, R. (1972c). "Statt eines Vorworts." In: C. W. Morris, *Grundlagen der Zeichentheorie. Ästhetik und Zeichentheorie* (pp. 7–13). Munich: Hanser.

Posner, R. (1974). "Diskurs als Mittel der Aufklärung—Zur Theorie der rationalen Kommunikation bei Habermas und Albert. In: M. Gerhardt, ed., *Linguistik und Sprachphilosophie* (pp. 280–303). Munich: List. (English translation: "Discourse as a Means to Enlightenment—On the Theories of Rational Communication of Habermas and Albert." In: A. Kasher, ed., *Language in Focus* [pp. 641–660]. Dordrecht, Boston, and London: Reidel 1976.)

Posner, R. (1982). *Rational Discourse and Poetic Communication. Methods of Linguistic, Literary, and Philosophical Analysis*. Berlin and New York: Mouton.

Posner, R. (1986a). "Syntactics." In: T. A. Sebeok, ed., *Encyclopedic Dictionary of Semiotics*. Berlin and New York: Mouton.

Posner, R. (1986b). "Charles W. Morris." In: T. A. Sebeok, ed., *Encyclopedic Dictionary of Semiotics*. Berlin and New York: Mouton.

Posner, R. & Reinecke, H.-P., eds. (1977). *Zeichenprozesse—Semiotische Forschung in den Einzelwissenschaften*. Wiesbaden: Athenaion.

Price, K. B. (1953). "Is a Work of Art a Symbol?" *The Journal of Philosophy*, 50:485–503.

Resnikov, L. O. (1977). "Zeichen, Sprache, Abbild." Trans. from the Russian by H. Siegel. Ed. w. introd., A. Eschbach. Frankfurt: Syndikat.

Roberts, L. (1955). "Art as Icon: An Interpretation of Charles W. Morris." *Tulane Studies in Philosophy*, 4:75–83.

Rochberg-Halton, E. & McMurtrey, K. (1983). "The Foundations of Modern Semiotic: Charles Peirce and Charles Morris." *American Journal of Semiotics*, 2:129–156.

Romeo, L. (1981). "Charles Morris and the History of Semiotics." In: Eschbach, 1981:227–234.

Rossi-Landi, F. (1953). *Charles Morris*. Milan: Bocca.

Rossi-Landi, F. (1967). "Sul modo in cui è stata fraintesa la semiotica estetica di Charles Morris. *Nuova Currente*, 42–43:113–117.

Rossi-Landi, F. (1975). "Signs about a Master of Signs." *Semiotica*, 13:155–197.

Rossi-Landi, F. (1976). "Über einige Fehlinterpretationen der ästhetischen Semiotik von Charles Morris." In: F. Rossi-Landi, *Semiotik, Ästhetik und Ideologie* (pp. 75–82). Munich: Hanser.

Rossi-Landi, F. (1978). On Some Post-Morrisian Problems. *Ars Semeiotica*, 3:3–32.

Rudner, R. (1951). "On Semeiotic Aesthetics." *Journal of Aesthetics and Art Criticism*, 10:67–77.

Sanctius, F. (= Francisco Sànchez de las Brozas) (1587). *Minerva: seu, De causis linguae Latinae*. Salamanca: Renaut.

Searle, J. (1969). *Speech Acts. An Essay in the Philosophy of Language*. Cambridge, England: Cambridge University Press.

Searle, J. (1975). "Indirect Speech Acts." In: P. Cole & J. Morgan, eds., *Syntax and Semantics III: Speech Acts* (pp. 59–82). New York: Academic Press.

Sebeok, T. A. (1981). "The Image of Charles Morris." In: Eschbach, 1981:267–284.

Sheldon, W. H. (1940). *The Varieties of Human Physique.* New York: Harper & Row.

Shibutani, T. (1961). *Society and Personality.* Englewood Cliffs: Prentice-Hall.

Skinner, B. F. (1938). *The Behavior of Organisms.* New York: Appleton-Century.

Steiner, P. (1977). "Jan Mukařovský and Charles W. Morris: Two Pioneers of the Semiotics of Art." *Semiotica,* 19, 3–4:321–334. (Reprinted in Eschbach, 1981:285–297.)

Steiner, W. (1981). "Ein Beispiel unklaren Denkens: Die Neokritizisten gegen Charles Morris." In: Eschbach, 1981:299–314.

Stokoe, W. C. (1977). "Die 'Sprache' der Taubstummen." In: Posner & Reinecke, 1977:167–179.

Tarski, A. (1935). "Der Wahrheitsbegriff in den formalisierten Sprachen." *Studia Philosophica,* 1:261–405.

Teigeler, P. (1968). *Verständlichkeit und Wirksamkeit von Sprache und Text.* Stuttgart: Nadolski.

Tolman, E. C. (1932). *Purposive Behavior in Animals and Men.* New York: Century.

Tranöy, K. E. (1972/75). " 'Sollen' impliziert 'Können': Eine Brücke von der Tatsache zur Norm?" *Ratio,* 14:111–125, 17:141–169.

Uexküll, J. von (1937). "Umweltforschung." *Zeitschrift für Tierpsychologie,* 1:33–34.

Watson, J. B. (1913). "Psychology as the Behaviorist Views It." *Psychological Review,* 20:158–177.

Watson, J. B. (1914). *Behavior—An Introduction to Comparative Psychology.* New York: Holt.

Watson, J. B. (1919). *Psychology from the Standpoint of a Behaviorist.* Philadelphia: Lippincott.

Watzlawick, P., Beavin, J. H., & Jackson, D. D. (1967). *Pragmatics of Human Communication.* New York: Norton.

Wilson, W. & Miller, N. (1968). "Repetition, Order of Presentation, and Timing of Arguments and Measures as Determinants of Opinion Change." *Journal of Personality and Social Psychology,* 9:184–188.

Wittgenstein, L. (1922). *Tractatus logico-philosophicus.* London: Kegan Paul.

CHAPTER 3

Ferdinand de Saussure and the Development of Semiology[1]

MARTIN KRAMPEN

1. ON THE BIOGRAPHY OF DE SAUSSURE[2]

De Saussure was born on November 26, 1857 into one of Calvinist Geneva's prominent patrician families. For generations, the de Saussures had excelled in the sciences, producing well-known botanists and mineralogists.[3] As a young boy, de Saussure was already fluent in French, German, English, Latin, and Greek, an achievement which was not unusual in cultivated families at that time. At the age of fifteen, he wrote an essay on the general system of languages ("Essai sur les langues", 1872) which clearly showed the influence of the historical linguist Pictet, a friend of the de Saussure family. From 1873 to 1875 he attended a *Gymnase*. Then, in accordance with the wishes of his parents, he began studying physics and chemistry at the University of Geneva. In 1876, however, with the permission of his parents, he switched to linguistics and transferred to the University of Leipzig. In the same year he became a member of the recently founded "Société de Linguistique de Paris," for which he wrote a series of specialized research papers.

Apart from a short interruption which led him to Berlin in 1878 to 1879, de Saussure stayed in Leipzig for four years. In 1878 his study of "the system of vowels in its generality," with special reference to the Indo-European vowel *a*, was published. This treatise already made reference to the concept of "opposition" of linguistic elements which was later to become one of the fundamental tenets of his theory of general linguistics.

In 1880, at the age of twenty-three, de Saussure obtained his doctoral

MARTIN KRAMPEN • Professor of Theory of Visual Communication, University of the Arts, Berlin, West Germany.

degree; his dissertation "De l'emploi du génitif absolu en sanscrit" received the
mention "summa cum laude et dissertatione egregia." His relationship to the
"Neogrammarians" among his professors having been rendered difficult by scientific controversies, de Saussure left Leipzig. After a study trip to Lithuania
he continued his career in Paris.

In Paris he attended the lectures of Bréal and Darmesteter. In 1881 he was
appointed lecturer for Gothic and Old High German at the École des hautes
études. In addition, he taught at the Sorbonne and continued to write specialized
papers for the Société de Linguistique.

In 1891 he took over as a "professeur extraordinaire" filling a chair at the
University of Geneva which had been created especially for him. In 1896 he
was appointed full professor for Sanskrit and Indoeuropean languages. In his
lectures he taught Sanskrit, the phonology of modern French, and various aspects
of the German language.

After his return to Geneva, his publications became rarer and rarer. He
worked on the *Nibelungen Song* and on the poetic form of the anagram. This
increasing silence has been attributed to his perfectionism. But it was precisely
during the period from 1890 to 1900 that his own inner struggle with the problems
of a theory of general linguistics must have been taking place. In a letter dated
January 4, 1894 he wrote to Meillet, his friend and successor at Paris, that he
was thinking about a book in which the whole terminology of linguistics would
be put into a new order.[4] In the same year, he was invited by the American
Philological Association to the first American congress of philologists, dedicated
to the memory of the linguist Whitney who had just died. De Saussure wrote a
seventy-page manuscript for that congress, but he never finished the paper and
did not go to the congress. In the manuscript de Saussure expressed his agreement
with Whitney's idea that language was a human institution. But he countered
the American's unrestrained conventionalism with his own thesis that linguistic
elements were related in a system: Speech sounds and meanings are not first
grasped directly, i.e. outside a language system, to be in a second moment
connected by convention into a unified whole, but exist to begin with in a pre-
established (arbitrary) connectedness produced by the language system.

The term "semiology" must have originated at the beginning of the same
decade. It appears as early as 1893/94 in de Saussure's notes for the book
mentioned in his letter to Meillet. Adrien Naville, dean of the faculty of Literary
and Social Sciences at the University of Geneva, explicitly attributes the invention
of the term "semiology" to de Saussure in his volume *Nouvelle classification
des sciences. Étude philosophique*, published in Paris in 1901.

In 1906 the faculty of Literary Sciences entrusted de Saussure, in addition
to his existing duties, with the teaching of general linguistics and of historical
and compared Indo-European languages.

During the following three years, he gave the three courses which would
provide the material for the famous *Cours de linguistique générale* edited by his
students Bally and Sechehaye in collaboration with Albert Riedlinger on the

basis of lecture notes taken by several students. (De Saussure used to throw away his lecture manuscripts.) The first course was held from January 15 to July 3, 1907. In it de Saussure paid special attention to the subjective and objective analysis of language (the former comprising the perception of speech sounds, the latter word roots, suffixes and other units of historical grammar) and to the physiology of speech-sound production. In the second course, which began in early November, 1908 and ended on the 24th of June, 1909, de Saussure defined the central terms of general linguistics (system, identity, value, synchrony, and diachrony). In the third course, which ran from October 29, 1910 to July 4, 1911, de Saussure integrated the analytical material of the first course with the theoretical concepts developed in the second, illustrating his ideas with concrete examples from various languages.

Despite the early international acclaim, the last years of his life seem to have been overshadowed by solitude and depression. His student Gautier wrote 1916 in retrospect: "Cet homme (. . .) a vécu solitaire" (quoted after de Mauro 1976: 358). In 1912 he had to quit teaching because of illness. At that time he withdrew completely from public life and retreated into the castle of his wife's family in Vufflens near Morges where he died on February 22, 1913.

2. SEMIOLOGY AND LINGUISTICS IN DE SAUSSURE

2.1. The Relationship between Semiology and General Linguistics

The importance of de Saussure for the development of (general) linguistics is seldom questioned today. The *Cours de linguistique générale* was translated successively into Japanese, German, Russian, Spanish, English, Polish, Hungarian, Portuguese, and Italian, and continues to be read all over the world.

Since Ogden and Richards (1923), however, some misunderstandings regarding the linguistic and semiotic concepts of de Saussure have appeared in the English-language literature. Thus, the abovementioned authors write about his semiology: "Unfortunately this theory of signs, by neglecting entirely the things for which signs stand, was from the beginning cut off from any contact with scientific methods of verification."

While important American linguists such as Bloomfield, Hockett, Wells, and Chomsky, have readily recognized de Saussure's contribution to the foundations of modern linguistics, it has become fashionable among some semioticians to pit the relatively elaborate semiotics of Peirce against de Saussure's semiology, which exists only in the form of a project. From this perspective, Bense (1976:144) writes: "Yet de Saussure did not develop a general theory of signs, but merely certain terms which are usable only to make the most primitive differentiations in language and which have been overemphasized in an irrational manner in Marxist structuralism."

Walther (1974:97) too mentions de Saussure only in passing in "Foundations of Semiotics" ("Grundlagen der Semiotik") in her chapter "Survey of the History of Semiotics from Plato to the Present." The probable reason for this neglect is given in the following sentence from the preface of her book: "Neither the studies of structuralist 'semiology' as they are carried out in France on the basis of de Saussure and Lévi-Strauss with the tools of linguistics and structuralism, nor the Marxist publications on semiotics based on psychology and sociology, are useful in the construction of a general theory of signs."

In fact, taking the explicit completeness of a system as a standard for the importance of a theoretical contribution and, in addition, not knowing de Saussure's original manuscripts (Engler 1974), as apparently is the case with the above mentioned authors, one does not find in de Saussure much more than the famous prophecy in the "Cours de linguistique générale" of a future "Semiology"—a science "that studies the life of signs within society" (Saussure 1964:16) and which will form part of social psychology and therefore of general psychology.

However, with the impetus provided by Engler's (1974) comprehensive publication of de Saussure's original notes, a Saussure renaissance began during the late seventies (cf. Jäger 1976, Stetter 1978, and Stetter without date). The "new look" of Saussure interpretation is based on the assumption that the *Cours de linguistique générale* is a first step in the direction of a "structuralist corruption" of de Saussure's authentic linguistic theory. The attempt is made, therefore, to reconstruct the "original" thoughts of de Saussure's semiology from his notes alone, especially from the so-called "notes item" (N15.1–19) which could not have been "distorted" by the editors of the *Cours*. This procedure is not without interest as a method, although it was, for the purpose of polemics against structuralism, immediately put into the service of another "ideology": it now serves the apologists of "pragmalinguistics." Pragmalinguistics, it will be recalled, is that direction in linguistics elaborating especially the influence of sign use, i.e. the "pragmatics" of speech use, on meaning. This puts it in a certain contrast to structuralism in which language is understood, independently from its use, as a system. Now, from a semiotic point of view, there is no reason to criticize the fact that pragmatic (and hermeneutic) considerations, perhaps with reference to Kantian apriorism, are given such an important function in the new interpretation of de Saussure's linguistics, as can be seen in the writings of Stetter (1978 and without date), although the overemphasis on these considerations does reveal an ideological aspect. It is to be deplored, however, that this new reception of de Saussure has led to conclusions concerning linguistics and philosophy of language only, but not general semiotics. In addition, the method itself proves to be too "radical."

The problem brings to mind the reconstruction of the "authentic sayings of Jesus" in New Testament philology. In the reconstruction of "what Jesus really said" some philologists like to rely on quotations of Jesus in the letters of Paul which are, of course, closer to the times of the historical Jesus. It is argued that the sayings of Jesus in the synopsis of the four gospels have been put together from various sources by editors and must be dated much later than Paul's letters. It seems nevertheless pointless to completely renounce the synopsis as a source, because a patent loss of information results from such a radical decision. This is equally true for the correct interpretation of de Saussure. Even if it was possible to reconstruct an "early" de Saussure from his own notes—would this be a more "authentic" de Saussure than the one who held the lectures from 1907 to 1911 in which his students took their notes? It seems advisable to draw on both, the synopsis of the lecture notes of the students (CLG) and the personal manuscripts of de Saussure as well, in order to describe his semiology.

Above all it is important that in the *Cours* (and in the lecture notes of the students George Degallier, Albert Sechehaye, and Francis Joseph) the relationship between linguistics and semiology is defined very clearly (Saussure 1964, 16, cf. CLG 33:46–49): "Language is a system of signs that express ideas, and is therefore comparable to a system of writing, the alphabet of the deaf-mutes, symbolic rites, polite formulas, military signals, etc. But it is the most important of all these systems (. . .). Linguistics is only a part of the general science of semiology; the laws discovered by semiology will be applicable to linguistics and the latter will circumscribe a well-defined area within the mass of anthropological facts."

This exact definition of the relationship between linguistics and "the science that studies the life of signs within society" has been frequently forgotten or even perverted by epigones of de Saussure. Thus Barthes (1964a) in the preface to his famous article on "Elements of Semiology" turns this relationship around: "(. . .) c'est la sémiologie qui est une partie de la linguistique" (it is semiology which is a part of linguistics).

A similar tendency to reduce semiology to linguistics is based on the interpretation of another passage in the *Cours de linguistique générale*, and therefore attributed to de Saussure. It reads: "Signs that are wholly arbitrary realize better than the others the ideal of semiological process: that is why language, the most complex and universal of all systems of expression, is also the most characteristic; in this sense linguistics can become the master pattern (French: *patron général*) for all branches of semiology, although language is only one particular semiological system" (Saussure 1964, 68). It is in gauging the importance of language within the framework of de Saussure's semiology that it becomes obvious how important it can be to go back to the synopsis of the students' lecture notes (cf. Baer in this volume, p. 186f). Reading only the passage of the "Cours" quoted above, language appears in fact to be the sign system which is given the role of the model of semiology by de Saussure. But reading the lecture notes of the students, things look a bit different.

The expression *patron général* stems from the copy book of Albert Riedlinger, which he kept during the lecture of 1908/09. It is not mentioned in the same context by the lecture notes of Léopold Gautier, François Bouchardy, or

Emile Constantin. But their lecture copy books were equally used by Bally and Sechehaye in the synthesis of the chapter on "the nature of the linguistic sign" in the *Cours de linguistique générale* (CLG 102:154) containing the passage in question. By the way, in the notes of Gautier we find at this point the following remark on the special role of language (langue) in semiology: "But this must be an accident: from the theoretical point of view it (language) is only a special case." In Bouchardy's notes we read similarly: "But this is an accident. Theoretically this is one case among others." In any event it is difficult to prove whether de Saussure ever used the expression *patron général* to describe the role of linguistics in semiology. But even if he had used it, the context in which this metaphor appears does not permit a linguistic reduction of semiology. If de Saussure ever assigned a special role to linguistics, he could only have meant that its methods, highly developed by his time, as well as some of its concepts, might be of help to the future work of those who would turn his prophecy into a scientific reality. In this sense the expression *patron général* would then better be interpreted "patron saint" than "commander-in-chief."

2.2. Basic Concepts of de Saussure's General Linguistics

With the logical primacy of semiology over linguistics having been indicated, the basic terms of de Saussure's linguistics can now be discussed. These terms are organically deducible from one another as a series of oppositions. It is not the goal here, however, to present the linguistics of de Saussure for its own sake, but to elaborate on the semiological core as the basis of his linguistic concepts. Therefore it will be demonstrated, in a further step, both that the linguistic terms can be semiologically generalized, and how they have in fact been generalized by authors of de Saussure's "school." But first let us begin with the basic terms of his linguistics.

The most important pair of terms in de Saussure's linguistics is the opposition between "speech" (human speaking activity) and "language" or language system (in French, the opposition *parole* vs. *langue*). De Saussure starts with the linguistic activity of human beings such as it reveals itself in the making and in the understanding of speech sounds. In comparison with speaking, writing as well as orthography are already secondary phenomena. The question is which "internal" laws form the basis of speaking and understanding speech. The answer is that in the concrete activity of speech an abstract system, language, expresses itself. One of the most important tasks of linguistics is therefore to investigate the "internal" laws of language as a system. It is not the prime concern of linguistics to busy itself with ethnological, cultural, historical, political, institutional, and geographical aspects of linguistic phenomena. De Saussure does not deny that investigations of this kind can be fruitful, but he maintains that language as a sign system can be described without these "external" data.

Language, the abstract system at the basis of concrete expression, is a sign system. The language signs exist "in the head" of the subject as associations between images of (perceived) speech sounds (not the "objective" sounds!) and concepts of things, for instance (e.g. imaginations, and not "objective" things). The images of speech sounds, the signifying part (signifier) and the concept, the signified part or meaning (signified) form an undivisible unity as do the two sides of a coin or a sheet of paper. It is this unity which is called a sign. One basic property of signifiers and signifieds as parts of signs, and of the signs themselves, is their relativity. Precisely because language is a system, the parts of signs and the signs themselves receive their identity only by belonging to such a system and, within the system, only by their difference from other elements of the system. A speech sound acquires its identity only by means of its difference from the properties of other speech sounds in a system of speech sounds. Concepts obtain their meaning only by differing from other concepts in a meaning system. A sign as a whole receives its "value" only by comparison with other signs in the sign system to which it belongs.

One of the basic properties of linguistic signs is, according to de Saussure, that they are absolutely arbitrary. This property is in opposition to the "motivated" quality of what de Saussure calls "symbols." The arbitrariness of a sign reveals itself in the arbitrary, unmotivated association of signifier and signified in the linguistic sign which is not based on any obvious principle.

On the contrary, in symbols there is a "rudiment of a natural bond between signifier and signified" (Saussure 1964, 68). In the symbolic representation of Justice, the pair of scales cannot be substituted by any other arbitrary object without loosing the motivation of this sign.

Aside from absolute arbitrariness de Saussure knew also the concept of relative arbitrariness. For instance, the numerical term "eleven" is totally unmotivated, whereas this cannot be said about the numerical terms thirteen, fourteen, fifteen, etc. One can recognize the elements of which the latter are composed (digits and the number of ten) and in which something of their meaning appears. A basic property of language is its linear and temporal sequential ordering. In this it differs from other systems, the signs of which can be displayed simultaneously in space or on a surface. The relation of signs in an ordering which de Saussure calls a "syntagm" differs from the associative relation of signs having similar meanings. Such signs could be substituted for each other in a syntagm without changing its meaning. The associative relation of signs is called "paradigm" by de Saussure. The syntagmatic and paradigmatic aspect of language must not be confused, however, with the development of language in time, its "diachronic" aspect, and its state as a system at a given moment, its "synchronic" aspect. The latter two terms designate two different perspectives in linguistics, the dynamic and the static one. Dynamic and static aspects of a language system depend in turn on the opposition between individual (and changes in his speaking activity) and society (and the relative stability of its language).

The circle of oppositions thus closes: Beginning with "speech" (parole) and "language" (langue) it has led us first to a differentiation between external and internal aspects of linguistics. The "internal" aspect of language as a system is defined by the unity of the sign, made up of a signifier and a signified. The identity of a sign is given only by virtue of its place in the structure of the system. Absolutely arbitrary language signs differ from relatively arbitrary ones, and both in turn from motivated symbols. The linear syntagms of language are contrasted by spatially concomitant orderings of other sign systems. The ordered relation of signs in general must be distinguished in turn from their paradigmatic association. Finally, the diachronics of changes in language are opposed to its synchronic description as a system, the individual aspects of speech to the social aspects of a language community.

3. ON THE SEMIOLOGICAL GENERALIZATION OF DE SAUSSURE'S BASIC CONCEPTS

3.1. "Parole," Signal, and Tool

The following presentation of the development of semiology up to our time is based on de Saussure's remarks on this "future" science and on those of his basic concepts which have proven utilizable for semiological generalization. In order to sketch the present state of semiology some amplifications of de Saussure's starting points, as they have been proposed after him by other authors, will be discussed in this connection.

One central property of de Saussure's linguistics which lends itself to generalization is his appropriation of concrete speech activity as a starting point. He proceeds from concrete utterances to the abstract language system, investigating how in a specific act of communication specific speech realizations come about and are understood. Expressed in more general terms, this means that semiology (like general linguistics) starts with the practice of communication or, even more generally, that the phenomenon of meaning is rooted in human practice and cannot be deduced from pre-established theories. The realizations of speech practice are summed up under the heading of "parole." In a semiology of communication, as it has been generalized beyond de Saussure's general linguistics by Buyssens (1943, 1970) and Prieto (1966, 1968), a realization of communication practice is called a "signal." According to Prieto (1966, 1968) signals pertain to the category of indices, i.e. to those immediately perceivable facts that carry not only information regarding themselves, but also information about other facts which are not immediately perceivable. Examples frequently given are the smoke giving information about a fire or the velocity of speech indicating the psychological state of the speaker, etc. All signals of communication are therefore always indices as well, because they convey something about the sender (or at least indicate that there is a sender). But not all indices are signals "artifically" produced for the express purpose of communication. Before Prieto, the concept of index had already been added to de Saussure's categories of sign and symbol by Piaget (1936).

"Parole" is therefore a special linguistic instance of signals. But even the signal can be regarded as a special case. If "semiology of communication" is only a part of an all-encompassing "semiology of signification" (Prieto 1975a), one is faced with the human practice of communication as only a special case. Human practice is carried out by means of "tools" (Prieto 1973, 1975a, 1975b). Thus, signals are a special type of tool applied in the practice of communication. This generalization from signal to tool has not been arbitrarily deduced from de Saussure's semiology. It is already present in the writings of Adolf Gotthard Noreen, a Swedish linguist and contemporary of de Saussure, whose work de Saussure certainly knew. In order to make clear not only the parallel between signal and tool, but also between the work of de Saussure and Noreen, an extensive passage from Noreen will be quoted here. In an article on "Correctness of Speech" Noreen (1888) writes:[6]

> Because language is on the whole an artificial product like garments, houses, tools, it must offer the same perspectives for analysis as any other artifact; the same perspectives indeed, i.e. that of the materials (meaning that which the product "represents" or that which it "deals with"; the task it must fulfill: its function) and the one of form (the manner in which the task is carried out by means of the material employed: the structure, the construction). These perspectives . . . define the main parts of grammar:
>
> 1. The science of speech sounds or phonology, dealing with the physical material which is constituted in the primary and most important language, i.e. spoken language, by "articulated sounds of the voice" through which the content of ideas is differentiated. Phonology must not be confused, as it sometimes has been, with one of its most important ancillary sciences, "phonetics," and is even more removed from the science ancillary to the latter known as "acoustics."
>
> 2. The science of meaning or semology,[7] which treats the psychic content of language: the ideas which are subdivided by means of the sounds of the voice and which thus on this basis constitute the "meaning" of the latter. Semology must not only be carefully distinguished from its most important ancillary science, "philosophy of language," but also from that part of psychology which treats of representations and contents of a higher level of consciousness, and at the same time and especially from "logic," the science of concepts as such (and not insofar as they have found an expression in language) and of the relationships between concepts (and not of the relationships between language expressions). It cannot be said, in fact, that a given concept corresponds to each language expression endowed with meaning, and the contrary is even less true. Certainly, this false conception and the confusion of the two sciences connected with it have had a damaging effect on grammar, but even more on logic; more or less in the same way as phonology has suffered (even if to a lesser degree) from the confusion between letter and sound, and from the resulting confusion between phonology and orthography.
>
> 3. The science of form or morphology, which endeavors to describe the manner in which the sound material is shaped into "linguistic forms" in the service of meaningful content. Morphology occupies the central and most important place in grammar, because thanks to morphology grammar differs from all other sciences.

This lengthy quotation clearly shows the similarity of the positions taken by de Saussure and Noreen (who incidentally coined the term "semology" prior to de Saussure). Following Noreen, in analogy to the realizations of language, any group of signals should be investigated as to its material, meaning-relations, and morphological constitution. Signals, in turn, should be considered only a special case of tool realizations for the special practice of communication, as Prieto (1973) later consequently deduced from de Saussure.

3.2. The Parallel between Signifier and Operant, Signified and Utility

How do certain language relationships come about or, respectively, how are they "understood"? Realizing or understanding comes about, according to de Saussure, when concrete elements of "parole" are conceptualized or recognized as members of abstract classes. To recognize a realization means, consequently, to classify it. In order to identify the sounds of which the words of a language consist, the subject must attribute very different realizations of the "same" sound, as they vary from one speaker to another, to one sole (abstract) class of sounds. These abstract classes of sounds were called "phonemes" by de Saussure, who took over this term from the French philologist Louis Harvet (Jakobson 1971b). Generalizing this process from the linguistics to the semiology of communication, different sound classes of language correspond to different signal classes of a "communications system." For these signal classes, and not only for phonemes, de Saussure coined the expression *signifiant* (signifier). If the same problem is looked at from an even more general point of view, i.e. in the framework of the semiology of signification, it becomes a question of tool classes which are called "operant" by Prieto (1973, 1975a). The signifiant (signifier) of de Saussure is thus a special case of the operant, and the phoneme of linguists a special case of the signifiant.

The common denominator logically permitting the generalization from the phonemes of linguistics, via de Saussure's signifiers of communication, to the operants or tool classes of human practice can be demonstrated by set theory. The terminology of set theory contains among others the three expressions universe (of discourse), set, and complementary set or complement. These terms are connected by the fact that each universe of objects is composed by a set and its corresponding complement. In the terms of set theory, different operants, signifiers or phonemes form different sets within their respective universes which can also be called "level of the signifier" or, with Hjelmslev (1968/71), "level of expression" (cf. Trabant in this volume p. 96f).

Since the pairs *universe* and *classification system, set* and *class* have the same meaning, de Saussure's starting point from the practice of communication implies the cognitive activity of classifying within classification systems or establishing sets within universes. The question is not, however, one of any classification or establishment of sets whatsoever, but one of cognitive activity which sorts sounds, signals, or tools according to their "relevant" properties—neglecting their non-relevant details. Thus the /a/ of a given speaker from a given region is recognized, despite its particular sound quality, as a member of the same phoneme class (as element of the same set) as the /a/ of a speaker from another region pronounced quite differently in comparison with the first.; or a round traffic sign with a diameter of 70 cm will be classified as an element of the same set (signifier) as one with a diameter of 50 cm, a pair of pliers with red handles as an element of the same set (operant) as one with blue handles.

The classification of speech sounds, signals, or tools according to their "relevant" properties cannot, therefore, be an end in itself, but necessarily constitutes a means to an end within a framework of a practice—the end being the production of social contacts by means of words or signals or solving a problem of any social practice in general by means of tools.

From de Saussure's notes dating back to 1893/94 one can deduce that phonemes and signals, and therefore tools and objects in general, can only be classified from a certain perspective, i.e. from a given point of view.[8] It would be possible, for instance, to have phonemes classified by a group of experts according to their beauty, signals according to the difficulty of their production, and tools according to the historical period of their invention. But for communication, or for an operation with a tool, this perspective would be irrelevant. Hence speech sounds are normally classified by subjects from the point of view of communication in a common language, signals from the point of view of making social contact by means of a communications system, and tools according to their function within the system of instruments in a given culture. This means that the classification of these objects is not made according to arbitrary properties which these objects possess among others, but according to those properties which render them relevant from the perspective of a given social practice—for instance a communication or an operation.

Which of the many possible points of view is relevant can be established as follows: The perspective of a given classification reveals itself in a second classification system, in a second universe. Hence one cannot establish sets within a universe without the help of another universe within which the "sense" of the establishment of sets in the first universe is classified. The latter universe confers its relevance upon the former, but receives in turn its own from it. Each universe of signifiers is insolubly connected with another universe. Likewise, each set in a universe of signifiers is coupled with a set in the correlated universe. This correlated universe (or this classification system) is de Saussure's level of the signified (signifié) or, following Hjelmslev (1968/71), the "level of content." Level of the signifier and level of the signified are thus coordinated for certain purposes—in the semiology of communication according to the perspective of communication practice, in the semiology of signification according to the perspective of human practice in general.

Signifier and signified, as two classes mutually conditioning each other and being situated in two coupled classification systems, form a dialectic unity which de Saussure calls sign (French: signe). With the definition of the sign as a unity of signifier and signified de Saussure definitely leaves the confines of general linguistics and advances into the realm of semiology, i.e. into the domain of all "signs within society" serving communication, among which he lists the signs of writing, of the deaf-mutes' alphabet, of symbolic rites, of polite formulas, of military and nautical signals, of customs, usage, fashion, of pantomime, etc. With the exception of writing, which he treated more extensively, rudimentary investigations of such different sign systems are found only in his discussions of literary problems (cf. de Mauro, 1976:348).[9]

Buyssens (1970:22–26) has expanded the catalogue of sign systems begun by de Saussure. He lists the following:[10] graphic signs of the exact sciences and logic, road signs, the gestures of the Trappists, and of the Indians, which are used for communication between tribes of different languages, bell-ringing devices of churches, bugle signals of the military, pictographs in timetables and tourist guides, geographic maps, proofreading signs of the printers, trademarks, shop signs, uniforms of soldiers and functionaries, radio station identification signals, clock faces, the red light of emergency exits, the brown or colorless bottles of the pharmacist, the skull and crossbones. Under certain circumstances, according to Buyssens, artistic manifestations are to be considered part of semiology— i.e., whenever they are understood by the public as signs of communication: Painting, perspective, sculpture, dance, music, architecture, rhetorical devices, literature, drama, poetry. "Symbols" such as the cross, too, may have a semiological character if they are used for communication. This is also true of photographs, movies, and the theatre.

A consistent generalization of de Saussure's sign concept beyond the domain of the semiology of communication into the realm of the semiology of signification has been proposed by Prieto (1973, 1975a): To the double-faced unity of the sign consisting of signifier and signified corresponds the double-faced unity of "operant" and "utility" of the "instrument." Signs are special cases of instruments—they are instruments of communication.

To the realization of a given signal in the set (or class) of a signifier a concrete "sense" is always connected, i.e. the concrete meaning pertaining to the set (or class) of the signified which is coordinated with that signifier. Likewise, the use of a given tool from the set (or class) of an operant is always connected with a given operation which belongs to the set (or class) of the utility coordinated with that operant.

3.3. System, Oppositional Structure, and Semiotic Structures

As far as language communication is concerned, it is, according to de Saussure, the ensemble of the signs, of the coupled sets pertaining to the two coordinated universes (that of the signifier and that of the signified) that form the language (French: *langue*). Language constitutes the basis of the concrete realizations produced by speaking activity (French: *parole*). More generally speaking, i.e. beyond the domain of linguistics within the framework of the semiology of communication, the signs of each communicative mode form a sign system or code (Prieto 1975a). Therefore language is also a sign system or code, as de Saussure explicitly states. Even more generally speaking, i.e. within the framework of the semiology of signification, the instruments of a given culture form an instrument system.

It is characteristic of such systems as language, as well as other sign systems or instrument systems in general, that the double-faced elements of these systems reciprocally furnish each other's "value," i.e. their meaning. This implies that the elements of these systems, whether they are signs of a sign system or more generally instruments of an instrument system, cannot be recognized directly by themselves, but only by means of their relationships within the system as a whole. De Saussure repeatedly stressed this point by using the example of the chess game (Saussure 1964:88–89, 107, 110):[11] In one passage of the *Cours* he says:

> Take a knight, for instance. By itself, is it an element in the game? Certainly not, for by its material make-up—outside its square and the other conditions of the game— it means nothing to the player; it becomes a real concrete element only when endowed with value and wedded to it. Suppose that the piece happens to be destroyed or lost during a game. Can it be replaced by an equivalent piece? Certainly. Not only another knight, but even a figure shorn of any resemblance to a knight can be declared identical, provided the same value is attributed to it. We see then that in semiological systems like language, where elements hold each other in equilibrium in accordance with fixed rules, the notion of identity blends with that of value and *vice versa*. In a word, that is why the notion of value envelopes the notions of unit, concrete entity, and reality.

Relating this "relativism" to the aforementioned levels of expression and content, the general conclusion results that, like a piece in a game of chess, each set in the universe of the signifier, or the operant, and each set in the universe of the signified, or utility, possesses its identity not by itself, but only in relation to its complement within the universe in question. As curious as this may seem at first, no index, signal, or tool is recognizable by itself, i.e. they possess no reality of their own except in relation to the whole universe in which they are assigned to a set differing from its complement. The same applies to the level of content, which is coordinated with the level of expression just mentioned: A meaning or an operation cannot be assigned to a set in the universe of the signified, or utility, by virtue of its own properties, but only with reference to the corresponding complements in the universes mentioned. Because of certain distinctive features the sets in these universes stand to each other in the contrasting relationship of "opposition." For instance, the signifiers of the European road sign system stand in opposition to each other because they are circular, triangular or rectangular and colored blue or white with a red frame. Coordinated with these signifiers are the influences which are intentionally exerted by road traffic laws, i.e. signifieds which stand in opposition to each other because they are euphorically or dysphorically informative, and negatively or positively injunctive. Two such oppositional structures articulated within themselves and correlated with each other form together a "semiotic structure" (Prieto, 1975a).

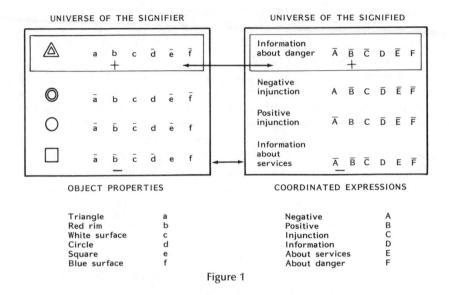

Figure 1

As the round and angular forms in the "communication tools" of road traffic regulation are connected with their corresponding messages of the authorities for the traffic participants, the tools of any tool box are coordinated equally with their corresponding operations. A sign system is thus a kind of "tool box for communication." The realizations of signifiers in the form of concrete signals, and of signifieds in concrete messages, "make sense," because signifier and signified belong indivisibly to a sign which obtains its value only within a sign system. Likewise the realizations of operants in concrete tools and of utilities in concrete operations possess functionality, because operant and utility belong indivisibly to an instrument which obtains its value only in an instrument system. A pair of pliers would make no sense without a hammer and nails.

Such structures are "semiotic" inasmuch as both oppositional structures involved confer relevance onto each other, i.e. each of the two oppositional structures mediates additional information over and above that which it contains by itself because it is coordinated with the other.

The basic idea of de Saussure that nothing can be classified without a certain point of view must now be consistently elaborated further to its ultimate consequences. According to Prieto (1975a) the level of the signified confers meaning upon the level of the signifier connected to it, but must itself be a level of the signifier in an additional semiotic structure, since there are no classification systems without a point of view. If the level of the signified is classified within itself, this classification must result from a point of view which means nothing else but that it is a class or set in another classification system. As a level of the signifier in this additional semiotic structure it is a classification system which must be considered logically prior to the forementioned one. Each level of the signified is thus classified twice—once as the signified of a signifier of which it constitutes the perspective of classification, and once as the signifier of another signified that in turn bestows its own perspective upon it. The level of the signified in this next semiotic structure is again a level of the signifier in a further semiotic structure, etc., until the chain of semiotic structures ends in the subject constituting a semiotic structure by a perspective of its own. This conception of Prieto shows that like Peirce the Saussurean tradition, too, makes use of a notion of "interpretant." The subject interpretant, however, is conceptualized by Prieto as a subject which is determined by society. The last source of interpretation is therefore always the dominating part of society with its practices which determine the subject. [12] In the Saussurean tradition the perspective of the subject is the interpretant, the position of the semiotic object within a classification system constitutes its "value," and the position of its signified with respect to other signifieds is its meaning as viewed from the subject's perspective.

3.4.   Syntagmatic and Paradigmatic Opposition

In language as a sign system which is realized linearly in time, signifiers and signifieds form two kinds of oppositions within their respective universes. These are called by de Saussure syntagmatic and "associative" (today one would say "paradigmatic") oppositions. De Saussure (1964:123–124, CLG 282) clarifies its implication by an example from architecture:

> From the associative and syntagmatic viewpoint a linguistic unit is like a fixed part of a building, e.g. a column. On the one hand, the column has a certain relation to the architrave that it supports; the arrangement of the two units in space suggests the syntagmatic relation. On the other hand, if the column is Doric, it suggests a mental comparison of this style with others (Ionic, Corinthian, etc.), although none of these elements is present in space: the relation is associative.

The syntagmatic opposition, i.e. the value position which an element takes on within a linear sequence, is therefore especially characteristic for language as a sign system. A typical sign system in the semiology of communication such as the road sign system contains equally rudimentary linear syntagms (e.g. the sequence of pre-warning and warning signs). As a rule, however, nonlinguistic sign systems are based on spatial syntagmatics (for example adjacency on a surface). Jakobson (1935, cf. also Jackobson & Halle 1956) has generalized the two principles of syntagm and paradigm into the two most important operations in language and poetic communication. Poetic communication is defined by him as a projection of elements from the paradigmatic level of association onto the syntagmatic level of composition. In doing this the operation of selecting from an associative complex is combined with a "chaining" or spatial composition of the elements selected. Thus for instance some sounds are taken from the paradigmatic "pile" of notes in the minor key and are "chained" together into a (sad) melody.

3.5. The Concepts of Arbitrariness, Motivation, and Symbol in de Saussure[13] and the Problem of Sign Classification

A further oppositional pair plays an important role in de Saussure's semiology: It results from the different possible relationships between signifier and signified in the sign. So far we have seen that the relationship among signifiers, on the one hand, and among signifieds on the other, is oppositional, since it is based on the presence or absence of distinctive features within the sets to which they belong. These distinctive features putting in opposition the signifiers in their universe as well as the signifieds in their universe do not seem to be formed by any special principle, but are obviously arbitrary. What represents a relevant phonological distinctive feature in one language, i.e. a phoneme, must not be a relevant feature, i.e. a phoneme, in another. This arbitrariness of the relevant distinctive features applying to the level of both the signifier and signified in different languages and other sign systems has its consequences: The sets in these systems can only be differentiated from each other by the opposition of their features; no other plausible reasons for their differentiation can be established —excepting the possibilities of human vocal articulation and perception of sound, which both have natural limits.

The coordination between signifier and signified in the sign as a whole may also be based on arbitrariness. There is no reason one can think of why the same concept, say "housing device," should be coupled in one language with the signifier /house/, in another with the signifier /maison/. As has been suggested before, however, there exist relationships between signifier and signified which are "motivated" to different degrees, meaning that "there is the rudiment of a natural bond between the signifier and the signified" (Saussure 1964, 68; cf. CLG 103 with the notes of Georges Dégallier, Albert Sechehaye, Francis Joseph, and Émile Constantin).

As one example among others of such a "natural" relationship between signifier and signified de Saussure quoted the phenomenon of onamatopoeia in language. However, although there are in language examples of this kind which must be described as "motivated," language remains a sign system resting primarily on arbitrariness, since its signs (even when they are in themselves motivated) receive their function only in opposition to other signs of the system. But de Saussure is convinced that in the future a fully developed semiology would also have to investigate communication systems such as pantomime, which are characterized by a high degree of motivation. Motivated connections between signifier and signified are called "symbols" by de Saussure.[14] With this nomenclature semiology is in direct contrast to Peirce's terminology (see Oehler in this volume p. 6) in which signs with an "arbitrary" connection between the representamen and the object represented are called symbols.[15] One of de Saussure's rare applications of semiology concerns literary symbols, and occurs in his studies on the *Nibelungen Song*. Because of the rarity of his remarks on symbols, the passage is quoted here extensively:[16]

- The legend is composed, in a sense to be further clarified, by a series of symbols.
- These symbols without doubt are subjected to the same vicissitudes and the same laws as all other series of symbols, such symbols, for instance, as the words of a language.
- They are all elements of semiology.
- There is no method by which one could show either that the symbol remains unaltered or that it must continuously change; probably it must change within certain limits.
- From the moment it turns into symbol, i.e. enters into the mass of society which determines its value at any moment, the identity of a symbol can never be fixed.

Thus the rune Υ is a "symbol." Its identity seems to be quite a tangible fact and consists, to be sure in an almost ridiculous way, in the following: It has the form Υ; it is read z; it is the eighth letter of the alphabet; it is called mystically *zann* and is sometimes quoted as the origin of the word. After a certain time . . . it becomes the tenth (letter) of the alphabet . . . , but here it already begins to assume a unity. Where is its identity now? To this question one is more likely to receive a smile, than an answer, so that the philosophical importance of the fact remains entirely unnoticed. It signifies no less than that, once it has entered into circulation (and each symbol exists only because it has been put in circulation), we are absolutely incapable at any moment of saying what the identity of a symbol will be at the next moment. It is with this general mental attitude that we tackle questions concerning any legend, because each of its characters is a symbol and one can—just as in the case of the rune—see the change (a) of the name, (b) of its position with respect to the others, (c) of its character, (d) of its function, its actions. When a name is transposed, the consequence may be that part of the actions is transposed as well, and vice-versa, or that the whole drama is changed by an accident of this kind.

3.6. Sign Classification in Semiology

Summarizing the generalizations based on the teaching of de Saussure, one finds that the fundamental sign concept is that of the index. Signals of communication are always indices as well. At the same time signifier and signified of the signs used in communication either may be arbitrarily connected or their connection may be motivated. Buyssens (1970) calls the former kind of connection *extrinsic*, i.e. a coding which is governed from the outside, the latter kind *intrinsic*, i.e. a coding defined from the inside (of the sign). Mutatis mutandis, by comparison with the Peircean trichotomy of sign-object relationships the a terminological table results (see Table 1).

As the table shows, parallels with the trichotomy of the sign-object relationship in the Peircean tradition are present in the Saussurean tradition. One can even recognize in de Saussure the concept that each sign may belong at the same time more or less to each of the three trichotomic levels.[17]

Table 1

De Saussure	motivated symbol	(index)	arbitrary sign
Piaget	symbol	index	sign
Buyssens	intrinsically coded	(index)	extrinsically coded
Prieto	motivated symbol	index	arbitrary sign
Peirce	icon	index	symbol
Morris	icon	index	symbol

3.7. Synchrony, Diachrony, and the Social Aspect of Sign Systems

The (relative) arbitrariness of the signs used in communication, i.e. the fact that they can be differentiated only in their opposition and by their organization into systems, but by no means primarily on the basis of natural reality, results from the fundamentally social aspect of sign systems (especially of language). The profoundly natural and biological aspect of sign systems is, to be sure, the fact that they are limited by the apparatus of perceptors and effectors in the human species. The possibilities for combining signifiers with signifiers, signifieds with signifieds and signifiers with signifieds, however, are within these limits infinite. These combinations are always socially defined, because they vary, depending on the purpose, from one group to another, between ethnic units, and between cultures.

This social determination of sign systems constitutes at the same time their historical character. Thus we find in de Saussure, side by side with the ahistorical synchronic inquiry into language or, more generally, into the state of communication systems, the diachronic investigation as a necessary complement. The accusation of ahistorical positivism sometimes raised against de Saussure conflicts with his central concept that language is arbitrary and has a systemic character marked by oppositions, inasmuch as this systemic character can only be explained by social and hence historical determination. Also Jakobson's (Jakobson & Waugh, 1979) criticism of the alleged static synchronism of de Saussure's general linguistics simply misses the point developed in the entire third part of the *Cours* under the heading "Diachronic Linguistics" (Saussure 1964, 140–190). De Saussure did not, to be sure, develop the concept of "dynamic synchronism" explicitly. But one cannot accuse him of having neglected the problem of diachronic changes in language.

The criticism of the Soviet psychologist Rubinstein, too, misses de Saussure's central conception of diachronic change and social determination although it remains, on the whole, rather temperate. Rubinstein writes:[18]

> If we consider the general conception of de Saussure, we cannot agree with his view
> of speech activity and language as ultimately psychological phenomena, with the mere
> difference that language is a part of social psychology and speech activity a part of

individual psychology. Unacceptable also are the reasons which de Saussure gives for differentiating language and speech activity, namely the opposition of the social and the individual.

But at this point Rubinstein qualifies his criticism with a footnote:

De Saussure's formulations regarding this question are not clear-cut. Thus he writes on p. 38 (*Grundfragen der allgemeinen Sprachwissenschaft*, Berlin and Leipzig, 1931): "In separating language from speaking we are at the same time separating: (1) what is social from what is individual . . ." Just next to this we find on p. 34 the correct statement: "Speech has both an individual and a social side, and we cannot conceive of one without the other."

Rubenstein then concludes his comment as follows:

But the differentiation between language and speech activity must be kept up, despite some opinions which have been voiced recently. The problem is only how and with regard to what they should be delimited one from the other. If one makes a difference between language and speech activity one must at the same time see their relationship. Only if both are conceived of as a unity can one understand their relationship with cognition correctly.

De Saussure's statements regarding this problem are unequivocal and can also be generalized from linguistics to the semiology of communication as a whole:

Language is speech, minus speaking. It is the whole set of linguistic habits which allow an individual to understand and to be understood. . . . But this definition still leaves language outside its social context; it makes language something artificial, since it includes only the individual part of reality; for the realization of language, a community of speakers (*masse parlante*) is necessary. Contrary to all appearances language never exists apart from the social fact, for it is a semiological phenomenon. . . . But under the conditions described, language is not living—it has only potential life; we have considered only the social, not the historical fact . . . , it is rather the action of time combined with the social force. If time is left out, the linguistic facts are incomplete and no conclusion is possible. If we considered language in time, without the community of speakers . . . , we would probably notice no change; time would not influence language. Conversely, if we considered the community of speakers without considering time, we would not see the effect of the social forces that influence language" (Saussure, 1964, 77–78, cf. CLG 114f. with the notes of George Dégallier, Albert Sechehaye and Emile Constantin).

As early as his first lecture at the University of Geneva in November 1891, de Saussure had stated almost in a programmatic fashion (N1.1): "Linguistics is a historical science and nothing else but a historical science."[18]

Prieto (1977) elaborated on the social determination of language (and hence of other sign systems) in differentiating between the truth of a linguistic utterance and its social relevance. Thus the two statements, that the neighbor is from Virginia and that he is a dentist, may both be true. But for the person with a toothache only the latter is relevant. The truth of a statement depends on the reality to which it refers, whereas its relevance depends on the human practice in which this reality is involved. To be sure, it is not the individuals who select this practice, because it is predetermined by society (as a rule, by the dominant classes). The relevance of a statement is therefore its social dimension. Insisting on the very truth of a statement may sometimes only serve the purpose of avoiding the taking of a social stance or even of hiding it.

It is by taking speech activity as his starting point by its foundation in social practice, and hence by his fundamental historicism that de Saussure differs from some of his structuralist followers. Not only the linguistics, as shown by de Saussure, but also through the study of non-linguistic sign systems, the connection between the change of sign systems and its social causes can be demonstrated, as has been shown for example in the case of road signs (Krampen, 1983). This example shows specifically the dependence of the code in question on historical-technical development and social conventions. In this case concrete international conventions developed under the auspices of the League of Nations and the United Nations play a special role.

4.   DE SAUSSURE'S SEMIOLOGY AND PROBLEMS OF STRUCTURALISM

4.1.   Some Problems with the Generalization of Basic Saussurean Concepts

So far the relationship between semiology and linguistics as well as the basic concepts of general linguistics in de Saussure have been discussed and subsequently the semiological generalizations rooted in his linguistics but transcending it have been pointed out. Now attention must be called to some dangers connected with attempts at generalizing de Saussure's linguistics. These dangers tend to appear when from the structure of linguistic meaning conclusions are transferred beyond the structure of communicative meaning to the meaningful structure of systems not (primarily) used for communication. There are precise differences in the functioning of sign systems used primarily for communication (of which language is one) and other sign systems in which communicative effects either are clearly not intended or at least need first to be proven. So far the attempt has been made here to respect this difference between signs belonging to the realm of the semiology of communication and tools pertaining to the semiology of signification, although the structural features common to both signs and tools have been stressed. In the following pages attention will be given to the difficulties, especially of a terminological kind, which arise if this difference is neglected.

4.2.   Hjelmslev and the Concept of Language

Such difficulties are already present in Hjelmslev, who certainly must be counted among those linguists who developed the basic ideas of de Saussure with particular consistency. It is precisely because Hjelmslev carried out one of the most interesting amplifications of Saussurean linguistics that his work deserves special attention (see the next chapter of this volume, p. 89ff). The following anticipatory remarks on Hjelmslev are necessary, because it is in connection with some of Hjelmslev's definitions that terminological difficulties of the kind alluded to can be demonstrated in the work of Roland Barthes.

Hjelmslev's theoretical starting point[19] is the assumption that all sign systems of language communication are formally isomorphic. This can be seen from his assertion that a general theory of language (singular!) constructed according to a formal model of natural languages (plural!) should be applicable to all sign systems (Hjelmslev, 1968/71:129 ff.). Such a conclusion brings about the danger of overlooking the difference between linguistics and semiology in de Saussure and ending up with that pan-linguistic—or at least metaphorical—view that every semiotic structure is a language.

It cannot and should not be excluded, of course, that all sign systems of communication, including languages, have common properties. But to reduce the different sign systems to a common basic linguistic model would not correspond with the intentions of de Saussure. If one follows de Saussure's definition according to which language is one sign system among others (such as writing, military and nautical signals, the alphabet of the deaf-mutes, but also symbolic rites and usages, customs, fashion, and pantomime) one direct implication is the task of elaborating on the differences between all these sign systems.

Hjelmslev defines language (singular) as a hierarchical system that can be subdivided on various levels into relational structures (Hjelmslev, 1968/71:135). This is correct, and also corresponds to de Saussure's concept of *langue*. But all hierarchical systems may be seen as founded on such a definition, which is so abstract that it could apply—as Mounin (1970:98) points out—to organic chemistry as well as to internal combustion engines. Furthermore, the characterization of the "natural languages" as systems into which all other languages (viz., sign systems) can be translated, because they constitute the model of "the language" (singular), has as a consequence that only the natural languages can give form to all meanings—an assertion for which Hjelmslev has not given any empirical proof nor even a reason (Hjelmslev 1968/71:138). In fact, Hjelmslev's few examples of non-linguistic sign systems (such as traffic lights, the telephone dial which features numbers and letters, the carillon of clocks, the tap sign-code of prisoners, or the Morse code in Hjelmslev 1968/71:179–231) are given as rather general descriptions which do not take into account the specificity of these sign systems.

A semiotically important development of Saussurean foundations was Hjelmslev's differentiation between the level of expression and the level of content in "language" which runs parallel to the concepts of signifier and signified. Following a suggestion of de Saussure, who held that the combination of speech sound and concept was a pure form and not a (formed) substance (CLG p. 157), Hjelmslev further subdivided both the level of expression and of content in language into (pure) form and (formed) substance. A similar subdivision was already present in Noreen.

It is precisely the concept of the formed substance of expression which could have given a point of departure for the specific analysis of non-linguistic communication systems, most of which are in fact different from the formed sound substance of expression typical of natural languages (cf. Wells, 1977).

Yet this possibility was not pursued by Hjelmslev. Instead he used this differentiation to distinguish between denotative and connotative "languages" and of "metasemiotics"—terms which were then picked up by Barthes (1964b:130–132) where, unfortunately, they did not contribute much to the clarification of semiotic problems. The next chapter in this book will show that a "language" is connotative in Hjelmslev's (1968/71:144) sense, if its level of expression is itself a "language" (thus also exhibiting a level of expression and a level of content). Metasemiotics arise if the level of content of a "language" is itself a "language."

Not only styles and stylistic registers such as archaic or vulgar manners of expression, but also code variants like speaking, writing, or gesticulating, are connotative languages according to Hjelmslev. Dialects and idiolects are also among the connotative languages (Hjelmslev 1968/71:145 f.). If, according to de Saussure, the criterion of semiology is however communication, whether by linguistic or non-linguistic signs, Hjelmslev's connotative "languages" are as a rule indices which in fact furnish information about the sender's state, but which were not emitted for the express purpose of communication. Obviously Hjelmslev had not yet envisaged a distinction between the semiology of communication and the semiology of signification (Prieto, 1975b) or "semiology of connotation," as Prieto (1975a) calls it with the intention of correcting Hjelmslev and Barthes.

4.3. Barthes

Barthes (1964b:130–132) took over the concepts of denotation, connotation, and metasemiotics from Hjelmslev. Typically, he also changed Hjelmslev's term "metasemiotics" into "metalanguage" (French: *metalangue*). For Barthes, connotation is the "tone" of a text, the manner in which it has been "doctored." In the final analysis, the signified of a "connotative sign" is for Barthes the "fragment of an ideology," the signifier, in turn, a "rhetoric," both going back to a "real system" via a metalanguage. Obviously even here no difference is made between communication and indication. Thus, for Barthes everything which furnishes meaning becomes a sign, and any group of signs becomes a system, although neither the existence of an intention to communicate, nor of a complete sign inventory, nor of combination rules or opposing features, is proven.

As for Hjelmslev, every system for Barthes, too, is a language. In this way, a whole host of social practices suddenly become languages, according to Barthes, and thus belong to semiology. And since de Saussure had postulated this with reference to polite formulas, customs, and fashion, his methods of general linguistics (as well as their development in linguistics, mind you) become, unawares, the working instruments of semiology. The subordination of linguistics to semiology is overlooked in this process and it is precisely the contrary which is proposed. Now, all of a sudden, one reads: ". . . *c'est la sémiologie qui est une partie de la linguistique*" (Barthes, 1964a:81) - "semiology is a part of linguistics." What Barthes investigates are not signs of communication; he looks perhaps at symbols (in the sense of literary semiology as occurring in de Saussure), but mostly at indices of sociological phenomena—certain manners of preparing food, of dressing, styles of furniture, cars, architecture, etc. Even for unequivocally communicative processes such as photography and film, Barthes is not interested in the specific semiological investigation of these media as sign systems, but, as Lindekens (1971:231–242) has pointed out, in the social phenomena presumably standing behind the signs. Now it is true that semiological objects can indeed be interpreted as indices of social conditions. In this case, however, it is not the semiology of communication which is at stake, but the semiology of signification (if a system of indices can be delimited), or probably even more a sort of "symptomatology" of social psychopathology.

A certain kind of food preparation becomes quickly a "language of the menu" and finally a "rhetoric of the menu," without any proof that a meal is actually (and regularly) a communicative message. In the semiology of signification one would have to demonstrate to begin with the systematic character of the indices of social circumstances. And even if such a system could be found, the indices would not by that token become signs, i.e. signs of communication.

4.4. Lévi-Strauss

Similar problems arise in the "structural anthropology" of Lévi-Strauss. Apparently Lévi-Strauss became acquainted with de Saussure's linguistics through Jakobson whom he met towards the end of World War II in the École des Hautes Études, which was transferred to New York at that time (cf. Mounin, 1970:200 f.). He subsequently used the linguistic model to discover and formulate laws in the realm of anthropology: "We must in fact ask ourselves whether various aspects of social life (including art and religion), for the investigation of which we already know that the methods and concepts of linguistics can be utilized, consist of phenomena the nature of which approach that of language . . . one should elaborate a universal law (French: *code*[!][20]) capable of expressing the common properties of specific structures depending on each aspect of it" (Lévi-Strauss, 1967:75). More specifically, Lévi-Strauss takes as his starting point the so-called "Prague phonology" developed by Trubetskoy and Jakobson, in which the speech sounds of a language are described by a classification system of phonemes standing in opposition to each other. Mounin (1970:203–207) has drawn attention to the fact that some misunderstandings slipped in when Lévi-Strauss adopted linguistics. Thus he calls the phoneme an "element of meaning" (élément de signification) or confuses occasionally the opposition synchrony/

diachrony with paradigm/syntagm (cf. Mounin 1970:205–207). But these details
are not that important. More important is the fact that from a metaphorical
application of linguistic concepts to anthropology some analogies result which
are difficult to prove (and are not proven in Lévi-Strauss). Thus in Lévi-Strauss
rules of marriage and systems of kinship become "languages" (e.g. Lévi-Strauss
1967:63) and, since language serves communication, they become communications, too (Lévi-Strauss 1967:74). Communications again, according to Lévi-
Strauss, are a kind of circulation (for instance of women) and circulation in turn
is a kind of exchange (Lévi-Strauss 1967:97). It must be assumed that for Lévi-
Strauss linguistic analogy is a heuristic device. If such a heuristic device is taken
over uncritically, however, and leads to statements which are not proven empirically (or are unprovable), this can lead to terminological confusion.

General linguistics according to de Saussure is a part of the semiology of
communication. If a linguistic analogy is to make sense, proof has to be given
that the analogon in fact belongs to the phenomena of communication. In the
event this proof cannot be given, the analogon in question may at best belong
to phenomena which can be subsumed under the semiology of signification, and
should be so labelled.

4.5.   Definition and Criticism of "Structuralism"

From the preceding remarks on Hjelmslev, Barthes, and Lévi-Strauss a
definition of structuralism can be derived which is different from the ones cir-
culating thus far. For example, what Bierwisch calls "structuralism" in his excellent article (Bierwisch, 1966) is actually "structural linguistics" derived from
de Saussure, i.e. linguistics based on the analysis of oppositional structures and
of semiotic structures in language which are constituted by them. The preceding
remarks suggest, however, a distinction between structural linguistics and structuralism. While structural linguistics, as a part of the semiology postulated by
de Saussure, investigates natural languages as sign systems, in structuralism,
instead, methods and terms of structural linguistics are generalized a priori and
applied to the realm of non-linguistic signs pertaining to the semiology of communication, and especially to the realm of indices in the semiology of signification. In addition to the empirically unproven (and unprovable) results frequently
derived from these conclusions by analogy, even absurdities sometimes follow
from them. Thus the correct statement that all languages consist of signs leads
to the unnecessary (and wrong) conclusion that all systems consisting of signs
or even indices are languages. The confusion continues with the term "syntax."
From the realization that all languages have a syntax and that each syntax is a
generative device, the conclusion is easily drawn that all products of generative
devices are languages. One can agree with Hjelmslev's construction that all
languages have a level of expression and a level of content which are each
subdivided by form and substance. But if from this statement the conclusion is

drawn that every sign system furnished with a level of expression and a level of content is a language, this is neither cogent nor necessary.

The memory of de Saussure is not well served by the introduction of linguistic analogies. He himself had conceptualized his semiology in a more extensive way. It is therefore recommendable as a rule to examine the soundness of the semiological investigations of the structuralists—despite their frequent reference to de Saussure.

This is best done by following in concrete semiological analysis a set of rules which bring to the foreground the special properties of the sign system (or of the system of signification) under investigation (cf. Eco in this volume, p. 118ff). Some of the most important rules for conducting these analyses (the list does not pretend to be complete) are:

- Distinguish between problems of communication and problems of signification
- Determine whether the semiotic structure is autonomous or not (the Morse code, for instance, is not autonomous, because it only transcribes the vowels and consonants of a natural language)
- Define the "formed substance" of the signifier or of the "indicating" (i.e. the sensory channel of perception) and of the signified or the "indicated"
- Establish whether the sign system under investigation is linear or non-linear, whether it has discrete or continuous sign complexes
- Make a complete inventory of all sets (or classes) by which the universes of the signifier and the signified are classified
- Indicate the differences of the sets within both universes in terms of distinctive features
- Classify the kind of connection between signifier and signified (i.e., establish whether the coding is intrinsic or extrinsic)
- List the elements in the sets (i.e. all possible variants of their distinctive features)
- Describe the relationship among the elements (are the variations of the distinctive features measurable by nominal, ordinal, or interval scaling?)
- Describe the composition rules ("syntax") of the sets (indicate which sets have predicative functions; find existing rules of exception), etc.

5. PERSPECTIVES OF SEMIOLOGY

The origin of Saussurean semiology is "anthroposemiotic" to begin with (cf. Sebeok 1976:3; 1977:183), although it cannot be reduced to linguistics. But there are even some attempts in the tradition of semiology to embrace the realm of "zoosemiotics" (cf. Sebeok 1976:3, 83–93). Benveniste (1952) for instance proposed some ideas on the communication of bees. Mounin (1970:41–56) has looked at the communication of ravens. He has also reviewed, from a semiological point of view, the experiments of the Premacks and Gardners in which chimpanzees learned to "communicate" with their trainers by gestures or arbitrary visual tokens (Mounin, 1976:1–21). Therefore semiology is not necessarily fixed in an anthroposemiotic direction. Mounin (1976:46) writes, for example: "In the case of ravens and bees we apparently have messages and communication: The dance of the bees, the cry of the ravens have their place in a general semiology or science of signal systems."[21] A more conservative proposition of coordinating non-anthroposemiotic phenomena with semiology has been made by Wells (1977:10 f.). He starts with the premise that according to de Saussure and Hjelmslev signs have a specific form of expression and of content as well as a substance of expression and of content. A new area of semiology to be worked out could therefore refer to the problem of which kinds of substances of expression could have facilitated the phylogenetic development of "higher" forms of expression (especially of the human kind). Such an investigation would have as its subject matter the genesis of the different human forms of expression from prehuman substances of expression.

According to Wells (1977) the human combination of forms of expression with those of content would have a full sign status, whereas pre-human sign substances would have to be described as potential forms of expression of potential signs.

The sign concept developed in the tradition of de Saussure is based on the assumption that each sign is an index, but that not all indices are signs of communication. Given the parallelism of sign and instrument, signifier and operant, signified and utility—ultimately of purpose and means—the capacity of elaboration and of generalization in semiology does not seem to be exhausted. With the introduction of the term "instrument" as a parallel to the term "sign" the problems of sign definition and sign classification, which have been central thus far, lose importance. In the future the attention of semiologists will be directed more to the analysis of the use of certain means to reach certain ends, and this not only in reference to human beings, but also to animals and to living beings in general.

NOTES

The alleged statements of de Saussure stemming from the lecture notes of his students are quoted according to Engler's (1968 vol. 1) critical edition of the *Cours de linguistique générale*, indicated as CLG with the page numbers of the first edition of 1916.

For the quotations from Saussure's own notes collected by Engler (1974, vol. 2, fasc. 4) the notation N 1–24 (with further decimal subdivision, if required) is used.

The direct and indirect statements of de Saussure collected by Godel (1969) under the title *Les sources manuscrites du Cours de linguistique générale de F. de Saussure* are quoted as SM, with the page number of the book.

1. The term *semiology* created by de Saussure for the general science of signs, is used throughout this article instead of the term *semiotics* which is today more generally accepted. On the history of these terms cf. Sebeok, 1976:47–58.
2. This biographical account is based on extensive investigations of the life and work of de Saussure carried out by Robert Godel (1969) and Tullio de Mauro (1976).
3. From a book review written by Charles Sanders Peirce which appeared on December 14, 1899 in *The Nation* it can be seen that he knew of the existence of the de Saussure family (especially Henri de Saussure, the father of Ferdinand). Peirce had also visited Geneva during two of his trips to Europe. There is, however, no evidence that he knew Ferdinand de Saussure (or his work) (cf. Sebeok, 1977b:27–32).
4. Some of the notes de Saussure wrote for this book, and a reference to a chapter on semiology, are preserved (cf. N9.1–2; SM:36 f.).
5. Translation by this author.
6. Translation from the French by this author (de Mauro 1976:393 f.).
7. Noreen seems to have coined the term *semology* before de Saussure introduced his term *semiology*.
8. Already in the notes of 1893/94 for his book de Saussure writes (SM:43, translation by this author): "There are different kinds of identity. . . . Outside of some kind of identity relation no linguistic fact exists. But the identity relation depends on the different points of view which one applies; there is then no trace of linguistic facts outside a certain point of view which precedes differentiation."
9. But beginnings of such investigations (for example on colors and forms) are found in the "notes item" (N 15, 3316–3318.9).
10. Summary by this author from the French original (Buyssens 1970:22–26).
11. The example of the game of chess already appears in the 1894 manuscript of de Saussure for his Whitney memorial lecture (N 10; SM:44).
12. The reproach of Ogden and Richards (1923:5) that in de Saussure the process of interpretation would be included by definition in the term sign cannot be maintained, in view of his teachings on the classifications of linguistic phenomena "from a certain point of view."
13. Cf. especially Engler, 1962 and 1964.
14. In this respect Ogden and Richards (1923:5) are again mistaken when they state that de Saussure excluded the term symbol for the designation of linguistic signs.
15. De Saussure's conception of the linguistic sign as arbitrary and of symbols as motivated was taken over by Piaget (1932, 1945, Piaget & Inhelder 1948, 1966) from the point of view of developmental semiotics. Piaget (Piaget 1968; cf. Smith 1977) preferred even later the terminology of de Saussure (motivated symbols vs. arbitrary sign) to Peirce's trichotomy (icon, index, symbol). But very early Piaget (1936) had also developed a semiological concept of index.

    Jakobson (1968) on the other hand has relativized, by means of the Peircean nomenclature, de Saussure's distinction between arbitrary signs and motivated symbols (cf. Eco in this volume p. 119): "Learned, conventional connections are copresent also in indexes and icons. The full apprehension of pictures and diagrams requires a learning process. No painting is devoid of ideographic, symbolic elements. The projection of the three dimensions onto a single plane through any kind of pictorial prespective is an imputed quality. . . . Any attempt to treat verbal signs as solely conventional, 'arbitrary symbols' proves to be a misleading oversimplification. Iconicity plays a vast and necessary, though evidently subordinate part in different levels of linguistic structure."

    De Saussure's discussion of motivated symbols (CLG 103) suggests nevertheless that he thought of motivated and arbitrary qualities as being relative and occurring also in mixed relationships.
16. Translation from de Mauro (1976:348) by this author.
17. Concerning the psychological relevance and the mixed occurrence of Peirce's trichotomic terms see the studies of Krampen, Espe and Schreiber (1981) and Krampen, Espe, Schreiber and

Braun (1983). These studies show that the subjects experienced the three-sign aspects of Peirce's trichotomy as co-occurring in a sign. But photographs and paintings are classified as predominantly iconic, drawings and pictographs as iconic and indexical, typographic products as predominantly symbolic.

18. See also the earlier remarks of de Saussure on linguistics as a historical science (N 15, 3309 and 3322.2), cf. especially Jäger, 1976.

19. To those who do not know Danish, Hjelmslev's programmatic work on linguistic theory *Omkring sprogteoriens grundlaeggelse* (Prolegomena to a Theory of Language) is only accessible in English or French translation. Both translations are accused of incoherences in the rendering of Hjelmslev's terminology (Mounin, 1970:95 f.). This is not without importance, since Hjelmslev's development of de Saussure's general linguistics into "glossematics" is based on an extensive introduction of new terms. Our studies are based on the French translation by Una Canger, a student of Hjelmslev's and later director of the Institute of linguistics of the University of Copenhagen.

20. Note by this author.

21. Translation by this author.

REFERENCES

Barthes, R. (1964a). *Éléments de sémiologie*. Paris: Éditions Gonthier.

Barthes, R. (1964b), "Éléments de sémiologie." *Communications*, 4, 91–144.

Beneviste, E. (1952), "Communication animale et langage humain." *Diogène*, 1, 1ff.

Bense, M. (1976), *Vermittlung der Realitäten*. Baden-Baden: Agis, p. 144.

Bierwisch, M. (1966), "Strukturalismus und Linguistik." *Kursbuch*, 5, 77–152.

Buyssens, E. (1943). *Les langages et le discours—Essai de linguistique fonctionelle dans le cadre de la sémiologie*. Bruxelles: Lebègue.

Buyssens, E. (1970), *La Communication et l'articulation linguistique*. Bruxelles: Presses Universitaires de Bruxelles.

Engler, R. (1962), "Théorie et critique d'un principe saussurien: l'arbitraire du signe." *Cahiers F. de Saussure*, 19, 5–66.

Engler, R. (1964), "Compléments à l'arbitraire." *Cahiers F. de Saussure*, 21, 25–32.

Engler, R., Ed. (1968), *Ferdinand de Saussure, Cours de linguistique générale. Edition critique*. Wiesbaden: Otto Harrassowitz.

Engler, R., Ed. (1974), *Ferdinand de Saussure, Cours de linguistique générale*. Édition critique, fasc. 4. Wiesbaden: Otto Harrassowitz.

Godel, R. (1969). *Les Sources manuscrites du Cours de linguistique générale de F. de Saussure*. Genève: Librairie Droz.

Hjelmslev, L. (1968/71), *Prolégomènes à une théorie du langage*. Trad. du danois par U. Canger. Paris: Éditions de Minuit.

Jäger, L. (1976). "F. de Saussures historisch hermeneutische Idee der Sprache." *Linguistik and Didaktik*, 27, 210–244.

Jakobson, R. (1935), "Randbemerkungen zur Prosa des Dichters Pasternak." *Slavische Rundschau*, 7, 357–374.

Jakobson, R., Halle, M. (1956), "Two Aspects of Language and Two Types of Aphasic Disturbances." In: *Fundamentals of Language*. The Hague: Mouton.

Jakobson, R. (1971a), "Language in Relation to Other Communication Systems." In: *Selected Writings*, Bd. II. The Hague and Paris: Mouton, pp. 697–708.

Jakobson, R. (1971b), "The Kazan' School of Polish Linguistics and Its Place in the International Development of Phonology." In: *Selected Writings*, Bd. II. The Hague and Paris: Mouton, p. 394 ff.

Jakobson, R., Waugh, L. (1979), *The Sound Shape of Language*. Bloomington and London: Indiana University Press, p. 76.

Krampen, M. (1983), "Icons of the Road." *Semiotica*, 43, 1/2, special issue.

Krampen, M., Espe, H., Schreiber, K., Braun, G. (1983), "Weitere Untersuchungen zur Mehrdi mensionalität visueller Zeichen." In: Tasso Borbé (Ed.), *Semiotics Unfolding*, Vol. III, Berlin, New York, Amsterdam: Mouton, pp. 1471–1482.

Krampen, M., Espe, H., Schreiber, K. (1981), "Zur Mehrdimensionalität ikonischer Zeichen— Ergebnisse einer Leitstudie." In: A. Lange-Seidl. (Ed.), *Zeichenkonstitution*. Vol. II, Berlin, New York: Walter de Gruyter, pp. 18–25.

Krampen, M., Espe, H., Schreiber, K. (1980), "Zur Mehrdimensionalität ikonischer Zeichen— Varianzanalytische Untersuchungen." *Zeitschrift für Semiotik*, 2, No. 2, 95–103.

Lévi-Strauss, C. (1967), *Strukturale Anthropologie*. Frankfurt a.M.: Suhrkamp. (French: *Anthropologie structurale*. Paris: Librairie Plon, 1958.)

Lindekens, R. (1971). *Éléments pour une sémiotique de la photographie*. Paris: Didier.

Mauro, T. de (1976), "Notes biographiques et critiques sur F. de Saussure." In: F. de Saussure, *Cours de linguistique générale. Édition critique préparée par T. de Mauro*. Paris: Payot, pp. 319–404.

Mounin, G. (1970), *Introduction à la sémiologie*. Paris: Les Éditions de Minuit.

Mounin, G. (1976), "Language, Communication, Chimpanzees." *Current Anthropology*, 17, No. 1, 1–21.

Noreen, A. G. (1988), *Om sprakriktighet*. Uppsala: Schultz.

Ogden, C. K., Richards, I. A. (1923). *The Meaning of Meaning*. New York: Harcourt, Brace & Company. 6th ed., 1946, pp. 4–6.

Piaget, J. (1932), *Le Jugement moral chez l'enfant*. Paris: F. Alcan. (English translation by M. Gabain: *The Moral Judgement of the Child*. New York: Harcourt, 1932.)

Piaget, J. (1936), *La Naissance de l'intelligence chez l'enfant*. Neuchâtel: Delachaux & Niestlé. (English translation by M. Cook: *The Origins of Intelligence in Children*. New York: International Press, 1952.)

Piaget, J. (1946), *La formation du symbole chez l'enfant*. Neuchâtel: Delachaux & Niestlé. (English translation by C. Gattegno and F. M. Hodgson: *Play, Dreams and Imitation in Childhood*. New York: Norton, 1951.)

Piaget, J. (1968), *Le structuralisme*. Paris: Presses Universitaires de France. (English translation and edition by C. Maschler: *Structuralism*. New York: Harper & Row, 1971.)

Piaget, J. & Inhelder, B. (1948). *La Représentation de l'espace chez l'enfant*. Paris: Presses Universitaires de France. (English translation by F. J. Langdon and J. L. Lunzer: *The Child's Conception of Space*. London: Routledge & Kegan Paul, 1956.)

Piaget, J. & Inhelder, B. (1966), *La Psychologie de l'enfant*. Paris: Presses Universitaires de France. English translation by H. Weaver: *The Psychology of the Child*. London: Routledge & Kegan Paul, 1969.

Prieto, L. J. (1966), *Messages et signaux*. Paris: Presses Universitaires de France.

Preito, L. J. (1968), "La sémiologie." *Encyclopédie de La Pléiade*. Vol. *"Langage."* Paris: Gallimard, pp. 93–144.

Prieto, L. J. (1973), "Signe et instrument." In: *Littérature, Histoire, Linguistique*. Recueil d'études offert à B. Gagnebin. Lausanne: L'Age d'Homme, pp. 153–161.

Prieto, L. J. (1975a), *Pertinence et pratique*. Paris: Éditions de Minuit. (Italian: *Pertineza e pratica*. Milano: Feltrinelli, 1976.)

Prieto, L. J. (1975b), *Études de linguistique et de sémiologie générales*. Genève and Paris: Librairie Droz.

Prieto, L. J. (1977), "Discorso e realtà." *L'Unità*, 4 ottobre, 3.

Rubinstein, S. L. (1972), *Sein und Bewusstsein*, Berlin (DDR): Akademie-Verlag.

Saussure, F. de (1964), *Course in general linguistics*. Translated from the French by Wade Baskin. 2d ed. London: Peter Owen, 1964.

Saussure, F. de (1968), *Cours de linguistique générale*. Édition critique par R. Engler. Wiesbaden: Otto Harrassowitz.

Saussure, F. de (1971), *Cours de linguistique générale*. 3rd ed. Paris: Payot.

Saussure, F. de (1976), *Cours de linguistique générale*. Édition critique préparée par T. de Mauro. Paris: Payot.

Sebeok, T. A. (1976), *Studies in Semiotics*. Bloomington, Ind.: Indiana University Press.

Sebeok, T. A. (1977a), "Ecumenicalism in Semiotics." In: T. A. Sebeok (Ed.), *A Perfusion of Signs*. Bloomington and London: Indiana University Press, pp. 180–206.

Sebeok, T. A. (1977b), "The French Swiss Connection." *Semiotic Scene*, 1, No. 1, 27–32.

Smith, M. D. (1977), Peirce and Piaget: A commentary on signs of a common ground. *Semiotics*, 19, No. 3/4, pp. 271–279.

Stetter, C. (1978), La Fonction des réflexions sémiologiques dans la fondation de la linguistique générale chez F. de Saussure. *Kodikas/ Code*, 1, 9–20.

Stetter C. (without year), *Grundlagen der Pragmatik—Untersuchungen zum Problem einer semiotischen Begründung der Linguistik*. Teil I: *Kant, Humboldt, de Saussure*. Unpublished manuscript.

Walther, E. (1974), *Allgemeine Zeichenlehre*. Stuttgart: Deutsche Verlags-Anstalt, pp. 7, 97.

Wells, R. (1977), Criteria for Semiosis. In: T. A. Sebeok (Ed.), *A Perfusion of Signs*. Bloomington and London: Indiana University Press, pp. 1–21.

CHAPTER 4

Louis Hjelmslev: Glossematics as General Semiotics

JÜRGEN TRABANT

1. *LA LANGUE* AS THE GENERAL PRINCIPLE OF SEMIOTIC STRUCTURE

1.1.

Not long ago, the author of a review of the recent German edition of Hjelmslev's major work, the *Prolegomena to a Theory of Language*, queried the need for the translation by asking whether Hjelmslev ought still to be read in linguistics courses (Kotschi, 1977). No clearer indication could be found of the disrepute into which glossematics, as an important school of European structuralism, has fallen. This general tendency, however, (to which the linguistics of Greimas stands as perhaps the only exception) ought to be combated on two grounds.

In the first place, Coseriu, one of the most eminent historians of linguistics, has placed Hjelmslev beside no lesser figure than Humboldt as one of the founders of general linguistics: "For we are convinced that glossematics marks a decisive point in the history of linguistics. It cannot be passed over, or regarded simply as a 'deviation' from the true course of linguistics, since it continues and develops a tradition that goes back to . . . Wilhelm von Humboldt. . . . It therefore seems to us that in this respect, Hjelmslev can be compared only with Humboldt . . . ," for, "like Humboldt, Hjelmslev sees the possibility of comprehending all human and cultural problems in terms of language" (Coseriu, 1954:175).

Translation by Iain Boyd Whyte.

JÜRGEN TRABANT • Department of Romance Languages, Free University of Berlin, Berlin, West Germany.

Secondly, I would offer the following argument against ignoring Hjelms-lev. Even if, as the reviewer cited above implies, one ought not to read Hjelmslev in a university linguistics course because glossematics—regardless of Coseriu's opinion—might justifiably be regarded as a "deviation" from the true course of linguistics, it seems to me nevertheless that Hjelmslev's work is indispensible in a university *semiotics* course. For in my opinion, and with all respect for Hjelmslev's importance as a linguistic scientist, the truly original aspect of his work is the development of a semiotic rather than a linguistic theory. For he is nothing less than the originator of that Saussurean desideratum, namely a general science of signs (*sémiologie*) *based on immanent and structural linguistics*.

1.2.

Although he described his new linguistic science as "structural linguistics" or "immanent linguistics," Hjelmslev also gave it the name *glossematics*, to distinguish it from traditional linguistics. Strictly speaking, glossematics is not a linguistic science at all: It is not a science of the "linguistic language" (*langue linguistique*—Hjelmslev, 1944:32) or of the "natural language," but rather a science of signs, a science of the general semiotic structure. In Hjelmslev's writings, "language" (*langue*), defined as a glossematic object, is substantially synonymous with "sign system" (which Hjelmslev calls "semiotic"). Excluded from this usage of the term *language* are those specific points at which the particularity of the linguistic language over the general semiotic structure is determined.[1]

In his programmatic editorial in *Acta Linguistica*, Hjelmslev makes it absolutely clear that the object of glossematics is not, in the final analysis, the "linguistic" language.[2] Following Saussure's model, he insists that the object of linguistics ("*l'objet auquel on vise*"—the goal) is not the *parole*, which is nevertheless the necessary starting point (*l'objet étudié*), but the *langue*. This object *langue* is defined more exactly by Hjelmslev as follows: "If the *parole* is the manifestation of the *langue*, then a *langue*, in turn, is the manifestation of the typological class to which it belongs, and ultimately the manifestation of that particular class of classes that is THE *langue*. . . . the species (*espèce*) *langue* is the actual and prime object of structural linguistics. A particular *langue* (*langue particulière*) is subordinate to the type, and the type subordinate to the species. We [the editorial board of *Acta Linguistica*] hope, therefore, that research into any particular language will be based on the structure of the type or the species *langue*, and will be aimed specifically at throwing light on this species" (Hjelmslev, 1944: 31 f.). From this ascending sequence: *langue particulière—type* (class)[3]—*species* (*espèce*, class of classes), it becomes clear that *langue* is something far more comprehensive than the structure of one historical language: As a species, *langue* embraces the linguistic universals.

Yet even with the species *langue*, Hjelmslev has not reached the end of his abstractions: *La langue* is extended further to become the structure of the class of all signs systems. The three levels of abstraction of spoken language are then only a special case within this general *langue*. Having established the sequence of *langue particulière*, type and species, and indicated the species as that which should be illuminated by structural linguistics, Hjelmslev continues: "This typological hierarchy, which ascends from the particular languages to the species language, theoretically ends only at the point at which one has arrived at the general principle of semiological structure. Both Saussure's theory and also the most recent researches in formal logic indicate that the linguistic language (*langue linguistique*) represents only one of the possible manifestations of *la langue*, when *la langue* is understood in the widest sense as embracing every sign system organized as a transformative structure" (ibid.) Figure 1 shows how we could depict the hierarchy of *langue*:

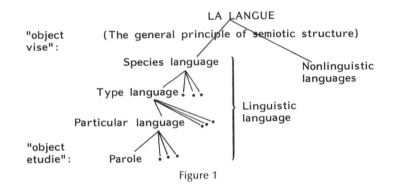

Figure 1

1.3.

The passage quoted above reveals a characteristic feature of Hjelmslev's writing: He tends to present the central ideas of glossematics and thus glossematics itself as the fulfillment of Saussure's intentions. Although we cannot provide a detailed account here of Hjelmslev's exegesis of Saussure, we can show, taking one point central to our argument, that this interpretation is by no means so self-evident as Hjelmslev would have us believe.

Saussure presented language as one particular sign system among many, and linguistics as one specific area within the proposed science of semiology. But he did not claim, as Hjelmslev does, that the linguistic language was only one manifestation of a very general *langue*. In the passage in the *Cours* to which Hjelmslev is presumably alluding in the quotation above, Saussure refers exclusively to the *linguistic* language. In fact he says that the spoken language—by which he means the *phonic* language—is one possible material manifestation of language. Beyond this material manifestation, "above the functioning of the various organs," there may be, says Saussure, "a more general faculty, the faculty which governs signs and which would be the linguistic faculty par excellence" (Saussure, 1916: 27). While this formulation of a "sign-governing faculty" appears to suggest Hjelmslev's wide-ranging definition of *langue*, it actually refers quite clearly and specifically in the passage cited only to the "*langue linguistique*." Whether or not, on the basis of the *Cours* text, the "*faculté linguistique*" can be extended to become a "*faculté sémiologique*" must remain an entirely open question. In my opinion, Saussure is still working here on the abstraction plane of *species* (linguistic) language, and not on the higher level of semiotic structure in general.[4] This also accounts for the other relevant passage where he insists that "the essence of language is alien to the phonic character of the linguistic sign" (Saussure, 1916: 21). The extension of the concept *langue* to mean specifically "semiotic structure" is characteristic of Hjelmslev's radical interpretation.

1.4.

In his analysis of glossematics, Coseriu (1954) shows quite clearly that the focus of Hjelmslev's attempt to establish a new linguistic science is not language itself, but rather sign systems in general.[5] This interpretation resolves, in particular, all those difficulties that arise when a given glossematic predicate (for example, the theorem of the independence of substance from form[6]) is applied to linguistic language or to other *specific* languages. In descending to the level of concrete sign systems, glossematics ceases to be glossematics, that is to say, a science of pure form.[7]

In certain respects, however, Hjelmslev himself appears to be apprehensive about the radicality and audacity of his reasoning. A symptom of this is the fact that only research into linguistic language is published in his *Acta Linguistica*, even though the journal was conceived as the organ of the all-embracing *langue* described above. He explicitly admits to this limitation as a concession forced by practical considerations,[8] but this concession cannot be justified in terms of his own theory. In other words, Hjelmslev himself has not carried his radical theory through to its logical conclusion. He appears to be implying that glossematics can, at the same time, be both a general theory of signs and a theory of language. But this distorted self-evaluation of glossematics prevents the truly novel aspect of the theory—the idea of a general theory of signs[9]—from bearing fruit. Furthermore, it creates new difficulties, such as the generalization of linguistic signs into signs per se—a question we shall go into later. Yet in spite of Hjelmslev's own evaluation of glossematics and the problems arising from his conception of signs, the appearance of glossematics must be seen as an important point in the development of modern semiotics, for it marks the point at which *linguistics* meets the broader science of semiotics.[10]

1.5.

Glossematics as semiotics represents not only a transition from one plane of abstraction to a higher one, but also the expansion on the higher plane of the data gathered at the lower level. For in glossematics, the structure of the linguistic sign is taken explicitly as the basis of the general sign structure: That is to say, the only things accepted as signs are those things that are structured in the same way as linguistic signs. In this respect glossematics is an agent of the so-called "linguistic imperialism" that has been increasingly challenged by those semi-oticians who feel that it is necessary to emancipate semiotics from its parent sciences.

Even if it is no longer possible today to grant the attribute "sign" only to those structures that, like linguistic signs, are "double articulated,"[11] there are still good arguments in favor of regarding the linguistic sign as the nucleus and guiding principle of semiotics.[12] This does not imply, however, that features specific to the linguistic sign should be elevated to the higher plane of abstraction of signs in general, as Hjelmslev has done.

2. THE DOUBLE-ARTICULATED OR TWICE-FORMED SIGN

2.1.

Something can only be called a sign when it is possible to distinguish in it a *signifiant* and a *signifié*. In place of the Saussurean terms Hjelmslev introduces the terms *expression* and *content*, which he calls the *planes* of the sign. In a further interpretation of Saussure the terms *form* and *substance* are introduced: Language, according to Saussure, is a form that initiates distinctions in both the "amorphous mass" of our thoughts (content) and also in the "plastic matter" (*matière plastique*, Saussure, 1916: 155) of sounds. Just how Saussure imagined the formation process of these two formless substances is shown in Figure 2, from the *Cours* (Saussure 1916: 156). Saussure wanted to portray language as *one* synthetic form located between two substances. Hjelmslev, in contrast, emphasizes the differing formation of the two planes of expression and content,

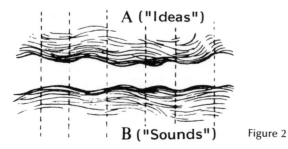

A ("Ideas")

B ("Sounds")   Figure 2

and defines this entity created out of *two* different forms as the definitive model of the sign.

The image used by Hjelmslev to illustrate the relationship between form and substance is that of a net (form), which is thrown over the unformed matter (called by Hjelmslev *purport*—also on the plane of expression—or *matière*), so that a *formed substance* is created by projecting non-substantial form onto the formless substance. It is necessary, therefore, to distinguish, on both planes of the sign, between matter (formless substance), (formed) substance, and (non-substantial) form. This leads, in Hjelmslev's model of the sign, to the following six major components: expression-purport, expression-substance (ES), expression-form (EF), content-form (CF), content-substance (CS), and content-purport. These can be represented in the following diagram (with the particular interdependences indicated by arrows):

$$\text{Expression-purport—ES} \rightarrow \text{EF} \leftrightarrow \text{CF} \leftarrow \text{CS—Content-purport}$$

Following on from another of Saussure's maxims, the sole object of glossematics is the pure, non-substantial form.

2.2.

2.2.1.

The relationship of form, substance and matter can be illustrated using Hjelmslev's now classic example (see Figure 3) from the area of *content*, concerning the naming of colors in English and Welsh (Hjelmslev, 1943/63: 53). A segment of the color spectrum as linguistically unformed matter is symbolized by a rectangle (I) (although the delineation of the limits of this area of reality is actually inadmissible, as it already seems to symbolize some sort of forming process). The various languages now throw their various "nets" onto this unformed area of reality (II). The net thrown by the English language over this area (solid lines) is different from that thrown over the same area by the Welsh language (dotted lines):

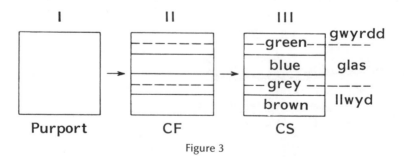

Figure 3

The area is given form in this way as a totality, and formed substances are created as divisible, distinguishable parts of the previously unformed substance. In the English language the content-form thrown over the matter produces distinguishable colors called *green, blue, grey* and *brown.*

2.2.2.

It is not always correctly understood, in interpretations of glossematics,[13] that content-substance is, among other things, what we tend to call "meaning." But content-substance also includes the so-called "referent," the actual aspect of reality designated by the meaning. According to Hjelmslev, the difference between meaning and reference is something that lies *within* the content-substance, and does not correspond to the difference between content-form and content-substance. In fact Hjelmslev himself (1954) differentiates within the substances between a physical, a sociobiological, and a collective-appreciative level, whereby the physical level of the content-substance approximates to the *reference*, and the other two levels to different conceptions of *meaning*. In contrast, glossematic content-form is only form. It is not "meaning," although constantly mistaken to be so: It is only the framework, the net, the constellation of differences. Whoever misunderstands this misunderstands the real intention of glossematics, namely to be a discipline that is independent of all substance, concerned only with *pure form*.

This primacy of pure form is based on two Saussurean tenets: firstly on his insistence that language is form and not substance,[14] and secondly on his definition of the formal character of language, which is derived from the view that in language there is nothing positive, only differences (Saussure, 1916: 166). Language as pure form is a radical, a priori hypothesis offered by Hjelmslev as an interpretation of Saussure. The true object of glossematics, it follows, is the *langue* as pure form. Substance is excluded from glossematic consideration, that is from linguistics seen from the glossematic viewpoint, and the study of substance is assigned to other, non-glossematic, that is to say non-linguistic, disciplines. Semantics, as the study of meaning—the study of content-substance— is thereby excluded completely from linguistics-glossematics.[15]

2.2.3.

The example of semantics makes it clear why glossematics creates difficulties by claiming to be a *linguistic* science rather than a *general science of signs*. If we regard glossematics, in the way Hjelmslev wants us to, as "linguistics," then we are confronted by the enormous problem posed by semantics. According to Hjelmslev, semantics, which without any doubt is an aspect of linguistics, must be regarded as a non-linguistic discipline, since it studies substance. But if we regard glossematics as general semiotics, then the exclusion of semantics from glossematics (= semiotics) becomes entirely logical and sensible, since a general theory of signs is not concerned with meaning within a particular "language" or sign system, but rather with the formal structural laws that might govern the content of the sign in general.

2.2.4.

As a science of general sign structures, glossematics is a science of theoretical possibilities and not of manifest realities. Hjelmslev's view of glossematics as a type of *algebra* should be viewed in this way, for like algebra, glossematics is a discipline of possible theoretical constructs that do not have to be made manifest in particular substances. Thus in the previous example, it is not the English color names that are suitable objects for glossematics (since they are substantial forms[16]), but rather the framework used in the diagram, as a possible way of structuring a given content area. Other, purely theoretical ways of structuring the same entity can be seen in Figure 4. These theoretically possible constructions may or may not occur in reality. As Hjelmslev himself says with regard to his science of the general *langue*: "All possibilities must here be foreseen, including those that are virtual in the world of experience, or remain without a 'natural' or 'actual' manifestation" (Hjelmslev, 1943/63: 106).

2.3.

2.3.1.

On the *expression* plane too, form acts as a net thrown onto the initially unformed matter. For example, if one imagines as unformed matter the potential for producing sounds by means of the vocal organs, then it becomes clear that every language forms this matter in different ways, and imposes different limits. One of Hjelmslev's examples concerns the continuum formed by the median profile of the roof of the mouth from the pharynx to the lips, as the area where

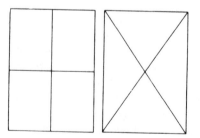

Figure 4

the voiceless occlusive consonants are articulated. In the usual European languages this matter is distributed over three areas, namely /p/, /t/, and /k/, whereas the Eskimo and Latvian languages distinguish between two /k/ areas, and many Indian languages have two /t/ areas (Hjelmslev, 1943/63: 55).

Once again we get the same picture here as with the content. The unformed matter is separated by the form into three areas, becoming formed substance or expression-substance. Here too, expression-form is not the phonological or phonetic structure of a language, but only the non-substantial net thrown over the unformed matter. Like the semantic and referential aspects on the content plane, so the phonological and phonetic aspects belong to the substance: these are different planes within the expression-substance,[17] and therefore not a matter for glossematics.

2.3.2.

Even on the expression plane the insistence that the new discipline should occupy itself exclusively with form is only tenable if we locate glossematics as a science of signs on a more general level. For as a general science of signs glossematics has nothing to do with the forming of a substance through a particular sign system, and it follows from this that phonology and phonetics, as the specific investigation of the specific sign system language, would not then be glossematic disciplines. On the other hand, if phonetics and phonology were to be banished from linguistics on the grounds that they were non-linguistic, then such glossematic formalism would rightly be seen as absurd.

As Coseriu has pointed out, ignoring the expression-substance of natural languages is even more anti-linguistic than ignoring the content-substance. For the material manifestation of language as an entity in the world is the sound; that is to say, the phonic substance is the substance of language. Without expression-substance the linguistic language would simply not exist: "The language form manifests itself and *is* immanently extant in the expression-substance." The content-substance—the world in general—also exists without language; the world "neither manifests nor makes material any language form"; through this form the world is merely organized. In other words, the world is made perceptible through language, but also exists without the language form (Coseriu, 1954:210).

2.4.

As expression-substance and content-substance are not necessarily linked to expression-form and content-form, respectively, (the forms are pure virtualities that do not need substantial manifestation),[18] the glossematic sign model is ultimately composed of only two of Hjelmslev's six major components, namely expression-form and content-form. The "sign function"—the characteristic dependence of signs—is the relationship between expression-form and content-form. As in Saussure's model, this relationship is close and reciprocal.[19] The sign in itself, dematerialized into pure form, remains the true object of glossematics.

2.5.

The need to distinguish between the two forms of the sign, the content-form and the expression-form, only occurs, of course, when the content-plane and the expression-plane are actually formed in different ways. There are structures in which the expression plane and the content-plane have one and the same form: Hjelmslev calls them "symbols." They are interpretable objects to which a content-substance can be assigned, but no content form that differs from the expression-form. These interpretable entities serve in Hjelmslev's argument as a background against which the specific characteristics of the sign, namely the differing forms of the two separate planes, stand out particularly well. Signicity consists not only in the mere distinctiveness of the two planes of expression and content (in symbols too, expression can be differentiated from content), but in the different form of the two levels.

Thus the expression-plane of the verbal sign *Tisch* (table) is constructed in a different way from that of its content. The expression-plane is made up of the units /t/, /i/ and /š/, while the content-plane is made up of the unified idea-complex *Tisch*. Even if one were to analyze the content of *Tisch* using various aspects of the content, such as "table," "singular," "nominative," it would still be impossible to assign each of these three content aspects to a corresponding unit on the expression plane, for example "table" to /t/, "singular" to /i/, or "nominative" to /š/. The content-plane has a different form to the expression-plane.

In contrast, there exists with symbols a one-to-one relationship between the expression-plane and the content-plane. An example is offered by chess pieces, in which every element of the expression-plane, that is every chess piece, corresponds to a unit on the content-plane, namely a particular function. In this case, therefore, it is unnecessary to submit the expression-plane and content-plane to separate analyses, as both planes present the same form. Hjelmslev gave other examples in a lecture delivered in London in 1947: the hourly chimes of a clock, whereby the number of chimes corresponds to the number of hours, and the lights of a traffic signal, in which each color corresponds to a function ("Stop!," "Go!," "Caution!"). According to Hjelmslev, symbols are not signs, as they do not display any difference in form between content and expression— indeed, he specifically calls them "interpretable, *non-semiotic* entities" (Hjelmslev, 1943/63: 114)—and thus are not the concern of glossematics.

Hjelmslev's definition of symbols embraces the iconicity, the similarity between *sign* and denotatum, which Morris sees in iconic signs (Morris, 1971:420), and also the "motivatedness" of Saussurean "symbols." As is shown in the example of the chess pieces, which share neither "similarity" nor "natural motivation" with their content (the chess knight bears no similarity to his function), Hjelmslev's definition goes much further and is much clearer, as it reduces both iconicity and symbolicity to the level of structural features, that is, to the feature of single-articulation (in contrast to the double-articulation of signs).

2.6.

The semiotic problem posed by glossematics when regarded as a general theory of signs lies, as we have seen, in the fact that the structure of the linguistic sign, the existence of different forms of expression and content (the double articulation) is considered to be a fundamental characteristic of any sign. This particular variant of "linguistic imperialism" is the result both of the strangely hybrid assessment which glossematics makes of itself, as described above, and also of the glossematic interpretation of Saussure's postulate of immanence, an interpretation that is radical in two ways. First, it excludes all "external" considerations, particularly psychological, social and ethnological considerations, which in current terms could be called the exclusion of the pragmatic dimension. Second, it excludes *substance* (formalism). If the pragmatic dimension remains suppressed and aspects like human conversation, the intentions of the communicators, and the actional character of signs do not come under scrutiny, but purely the sign alone, the sign as a thing, then the immanent structure of this reified entity must provide its definitional criteria. Furthermore, as concern for substance, for the materiality of the sign-entity is excluded, the way in which the sign is articulated remains for Hjelmslev the sole criterion of signicity.

That this is a bad criterion of signicity can be demonstrated from the broader pragmatic viewpoint, using Hjelmslev's own example. Seen from their actional aspect, the traffic signals that Hjelmslev counts as symbols (and thus excludes from glossematics-semiotics) should without doubt be regarded as signs, even though they are single-articulated. In contrast, the actional character of telephone numbers makes it difficult to agree with Hjelmslev's proposition, made in the 1947 London lecture, that such numbers are signs.[20]

Even if contemporary semiotic research is not reduced to the immanent syntactic-semantic approach of European structuralism and tries to look at the sign from a pragmatic viewpoint, the immanentist approach has achieved a deeper understanding of the inner structure of signs and created an indispensible basis for further work. Nobody before Hjelmslev had comprehended so clearly the structure of single-articulated and double-articulated entities. Dialectically conserved in a pragmatically-based semiotic theory, these differences in articulation remain important features for a sign classification, and important criteria of the efficiency of sign systems. It is not mere chance that a double-articulated sign system, namely "natural" language, is the richest, most important, and most universal of all sign systems.

3. CONNOTATION AND METASEMIOLOGY

3.1.

In the following section I would like to discuss two further consequences of the highly immanent and formalistic nature of glossematic sign theory. Both are relevant to current semiotic research, and are concerned with aspects of semiotics that are explicitly excluded by glossematics.

1. The (general structuralist) exclusion of "*external*," in the wider sense *pragmatic*, facts leads to the characteristic glossematic doctrine of the *connotative* sign.
2. The typical glossematic exclusion of *substance* makes it necessary for the analysis of substance to be linked to (formal) glossematic analysis as *metasemiology*.

3.1.1.

In spite of Hjelmslev's exclusion of the pragmatic dimension (which is by no means unique to him), he is not blind to the reality of language and to differences in languages and sign systems that derive from real speakers and real listeners. Hjelmslev tries to link this awareness to the specifically structuralist immanence postulate[21] by incorporating the pragmatically determined differences in semiotic material (differences between nations, classes, regions, communicative situations, and individuals) by means of his theory of the connotative sign, according to which the excluded "external" information about the speaker and listener reappears as an immanent quality of the sign. This takes place on an additional *content-plane,* which vaults over the *denotative* sign to form the expression-plane of the *connotative* sign. As an expression of the connotative content can serve the substances or the forms, or the forms *and* substances of the denotative sign.

By "connotation" Hjelmslev is not referring to the so-called *emotive meaning*, the psychological appraisal of a particular thing,[22] but to something far more general, namely everything that the sign says about the speaker: "He is an Englishman, he comes from London, he is a linguist, he expresses himself carefully" and so on. Following the immanence postulate, this information about the speaker is comprehended as something that the *sign* says about itself: "I am

English, from London, linguistically employed, represent refined speech" etc. In this extended concept of "connotation" every sign participates as a matter of principle in several connotative semiotic structures.

Now if the connotative structure is to be a sign, it must be built like a sign and must have the strata of a sign: expression-substance, expression-form, content-form, and content-substance. Above all, it must possess differently formed planes of expression and content, that is to say a *connotative expression-form* and a *connotative content-form*, as in Figure 5:

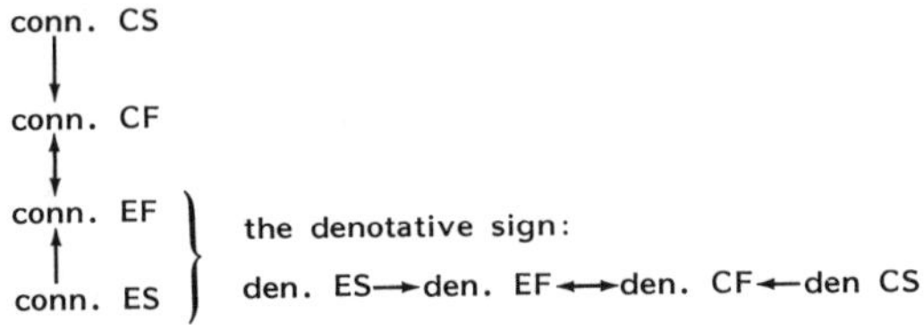

```
conn. CS
   ↑
conn. CF
   ↑
conn. EF   ⎫  the denotative sign:
   ↑       ⎬
conn. ES   ⎭  den. ES→den. EF↔den. CF←den CS
```

Figure 5

The assumption that the connotative expression-plane and the connotative content-plane are differently formed, in other words the assumption of a sign-like structure of connotation, is one of the most problematic concepts in glossematic sign theory.[23] For it must be questioned whether the connotative entities do actually manifest different forms of expression and content, or whether they are symbol-structures, that is to say "interpretable" structures to which only content-*substances* can be assigned, standing in a one-to-one relationship to the interpreted entities, like the traffic regulations to the traffic signals. As a simple and illuminating example one can assign to a given word or text the connotative content-substance "German," that is to say the "actual notions of social or sacred character that common usage attaches to the concept 'German language' " (Hjelmslev, 1943/ 63:119). Taken this way, this relationship would be identified as a "symbol." But since it is supposed to be a "sign," a content-*form* must be assumed.

What is the form of the connotative content "German"? Hjelmslev's answer would be: the mutual dependences (*functions*) of connotative contents, for example the relationship between the content "German" and the content "French," "Russian" and so on. Unfortunately, Hjelmslev does not indicate what such a formal, mutual demarcation of connotative contents would look like.[24]

Be that as it may, he does put content-form in a connotative context, and here too the real glossematic analysis of the connotative sign is an analysis of form. After the analysis of denotative signs (seen as connotatively homogeneous) is concluded, the connotative contents—which had hitherto been systematically excluded—are exposed to the same formal analysis: "After the analysis of the denotative semiotic is completed, the connotative semiotic must be subjected to an analysis according to just the same procedure" (Hjelmslev, 1943/63: 119).

The glossematic interest in the connotative sign is an interest in the *forms* of the connotative sign (see Figure 6):

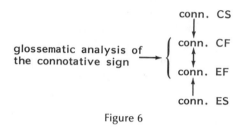

Figure 6

The connotative sign-form does not itself contain the (substantial) interpretations but only the rather dubious mutual dependences of such interpretations. It is, in other words, an "empty" form. For this reason, the excluded pragmatic information itself is not considered in the course of the glossematic (in the narrow sense) treatment of connotative signs. This is only done in the analysis of connotative content-*substance*.

Although the analysis of substance is not a *glossematic* task, Hjelmslev does not banish it entirely from science, but rather categorizes it as a separate, non-glossematic discipline that has to be linked with the glossematic analysis of form. This holds both for the denotative and the connotative sign. Just how this analysis of substance is related to the analysis of form will be shown in section 3.2.

3.1.2.

Today the pragmatic and actional character of language and of signs is considered to be of such central importance, that attempts have been made to define signs in terms of actional structures. In such attempts the sign and the language are from the outset much more intimately linked with the acting man than in Hjelmslev's structuralistically immanent method, in which the pragmatic aspect of signs is admitted to exist, but regarded as an extra dimension of the sign that disturbs the functional homogeneity of the object and is therefore initially excluded from the true core of linguistics and semiotics. Only *after* it has performed its own specified task does glossematics turn to the connotative aspects (and even then only very formally!).

Clearly "denotation," essentially meaning "meaning," and, on the level of speech, "reference" (or what Bühler has called "representation"), is the principal function of the linguistic sign. In this respect the characteristic method of structuralism in proceeding from denotation, and the neglect of the additional, "pragmatic" aspects of communication, is understandable. Yet it should also be emphasized that the act of denotation, the representation of reality by means of the signs, is also an *actional* process. And it is an action carried out with respect to the *others*, so that the dimension of acting persons—the pragmatic dimension—cannot be seen as something added or extra, but as something essential to the sign.[26]

3.2.

3.2.1.

Although he has banished substances from the glossematic paradise, Hjelmslev nevertheless considers the analysis of the substance of signs to be an important and socially significant scientific activity. He does not consider it to be *unscientific*, merely *unglossematic*. In his impressive Vice Rectorial address of 1953 on linguistic content-form as a social factor (Hjelmslev, 1953), he drew attention, for example, to the political relevance in our time of scientific research into meaning (content-substance). Hjelmslev relates substance analysis to the glossematic analysis of the pure forms of language and signs in a complicated way, namely via a third-level sign structure, the so-called *metasemiology*.

Linguistics-glossematics as a scientific metalanguage, whose object-language is a sign system, is a *second*-level sign structure similar to the connotative sign. In contrast, however, to the connotative sign, in which the *expression*-plane is made up of signs (out of the substances or forms of the signs, or both), linguistics as a sign structure has a *content*-plane of signs, but only the *forms* of the signs, as the substances are by definition not a matter for linguistics. The scientific meta-sign-structure is called by Hjelmslev *semiology*. Linguistics is a semiology, whose structure reflects the pattern see in Figure 7 (whereby we are differentiating here in meta-sign only between the planes and not, in addition, between form and substance):

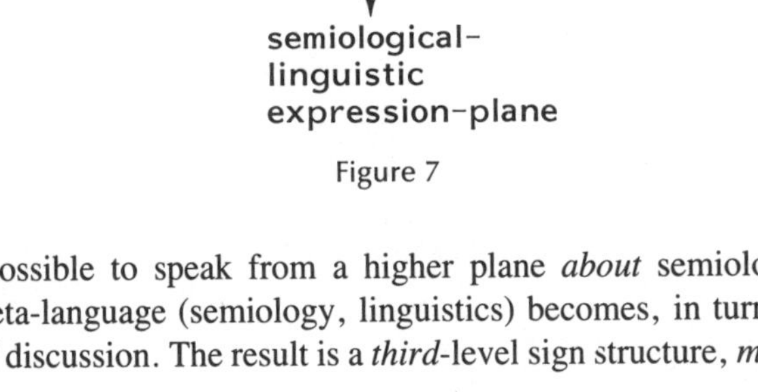

$$\text{den. ES} \longrightarrow \text{den. EF} \longleftrightarrow \text{den. CF} \longleftarrow \text{den. CS}$$

semiological-
linguistic
content-plane

$\updownarrow$

semiological-
linguistic
expression-plane

Figure 7

Now it is possible to speak from a higher plane *about* semiology itself: the scientific meta-language (semiology, linguistics) becomes, in turn, a content—the object of discussion. The result is a *third*-level sign structure, *metasemiology*.

In this discussion on semiology it finally becomes possible, following Hjelmslev, to speak about those things that had to be excluded, that is, the substances. Since a discussion of the semiotic treatment of the linguistic form would merely repeat what has already been said, metasemiology can even be dedicated primarily to substance. The substances that were excluded from the glossematic treatment of object languages can finally be described on a meta-plane. Figure 8 depicts this complex relationship. The disciplines that describe the denotative sign substances— phonetics and phonology on one side, and semantics on the other—are not integrated into linguistic-glossematics, but layered, as it were, on top of it. The semiotic disciplines concerned with substance emerge in the hierarchy *above* the layers of semiotic analysis concerned with form. Phonetics/phonology and semantics are not the customary partial metalanguages, but partial meta-metalanguages.

But to regard phonetics/phonology and semantics not as straightforward linguistic disciplines, but rather as meta-investigations loosely related to lin-guistics, is a total distortion of normal linguistic research. The metaglossematic rescue operation aimed at saving substance analysis, and the attempt to reunite with glossematics those disciplines that, in any case, are barely conceivable as non-linguistic, would all be unnecessary if Hjelmslev did not persist in viewing linguistic language (and other concrete sign systems) as pure form. If he were to retain on the plane of pure form only the general semiotic structure, the *langue* as described above in 1.2, then the linguistic language could settle where it

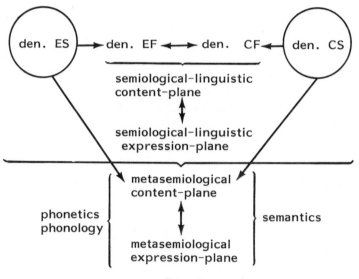

Figure 8

belongs, on the lower plane of formed substances, and phonetics/phonology and semantics would be what they actually are, namely linguistic disciplines.

3.2.2.

As we have seen, the true glossematic study of connotative signs limits itself to the analysis of form. The study of the excluded substance is related to the analysis of pure form (substance here means *content*-substance, as the connotative expression-substance is analyzed in any case, since it is the denotative sign) in the same way as with denotative signs, via a *metasemiology*: "Just as the metasemiology of denotative semiotics will in practice treat the objects of phonetics and semantics in a reinterpreted form, so in the metasemiotic[27] of connotative semiotics, the largest part of specifically sociological linguistics and Saussurean external linguistics will find their place in reinterpreted form" (Hjelmslev, 1943/63:125). The metasemiology of connotative signs analyzes the various "geographical and historical, political and social, sacral and psychological content-purports" (ibid.), which are linked to the nation, region, style, personality, mood, etc. Hjelmslev singles out sociology, ethnology, and psychology as the disciplines that contribute most to the analysis of connotative content-substance.

Figure 9, a representation of connotative metasemiology, is complicated by the fact that the connotative sign is itself a second-level sign structure, making connotative semiology a third-level sign structure and connotative *metasemiology* a fourth-level sign structure:[28]

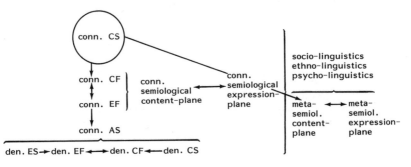

Figure 9

The criticism made above with respect to phonetics/phonology and semantics can also be applied in part to the analysis of connotative sign-substance. For glossematic formalism demands that substance, which has been excluded from the *formal* core of semiology, be approached via a higher meta-plane, which would be entirely unnecessary but for the a priori exclusion.

On the other hand, it cannot be said that the disciplines described as "connotative metasemiology" are generally considered to be *linguistic* disciplines in the way that phonetics/phonology and semantics are. These disciplines, for which names like socio-linguistics, ethno-linguistics, psycho-linguistics, pragma-linguistics, and so on have been found, are certainly not regarded by many linguists as belonging to the inner core of linguistics. Although no other direction in modern linguistics has supported Hjelmslev's extreme formalism, it has never-theless been characteristic of large sections of structuralist research from Saussure to Chomsky to exclude from true linguistics the so-called "external factors"— the pragmatic elements taken in a very wide sense. Hjelmslev's proposal of a connotative metasemiology, in contrast, is an attempt to overcome the exclusively immanent viewpoint, a fundamental attempt, as Coseriu has pointed out, "to comprehend all human and cultural problems in terms of language." Today's hyphenated disciplines could be seen as further, single steps towards overcoming the immanent viewpoint. The hyphens in the current titles of these disciplines "symbolically" reflect the fact that these efforts are still regarded as something alien, grafted on to the true inner core of linguistics, which, in the structuralist tradition, still prefers to exclude the disturbing facts concerning the speaker and the listener.

But only from a linguistic standpoint that integrates these "external" factors is it possible to supersede the opposition of "external" and "internal." Only when this opposition is removed will the scientific treatment of the "external" factors of language become a central concern, and only then will the analysis of the connotative content-substance emerge as a true linguistic endeavor rather than something peripherally related to linguistics.

NOTES

1. Cf. Hjelmslev, 1943/63: 109 f.
2. Hjelmslev, 1944. See also Chapt. 21 of the *Prolegomena*, which argues that glossematics is concerned with "language in a far broader sense" (102), namely with "any structure whose form is analogous to that of a 'natural' language" (102), "any semiotic—any structure that is analogous to a language and satisfies the given definition" (107). Thus glossematics, as "linguistics in the broader sense," is " 'semiology' on an *immanent* basis" (108), the explicit realization of the Saussurean semiology desiratum (107 f.)
3. On Hjelmslev's conception of "language type," see Hjelmslev, 1968: 112.
4. Coseriu's placement of Saussure's "faculté linguistique par excellence" on the same plane of abstraction as Hjelmslev's *langue* (Coseriu, 1954: 201) should be qualified. In my view Hjelms-lev's *langue* is located one plane of abstraction higher.
5. See Coseriu 1954: especially 201, 218.
6. See above 2.2.3. and 2.3. Also compare Coseriu, 1954 and Trabant, 1970.
7. Cf. Coseriu, 1954, especially 227 ff.
8. "Ici s'impose cependant une réserve d'ordre pratique. C'est la *langue linguistique* qui constitue le domaine de notre revue. On ne sait pas dans quelle mesure cette restriction, imposée par la tradition, correspond à une réalité . . . C'est ainsi que notre organe se consacre à la langue

linguistique, et qu'il n'admettra les recherches sur les langues non linguistiques que dans la mesure où ces recherches contribuent directement à l'étude linguistique proprement dite" (Hjelmslev, 1944: 32).

9. If Hjelmslev had really conceived his *Acta Linguistica* as "Acta Semiotica," then research into semiotics would have taken a quite different course, having had its own journal for thirty years prior to the appearance of *Semiotica* (i.e. since 1939).

10. Apart from Saussure's preparatory comments on a general science of signs, glossematics remains the principal European contribution—which is, at the same time, the contribution of linguistics— to modern general semiotics. The American contributions to semiotics derive from philosophy and possibly psychology.

11. Cf. Eco, 1972:231ff.

12. Through the analysis of linguistic signs, I have abstracted certain actional criteria as definitive criteria for signs in general; see Trabant, 1976.

13. For example Greimas, 1966: 25, 106; see also Trabant, 1977:9f.

14. Saussure 1916: 157. On the various ways of interpreting this sentence see Coseriu, 1954: 220, 231.

15. Hjelmslev, 1943/63: 79: "Linguistics must see its main task in establishing a science of the expression and a science of the content on an internal and functional basis; it must establish a science of the expression without having recourse to phonetic or phenomenological premises, a science of the content without ontological or phenomenological premises . . . Such a linguistics, as distinguished from conventional linguistics, would be one whose science of the expression is not a phonetics and whose science of the content is not a semantics."

16. Coseriu, 1954: 216: "As soon as he introduces *examples* he leaves this plane [of algebra], and cannot avoid the difficulties that arise from his attempt to apply the algebra of pure form to 'forms of substance' [i.e. the examples]."

17. The abstraction level of the Prague school's phonology comes off badly with Hjelmslev, who dismisses exactly this level of functional language description as "fiction," that is as a nonsensical step in the formalization of the expression-plane, as a step which should, therefore, be eliminated. For him only the phonetic plane is valid as "usage" (see Hjelmslev 1943: 88f.).

18. According to the glossematic classification of functions, the relationship between substance and form is one of "determination," that is to say, a relationship between one variable (substance) and one constant (form) (see Hjelmslev 1943/63: 41), which is symbolized by an arrow →.

19. A relationship between two constants, an "interdependence" is symbolized by a double-headed arrow ↔.

20. For an attempt to define the concept of the sign on the basis of actional theory, see Trabant, 1976. There are certainly sections in Hjelmslev's writings in which signicity is not fully identified with the internal structure of the double-articulated sign, but where rather the function of *designation*, of the "relationship to the non-linguistic factors which surround it" appears to be taken as definitive for signicity in general (Hjelmslev, 1943/63: 47). This opposition of a structural and—*cum grano salis*—an "actional" definition of signs is intimated in the formulation of language as a "figurae system with sign-purpose" (ibid.: 102).

21. Cf., for example, Hjelmslev, 1943/63: 4ff.

22. According to Hjelmslev, 1954: 60, this is rather an element of the denotative content-substance.

23. I have myself applied the idea of the connotative sign to the structure of literary texts; see Trabant, 1970. I now have doubts, on the one hand, whether literary texts should, in the context of *actional theory*, be regarded as signs at all; see Trabant, 1976: 95ff. On the other hand, the *structural* signicity of the connotative sign, that is to say the assumption of a connotative content-form differing from the form of the expression on which the signicity of the connotative sign depends, seems equally problematical.

24. Cf. Hjelmslev, 1943/63: 119. The relationship between connotative contents is probably a relationship between variants ("constellation"). According to the glossematic interpretation, such relationships are not scientifically describable as they amount to the absence of dependences. Cf. Hjelmslev, 1954/63: 83, and Trabant, 1970: 29, n. 28.

25. For example Trabant, 1976.
26. On the relationship of pragmatics to the other semiotic dimensions, and in particular on the "integrative" pragmatic standpoint, see Trabant, 1976: 46f.
27. Hjelmslev is not quite precise here: As the analysis of the *form* of connotative signs is itself a "metasemiotic of connotative signs," Hjelmslev should speak of a "meta-metasemiotic of connotative signs" or of a "metasemiology of connotative signs."
28. Hjelmslev regards any meta-levels above the level of metasemiology to be meaningless (Hjelmslev, 1943/63:125).

REFERENCES

Coseriu, E. (1954). "Forma y sustancia en los sonidos del lenguaje." In: E. Coseriu, *Teoría del lenguaje y lingüística general*. Madrid, 1962: 115–234.
Eco, U. (1972). *Einführung in die Semiotik*. Munich.
Greimas, A. J. (1966). *Sémantique structurale*. Paris.
Hjelmslev, L. (1943/63). *Prolegomena to a Theory of Language*. Madison, Wisc. 1963² (Danish: 1943).
Hjelmslev, L. (1943). "Langue et parole." In: Hjelmslev, 1971: 77–89.
Hjelmslev, L. (1944). "Linguistique structurale." In: Hjelmslev, 1971: 28–33 [= Editorial of Acta Linguistica].
Hjelmslev, L. (1947). "La structure fondamentale du langage" (French translation of a London lecture of 1947). In: L. Hjelmslev, *Prolégomènes à une théorie du langage*. Paris, 1968/71: 177–231.
Hjelmslev, L. (1953). "La forme du contenu du langage comme facteur social." In: Hjelmslev, 1971: 97–104.
Hjelmslev, L. (1954). "La stratification du langage." In: Hjelmslev, 1971: 44–76.
Hjelmslev, L. (1968). *Die Sprache*. Darmstadt (Danish: 1963).
Hjelmslev, L. (1971). *Essais linguistiques*. Paris.
Kotschi, T. (1977). Review of L. Hjelmslev, *Prolegomena zu einer Sprachtheorie* (Munich, 1974) and L. Hjelmslev, *Aufsätze zur Sprachwissenschaft* (Stuttgart, 1974), *Historiographia Linguistica*, 4(1), 97–105.
Morris, C. W. (1971). *Writings on the General Theory of Signs*. The Hague.
Saussure, F. de (1916). *Cours de linguistique générale*. Paris, 1962.⁵
Trabant, J. (1970). *Zur Semiologie des literarischen Kunstwerks—Glossematik und Literaturtheorie*. Munich.
Trabant, J. (1976). *Elemente der Semiotik*. Munich.
Trabant, J. (1977). "Semiotik der Poesie in Frankreich." In: A. Noyer-Weidner (Ed.), *Aufsätze zur Literaturwissenschaft*, I. Wiesbaden: 1–32.

CHAPTER 5

The Influence of Roman Jakobson on the Development of Semiotics[1]

UMBERTO ECO

1. THE HISTORY OF AN OSTRACISM

The project of a science studying all possible varieties of signs and the rules governing their production, exchange, and interpretation is a rather ancient one. Pre-Socratic poetry and philosophy are frequently concerned with the nature of natural signs and divine messages. The Hippocratic tradition deals with the interpretation of symptoms, while the Sophists were critically conscious of the power of language. Plato's *Cratylus* is a treatise on the origins of words, and the *Sophist* can be considered the first attempt to apply a binary method to semantic definitions.

I can also cite the impact of Aristotle's *Poetics* and *Rhetoric* on the study of dramatic plot, metaphorical substitutions, "discourse analysis" and "conversational rules," and the role played by the Stoics in analyzing the fundamental distinction between *semaínon, semainómenon,* and *pragma.* The discussion on signs became particularly important during the patristic period and reached a high level of subtlety from the Modistae to Ockham.

In brief, the entire history of philosophy could be re-read in a semiotic perspective. Let me mention only the *General Grammar* of Port-Royal, the seventeenth-century discussion on the possibility of an *ars signorum,* diversely called "semaelogia" (Wilkins), "semeiotiké" (Wallis), "sematology" (Dalgarno), or "semeiologia" (Kircher), until the fundamental proposal of Locke, who in the last book of his *Essay* (1690) defines "semiotic" as one of the three aspects of science (along with physics and ethics), as a discipline equal to logic, "the

UMBERTO ECO • Department of Semiotics, University of Bologna, Bologna, Italy.

busines whereof is to consider the nature of signs the mind makes use of for the understanding of things, or conveying its knowledge to others."

Even without considering the philosophies of Hobbes, Hume, Berkeley, and Leibniz as explicit contributions to modern semiotics, and even disregarding (as has been frequently done outside Italy) that impressive archeology of human languages which is *La Scienza Nuova* by Giambattista Vico, the unquestionable statements of Locke should have been enough to make semiotics an institutionalized science. Yet on the contrary, this discipline has been ostracized as such by the scientific milieu over the following centuries.

No one has sufficiently evaluated the work of Jean Henri Lambert, *Semiotik oder Lehre von der Bezeichnung der Gedanken und Dinge* (1764), nor has anyone remarked that "Semiotik" is the title of one of the chapters of Bolzano's *Wissenschaftslehre* (1837). Husserl in 1890 wrote an essay entitled *Zur Logik der Zeichen (Semiotik),* but this text remained unpublished until 1970.[2] The last and most paradigmatic example is the academic misfortune of C. S. Peirce, which made it possible for a substantial part of his work to have remained undiscovered until no more than four decades ago. Even after this date the "father of semiotics" has continued to be better known as a metaphysician, a logician, or a philosopher of pragmaticism, without consideration being given to the fact that his thought cannot be really understood unless it is interpreted from a semiotic point of view.[3]

As far as the present century is concerned, four authors have systematically outlined the principles of a semiotic theory: Saussure, Morris, Hjelmslev, and Buyssens. But Saussure, Hjelmslev, and Buyssens have always been considered as linguists, and Morris has been considered as a philosopher.

Morris's proposals have been partly accepted by logical positivists and logicians (more the distinction between syntactics, semantics, and pragmatics than his skillful classification of various types of signs). A long series of thinkers has connected those problems to the ideas of Frege and to the questions raised by extensional semantics via Wittgenstein's *Tractatus,* and Wittgenstein's *Philosophical Investigations* (which contains a number of important insights on the problems of iconic and ostensive signs, context-sensitivity, and so on) has produced many inquiries into the logic of natural languages. But it would be daring to assert that these problems have been compared on the one hand with those raised by structural linguistics and on the other with investigations into nonverbal languages (De Jorio, Kleinpaul, Mallery, and Efron, to cite only pioneers) as well as with the analyses of poetry, folklore, painting, movies, and theater made by the Russian Formalists and their congeners.

Linguists have continued to recognize that, following Saussure, language should have been inserted into a more general framework. But Saussure only foresaw the *droit à l'existence* of his *sémiologie* without going further, and limited himself to listing some possible applications.[4] Therefore linguists continued for years to pay their tribute to the myth of *la sémiologie* and to study with structural methods the nature of verbal language only. Buyssens, who in 1943 tried to extend linguistic principles to other communicative behavior, met with a polite *fin de non recevoir*.

The only author who could have succeeded in proposing a general theoretical framework for a semiotic theory was Hjelmslev, but his theory was too abstract, his examples concerning other semiotic systems very limited and rather parenthetical, and his glossematic jargon impenetrable. Hjelmslev as a semiotician has been highly influential in the last two decades, but in order to arrive at this state of the art something had to happen: an interdisciplinary earthquake, a methodological dissemination, a sudden twisting of scientific curiosity, a reversal of the trend, a new feeling, a sort of new philosophical *Kunstwollen* capable of producing a culture that was fundamentally sign-oriented.

Today, semiotics exists as a discipline (be it a unified science or a unifying point of view methodologically focusing on a given "object" common to different sciences). It is considered an academic discipline in many universities, and in some countries is even proposed as a powerful pedagogical tool in primary and high schools. There is an International Association for Semiotic Studies, many reviews, international meetings, and national societies. This "revolution" has developed only during the last two decades, and one may wonder why such a disciplinary coalescence has taken place just now.

There is an anthropological and historical answer, no doubt; through the pressure and the technological development of mass media, the problem of communication has proved to be the central one of our civilization, and it is understandable why many disciplines have converged to study the general laws of human and natural signification. But this is not enough: for years the disturbing presence of mass media had only succeeded in producing a lot of sociological theories and a qualitatively irrelevant quantity of empirical research.

Moreover semiotics, even if it has devoted some energy to the study of mass media, has had its real effect by going deeper and outlining those "primitive" systems of significant interaction upon which mass media also rely, comprehending animal and natural processes (such as genetic information) or machine-to-machine interaction. Therefore the anthropological-historical explanation is not fully satisfactory: when speaking of an academic "dissemination" we must also consider the catalyzing influence of given schools and individual works.

The aim of the present paper is to demonstrate that the major "catalyst" in the contemporary "semiotic reaction" was Roman Jakobson.[5]

2. THE QUEST OF SEMIOTICS

Ransacking Jakobson's immense bibliography to seek out an item explicitly devoted to semiotics may be disappointing. The only bibliographical item clearly labeled in this way is the introductory speech to the First Congress of the IASS,

June 1974, "Coup d'œil sur le développement de la sémiotique." Going backwards from 1974, one realizes that Jakobson also wrote two fundamental essays which outline a semiotic landscape, but they appear at first glance to be a generous and comprehensive picture of the state of "linguistic" sciences. Moreover these two essays are quite late: "Language in Relation to Other Communication Systems" (1968) and "Linguistics" (1970) (now in *Main Trends in the Science of Language*, 1974). This last essay actually is a little treatise on semiotics under a misleading title. When reading the other items of Jakobson's bibliography, one realizes that despite his frequent use of the word "semiotics," some of the pages which have most influenced the development of this discipline fail to mention it.

Let me assume that the reason Jakobson never wrote a book on semiotics is that his entire scientific existence was a living example of a Quest for Semiotics. His well-known coat of arms (*linguista sum: linguistici nihil a me alienum puto*) should be rephrased as *linguista sum:* nihil *a me alienum puto*. Aiming at understanding the phenomenon of language in all its manifestations, Jakobson demonstrates that it is impossible to isolate it from the rest of human behavior, the whole of this behavior being always SIGNIFICANT. For instance, Jakobson does not start from verbal language to arrive, *après coup*, at discovering certain analogies between language and folklore. Jakobson meets Petr Bogatyrev "le premier jour des mes études universitaires . . . et aussitôt nous avons discuté le besoin d'un cercle de jeunes pour chercher à pénétrer les replis du langage et de la poésie écrite et orale."[6] This was in 1915. In 1929 Jakobson and Bogatyrev wrote "Die Folklore als eine besondere Form des Schaffens,"[7] in which some fundamental principles are vigorously stressed: (a) any linguistic innovation can work only when accepted and integrated by social consensus, and the same happens with the other communicative systems; (b) any semiotic system is submitted to general semiotic laws and functions as a code; but such codes are also linked to specific communities (from village to ethnic unit) in the same way in which a language produces its subcodes linked to given professions or activities; (c) the study of a code is concerned with both its synchronic laws and with their diachronic formation and transformation. Notice that the essay does not say that the creations of folklore are products of the language; it says that folklore is the product of the code of folklore, an independent system whose laws are of the same nature as those of language. Obviously a folkloric poem is also made of words and therefore follows verbal rules, but the linguistic "competence" is used in order to "perform" another "competence."

According to the famous text written in 1928 by Jakobson and Tynyanov ("Problemy izučenija literatury i jazyka"),[8] it is impossible to understand the literary series without comparing it to the immanent laws of the other series, just as it is impossible to understand the laws of verbal language without considering their interaction with the laws of the other semiotic systems.[9]

A superficial observer might say that Jakobson has arrived at linguistics after studying avant-garde poetry,[10] painting,[11] or folklore; the truth is that Jakobson was always studying semiotics when analyzing cubist and futurist painting or the structure of contemporary and ancient verse, just as he was studying painting, poetry, or cinema when speaking of the laws of language. Jakobson was semiotically biased from his early years: he could not focus on the laws of language without considering the whole of their behavioral background. Language and the whole culture are mutually implicated and it is difficult to isolate linguistics from cultural anthropology.[12]

It is probable that Jakobson became definitely convinced of the possibility of a general semiotics when, having discovered the binary structure of phonological systems, he encountered the results of information theory. From this point on his references to the whole semiotic field became more and more frequent, and Jakobson's influence on anthropologists (Lévi-Strauss) or psychoanalysts (Lacan) became more and more intense. This interdisciplinary conscience reaches its peak between the forties and the early fifties. After this, three fundamental contributions follow: the closing statements to the Conference of Anthropologists and Linguists at Bloomington, *Fundamentals of Language*[13] (with its enlightening comparison between aphasic disturbances, linguistics, rhetoric, magic, and aesthetic activity), and the paper "Linguistics and Communication Theory."[14] The semiotic design is quite complete. It is not by chance that precisely in the early sixties there appeared the first systematic outlines of a semiological theory: 1964 is the year of the first draft of *Elements of Semiology* by Roland Barthes and of the publication of *Communication* 4. From that moment on, *sémiologie* or "semiotics" became a conversation-piece. But the ease of such a discussion (which many highbrow critics have mistaken for mere fashion and charged with impudence) belied something more solid in its background: two thousand years of continuous appeals and the catalyzing activity of Roman Jakobson, whose work, so to speak, at last entitled other scholars "to try semiotics." By the early sixties semiotics was no longer an impossible dream: it was the result of a successful quest.

3. THE BASIC ASSUMPTIONS

Let me try to list eight assumptions on which contemporary semiotic research is basically founded. It is easy to see how the work of Jakobson has been of invaluable importance in making each of them widely accepted by the scientific milieu. Since I have assumed that contemporary semiotic research arrived at its definitive state at the beginning of the sixties, I shall take into account those texts Jakobson wrote before this. References to more recent papers will be given only as examples of more systematic formulation of those early ideas.

(1)   There is a sign every time there is a *"rélation de renvoi,"* a "sending-back" relation, in other words, when *aliquid stat pro aliquo.*

The structure of sign-phenomena as a dialectics between *signans* and *signatum* was not invented by Jakobson, but the whole work of Jakobson is centered on this "dramatic" relationship: "Le rapport du signe à l'objet signifié, et en particulier le rapport de la réprésentation au réprésenté, leur identité et leur différence simultanée, son l'une des antinomies les plus dramatique du signe."[15] To summarize the profound sense of this basic definition, there is the formula proposed in 1974: "Tout signe est un *renvoi* (suivant la fameuse formula *aliquid stat pro aliquo*)." I think there is no other way to define semiotics than as the discipline which studies all phenomena (even though they constitute the object of another discipline) which are based upon a relation of referring back ("sending back") to something else. It is a very simple idea, indeed, but it represents the core of the semiotic enterprise, and it represents at the same time the core of all linguistic, aesthetic, and scientific curiosities of Jakobson.

(2)   Signification is a phenomenon encompassing the entire cultural universe. There are signs everywhere outside verbal language.

As has been previously said, in Jakobson's work every discussion on verbal language is always connected with other communicative phenomena. Jakobson very early analyzes, along with poetic expression, painting.[16] folklore,[17] music,[18] film and theatre,[19] ostensive signs,[20] the mutual influence between various arts during a given historical period,[21] the symbolism of sculpture,[22] the grammar of traffic signals,[23] and the essentials of culinary art.[24] He has been the first among the linguists to point to Peirce's trichotomy (Symbol, Index, and Icon) as a basic tool for comprehension of the differences and identities among various types of signs.[25] A more comprehensive list of all systems of possible signs came later,[26] and the first investigation of gestural signs seems to be the study on head positions in "yes" and "no."[27] But the early writings as well as the investigations of phonetic behavior, child language, and aphasia[28] are full of minor observations on the various systems of signification. Approaches to anthropology are explicit in "Franz Boas' Approach to Language,"[29] and stimulating ideas about the communicative nature of anthropological and sociological systems (fully developed in "Language in Relation to Other Communication Systems" and "Linguistics"[30]) appear in "Results of a Joint Conference of Anthropologists and Linguists" (1952). But it is not by chance that in 1945 Claude Lévi-Strauss, outlining his communicative approach to anthropological phenomena, quotes Jakobson as one of his main sources of inspiration.[31]

As for the communicative aspects of natural life and mechanical appratuses—or the analogies between human languages and "languages" in biology and mathematics—it is sufficient to mention the first of Jakobson's approaches to communication theory[37] just three years after the publication of *The Mathematical Theory of Communication* by Shannon and Weaver, as well as the recent attention to the genetic code.[33]

(3) Since there are many types of signs, each embodying a *rélation de renvoi*, semiotics must operate with an interdisciplinary transference of laws in order to isolate constant or universal mechanisms of signification.

The whole bibliography of Jakobson is a living instance of such a procedure. This principle is solemnly stated in 1952 when Jakobson, recalling Saussure and Peirce, points out the necessity for a comparative study of all semiotic systems: the mathematical theory of communication should back linguistics and anthropology in a task to be realized without fearing either new and sophisticated terminologies or those "analogies" which can prove their fecundity. As a living example of this interdisciplinary energy, let me cite six lessons given in 1942[34] where Jakobson analyzes at the same time Poe's poem *The Raven*, its commentary (The Philosophy of Composition"), and the case of two persons speaking of the performance of the poem itself, given by an actor and broadcast by radio. Jakobson indicates in a masterly way in this multiple interaction of messages a sort of model of a complex network of communicative acts: "L'éffet decisif du *Corbeau* vient de son audace à mettre en œuvre les problèmes les plus complexes de la communication."

In this line Jakobson has realized the most daring interdisciplinary transferences. Let me list some of these methodological "transplants," which constitute veritable milestones in our discipline:

(a) The linguistic criterion of PERTINENCE applied to music, cinema, folklore, and so on.

(b) The psychological notion of FRUSTRATED EXPECTATION[35] applied to metrics and to poetic devices in general,[36] consequently the opposition information/redundancy viewed as essential to the poetic principle ("l'inconnu surgit et frappe seulement sur le fond du connu"),[37] reformulated as the double order of norm and deviation,[38] and definitively organized in 1958.[39]

(c) The FUNCTIONS OF LANGUAGE (inspired by Bühler), forecast in 1921 in *Novejšaja russkaja poèzija*, splendidly reproposed in the essay on poetry,[40] developed in an interdisciplinary context in "Results of a Joint Conference of Anthropologists and Linguists," and more systematically stated in "Concluding Statement: Linguistics and Poetics." This system of functions, bringing together psychology, information theory, the logical notion of metalanguage, and the aesthetic definition of the self-focusing quality of works of art, has profoundly influenced the development of semiotic studies all over the world.

(d) The extension of so-called BINARISM from phonology (which was encountering the results of mathematical inquiries on the nature of information) to a number of other systems. It could be said that in this case Jakobson has had too much influence, beyond his own wishes, because semioticians have frequently superimposed binary networks upon phenomena strenuously resistant to them. In any case, among the most famous applications of this principle rank that of Lévi-Strauss (structures of kinship and the culinary triangle) and that of Lacan, where the notion of binary opposition joins the emblematic Freudian alternative "Fort-Da!"

(e) The concept of DISTINCTIVE FEATURE, closely connected with the preceding one, more or less extended to a number of other significant phenomena. Jakobson himself has promoted the extension of this principle to grammar,[41] and I think that, even having allowed many semanticists to reformulate their analyses, this proposal has not yet been taken into full account by generative semantics and deserves further attention.

(f) The extension of the pair CODE/MESSAGE from the theory of communication to the entire realm of semiotics. This point will be dealt with in 3.4.

(g) The extension of the pairs SELECTION/COMBINATION and METAPHOR/METONYMY to magic, cinema, visual arts, literature, and aphasic disturbances.[42] Barthes and Lacan have ingeniously translated this notion into other fields, from fashion and advertising to psychoanalysis. Many others have applied the same pairs to architecture, objects, cultural behavior, and so on. It must be stressed, however, that the first comparison between rhetorics and magic appears in 1937 (in the analysis of the myth of the statue in Pushkin).

(h) The extension of the principles of Prague POETICS to different forms of art, thus establishing the bases of a semiotically oriented aesthetics. Particularly important from this point of view are the principles of the ambiguity and self-focusing quality of aesthetic messages.[43] The following quotation can witness to the work done by Jakobson in this field and is a program for many of the future investigations made by many semiotic analysts of art and literature:

> It is evident that many devices studied by poetics are not confined to verbal art. We can refer to the possibility of transposing *Wuthering Heights* into a motion picture, medieval legends into frescoes and miniatures, or *L'Après-midi d'un faune* into music, ballet, and graphic art. However ludicrous may appear the idea of the *Iliad* and the *Odyssey* in comics, certain structural features of their plot are preserved despite the disappearance of their verbal shape. The question whether Blake's illustrations to the *Divina Commedia* are or are not adequate is a proof that different arts are comparable. The problems of baroque or any other historical style transgress the frame of a single art. When handling the surrealistic metaphor, we could hardly pass by Max Ernst's pictures or Luis Buñuel's films, the *Andalusian Dog* and *The Golden Age*. In short, many poetic features belong not only to the science of language but to the whole

theory of signs, that is, to general semiotics. This statement, however, is valid not only for verbal art but also for all varieties of language since language shares many properties with some other systems of signs or even with all of them (pansemiotic features).[44]

Many other transplants could be cited. In the most recent essays, of enormous importance is the strong effort to link human semiotics to the biological transmission of information, mainly to the phenomena of genetic coding and decoding,[45] and therefore the exploitation of the Peircian notion of index for all cases in which there is neither intentional sender nor intentional receiver. This reference to Peirce is extremely important at this point in our review, since one of Jakobson's great historical merits has been precisely that semiotics can be considered today an "adult" discipline because he imposed the convergence between linguistic structuralism and Peirce. It has been also demonstrated—by Holenstein—that Jakobson, perhaps less ostensibly, merged structural linguistics with Husserlian phenomenology; but the short-circuit Peirce–Prague has been more than a merging: it has been a rescue, a restitution, a historical scientific event whose possibilities have still to be definitely exploited.

(4)   All semiotic systems can be described from a unified point of view if they are considered as systems of rules (codes) allowing the generation of messages.

It was Saussure who spoke of "*code de la langue,*" but it has undoubtedly been Jakobson who extrapolated those categories from information theory and extended them to linguistics and semiotics at large. Any further commentary or demonstration would be preposterous. There is, however, one point which deserves some attention. At first glance Jakobson seems to be responsible for a confusing generalization by which the term "code" indicates both a syntactic system of purely differential units devoid of any meaning (for instance, phonological codes; cf. *Fundamentals of Language*) and correlation of two series of elements systematically arranged term to term or string to string, the items of the first standing for the items of the second. As a matter of fact, in the act of proposing the acceptance of this notion,[46] Jakobson appeared clearly conscious of this difference: there is a code only when there is an ensemble of forecasted possibilities based upon the correlation of a given signifier to a given signified. But "the exceptionally rich repertoire of definitely coded meaningful units (morphemes and words) is made possible through the diaphanous system of their merely differential components devoid of proper meaning (distinctive features, phonemes, and the rules of their combinability). These components are semiotic entities *sui generis*. The signatum of these entities is bare otherness, namely a presumably semantic difference between the meaningful units to which it pertains and those which *ceteris paribus* do not contain the same entity."[47] It would then be more fruitful to call those systems *sui generis* simply "systems," reserving the name "code" for the correlations between the elements of two different systems.[48] But frequently Jakobson speaks of codes in both cases.[49] The reason is, I think, rooted in the basic concrete attitude that Jakobson (faithful to his phenomenological inspiration) has always showed. The notion of a purely distinctive and differential system is a rather abstract one and could be considered an isolation only from the standpoint of an "algebraic view" such as that of Hjelmslev (see Jakobson and Halle, *Fundamentals of Language*). The main object of all of Jakobson's research is, on the contrary, "language in action." The *langue* is a theoretical tool useful for explaining why and how *language* works. Therefore Jakobson cannot think of a phonological system (or of any semiotic analogon of it) as anything other than something designed for signification. People do not invent phonemes in order to utter them without any intention of signifying (nor in order to contemplate the system without using it): a phonological system takes its form in order to compose words (endowed with meanings, and therefore ruled by a code in the full sense of the term). "À l'origine du langage phonique ne se trouvent pas des associations d'éléments dépourvus de sens qui présentent par la suite un sens ou sont chargés de sens. À l'origine se trouvent bien au contraire des associations de sons qui reçoivent leur forme spécifiquement linguistique précisément en vue d'une fonction de signification et qui ne peuvent être définies sans recours à cette fonction de signification . . . Un phonème est défini par sa fonction de signe."[50]

Thus, playing on this double sense of code, Jakobson has given up trying to emphasize a sharp methodological distinction in order to preserve the unity of language in action. In many authors who have been inspired by Jakobson this sense of concreteness has been lost, and there has remained only a sort of imprecise oscillation between two linguistic usages of the word "code" (see also 3.6).

Jakobson has made many contributions to the best comprehension of the notion of code. Without discussing his well-known analyses in linguistics, let me recall at least three points: the introduction of the notion of "subcodes"; the important distinction between "coded words" and "coded matrices of sentences,"[51] which enlarges the notion of code to the one of generative grammar and to the many problems of textuality which will be discussed in 3.8; and the decision to study the specific functioning of different types of codes, as will be shown in 3.5

(5) Since there are many types of signs and of codes, behind their homogeneity, diversities should be isolated and described in their mode of production, in their way of "sending-back," in their mode of perception and memorization

Jakobson has always been attentive to this problem, carefully distinguishing the mode of being of different signs especially when other scholars were insisting more than necessary on the absolute identity between all semiotic phenomena (see, for instance, the outlines of the differences between visual and auditory signs).[52] The passionate proposal of Peirce's central trichotomy stresses exactly this *unitas varietatis* "L'index est un renvoi du signifiant au signifié en vertu d'une contiguité effective, l'icone est un renvoi du signifiant au signifié en vertu d'une similarité effective; le symbole est un renvoi du significant au signifié en vertu d'une contiguité assignée (*'imputed'*), conventionnelle, habituelle."[53] In this concise formula the traditional concepts of Peirce are rephrased so as to stress two typical Jakobsonian positions: (a) if there is signification there is a code, and codes are not phenomena limited to verbal language or intentional signs; (b) the presence of a code does not necessarily entail a total arbitrariness, not even in verbal language. Therefore iconism and indexicality are present also in verbal language, but coded rules are at work also in iconic and indexical signification: "Learned, conventional connections are co-present also in indexes and icons. The full apprehension of pictures and diagrams requires a learning process. No painting is devoid of ideographic, symbolic elements. The projection of the three dimensions onto a single plane through any kind of pictorial perspective is an imputed quality . . . Any attempt to treat verbal signs as solely conventional, 'arbitrary symbols' proves to be a misleading oversimplification. Iconicity plays a vast and necessary, though evidently subordinate part in different levels of linguistic structure."[54] In this same perspective, even though he has always advocated the preeminence of language among other systems of signs, Jakobson in his most recent essays has more and more said that the mechanism of other signs cannot be reduced to that of language. In "Linguistics"[55] he still stresses that "since, however, 'the most general matrix of symbolic system . . . is language', linguistics actually appears to offer the most helpful model for such an analysis." but in *Coup d'œil sur le développement de la sémiotique* he makes clear that "ceux qui considèrent le système de signes de la langue comme le seul ensemble digne d'être l'objet de la science des signes commettent une pétition de principe. L'égocentrisme des linguistes qui tiennent à exclure de la sphère sémiotique les signes organisés de façon différente qui ne le sont ceux de la langue réduit en fait le sémiotique à un simple synonime de la linguistique."

Studying the phenomenon of film in his astoundingly pioneering paper "Úpadek filmu?" he says that, provided that the matter of every art is the sign, cinema and theatre are characterized by the fact that they use as signs real things, therefore implicitly elaborating the notion of *ostensive sign* (in the same paper he points out the specific nature of pictorial signs as a mixture of similarity and convention). In fact film only *seems* to display real things, since it produces signs by inserting those things within the semiotic correlation of montage. Quoting Kulečov, Jakobson says that "a filmic plane works as a sign, as a letter." The "real thing" is not, however, assumed as such by film but is "modified as a sign" and only in this way becomes suitable material for cinema. To show only a part of a human body to signify the entire human being is an example of a rhetorical device (*pars pro toto*); working by resemblances and connections, film realizes both the principles of metaphor and metonymy. Maquillage interacting with light effects is another instance of a semiotic device. Every phenomenon of the external world is transformed into a sign on the screen. Here silence, as opposed to music, acquires semiotic purport. There is a shifting in semiotic laws (at the level of discourse—or, as it is said today, at the level "de la grand syntagmatique du film") in the passage from silent screen to sound film (the first following the laws of *vaudeville*—visual sketches with written intermissions—the second following those of opera—an uninterrupted sequence of visual, verbal, and musical textures). Montage realizes rules of temporal and causal signification; in sound film it follows the rules of the ancient epic poetry. In theatre—on the contrary—human behavior, rather than real things, is to be semioticized.

Even though in this short essay Jakobson is considering the opinions of many film theorists of his time, his paper is the first attempt to organize the paraphernalia of early film theory into a real *code*. What is even more amazing is that this paper contains virtually all the elements of the semiotic theories of film born in the early sixties. At the same time this paper solemnly states that there are codes other than verbal ones and that each of them follows specific rules: "Dans l'art, ce fut le rôle du cinéma qui révéla clairement et nettement . . . que la langue n'est qu'un des systèmes sémantiques possibles, comme l'astronomie révéla autrefois que la terre n'était qu'une planète parmi beaucoup d'autres et permit aussi une révolution complète de notre vision du monde."

(6)   A semiotic theory must naturally be concerned with the syntactic structure of the sign-vehicles of the different systems; but it also must take into account the fact that those systems, even though appearing as purely syntactic, allow the semantic interpretations of their combinatory possibilities.

In 1919, speaking of futurism, cubism, and non-representational painting,[56] Jakobson substantially anticipates (without making recourse to semiotic terminology) what is better defined in *Coup d'œil sur le développement de la sémiotique* (1974), that is, the function of internal and mutual *renvoi* performed by all the elements of a purely syntactic sequence: "La signifiance demeure sous-jacente à toutes le manifestations de l'artifice." In 1932[57] speaking of musicology and linguistics, Jakobson assigns the musical sounds to the kingdom of signs by a sort of Husserlian definition: the elements of music are not simple sounds (sonic substances) but count insofar as they are the goal of an *intentional* act. Sounds in music work as elements of a system and acquire a value according to specific criteria of pertinence: a primitive who makes timbre pertinent instead of pitch perceives as the same melody what a European feels as two different melodies played on two different instruments. In this essay the phonological concept of opposition is presented as a capital tool for the study of musical systems. It is from this essay, as well as from the investigations of the phonemic entities,[58] that a quarter of century later there springs the first significant interests in a linguistic approach to music (see mainly Springer, Ruwet, Lévi-Strauss, Schaeffer, and Natticz).[59]

For this reason Jakobson, even though admitting that there are purely syntactic systems such as chess (what Hjelmslev called *symbolic* systems, as opposed to the semiotic ones), immediately tries to find within them the possibility of an internal signification: "Le renvoi d'un fait sémiotique à un fait équivalent à l'interieur du même contexte . . . Le renvoi musical qui nous conduit du ton présent au ton attendu ou gardé dans la mémoire se trouve remplacé dans la peinture abstraite par un renvoi réciproque des facteurs en jeu."[60] When there is, as in music, "un langage qui se signifie soi-même," "diversely built and ranked parallelisms of structure enable the interpreter of any immediately perceived musical signans to infer and anticipate a further corresponding constituent (e.g., series) and the coherent ensemble of these constituents . . . The code of recognized equivalences between parts and their correlation with the whole is to a great degree a learned, imputed set of parallelisms which are accepted as such in the framework of a given epoch, culture, or musical school."[61]

(7) A semiotic theory is not only concerned with the structure of sign-vehicles but also with the structure of the universe of vehiculated contents. There cannot be a semiotics without incorporating a semantics. This semantics is not only an extensional one (as is the study of the correspondence between signs and things or states of the world) but also and especially an intensional one, that is, the study of the way in which the universe of sense is culturally organized.

Jakobson has always refused to exclude the study of meaning from linguistics, according also to his Husserlian inspiration and to the explicit assumption of the Prague Circle principles which he elaborated jointly with his Czech and Russian friends.[62] Therefore he repeatedly states that (a) there is a substantial difference between sense or meaning or signified and mere denotata[63] and (b) the nature of the signified cannot be explained but by making recourse to Peirce's notion of "interpretant":[64] against the naive confusion between "interpretant" and "interpreter" Jakobson demonstrates that to interpret a semiotic item means to "translate" it into another item (maybe an entire discourse) and that this translation is always creatively enriching the first item,[65] this continuous creativity being the main result of Peirce's "unlimited semiosis."[66] It is rather astounding to find a first suggestion of the compositional analysis of "bachelor" in a text[67] where semantic markers are viewed as Peircian interpretants, while the identity between interpretant as pure synonymy is denied. And in 1952[68] Jakobson stressed that a structural analysis of meaning consists in an investigation of semantic invariants just as a structural analysis of signifiers in language consists in a structural analysis of phonological invariants. More recently, after years of semiotic Olympic games on unmarried men, seals, and young knights, it it still Jakobson who has isolated in the most concise way the invariant underlying all the senses of "bachelor," that is, "quelqu'un dont la carrière est inachevée."[69] Finally the text on Pushkin of 1937 represents one of the first examples of the analysis of semantic structures at work within a text: rest and movement, death and life, living and still matter. Viewed as abstract roles assumed by the image of the statue in Pushkin's poetry, this work is a satisfactory—even though not yet formalized—instance of *analyse actancielle* recalling Lévi-Strauss's organization of mythic content, Lotman's analyses of cultural typologies, and Greimas' structural semantics.

(8)   In every sign exchange there are not only isolated items: semiotics must, as does contemporary linguistics, shift from a theory of single terms and "phrases" to a co-text and context theory. This also means that semiotics should incorporate not only syntactics and semantics but also pragmatics.

A scholar who has always been concerned with language in action cannot but have continuously offered suggestions about the problem of context sensitivity and utterance-in-circumstance. It is enough to quote, as a linguistic and semiotic introduction to pragmatics, the research on the shifters[70] where Jakobson subsumes within the framework of linguistic research suggestions coming from Husserl, Russell, and Carnap. In any case, the earliest studies on the Russian verb[71] seem to take into full account the problems that are today discussed by many disciplines under the heading of the pragmatics of natural languages, presupposition, and semantic entailment. All these interests are revisited in a more systematic and propulsive way in "Language in Relation to Other Communication Systems" (the problem of context-sensitivity and of the difference between *idiomorphic* signs and signs capable of building propositions) and "Linguistics" (higher units of discourse as "ready made" and coded texts, discursive competence, or competence in dialogic rules).

4. THE FINAL DESIGN

In 1933, commenting on the activity of the Prague Circle, Jakobson underlined the fact that that group had worked in a structural and phenomenological perspective in order to make available a rich material for a general theory of signs or semiology.[72] In 1970 he set up a sort of general definition of semiotics that every student could today take as a suitable characterization of his discipline and as a program for further enquiries:

> The subject matter of semiotic is the communication of any messages whatever, whereas the field of linguistics is confined to communication of verbal messages.

Hence, of these two sciences of man, the latter has a narrower scope, yet, on the other hand, any human communication of non-verbal messages presupposes a circuit of verbal messages, without a reverse implication. If the cycle of semiotic disciplines is the nearest one to encompass linguistics, the next, wider concentric circle is the totality of communication disciplines. . . . It was Lévi-Strauss who gave the clearest delineation of this subject matter and who launched the most promising attempt "à interpréter la société dans son ensemble en fonction d'une théorie de la communication." He strives toward an integrated science of communication which would embrace social anthropology, economics, and linguistics, or let us replace the latter concept by a wider notion of semiotic. . . . In any event semiotic occupies a central position within the total science of communication and underlies all other provinces of this science, while semiotic, in turn, comprises linguistics as its central section which influences all other semiotic provinces. Three integrated sciences encompass each other and present three gradually increasing degrees of generality:

1. Study in communication of verbal messages = linguistics;
2. Study in communication of any message = semiotics (communication of verbal messages implied);
3. Study in communication = social anthropology jointly with economics (communication of messages implied).[73]

I wonder if even the third level should not fall under the heading of semiotics, at least as far as relations of *renvoi* can be found here. But the thought of Jakobson is an intimately dialectic one, and the growing of the inner radius in this concentric diagram does not exclude the possibility that from a narrower circle the widest ones can be focused.

In any case, if one accepts this proposal of a semiotic design as a definition of the state of the art and as a promise for the future, one should say that from 1914[74] until now—sixty-two years in all—Roman Jakobson has coherently worked to make both this proposal and this promise suitable.

NOTES

1. The International Association for Semiotic Studies, established in 1969, has agreed to used the word "semiotics" instead of "semiology" or "semiotic." However, Jakobson originally followed Peirce and Morris in using "semiotic." In the present essay I shall metalinguistically use "semiotics" to speak of the object "semiotic" such as it is named by the author I am studying.
2. Roman Jakobson re-evaluated the role played by these last three works in "Linguistics," *Main Trends of Research in the Social and Human Sciences* I (The Hague-Paris, 1970), pp. 419–63, and *Coup d'œil sur le développement de la sémiotique* (the opening speech at the First International Congress of the International Association for Semiotic Studies [1974]) = *Studies in Semiotics* 3 (Bloomington, Ind.: Research Center for Language and Semiotic Studies, 1975). On links between Jakobson and phenomenological tradition, see Elmar Holenstein, *Jakobson* (Paris: Seghers, 1974).
3. Substantial reappraisals of Peirce are in Jakobson, "Results of a Joint Conference of Anthropologists and Linguists" (1952), *Selected Writings* II (The Hague, 1971), pp. 554–67; "Concluding Statement: Linguistics and Poetics" (1958), *Style in Language*, ed. Thomas A. Sebeok (New York, 1960), pp. 350–77; "À la recherche de l'essence du langage," *Diogène*, 51 (1965)

and *Problèmes du langage* (Paris, 1966), pp. 22–38 [see also "Quest for the Essence of Language," *Diogènes*, 51 (Montreal, 1966), 21–37, and *Selected Writings* II, pp. 345–59]; "Language in Relation to Other Communication Systems," *Linguaggi nella società e nella tecnica*, Convegno promosso dalla Ing. C. Olivetti and Co., S.p.A. per il centenario della nascità di Camillo Olivetti (Milan, 1970), pp. 3–16; "Linguistics," *Main Trends of Research in the Social and Human Sciences* I; and *Coup d'œil sur le développement de la sémiotique*.

4. "La contribution apporté par Ferdinand de Saussure au progrès des études sémiotiques est évidemment plus modeste et plus restreinte . . . Contrairement à Peirce et à Husserl, tous les deux conscients d'avoir jeté les fondements de la sémiotique, Saussure ne parle de la sémiologie qu'au futur." (Jakobson, *Coup d'œil sur le développement de la sémiotique*).

5. Sharing a precise theory of human history as a collective product, I believe that the development of the historical novel would have been nearly the same even without the existence of Walter Scott (only logicians would have changed their examples apropos of the author of *Waverley*). But there is some difference between a cult of personality and the respect accorded a matter of fact.

6. "De la poésie à la linguistique," *L'Arc*, 60 (1975).

7. *Donum Natalicium Schrijnen* (Nijmegen-Utrecht, 1929), pp. 900–13; also in R. Jakobson, *Selected Writings* IV (The Hague: Mouton, 1966), pp. 1–15.

8. *Novyj Lef*, 12 (1928), 36–37, and *Readings in Russian Poetics*, ed. L. Matejka (Ann Arbor, 1962), pp. 99–102.

9. Cf. the way in which the poems of Pushkin are understood in the light of a reference to sculpture (Jakobson, "Socha v symbolice Puškinově," *Slovo a slovesnost* III [1937], 2–24; see also "La statue dans la symbolique de Pouchkine," *Questions de Poétique* [Paris: Editions du Seuil, 1973], pp. 152–89, and *Puškin and His Sculptural Myth* [The Hague: Mouton, 1975]): literary signs speak of visual signs, both referring back to a semantic system of metaphysical oppositions, such as Life and Death.

10. *Novejšaja russkaja poèzija* (Prague, 1921); see also "Fragments de 'La Nouvelle poésie russe'," *Questions de Poétique*, pp. 11–24.

11. "Futurizm," *Iskusstvo*, 7 (August 2, 1919), also in *Questions de Poétique*, pp. 25–30.

12. "Results of a Joint Conference of Anthropologists and Linguists," "Again and again one may quote Sapir's still opportune reminder that 'every cultural pattern and every single act of social behavior involves communication in either an explicit or implicit sense'" ("Language in Relation to Other Communication Systems," *Linguaggi nella società e nella tecnica* [Milan, 1970]).

13. Written jointly with M. Halle and published as Janua Linguarum, series minor, 1 (The Hague: Mouton, 1956).

14. *Structure of Language and Its Mathematical Aspects*, ed. R. Jakobson [= *Proceedings of Symposia in Applied Mathematics*, XII] (American Mathematical Society, 1961), 245–52.

15. "Socha v symbolice Puškinově." "Pourquoi faut-il souligner que le signe ne se confond pas avec l'object? Parce qu'â côté de la conscience immédiate de l'identité entre le signe et l'objet (A est A), la conscience immédiate de l'absence de cette identité (A n'est pas A) est nécessaire: cette antinomie est inévitable, car sans contradiction, il n'y a pas de jeu de concepts, il n'y a pas de jeu des signes, le rapport entre le concept et le signe devient automatique, le cours des événéments s'arrête, la conscience de la réalité se meurt" ("Co je poesie?" *Volné směry*, 30 [Prague, 1934], pp. 229–39; "Qu'est-ce que la poésie?" *Questions de Poétique*, pp. 113–26).

16. "Futurizm," *Iskusstvo* 7 (August 2, 1919).

17. With P. Bogatyrev, "Die Folklore als eine besondere Form des Schaffens" (1929).

18. "Musikwissenschaft und Linguistik," *Prager Presse*, December 7, 1932; see also "Musicologie et linguistique," *Questions de Poétique*, pp. 102–04.

19. "Úpadek filmu?" *Listy pro umémí a kritiku* I (Prague, 1933), 45–49; see also "Décadence du cinema?" *Questions de Poétique*, pp. 105–12.

20. *Ibid.*

21. "The Dominant" (1935), *Readings in Russian Poetics: Formalist and Structuralist Views*, ed. L. Matejka and K. Pomorska (Ann Arbor, 1971), pp. 82–87.
22. "Socha v symbolice Puškinově."
23. "Concluding Statement: Linguistics and Poetics" (1958).
24. "Szczupak po polsku," *Prace Polonistyczne*, 20 (1965), 132–41 [Italian translation: *Premesse di storia letteraria* (Milano: Saggiatore, 1975)].
25. "Results of a Joint Conference of Anthropologists and Linguists" (1952); "On Visual and Auditory Signs," *Phonetica*, 11 (1964), 216–20, and *Selected Writings* II, 334–37; "Quest for the Essence of Language" (1966); and "About the Relation between Visual and Auditory Signs," *Models for the Perception of Speech and Visual Form*, ed. W. Watten-Dun (Cambridge, Mass., 1967), pp. 1–7, and *Selected Writings* II, pp. 338–44.
26. "Language in Relation to Other Communication Systems" (1968); "Linguistics," *Main Trends of Research in the Social and Human Sciences* I (1970); and *Coup d' œil sur le développement de la sémiotique* (1974).
27. "Da i net v mimike," *Jazyk i čelovek*, ed. V. A. Zvegincev (Moscow, 1970), pp. 284–89, and *Selected Writings* II, 360–65; see also "Motor Signs for 'Yes' and 'No'," *Language in Society*, 1 (1971).
28. *Kindersprache, Aphasie und allgemeine Lautgesetze* (Uppsala, 1941), and *Selected Writings* I (2nd ed: The Hague: Mouton, 1971), 328–401; see also *Child Language, Aphasia, and Phonological Universals* [= Janua Linguarum, series minor, 72] (The Hague: Mouton, 1972).
29. *International Journal of American Linguistics*, 10 (1944), 188–95; *Portraits of Linguists* II, ed. T. A. Sebeok (Bloomington: Indiana University Press, 1966), 127–39; and *Selected Writings*, II, 477–96.
30. Cf. note 26.
31. C. Lévi-Strauss, "L'analyse structurale en linguistique et en anthropologie," *Word*, 1, 2 (1945). By examining the footnotes of many books and papers one rather frequently discovers that a lot of provocative ideas have come from a "personal communication" by Roman Jakobson. This generosity in giving fresh suggestions, whether to old colleagues or to young students, is one of the main features of Jakobson's personality.
32. "Results of a Joint Conference of Anthropologists and Linguists" (1952).
33. "Linguistics," *Main Trends of Research in the Social and Human Sciences* I.
34. Later published as "Language in Operation," *Mélanges Alexandre Koyré* I (Paris, 1964), 269–81.
35. "Concluding Statement: Linguistics and Poetics" (1958).
36. *O češskom stixe preimuščestvenno v sopostavlenii s russkim* [= *Sborniki po teorii poètičeskogo jazyka* V] (Berlin-Moscow, 1923); "Concluding Statement: Linguistics and Poetics" (1958); "Linguistics and Communication Theory" (1961).
37. *Novejšaja russkaja poèzija* [see note 10].
38. "Randbemerkungen zur Prosa des Dichters Pasternak," *Slavische Rundschau* VII (1935), 357–74.
39. "Concluding Statement: Linguistics and Poetics."
40. "Co je poesie?" (1934) [see note 15].
41. "Zur Strukur des russischen Verbums," *Charisteria Gvilelmo Mathesio* (Prague, 1932), pp. 74–84, and *Selected Writings* II, 3–15; "Beitrag zur allgemeinen Kasuslehre," *Travaux du Cercle Linguistique de Prague*, 6 (1936), 240–88, and *Selected Writings* II, 23–71; and "Boas' View of Grammatical Meaning" (1959).
42. *Fundamentals of Language* (1956).
43. "Concluding Statement: Linguistics and Poetics" (1958).
44. "Concluding Statement: Linguistics and Poetics," *Style in Language* pp. 350–51. Apropos of one of the poetic devices most brilliantly pointed out by Jakobson, parallelism, it should be

remarked that he has devoted considerable effort to elucidating the semiotic role of the various types of symmetry reflected in the diverse uses of parallelism. Cf. "Grammatical Parallelism and Its Russian Facets," *Language*, 42 (1966), 399–429, and "The Modular Design of Chinese Regulated Verse," *Échanges et Communications: Mélanges offerts à Claude Lévi-Strauss* (The Hague: Mouton, 1970), pp. 597–605, where he stresses the striking similarity between the types of symmetry in Chinese classical verse and the approach to these problems in the theories of Chinese physicists.

45. "Language in Relation to Other Communication Systems" (1958); "Linguistics" (1970).
46. "Linguistics and Communication Theory" (1961).
47. "Language in Relation to Other Communication Systems" (1968).
48. See my proposals (U. Eco, *A Theory of Semiotics* [Bloomington: Indiana University Press, 1976]) for distinguishing between s-codes (or codes as systems) and codes *tout court*.
49. For instance in "Language in Relation to Other Communication Systems," *Linguaggi nella società e nella tecnica* (Milan, 1970), 1.4: "This code includes all the distinctive features to be manipulated, all the admisible combinations into bundles of co-occurrent features termed *phonemes*, and all the rules of concatenating phonemes into sequences—briefly, all the distinctive vehicles serving primarily to differentiate morphemes and whole words."
50. Holenstein, *Jakobson*, pp. 96, 202.
51. "Linguistics," *Main Trends of Research in the Social and Human Sciences* I (1970).
52. "On Visual and Auditory Signs" (1964) and "About the Relation between Visual and Auditory Signs" (1969) [see note 25].
53. *Coup d'œil sur le développement de la sémiotique* (1974).
54. "Language in Relation to Other Communication Systems" (1968).
55. *Main Trends of Research in the Social and Human Sciences* I (1970).
56. "Futurizm," *Iskusstvo* 7.
57. "Musikwissenschaft und Linguistik" (1932).
58. See, for instance, "On the Identification of Phonemic Entities," *Travaux du Cercle linguistique de Copenhague*, 5 (1949), 205–13 (also in *Selected Writings* I, 418–25); and *Fundamentals of Language*.
59. For an introductory bibliography, see *Musique en Jeu*, 5 (1971).
60. *Coup d'œil sur le développement de la sémiotique* (1974).
61. "Language in Relation to Other Communication Systems" (1968).
62. Thesis 8 in "Thèses présentées au Premier Congrès des philologues slaves," *Travaux du Cercle Linguistique de Prague* I (1929), 5–29; also in *A Prague School Reader in Linguistics*, ed. Joseph Vachek (Bloomington: Indiana University Press, 1964), p. 55.
63. "La phénoménologie moderne démasque systématiquement les fictions linguistiques et montre avec lucidité la différence fondamentale qui sépare le signe de l'objet signifié, la signification d'un mot et le contenu que vise cette signification." "Co je poesie?" (1934).
64. "Results of a Joint Conference of Anthropologists and Linguists" (1952).
65. "On Linguistic Aspects of Translation" (1959) [see note 66].
66. See specifically "On Linguistic Aspects of Translation," *On Translation* (Cambridge, Mass.: Harvard University Press, and New York: Oxford University Press, 1966), pp. 232–39, with the list of various types of interpretation: intra-linguistic translation or rewording, interlinguistic translation, intersemiotic transmutation. Apropos of the possibilities of intersemiotic transmutation (transposition from verbal to visual and so on), see the remarks in *Essais de linguistique générale* (Paris, Minuit, 1963) (on aphasic impairments in children). On the creativity of every interpretation, see in "Randbemerkungen zur Prosa des Dichters Pasternak" a provocative definition of metaphorical and metonymical substitutions in poetry as "interpretations" (Peircian terminology is still absent, but here one witness an enlargement of the notion of interpretant to poetic procedures).

67. In "On Linguistic Aspects of Translation."
68. In "Results of a Joint Conference of Anthropologists and Linguists."
69. "Louvain Lectures" (see M. van Ballaer, *Aspects of the Theories of R. Jakobson*, memoir (Kattolieke Universiteit te Leuwen, 1973 [mineographed]).
70. E.g., *Shifters, Verbal Categories, and the Russian Verb* (Harvard University Department of Slavic Languages and Literatures, Russian Language Project, 1957 [mimeographed]); also in *Selected Writings* II, 130–47.
71. "Zur Struktur des russischen Verbums" (1932).
72. "La scuola linguistica di Praga," *La Cultura*, 12 (1933), 633–41; see also "Die Arbeit der sogenannten 'Prager Schule'," *Bulletin du Cercle Linguistique de Copenhague* III (1938), 6–8 (also in *Selected Writings* II, pp. 547–50).
73. "Linguistics," *Main Trends of Research in the Social and Human Sciences* I.
74. In order to establish the beginning of the activity of Jakobson as a writer, I rely on *Roman Jakobson: A Bibliography of his Writings*, ed. C. H. van Schooneveld (The Hague: Mouton, 1971).

CHAPTER 6

Karl Bühler

THOMAS A. SEBEOK

1. BACKGROUND

People who undertake to reassess the diacritic flavor and scholarly quality of great figures of the past soon find themselves engaged in a free-for-all from which they are more likely than not to emerge by delineating the distinctive features of merely their own contributions. This process of self-definition may apply with special force when we attempt to reinterpret personalities who flourished in the decades following the political and cultural wreckage of the Habsburg *Hausmacht*—an epoch of imperial decay that has justly been described as "always desperate, but never serious"—because some of us were ourselves saturated in that selfsame ambience throughout our formative years. The ensuing era was one of infinite possibilities for the building of novel institutions and social practices, in brief, the new Austrian Republic. In this modern Austria, plenty of opportunities existed for intellectuals to put an effective system of social democracy into working order, something which had been unattainable during the times of Habsburg ultraconservatism. It was in this unprecedented atmosphere of social crisis that Bühler, with his ideas (germinated a decade or so earlier) about "imageless thought" and "rule awareness," began to play the role of chief theoretician in the movement underlying curricular reform in Austria (Bartley, 1973:144). Karl Popper and Ludwig Wittgenstein were among the budding giants who enrolled in the resulting teacher-training courses (Janik and Toulmin, 1973:288). Much of this constructive development was, of course, poignantly swept away with the coming of the Second World War. Still, the exercise of looking back upon the intervening decades is salubrious, for it at least reduces our complacency and melts away the comforting fat of self-delusion about the

Delivered in Vienna, *viva voca,* in the series "Wiener Erbe," on July 5, 1979.

THOMAS A. SEBEOK • Director of the Research Center for Language and Semiotic Studies, Indiana University, Bloomington, Indiana.

total innovativeness of our surviving contemporary heroes. As we thus casually journey back to the Vienna of the interwar period, we must, withal, be mindful of two basic facts: first, that we cannot escape the tendency of all travelers, whether in space or in time, to seize upon a dramatic moment here and there in order to generalize from this by the imposition of our own prejudices upon each such vivid flash; and second (to paraphrase your own extraordinary satirist, Karl Kraus, about his contemporary bourgeois Vienna), that this city was, during the time of Bühler's residence, already a proving ground for world destruction. George Steiner (1979:101) summed it up well: "As the waltz tune has it, *Wien, Wien, nur du allein*. Vienna was the capital of the age of anxiety, the hub of Jewish genius, and the city from which the Holocaust would seep." All this was foreshadowed in the scientific arena, with rare subtlety, in Bühler's *Die Krise der Psychologie*, first published in book form two years before the global economic catastrophe of 1929 (see also Wellek, 1959).

The objective of the lecture series, on the "Viennese Heritage," that I am presently assisting in is to commemorate and celebrate Austria's multiform yet distinctive role in the development of modern semiotic inquiry. My particular assignment is to observe the contribution of Karl Bühler, who was neither born nor educated in Austria, and who—although he was of small peasant stock and profited from a religiously broad-minded upbringing (his father, Ludwig, being a Protestant, his mother, Berta, in whose faith the young Karl followed, a Catholic)—was forced to flee this country and to settle down uneasily in America after 1938. He nevertheless achieved his international reputation in Vienna, where he chiefly functioned during sixteen of the most maturely productive years of his life, beginning in 1922 (Lebzeltern, 1969:25).

Bühler was born on May 27, 1879, in Meckesheim, in the vicinity of Heidelberg, and eventually matriculated at the University of Freiburg im Breisgau. In 1903, he was awarded an M.D. under the famous physiologist, Johannes von Kries, with a dissertation dealing with theories of color vision, experimentally researched, namely, the question of the limits of the eye's adaptability for light and darkness. His life-long interest in psychology was, furthermore, nourished at Freiburg, although eventually crowned with a Ph.D. at the University of Strassburg, where, in 1904, he presented, to Clemens Bäumker, a second dissertation on the physiological prolegomena that Lord Kames (Henry Home), the 18th century thinker, believed aesthetics required. It is interesting to speculate, at least in passing, about the influence on Bühler of Kames, with specific regard to the Scottish moral philosopher's arguments about the laws of association and the relational qualities that he was concerned with, such as contiguity in time and space (the domain that some of us now call indexicality), and resemblance and dissimilitude (or iconicity), as well as classic notions of signification based on cause and effect (Miller, 1979) and of surface variation against a background of global uniformity.

For a short time, Bühler then seems to have practiced medicine in Strassburg, specializing in opthalmology (Lebzeltern, 1969:13).

Bühler next became an assistant to Kries, in Freiburg, then went on to study, in Berlin, under Benno Erdmann, the logician and psychologist remembered chiefly for his work in respect to Kant, and his view (1907) of judgment at the core of which is a predicative relationship—a prototype illocutionary act, as it were, performed *in* the uttering of a sentence—a formulation, moreover, critically influenced by semiotic considerations, and to work, as well, under Carl Stumpf, often regarded (having brought experimental phenomenology into psychology) as one of the most important precursors of Gestalt psychology. Stumpf was also co-founder, in 1900, of Berlin's *Verein für Kinderpsychologie*, a field in which Karl became active eight years afterward, although not as much so as Charlotte Bühler.

2. BÜHLER AND INTIMATIONS OF SEMIOTICS

In 1906, Bühler moved on to an assistantship, and close collaboration, in Würzburg, with Oswald Külpe (who had himself served as Wilhelm Wundt's second assistant), and obtained his habilitation as a *Dozent* in philosophy. This monograph, published as a series of three consecutive articles in the *Archiv für die gesamte Psychologie*, in 1907–1908, was based upon Bühler's experimental studies on the psychology of thought processes, and bore the overall title, "*Tatsachen und Probleme zu einer Psychologie der Denkvorgänge.*" Bühler's analysis of "what is thought" was strongly influenced by Külpe's original concepts pertaining to *imageless knowledge* (or, in Bühler's terminology, "thought"), *determining tendency* (Narziss Ach's 1905 coinage to describe the unconscious process, hidden from introspection, that guides thinking along its proper course; see Rapaport, 1951, *passim*), *awareness, task set* (Aufgabe), *set* (Einstellung), and the technique of systematic *experimental introspection*. A substantial section of Part II (excerpts from which were—although not until 43 years later—published in England as well [Rapaport, 1951:39–57]) was devoted to the apprehension (*Auffassen*) of thought and the comprehension (*Verstehen*) of sentences (a function semioticians might well translate either as "understanding" or as "interpretation"). One of Bühler's important conclusions was that *Verstehen* takes place between the integral wholes. He immediately recognized that this experience is the inverse of a problem encountered in the psychology of language, to wit: how does the unitary thought differentiate into the meanings of the concatenation of words whereby it is expressed, or, to reverse this again, how do word-meanings build up to a totality the thought to be grasped? To put it yet another way, the question—which Bühler's data were insufficient to resolve—brings up the wider issue of the genesis of Gestalt, a lengthy and complex chapter in the history of ideas that can barely even be touched upon here (cf. the extended treatment by the man he considered his *"Hauptschüler,"* Egon Brunswik, 1929). This and kindred matters concerning "a rich scale of tensions between wholes and parts" involved in the constitution of language and other varieties of semiotic strings, were unerringly identified by Jakobson (1963), who alludes (1971b:715) to Bühler's seminal ideas in this connection, while more prominently adducing those of Peirce, Frege, Husserl, and, of course, Sapir. Bühler afterward—in the late 1920s and early 1930s—returned (on at least four separate occasions) to the characteristic experience of sentence comprehension as a consummatory operation climaxing the emergence of conscious relationships.

Külpe's own experiments eventually moved him from the elements of Wundt towards the acts of Brentano, but it was Bühler's study which gave impetus to a far-reaching controversy with Wundt, focusing on the methodological legitimacy of nonexact experiments and retrospective introspection, arguments about the empirical value of which, and more generally, about introspection and the mind, are still very much alive (e.g., Lieberman, 1979). According to Lebzeltern (1969:15), it was Bühler's prolonged discord with Wundt that made the junior scholar *"in der Fachwelt gleichsam über Nacht berühmt."* The main points of their argument were clearly summarized by Blumenthal (1974:1114–1116), and need not be recounted here. Bühler's views, that thoughts seem to be independent of the verbal manifestations in which they are cast, and that sentence-meaning hierarchically outranks word-meaning (a principle on which, by the way, he and Wundt thoroughly agreed), eventually matured, after 1919, into his brand of a semiotically tinged theory of speech.

When Külpe progressed to Bonn, in 1909, and eventually in 1913 on to Munich, Bühler followed him; there, he obtained an untenured appointment as an Associate Professor. In 1916, the 37-year-old Karl married Charlotte Malachowski, then 22, a fellow student of his, and a former disciple of Husserl's, who herself eventually became a famous psychologist. After the First World War was over, Bühler accepted an appointment as a full Professor at the Dresden Institute of Technology, and, four years later, the couple—lured by Otto Glöckel and his colleagues—moved to Vienna, where he became Professor, with Charlotte his assistant. The Institute of Psychology he established in this city—incidentally, with a supplemental ten-year grant from The Rockefeller Foundation—and directed, with his wife's support, until 1938, quickly gained world-wide recognition. He concurrently held a post as Adjunct Professor at the Pedagogical Institute of the City of Vienna. The Bühlers' salon, at Weimarer Strasse 100, soon became a mecca of social and intellectual life for visitors to Vienna from the world over; thus, by 1937, Bühler had attracted doctoral candidates from 18 countries.

On March 23, 1938, he was arrested by the Nazis, but released before long (on May 7) upon the intervention of influential friends, with whose help he then emigrated, next year, via Oslo, to the United States, a country where he had previously taught, in 1927–28 (at Stanford, Johns Hopkins, and Harvard), and, again, in 1929 (at Chicago); in 1930, he had held the MacDougall Professorship at Harvard and simultaneously served in Radcliffe. However, as Charlotte Bühler (1965:187) explicitly related years afterward, "*Da wir beide Wien sehr liebten, zogen wir es vor, in Wien zu bleiben.*" [Since we both loved Vienna very much, we resolved to remain in Vienna.] This decision proved, in retrospect, to have been a costly mistake, for, after his exile of a quarter of a century, which, as fate decreed, became irreversible after his 60th year, he was unable to secure a post suitable to his eminence, and was obliged to teach psychology in a succession of small Catholic undergraduate colleges, in Duluth and St. Paul, Minnesota. When the Second World War came to an end, in 1945, the Bühlers settled in Los Angeles for good, where Karl served, until 1955, as an Assistant Clinical Professor of psychiatry in the Medical School of the University of Southern California in 1963. "*Wir waren politisch so naiv,*" Charlotte wistfully added after Karl's death, "*dass wir Österreich für sicher hielten.*" [We were politically so naive, that we considered Austria secure.] Unfortunately, even his relatively brief, six-week incarceration in the hands of the Gestapo had, it seemed, incurably shattered his personality: realization that his own people would mistreat him in this way wounded him for life. He became withdrawn and suffered from such an abiding depression that the rich wellsprings of his creativity were effectively consumed. I believe that the sole reason for his persecution by the Nazis was that Charlotte—although raised a Protestant—came from a predominantly Jewish ancestry, and that, had he consented to divorce her, he could have kept his academic posts and social position.

In tracing the post-War diaspora of Bühler's "school," Charlotte (1965:193) makes the interesting, startling, and, I fear, exaggerated observation that "*er keinen bedeutenden Wiener Schüler auf dem Gebiete der Sprachpsychologie hatte . . . Es ist wahrhaft tragisch, dass er den allmählichen Triumph seiner Sprachtheorie nicht mehr erlebte.*" [he did not have any significant Viennese pupils in the field of the psychology of language . . . It is truly tragic that he did not survive to witness the gradual triumph of his theory of language.] The widow then follows up on her assessment with a shockingly ungracious, petulant, and certainly counterfactual remark, that Roman Jakobsen [sic], "*der in seinen Werken sich weitgehend auf Karl stützte, erwies ihm nicht die gebührende Anerkennung für das, was er Karl dankte.*" [who in his works leaned extensively on Karl, (yet) did not befittingly acknowledge his debt to Karl.] As a matter of fact, in Jakobson's *Selected Writings I–II* (1971a, 1971b) alone, Bühler is cited— almost always with approbation, and, what is more interesting for us, all but invariably in a semiotic context—no less than 20 times. The opening sentence of Jakobson's celebrated *Kindersprache* (1971a:328) is a direct quotation from a 1935 paper of Bühler's, and, as late as 1967 (1971b:671), Jakobson still

characterized Bühler's *Sprachtheorie* as being "for linguists probably the most
inspiring among all the contributions to the psychology of language." It is certainly no secret that Jakobson's initial exploration of the functions of language,
the essence of which lay in the distinction between everyday parlance (both
practical and emotive, but always oriented toward the signified) and poetic
language (manifested in the set toward the sign as such), a distinction which
dates back to 1921, was much later conflated with Bühler's frequently cited
triadic organon model of 1934 (as explicitly credited in Sebeok, 1960:355), but
which Jakobson, in turn, creatively expanded by three further factors of the
speech event, each corresponding to a specific communicative function.

Charlotte, curiously, charges a student of Jakobson's, Paul L. Garvin,
whom she mischaracterizes as *"ein junger Semantiker,"* ["a young semanticist,"]
with responsibility for the posthumous publication of Bühler's *Sprachtheorie* in
English, as a matter of fact, via the facilities of my Research Center. However,
no such manuscript was ever received by me, nor, so far as I am aware, has
ever appeared anywhere else. Garvin did write a brief necrology, where he
stressed (1964:633) that Bühler's "field-theory of language is an adaptation of
the Gestalt-theoretical ideas of figure and ground to the psychology of language."
He suggestively rendered *organon*—the term is heavily laden with Aristotelian
connotations and, of course, echoes Bacon—as "tool"—a tool composed of signs,
operating deictically (in a *Zeigfeld*) or symbolically (*Symbolfeld*), the two surrounds bearing the cover-term *Umfeld*. This word instantly evokes Jakob von
Uexküll's terminology (Sebeok, 1979, Ch. 10), and what is especially interesting
is that Bühler explicitly recognized its semiotic import. In 1934 (p. 27), for
example, he remarked that Uexküll's thesis *"vornherein in seinen Grundbegriffen
'Merkzeichen' und 'Wirkzeichen' sematologisch orientiert ist."* [is semiotic in
its orientations as to its fundamental concepts of *Merkzeichen*, or perceptual
signs, and *Wirkzeichen*, or operation signs.]

It should now be noted, as a terminological aside, that Bühler most frequently used Benjamin H. Smart's coinage, introduced in an anonymous work
of his entitled *Outline of Sematology* (1831:1), for what we call semiotics. Smart,
following Locke's tripartite division of the entirety of knowledge, suggested that
"all instruction for the use of *ta semata*, or the signs of our knowledge, might
be called *Sematology*." He further stated (Smart, 1831:2, n.) that "As to Sematology, the third division, it is the *doctrine of signs*, showing how the mind
operates by their means in obtaining the knowledge comprehended in the other
divisions." Smart continued to use this terminology in later books, notably in
his *Sequel to Sematology* (1837); it was picked up by Archibald H. Sayce and
then propagated by the most influential English lexicographer of all, James A. H.
Murray, both via the *OED* and an article he published in the early 1880's. Smart
was widely read in his time—among others, by Charles Darwin, whose philosophical views on language were compatible with Smart's (as well as with such
other authors as Dugald Stewart). However, *sematology* has all but vanished in

the present century, save for Bühler's idiosyncratic Teutonization. I find it particularly strange that he did not favor his Viennese colleague's, Heinrich Gomperz', competing term, *Semasiologie* (1908)—originally believed to have been created by Christian Karl Reisig, in Halle, to rhyme with *Etymologie*—because many of Bühler's semiotic notions closely resemble those of Gomperz, as traced in some detail in an unpublished master's thesis by Günther (1968); but Bühler continued habitually to employ *Semiotik* (e.g., 1968:16, 18, 19, 162), usually in a classical context.

It is true, as Charlotte (1965:195) remarked of her late husband, that *"Karl ist ein Enzyklopäde, den man nicht rubrizieren kann."* [Karl is a polymath who cannot be categorized.] He touched on so many areas of psychology that, indeed, he stood tall as *"einer der umfassendsten Forscher seiner Zeit."* [one of the most wide-ranging researchers of his time."] One could, for instance, devote a treatise to an assessment of Bühler's work in the field of child psychology—which influenced the school-reform movement from the outset (Bartley, 1973:146), including particularly his pioneering observations on the ontogenesis of verbal signs, notably in his daughter, Inge (1918:224). According to his wife's hardly unbiased survey of the field of child psychology (Charlotte Bühler and Hetzer, 1929:221), its development reached *"ihre prinzipiellste und umfassendste Ausgestaltung bei Karl Bühler,"* [its most fundamental and comprehensive formation in the work of Karl Bühler.] but the radically different approach—combining structure with genesis, or a model of rationalism with a role for experience—of Piaget, of the early 1920s, had already had its impact on the German investigators of that decade.

Too, it must be remembered that Bühler's Vienna was likewise and simultaneously the city of Freud and of Adler, rampant with psychoanalytic theories and deeply engrossed in bitter internecine doctrinal imbroglios. Bühler himself had close ties—given his medical training—with the University's Institute of Psychiatry, where many analysts attended his lectures and seminars. As Charlotte (1965:196) perceived it, *"Im Unterschied zu Freud hielt ich es für grundlegend wichtig, die Interpretation menschlicher Strebungen von seelisch gesunden statt von seelisch kranken Entwicklungen abzuleiten,"* [In contrast to Freud, I considered it fundamentally important to derive from sound minds rather than from sick minds the interpretation of the development of human endeavors.] and, in this, she shared her husband's point of departure. Lebzeltern's (1969:39) perspective seems also to have been generally correct, that Bühler *stand in der gesselschaftlichen Achtung und wissenschaftlichen Anerkennung turmhoch über Freud."* [towered over Freud in social esteem and scholarly recognition.] Their relative contemporary positions and seemingly unbridgeable apartheid notwithstanding—in the light of Freud's peripheral position vis-à-vis academic psychology, in contrast to Bühler's own centrality—Bühler generously characterized Freud (1927:178) as a *grosse[r] Zauberer, der alle seine 'legitimen' Schüler in einen Bannkreis gefangenhält."* [great magician who held all of his

'legitimate' students captive within his sphere of influence.] My personal opinion
is that the formidably entangled relationships between these two outstanding
residents of two quite different Viennas have not yet begun to be unravelled,
beyond the most superficial attempts.

In what follows, I prefer not to scrutinize anew ground which is sure to
be amply familiar to all at home with Bühler's *Sprachtheorie* (1934), considered
by many his single most enduring contribution. Having been well analyzed by
Krug (1929) in its historical setting, this field-theory of language has, further,
been thoroughly probed in Kamp's recent (1977), remarkably helpful monograph.
Bühler's reputed chef d'oeuvre was meant to be read along with, or to amplify,
his brilliant anticipatory essay, purporting to constitute an axiomatization of
linguistic inquiry (1933) in terms of four *Grundsätze*, i.e., rudimentary principles
(a monograph republished 36 years later, in somewhat abridged form but with
an extensive new introduction and commentary by Elisabeth Ströker, all lately
rendered into English by Robert E. Innis). Both works revolve around the polestar
of his semiotically based "organic" model of language, but I shall rather focus
my observations upon some more neglected aspects of Bühler's notions about
Zeichenverkehr, or the exchange of messages, that I myself find most arresting,
as well as of abiding interest to the field. It will be appreciated that even this
topic cannot be presented exhaustively here; Bühler's semiotic, in all of its
implications, and particularly so in the context of his work as a whole, awaits
extended treatment much more detailed than has been accorded it in Günther's
(1968) aforementioned thesis, creditable but hardly analytic, and fabricated to
compare Bühler's *Zeichenbegriff* specifically with that of George H. Mead.

In Bühler's view, as is generally known, it was the representative function
that distinguished language from semiotic processes in the speechless creatures.
Taking his point of departure from the speech act, he defined the criterial attributes of language as the combined realization of *Kundgabe* (announcing), or the
expressive function, which correlates the sign with the message source, *Appell*
(eliciting), or the appeal function, which correlates the sign with the message
destination, and *Darstellung* (the representing function), which correlates the
sign with its context (or, to repeat, *Zeigfeld* and *Symbolfeld* combined). Object-
relationships are, in other words, represented as a result of the speaker's dec-
laration of what goes on in him, which evokes a psychological process in the
listener. It was apropos these three aspects of each linguistic utterance that
Trubetzkoy (1939:17–18)—Bühler's close associate at the University of Vienna,
who himself died some months prior to the westward exodus of his psychologist
friend—observed: "*Es ist das grosse Verdienst Karl Bühlers, diese scheinbar
einfache und trotzdem so lange übersehene Tatsache ins richtige Licht gestellt
zu haben.*" [It is the great service of Karl Bühler to have shed proper light on
this seemingly simple and yet so long overlooked fact.] It is amply clear by now
to most linguists that to make sense of an utterance implies taking into account
the cognitive structures in terms of which the addresser's and the addressee's

worlds are organized, and how language maps into those structures. (Bühler's theory on the functions of language as an attempt toward a psychological solution of linguistic problems is interestingly discussed by Pazuchin [1963].)

This tripartite scheme, or one very much like it, was already present in the works of Husserl and Porzig, but Bühler connected it further with the principle of "abstractive relevance," which implies that only certain features of the total situation (*Gegenstände und Sachverhalte*) participate in semiosis; (this distinction is akin, *mutatis mutandis*, to that which Peirce sometimes drew between "object" and "ground"). Bühler attributes a representing function to the verbal sign as the direct consequence of this relevance, a conclusion which he no doubt elaborated from Gomperz' reinterpretation of the scholastic formulation *aliquid stat pro aliquo*. The abstractiveness can simultaneously serve the three functions enumerated, although it is assumed that, in any given message, one of the factors will be predominant while the other two, depending upon the total envelope of the goal-directed speech act (*la parole*), are hierarchically subordinate. This, in turn, is also tripartite, consisting of the actor, the field of action, and the needs and opportunities of the actor. It is in this emphasis upon the strong social moment of the speech act that Bühler departs from Husserl's subjectivistic act theses, although the influence of the *Logische Untersuchungen*—to say nothing of the philosophical writings of Alexius Meinong (especially 1977)—is palpable throughout Bühler's works. Directly following Husserl, Bühler distinguished between meaning and reference. An expression with its meaning unaltered may refer to various objects, and *vice versa*: expressions with divergent meanings (e.g., *George Washington* and *The First President of the United States*) may refer to the identical object. To restate this in another way—and here I follow an exposition and critique by Laziczius (1942:22–23)—behind Bühler's argument lurks another divergency, that between "meaning" and "the intention to mean," which implies this four-way matrix (see Figure 1):

	I.	II.
1.	Sprechhandlung (parole)	Sprachwerk (ergon)
2.	Sprechakt (energeon)	Sprachgebilde (langue)

Figure 1.

The entries under I.—that is, the concrete verbal messages and the "speech act"—are both *subjektsbezogen*; those under II.—that is, the product of the sender and the linguistic structure—are both *subjektsentbunden*. Those under 2. comprise hierarchically superior manifestations in oppostition to those under 1. Laziczius was first to show, in a careful analysis (1939) of this, Bühler's so-called

Third Axiom, that what he presented here was, in the form of a vicious circle, a thesis, *"deren Unhaltbarkeit ganz offenbar ist,"* [whose untenableness is perfectly obvious,] a telling criticism one is compelled to uphold (although other readers may disagree with this reading).

Bühler's implied distinction between "meaning" and "the intention to mean" goes to the heart of homonymy. When I utter the isolated English vocable /baer/, whether I use it as a synonym for "to support," "naked," or a mammal of the family *Ursidae* depends on my "intention," which the addresee can only guess at with a certain probability, depending on how much verbal and/or nonverbal context is supplied. For me, as a speaker, homonymy does not exist, since I already know what I mean; but for my interlocutor intention comes into play, more accurately called by Jakobson (1971b:575) "the conditional probabilities of the context."

It is equally well known that Bühler's consequent classification of sign functions yields the symptom, dependent upon the source whose introspection it expresses on the surface, the signal, constituting a guide for the destinations's inner and outer behavior, and the symbol, which is contingent upon contextual circumstances. No doubt it should be underlined, before leaving this subject, that the list of functions postulated by Bühler, and hence his classification of signs, is regarded by modern scholarship as very far from comprehensive; this was realized as long ago as 1937 by Petr N. Bogatyrev (1971, Ch. 19), in his discussion of "the function of the structure of functions," meaning by this awkward phrasing to call attention to a semiotic function of a higher order, to wit, the concerted operation of the whole complex knot of functions—in short, a metafunction. This fruitful notion was eventually and variously extended to other domains, for instance, by the linguist Karl Horálek (1948), and eventually by others.

In Bühler's conception, language is an epiphenomenon to the phenomena of activity and, more specifically, expression. Accordingly, in several interesting respects his book on expressive behavior—originally published in 1933 and reprinted unchanged in 1968—can be read as his quintessential contribution to semiotics. Yet it is hardly ever cited in either the immense, sprawling Anglo-American literature on the subject, or, more surprisingly, in West European works on nonverbal communication—including particularly German—which, in this respect, appear to ignore their autochthonous heritage.

The study of expressive behavior has a composite, essentially dual, origin in psychodiagnostics and in rhetoric—quite specifically, that of Quintilian (Bühler, 1968:227–235). The point (*"tragende Behauptung"*) of Bühler's book is to demonstrate that the history of those aspects of behavior which manifest motivational states—emotional attitudes and moods, cognitive states, such as attention and concentration, activation states, such as arousal and fatigue, and quasi-personal attributes, in other words, matters that are functionally quite different—do nevertheless constitute, by and large, a *"sachgerechtes System."* These are all commonly classed together by the misleading term, "expressive behavior," (thus,

for example, verbal behavior and expressive movement), which, however—as
Ekman and his collaborators (1969), following David Efron's scintillating and,
in many ways, pioneering work (1941, 1972) have shown—involves multiple
categories of enormous complexity. The link between verbal behavior and expressive movement is on a quite abstract level, which is precisely semiotic. Thus,
for instance, Bühler, in discussing the ancient art of physiognomy—the art of
judging human character from facial features (including as a means of divination)—
tries to disentangle the distinctive characteristics of this art, and finds, among
half a dozen contributory impulses, Aristotelian semiotics, as this had actually
been denominated in and after the 18th century (1968:16, n. 2). as *"eine durch-
sichtige Anwendung antiker Semiotik"* [a clear application of Classical semiotics].
Bühler cites (1968:18) a striking judgment by Saint Gregory against the Emperor
Julian. In *Adversus Julianum*, Gregory anticipated from Julian's physiognomy,
based on the following theatrical depiction, his animosity toward Christians:

> He had a straight, rigid head firmly situated upon his shoulders, his gaze was unsteady,
> wild and confused; his gait was unsure, his feet always in motion; his nose displayed
> scorn, impertinence, and pride; his laughter was noisy; he was restless, unruly; always
> responded with a yes and no; he always posed bothersome questions, and seldom
> gave a decisive or timely answer.

Gregory constructs Julian's character out of seemingly random but distinctive
chunks—signifiers, if you like—to form a sort of personal mosaic, the tacit
inference being that his accretive procedure will correspond to a unitary *"Bezeich-
netes,"* i.e., that the traits will signify the Emperor's inner coherence. Bühler
correctly contends that the charge leveled against Classical semiotics as being
"atomisierend" (as opposed to structural), is more often than not inaccurate, and
lucidly explains what is actually involved in the course of its history. For instance,
he makes highly interesting observations about insights gained, especially by
Johann Jakob Engel, from the theater (Ch. 3), and notably goes on to develop,
with much understanding and sympathy, Charles Darwin's special frame of
reference fusing *"Gesamtausdrücke an Tieren und Mensch"* ["The entire repertoire of expression in animals and man"] (Ch. 6), general ethology with human
ethology, or, in other words, the integration of zoosemiotics into a comprehensive
science of signs. It was Engel who established the basic distinction between
representation and expression in semiotic concepts, and Bühler (1968:40) praises
this procedure as the *"axiomatische Angelpunkt"* in the apprehension of mimicry.
He insistently calls for an *"umfassend neuer Plan in diesen Dingen der beherrscht
und getragen sein müssen von einer vertieften sematologischen Axiomatik"* [a
comprehensive new plan of these matters which must be commanded (controlled)
and carried by a deepened sematological axiomatic] (p. 88).

In reviewing the *"Ausdruckslehre"* of Ludwig Klages (Ch. 9), Bühler brings
up the seldom discussed teleological question of the relationship of expressive
behavior to free will. The argument—anticipated to a degree by Martinak (1901:27,
80–83)—is as intricate as it is erudite, but what attracted me to it was Bühler's
recognition of *"ein altes Deutungsproblem der Semiotik"* [an old problem of

meaning and semiotics], and more: not only did this issue engage the so-called Aristotelian *physiognomonica*, but it was newly and vigorously embodied in Wundt's experimental analyses of curves displaying pulse and breathing rates, in short, components of polygraphic "lie detector" tests (the juridical admissibility of which is still being debated—cf. Lykken, 1974).

Bühler's summative chapter (Ch. 10) about the "present" state of the art, and particularly his vision of future researches in the area of *der Ausdrucksforschung*, clearly anticipates a unitary semiotic blueprint:

> *Was der Ausdruckstheorie heute am dringendsten nötig wäre, um dabei ein klares Wort mitsprechen zu können, wäre der Ausbau einer wohlfundierten Synsemantik. Die im Ausdruckslexikon isoliert, wie die Wissenschaft es tun muss, kodifizierten fruchtbaren Momente des mimischen Geschehens stehen, wo immer sie das Leben erzeugt, in einem semantischen Umfeld; ihre pathognomische und physiognomische Valenz ist kontextgetragen. Es ist sematologisch gesehen mit den Ausdruckssymptomen wie mit den Wörtern der Lautsprache oder wie mit den Bildwerten der Farbflecken auf einem Gemälde.* (pp. 213–214). [What the theory of expression most urgently needs today, in order to impart to it some clarity, would be the development of a well founded "synsemantics." As isolated in the lexicon of expressivity, as must be done by science, productive moments of mimic events stand whereever they engender life in a semantic field; their pathognomic and physiognomic valency is derived from the context. They must be viewed, sematologically, as manifested symptoms just as words are in speech or as are the pictorial values of specks of color on a painting.]

It is therefore very much to be regretted, that, on the one hand, what little Bühler scholarship exists has tended either to discount, or more often to entirely disregard, his masterful chronicle, embedded in theory that is at once consequential and fertile; and, on the other, that a multitude of investigators in this area, whether toiling in American and European workshops, are scarcely aware that they are standing on Bühler's broad shoulders. I am not exaggerating when I assert that I have never met a single student of nonverbal communication who confessed to even a passing acquaintance with the *Ausdruckstheorie*, itself a milestone the antecedents of which go back at least as far as Quintilian. While the book is listed, for example, (and exceptionally), in the bibliography by Desmond Morris and his collaborators (1979:278) *pro forma*, there is no evidence in their text that any of the authors have actually consulted it. This neglect is an especial embarrassment for German-language scholarship, and it should be promptly remedied.

Another facet of Bühler's concerns with the theory of signs consists of its foundations in corrective change, homeostasis, or cybernetics *avant la lettre*. Problems with control, recursiveness, and information pervade his writings, with consequences that were examined by Ungeheuer (1967) with respect to the *Sprachtheorie*, but that could be usefully extended to his *Zeichentheorie* as a whole, as well. Bühler was certainly familiar with the ideas of Eduard Pflüger and Claude Bernard, developed virtually at the same time in the late 1870s, with the latter's key observation that any animal's *milieu interne* was balanced, or self-correcting, but the homeostatic concept, later elaborated by Cannon, seemed to Bühler ultimately insufficient to fully describe human psychic life. All the same, I call attention to a remark of Bühler's (1969:188) that only came to light ten years after his death:

> Nach einer Belehrung aus der Geschichte wird das eigene konstruktive Denken den Milieubegriff erörtern und über ihn hinweg zu der entscheidenden Idee fortschreiten, die ich den Sachverständigen vorlege. Es ist die Annahme, dass ein echtes Signalwesen im Bereich der innerkörperlichen Regulationen enthalten ist. Die Frage, was das heisst, wird aber erst im erweiterten Rahmen des letzten biologischen Modellgedanken, den wir formulieren und durchsprechen, wieder aufgenommen und, soweit wir es vermögen, zu Ende gedacht.
>
> [Following a lesson from history, constructive thinking argues for the notion of milieu and by means of this reaches the decisive idea which I am proposing to the specialist. This is the postulate that a genuine signaling capacity exists in the realm of regulations within the body. The question of what this means must be reconsidered in the widened framework of the latest biological model of thought which we reformulate and debate again, and, as far as possible, think through to its conclusion.]

As he himself was very much aware (1968), the decisive elements for the semiotic alterity that Bühler drew between representation and expression were emphasized by certain English classical logicians, advanced substantially by Frege and, following him, Marty, Martinak, Husserl, Gomperz, and especially Meinong (see, in particular, 1977, his theory of suppositions, written in reaction to a pair of Brentano's theses). Bühler deemed all of these predecessors to have been in such agreement with himself, "that I scarcely need to add anything to what I have myself written on the subject since 1918." (Meinong's *Über Annahmen*, by the way, was itself an important statement about communication, and such other semiotic topics as the nature of play and of games, and the conformation of interference; to grasp Bühler's thought, you must understand Meinong's!) To the listing of these primary sources, one may well add Plato's *Kratylos*, Aristotle, Quintilian, and, above all, Kant, whose semiotic ideas are still consistently misunderstood and certainly underestimated, as well as Humboldt, Cassirer, and Saussure (Haller, 1959:154). In turn, Bühler's influence on Trubetzkoy, which began as far back as 1931, and the continuing "fruitful discussions" (Jakobson, 1971b:715) between the two, the results of which diffused among other members of the Prague School generally, are common knowledge. His Second Axiom, which asserted that verbal phenomena are to be subsumed under the vaster domain of semiotic phenomena, was widely accepted by linguists of the time. The sign function was subsumed by Bühler under his notion of representation, giving rise to yet another triad: objective meaning, the phonemic mark (or *Mal*), which is but a "relevant" component of the sign, and the "field signs" that emerge in and from the context (a notion elaborated, e.g., by Jost Trier). Representation is, of course, opposed by Bühler to expression, which, in the guise of the "indexical function," persistently reappears in the *Funktionslust* (as Bühler called it) of Prague School linguists and with particular force after Jakobson's "discovery" of Peirce.

3. OPEN QUESTIONS

In passing, it should also be noted that Bartley (1973:148) was of the opinion that, although Wittgenstein's name appears in no list of Bühler's students, it seems that he was "the most eminent of those who learned from" him (although, from time to time, Wittgenstein would also denounce Bühler as a charlatan). This notwithstanding, there are "striking similarities between some of Bühler's leading ideas and those of the later Wittgenstein" (Bartley, 1973:149).

Bühler's writings are characterized by a pedantic density which requires a modicum of familiarity on the part of the modern reader not merely with the history of modern psychology but with the entire stream of its philosophical pedigree. The dialectic movement underlying all of his work can, however, be reduced to rather simple terms. It was his cardinal thesis, rather facile but nonetheless subtly argued, that a correspondence exists between certain well-defined states—*Regelbewusstsein*, or "consciousness of rules"—and given logical structures. He failed, of course, to prove the existence of any such isomorphism—even partially—between the subject's logic (the business of the psychologist) and that of the logician (who casts his net far beyond the former). This idea, in turn, rested upon two radically antithetical terms: the inanimate, that is mindless, *pleroma* (Plenitude)—as Jung, following the Gnostics, called it—versus the animate, or *creatura*, with its inherent tension between two polarities: the creative nature of human thought, the spark (*pneuma*) emerging from and operating atop a biologically governed foundation. In the last analysis, the latter two belong in essence together, for the creative nature of the mind, and *vice versa*, and both are in fact separated from the ordinary material universe. In the summative words of Albert Wellek (1968:201), "His final conclusion was that what is essentially human—thought and reason, gestaltic and holistic experience—is independent of the machine, or the mechanical principle, and also independent to some extent of what is merely biological in the animal kingdom."

In view of this judgment, it may perhaps appear surprising that, toward the end of his career, Bühler wrote a posthumously published (1969) study on spatial orientation, or steering, in man and animals, under the main title, *Die Uhren der Lebewesen*. This little monograph deals with the problem of biological clocks and "cognitive maps," which Bühler always had assumed his fellow men and animals—whether a navigating Lindbergh or a bee flying long-distance— to experience alike. As his student, Konrad Lorenz, testified (1971:324), this assumption is not at all based on "analogization." In fact, he regarded it among Bühler's greatest achievements to have realized that this train of reflection is "a genuine *a priori* necessity of thought and experience," in brief, has the evidentiary force of a Bühlerian axiom. In fact, Bühler dubbed this the *Du-Evidenz*, the attestation adduced from the addressee. Lorenz (1971:268) is led by his teacher's arguments to opt, among several alternative approaches toward a resolution of the body–soul dichotomy, for the postulate of indubitable identity. While for the practical purposes of psychophysiological researches it may indeed be irrelevant which position one takes in regard to this apparent partition, our view of the relationship between the observer and the thing observed has, as I have tried to show elsewhere (Sebeok, 1979, Ch. 5), very far-reaching consequences for this kind of semiotic researches we engage in. To paraphrase one of Bühler's very last antemortem paragraphs (1969:157), such inquiries are "*reizvoll und brennend*" ["intriguing and urgent"], and certainly once again exceedingly timely.

I want finally to return to Egon Brunswik, whom, as I have already noted, Bühler at one time considered his *Hauptschüler*. Brunswik contributed a remarkable tract, on "The Conceptual Framework of Psychology," to the *International Encyclopedia of Unified Science*. Substantial portions of his discourse were devoted to an objective functional approach to psychology, cybernetics, and communication theory. Brunswik was, moreover, thoroughly familiar with Charles Morris' work on semiotics as well. The only two references to Bühler that I was able to detect in his piece are one in connection with the picture he presents of "nineteenth-century psychology as an intersection of introspectionist, elementarist, sensationist, and associationist tendencies," and another, concerning Bühler's early studies in color consistency (Brunswik, 1955:711, 728). It remains to be determined whether Bühler—certainly a transitional figure in the history of semiotic studies, although, to be sure, a scholar, richly endowed with technical virtuosity—will be promoted to more than an outstanding footnote when the annals of this wide-ranging field are at last set forth.

REFERENCES

Bartley, William Warren, III (1973). *Wittgenstein*. Philadelphia: J. B. Lippincott.

Blumenthal, Arthur L. (1974). "An Historical View of Psycholinguistics." In *Current Trends in Linguistics: Linguistics, and Adjacent Arts and Sciences*, Thomas A. Sebeok (ed.), 12:1105–1134. The Hague: Mouton.

Bogatyrev, Petr (1971). *The Functions of Folk Costume in Moravian Slovakia*. The Hague: Mouton.

Brunswik, Egon (1929). "Prinzipienfragen der Gestalttheorie." In Brunswik *et al.*, *Beiträge zur Problemgeschichte der Psychologie: Festschrift zu Karl Bühler's 50 Geburtstag 1929*. Jena: Gustav Fischer, pp. 78–149.

Brunswik, Egon (1955 [1952]). "The Conceptual Framework of Psychology." In *International Encyclopedia of Unified Science*, Otto Neurath, Rudolf Carnap, and Charles Morris (eds.), 1:10:655–760.

Brunswik, Egon, *et al.*, eds. (1929). *Beiträge zur Problemgeschichte der Psychologie: Festschrift zu Karl Bühler's 50 Geburtstag*. Jena: Gustav Fischer.

Bühler, Charlotte (1965). "Die Wiener Psychologische Schule in der Emigration." In *Psychologische Rundschau*, 16:187–196.

Bühler, Charlotte *z.*nd Hetzer, Hildegard (1929). "Zur Geschichte der Kinderpsychologie." In Brunswik *et al.*, 1929:204–224.

Bühler, Karl (1905–08). "Tatsachen und Probleme zu einer Psychologie der Denkvorgänge." *Archiv für die gesamte Psychologie*, 9:297–365 (1907); 12:1–23, 24–92 (1908).

Bühler, Karl (1918). *Die geistige Entwicklung des Kindes*. Jena: Gustav Fischer.

Bühler, Karl (1927). *Die Krise der Psychologie*. Jena: Gustav Fischer.

Bühler, Karl (1933). "Die Axiomatik der Sprachwissenschaften." *Kantstudien*, 38:19–90.

Bühler, Karl (1934 [1965²]). *"Sprachtheorie: Die Darstellungsfunktion der Sprache."* Stuttgart: Gustav Fischer.

Bühler, Karl (1968² [1934]). *Ausdruckstheorie: Das System an der Gesichte aufgezeigt*. Stuttgart: Gustav Fischer.

Bühler, Karl (1969). *Die Uhren der Lebewesen: Studien zur Theorie der Raumzeitlichen Orientierung*. In *Österreichische Akademie der Wissenschaften, Philosophisch-Historische Klasse, Sitzungsberichte*, 265:3:10:73–160. Vienna: Hermann Böhlaus Nachf.

Efron, David (1972 [1941]). *Gesture, Race and Culture*. The Hague: Mouton.

Ekman, Paul and Friesen, Wallace V. (1969). "The Repertoire of Nonverbal Behavior: Categories, Origins, Usage, and Coding." *Semiotica*, 1:49–98.

Garvin, Paul L. (1964). "Note." *Language*, 40:633–635.

Garvin, Paul L. (1966). "Karl Bühler's Contribution to the Theory of Linguistics." *Journal of General Psychology*, 75:212–215.

Gomperz, Heinrich (1908). *Weltanschauungslehre 2/1: Einleitung und Semasiologie*. Jena: E. Diederichs.

Günther, Arnold Fritz (1968). "Der Zeichenbegriff bei K. Bühler und G. H. Mead." In *Forschungsbericht* 68:2/4, Institut für Phonetik und Kommunikationsforschung der Universität Bonn. Hamburg: Helmut Buske.

Haller, Rudolf (1959). "Das Zeichen und die Zeichenlehre in der Philosophie der Neuzeit." *Archiv für Begriffsgeschichte*, 4:113–157.

Hofalek, Karel (1948). "La fonction de la 'structure des fonctions' de la langue." *Recueil Linguistique de Bratislava*, 1:39–43.

Jakobson, Roman (1963). "Parts and Wholes in Language." In: *Parts and Wholes*, Daniel Lerner (ed.), New York: The Free Press of Glencoe, pp. 157–162.

Jakobson, Roman (1971a). *Selected Writings I: Phonological Studies*. The Hague: Mouton.

Jakobson, Roman (1971b). *Selected Writings II: Word and Language*. The Hague: Mouton.

Janik, Allan and Toulmin, Stephen (1973). *Wittgenstein's Vienna*. London: Weidenfeld and Nicolson.

Kamp, Rudolf (1977). *Axiomatische Sprachtheorie: Wissenschaftstheoretische Untersuchungen zum Konstutionsproblem der Einzelwissenschaften am Beispiel der Sprachwissenschafttheorie chattheorie Karl Bühlers*. Berlin: Duncker & Humboldt.

Krug, Josef (1929). "Zur Sprachtheorie." In Egon Brunswik *et al.*, *Beiträge sur Problemgeschichte der Psychologie: Festschrift zu Karl Bühler's 50 Geburtstag*. Jena: G. Fischer, pp. 225–258.

Laziczius, Julius von (1939). Das sogenannte dritte Axiom der Sprachwissenchaft. *Acta Linguistica* 1:162–167. Reprinted in Thomas A. Sebeok, *Selected Writings of Gyula Laziczius*, 64–70. The Hague: Mouton.

Laziczius, Julius von (1942). *Általános nyelvészet: alapelvek és módszertani kérdések*. Budapest: Magyar Tudományos Akadémia.

Lebzeltern, Gustav (1969). "Karl Bühler—Leben und Werk." In *Österreichische Akademie der Wissenschaften, Philosophisch-Historische Klasse, Sitzungsberichte*, 265:3:10:7–70. Vienna: Böhlaus Nachf.

Lieberman, David A. (1979). "Behaviorism and the Mind: A (Limited) Call for a Return to Introspection." *American Psychologist*, 34:319–333.

Lorenz, Konrad (1971). *Studies in Animal and Human Behaviour 2*. Cambridge: Harvard University Press.

Lykken, David T. (1974). "Psychology and the Lie Detector Industry." *American Psychologist*, 29:725–739.

Martinak, Eduard (1901). *Psychologische Untersuchungen zur Bedeutungslehre*. Leipzig: Johann Amrosius Barth.

Meinong, Alexius (1977). *Über Annahmen*, Rudolf Haller (ed). Graz: Akademische Druck- und Verlagsanstalt.

Miller, Eugene F. (1979). "Hume's Reduction of Cause to Sign." *The New Scholasticism*, 53:42–75.

Morris, Desmond, Collett, Peter, Marsh, Peter, and O'Shaughnessy, Marie (1979). *Gestures: Their Origins and Distribution*. New York: Stein & Day.

Pazuchin, Roscislaw V. (1963). "Učenie K.Bjulera o funkcijach jazyka kak popytka psiochologičeskogo resenija linvističeskich problem." *Voprosy Jazykoznanija*, 5:94–103.

Rapaport, David (ed.) (1951). *Organization and Pathology of Thought: Selected Sources*. New York: Columbia University Press.

Sebeok, Thomas A., ed. (1960). *Style in Language*. Cambridge: The Technology Press of the Massachusetts Institute of Technology.

Sebeok, Thomas A. (1979). *The Sign & Its Masters*. Austin: University of Texas Press.

Smart, Benjamin H. (1831). *Outline of Sematology*. London: John Richardson.

Steiner, George (1979). "Wien, Wien, Nur Du Allein." *The New Yorker*, June 25, 101–105.

Trubetzkoy, Nikolaj Sergeevič (1939). *Grundzüge der Phonologie*. (Travaux du Cercle Linguistique de Prague 7.) Prague.

Ungeheuer, Gerold (1967). Die kybernetische Grundlage der Sprachtheorie von Karl Bühler. In *To Honor Roman Jakobson: Essays On the Occasion of His 70th Birthday* 3:2067–2086.

Wellek, Albert (1959). "Ein Dritteljahrhundert nach Bühlers 'Krise der Psychologie.' " *Zeitschrift für Experimentelle und Angewandte Psychologie*, 6/1:109–117.

Wellek, Albert (1968). "Karl Bühler." *International Encyclopedia of the Social Sciences*, 2:199–202.

CHAPTER 7

The Sign Theory of Jakob von Uexküll

THURE VON UEXKÜLL

1. PERSONAL HISTORY AND FIELD OF RESEARCH

Jakob von Uexküll was born in Keblas, Estonia in 1864. After completing his studies in zoology at Dorpat (now Tartu, Estonia) he worked at the Institute of Physiology of the University of Heidelberg and at the Zoological Center in Naples. In 1907 he was given an honorary doctorate by the University of Heidelberg for his studies in the field of muscular physiology. His later work was devoted to the problem of how living beings subjectively perceive their environment and how this perception determines their behavior. He developed a specific method which he termed "Umwelt-research." In 1926 Uexküll founded the Institute of Umwelt-Research at the University of Hamburg. He died on the island of Capri, Italy in 1944.

Uexküll's field of research was the behavior of living organisms and their interaction as cells and organs in the body or as subjects within families, groups, and communities. He is recognized as one of the founders of behavioral physiology (ethology) later to be further developed, notably by Lorenz and Tinbergen.[1]

Of particular interest to Uexküll was the fact that signs are of prime importance in all aspects of life processes. He developed an original and integrated theory of sign processes, which was, however—and still is—open to misinterpretation, since it cannot be classed among any of the established sciences. Thus it concerns itself neither with physiology—even behavioral physiology, although the latter comes close to his theory in many aspects—nor with psychology, although subjects and their perceptual and behavioral activities are of central importance to it. Moreover, it cannot be placed within those boundaries which separate the human sciences (*Geisteswissenschaften*) from the natural

THURE VON UEXKÜLL • Professor Emeritus of Internal Medicine and Psychosomatics, University of Ulm, Ulm, West Germany.

sciences (*Naturwissenschaften*). Uexküll himself referred to his field of research as "biology," though he did not use the term in the narrowly defined sense applied to it today, but understood it as the science of the life of plants, animals, and human beings. Many misinterpretations can be overcome if his theory is classified as "general semiotics." Yet at the same time it becomes obvious that general semiotics also falls into an area between the boundaries of the established disciplines. A science which embraces the natural sign systems alongside and before the human sign systems we call "language" must at the same time break down the traditional division between the human sciences and the natural sciences. However, the attempt to classify Jakob von Uexküll's theory as general semiotics also presents us with some difficulties. As he knew neither Peirce nor Saussure and did not use their terminology, his theory cannot easily be accommodated to any of the known semiotic schools of thought.[2] Thus it long remained unknown to those semioticians who trace their origins to linguistics. Sebeok (1979: 187–215) was the first to recognize Uexküll's contribution to general semiotics.

The differences in terminology, however, are not to be regarded simply as a source of difficulty; they may also prove helpful in shedding light on those points where the various semiotic theories diverse.

2. WHAT IS UMWELT RESEARCH?

The negative conclusion that Umwelt-research is neither psychology, nor physiology (not even behavioral physiology), nor biology (if confined to molecular biology) must, however, be further supplemented: In many dictionaries of philosophy the Umwelt theory is described as neo-vitalism, and thereby labeled as some kind of a romantic philosophy of nature. This leads to further misunderstandings, because we are concerned with research here, empirical research which, though differing from the so-called exact sciences, does have its own presuppositions, methodology, and objectives.[3] I shall briefly attempt to outline these three points:

1. *The presupposition* on which Uexküll's theory is based reverses the classification of reality held in the traditional philosophy of science: Reality, to which all is subjected and from which everything is deduced, is not to be found "outside," in infinite space, which has neither beginning nor end, and which is filled with a nebulous cloud of elementary particles; nor is it to be found "inside," within ourselves and the indistinct, distorted images of this external world created by our mind. Reality manifests itself in those worlds—described by Uexküll as Umwelten (subjective-self-worlds) with which sense perception surrounds all living beings like a bubble—clearly delineated but invisible to outside observers. These "subjective—self-world bubbles" like Leibniz's monads, are the elements of reality which form themselves into a synthesis of all subjects and their subjective self-worlds at the same time undergoing constant changes in harmony

with one another. This ultimate reality—Uexküll uses the term *Natur*—which lies beyond and behind the nature conceived of by physicists, chemists, and microbiologists, reveals itself through signs. These signs are therefore the only true reality; and the rules and laws under which the signs and sign processes communicate themselves to our mind (*Gemüt*) are the only true laws of nature.

"As the activity of the mind is the only aspect of nature immediately known to us, its laws are the only ones which may rightly be called laws of nature." (Jakob von Uexküll, 1973: 40)[4]

Since Uexküll believed that this activity of the mind consists in the reception and decoding of signs, the mind—in the final analysis—is an organ created by nature to perceive nature. Nature may be compared to a composer who listens to his own works played on an instrument of his own construction. This results in a strangely reciprocal relationship between nature, which has created man, and man, who not only in his art and science, but also in his experiental universe, has created nature.

2. *The approach of Umwelt-research*, which aims to reconstruct creative nature's "process of creating," can be described as "participatory observation," if the terms *participation* (Teilnahme) and *observation* (Beobachtung) are defined more clearly: Observation means first of all ascertaining which of those signs registered by the observer in his own experiential world are also received by the living being under observation. This requires a careful analysis of the sensory organs (receptors) of the organism in question. After this is accomplished, it is possible to observe how the organism proceeds to decode the signs it has received. Participation, therefore, signifies the reconstruction of the *Umwelt* ("surrounding-world") of another organism, or—after having ascertained the signs which the organism can receive as well as the codes it uses to interpret them—the sharing of the decoding processes which occur during its behavioral activities. Participation is not, therefore, "sympathetic understanding" (*Einfühlen*), and depth psychology might well profit from this semiotic analysis in its use of the term *empathy*. Uexküll repeatedly emphasized that, where empathy is concerned, the approach of psychology runs counter to the methods of biology (1973:167).

3. *The objective of Umwelt-research* is to develop a theory of nature's composition, or to reconstruct the score to the "symphony of meanings" that nature composes out of the innumerable surrounding-worlds (*Umwelten*) and plays, as it were, on a gigantic keyboard, of which our life and our surrounding-world is but one key (1970b, 176).

3. UMWELT RESEARCH AND LINGUISTICS

The formula of the reciprocal relationship between man, who must, in his self-world, create nature, and nature, which has brought forth the human species, requires us to consider the relationship between sign processes in nature and in language. Uexküll was primarily interested in one particular aspect of the relationship between Umwelt-research and linguistics, namely the question of the extent to which words, sentences, or numbers[5] in human language may have meaning as signs in animal surrounding-worlds.[6] The works of Peirce, Saussure, Levi-Strauss *et al.*, with which Uexküll was not familiar, call, however, for a more ·fundamental consideration, since the puzzling formula of reciprocities which expresses the relation between nature and man, bears a surprising analogy to the formula developed in linguistic research to explain the relationship between language and man, and which states that while man has created language, language has created man.

Thus, we are faced with the basic problem of how to interpret this analogy between language and nature, between human and biological sign systems or between linguistic laws and the laws of nature. Are these similarities only coincidental and of a purely superficial kind? Is the analogy merely the result of a romantic, anthropomorphic interpretation of nature? Or are we confronted here with a case of homomorphy, i.e. a fundamental principle which recurs on different levels of complexity, in different ways, yet always in basically the same form—a principle which perhaps involves a hidden genetic correlation?

Accepting this last alternative, Saussure's distinction between *langue* and *parole* (or the more general distinction between code and message) may be viewed as an illustration of Uexküll's own distinction between an active plan and a concrete living phenomenon. When viewed together, *langue*, or code, is the synchronic system underlying the *parole*, or message, in whose spoken words and sentences it is concretely manifested for discursive observation. *Langue* has no other existence than in the step-by-step sequence of speech, but it determines each of these steps. In order to learn about the laws that govern the system our speech is based on, it is necessary to observe the *parole*, the actual spoken language of the people. This is analogous to Uexküll's "plan.": "Our mind (*Gemüt*) possesses an inner plan that is revealed only when it is in action. Therefore, the mind must be observed when it is applying itself to the reception and processing of impressions" (1973:10) And: "*Gestalt* (form) is never anything else than the product of a plan within indifferent matter—matter which could have taken shape in some other form." (1973:183).

Both the concept of speech, or code, and the concept of the plan of nature look like a final resolution of the age-old question of which came first, the chicken or the egg: as concrete phenomenona following one after the other, the chicken and the egg are only the manifestation of an underlying plan or system which determines each phase of development.

However, this interpretation of the analogy between the developmental laws that govern the human and the natural sciences is immediately subject to serious objection. The laws of speech are acquired[7] and practiced by living subjects who are adequately equipped with a capacity which is both biological and intellectual—consisting of brain *and* memory, the larynx *and* the ability to vocalize—and who have at their disposal the historical past of the culture in which their language has developed. All these qualities are lacking in the developmental laws upon which metabolism and cell differentiation in the development of living beings, as well as their reactions to stimuli, are assumed to be based. Is it therefore advisable to risk, with the kind of interpretation that models the laws of nature up on the laws of language, an anthropomorphic distortion of the laws of natural sciences, which regulate the behavior of molecules, membranes, and diffusion processes?

4. THE PROBLEM OF THE SIGN-RECEIVER, THE LAW OF "SPECIFIC LIFE-ENERGY," AND THE "ELEMENTARY SELF"

Uexküll rejects this objection as invalid, because it might just as well be raised against the existence of laws in the human/social sciences. No one can, in fact, contend that language invalidates the laws of physics, chemistry, and the molecular biology of air waves, the processes of the inner ear or the auditory nerve, etc. These natural laws, however, are insufficient for understanding the process of education within the scope of human culture. Here the structural laws of linguistics, which apply to living people and are concerned with significant and meaningful sign processes—not, or at least not only, with supposed physical and biochemical processes as in the field of biology—can be an aid in orientation. Two observations are essential at this point to the understanding of the Umwelt-theory:

1. The Umwelt-theory postulates that the laws of the natural sciences are not laws of nature, but rules which we derive for our own objectives from our confrontation with natural phenomena. In saying this, however, there is no attempt to deny their validity; it is only being maintained that a consideration of their validity must also include the contributions of man's perceptual organization, his intention, and his efforts toward abstraction.
2. The Umwelt-theory draws the line not between nature and man, but between animate and inanimate nature. The structural laws which it postulates as nature-plans, and which are analogous to the structural laws of linguistics,[8] are applicable only to living organisms.

"The ultimate aim in physiology . . . is to reduce biological processes to problems of a physical and chemical nature . . . The fundamental activities of tissue, e.g. the contraction of muscles, . . . serve as the basis from which physiology, by way of electrical or osmotic processes, etc., seeks to reduce the manifestations of life to the laws of inorganic matter.

Biology has pursued precisely the opposite path. . . . Its constituents are . . . biological elements [whose interaction it takes as the basis for understanding the life of an organism as a whole]. Therefore, in biology the question of the relationship between animate and inanimate is of no consequence." (1902:229)

The line drawn between organic and inorganic nature is not determined on the basis of random distinctive features, such as chemical makeup, size, complexity, or the form of the structure in question, but on the basis of a characteristic quality which can first be observed among living things and which is inherent even in the simplest forms of life, the protozoans. This inherent characteristic is the ability of an organism to react to stimuli, not just in a causal-mechanical way, but with its own specific reaction. From this point of view, all living organisms are considered autonomous, while the inorganic, including the tools and machines we use, remain heteronomous. This characteristic, which clearly and definitely marks the difference between the organic and inorganic, was, as Uexküll has emphasized, first described by Johannes Peter Mueller (1801–1858), a contemporary of Goethe:

> Sense impression is not the transmission to consciousness, of a quality or condition of external objects, but rather the transmission of a quality or condition in a sensory nerve, caused by external factors. These qualities, differing in the diverse sensory nerves, are called sensory energies. (1840:254)

In reference to the above statement Uexküll writes: "One hundred years ago Johannes Mueller evolved the theory—which has survived only as a mere torso in contemporary physiology that the behavior of every organic substance is fundamentally different from that of inorganic matter extended in space. A particular inorganic object, whether it consists only of a number of unrelated parts or whether it is a well-made machine based on a thoroughly coordinated plan, reacts toward the external world in a manner distinctly different from organisms and organs which are made up of living cells, because the living cell is autonomous and not heteronomous.

If a machine, for example an automobile, is subjected to external influences of a chemical or physical nature, it only reacts as a coordinated object and can only be set in motion if a gear or pedal is engaged. Under all other circumstances it reacts as an accumulation of metal; its parts move only when pushed, become warm only when heated, and rust when acids are poured onto them.

Mueller pointed out that a muscle reacts in a substantially different fashion. Never does it respond to any external impulse, be it of a mechanical, electrical or chemical nature, like a mass of separate parts, but always as a whole—as a muscle—with a contraction. Mueller called this "specific energy." At that time the word *energy* denoted vital energy, i.e. an immaterial factor that has nothing in common with physical energy. Furthermore, specific energy is not subject to the law of the conservation of energy which was postulated at a much later date. It could also be described as "holistic energy"—an energy that is non-transferable." (1931:208f.)

This means that all living organisms, including cells, behave as subjects, responding only to signs and—for as long as they live—not to causal impulses.[9]

Since all living organisms are of cellular composition, both physical development and the confrontation with the environment in its later life can only be understood as responses to signs. All living organisms, as one can also put it, code physical and chemical stimuli as signs.

In emphasizing the autonomy of each and every living organism, another conclusion may be drawn: A sign is never found alone, but always as part of a circular process in which a receptor receives stimuli, codes them as signs, and responds to them as such. The most elementary sign process, the "semiotic atom,"[10] so to speak, is therefore that code which governs the life of the cell. The cell furnishes every influence it responds to with a specific meaning, or translates it into its own specific code and then reacts with a specific response. This is the first instance in nature where a quality which we describe by the term "self" appears, namely the ability of an organism to differentiate between self and non-self and to bring them into relation.

The most primitive sign relationship—self and non-self—(in which each is indicative of the other) is also the most universal. In the course of the evolution of life this sign-relationship differentiates between the non-self as prey, food, enemy, etc., corresponding to the differentiation of the self as hunter, the hungry self, the threatened self, etc. The basis of all these relationships is the self and the non-self (see 9.2). Johannes Mueller's "specific energy" is what defines (in semiotic terminology) the "elementary self."

As soon as we realize that Umwelt-research is the exploration of sign processes that govern the behavior of living subjects, beginning at the cellular level, we can see that there does exist a real analogy between the structural laws of linguistics and biology, which, in the final analysis, abolishes the distinction betw· n the human and the natural sciences. If science is understood as the attempt to identify the factors which determine the behavior of phenomena in relation to each other and toward man, then Dilthey's famous distinction is no longer valid for a theory of signs. "Explaining" (*Erklären*), which according to Dilthey is restricted to the natural sciences, becomes identical with "understanding" (*Verstehen*), which he reserved for the human sciences.

Thus, we can compare terms such as system, structure, unit, code, etc., which have been taken from linguistics, to the terminology of the Umwelt-theory, because the linguistic terms seem to illustrate the concepts of the Umwelt theory in a more precise manner than do the illustrations drawn from music, which Uexküll favored.[11]

5. THE "PRIVATE" NATURE OF SIGNS

There is one more characteristic quality of sign processes that must be considered, which is also of fundamental importance to an understanding not only of the Umwelt-theory, but also of every other theory of signs.

It may be said that every sign is, in the strictest sense of the word, "private," or, in other words, there is no such thing as an objective sign. There are only sign systems with the same structure and the same code for different receivers. This conclusion is the counterpart to the autonomy of living organisms. What each sign means to the subject as a receiver is registered only by the subject itself or, as Uexküll has stated: "A living cell possesses its own ego-quality (*Ichton*)." (1931:209)

This conclusion has far-reaching consequences that can be reduced to a common denominator: the inevitability of self-experience if one understands by this the conclusion—which in various ways and degrees has agitated all philosophers—that in everything experienced, we are simultaneously experiencing ourselves, Uexküll has confronted this fundamental problem with reference to Kant. He writes:

> Kant categorically rejected the idea of the naive observer with his thirst for knowledge of the physical forms around him, studying and comparing their effects upon one another. Examine first what you yourself as a subject bring into nature before you start to examine the nature of things that surround you. Examine your own perception before you make a critical interpretation of what you have examined!

Kant now taught him that time and space are not objects that can be removed from the mass of other objects to be examined and touched by themselves, but that they are forms of our perception. From the very moment we turn our interest to the study of nature, we necessarily include time and space in our observation as a flexible framework, which completely encompasses all the phenomena present in each case, and in which all things—large and small, far and near, past and future—are set.

The qualities of all things, as Kant further states, are not their own, but of our own projected perception. The range of qualities present in all things extends just so far and no farthur than the range of our sensations." (1947:6f)

In other words, what we experience of nature is cloaked under the guise of our self-perception, or:

> All reality is a subjective appearance. This must form the major fundamental understanding in biology as well . . . With this recognition we are standing on the solid ground which was uniquely prepared by Kant to support the edifice of all the natural sciences. Kant has placed the subject called man in opposition to the objects, and has outlined the basic principles according to which the objects are formed in our mind.
>
> The task of biology is to expand the result of Kant's research along two lines: (1) To consider the role of our body, particularly our perceptual organs and the central nervous system and (2) to study the relationship of other subjects (animals) to their objects. (1973:9f.)

With these two imperatives Uexküll defines the scope of his theory of signs. The theory proceeds on the assumption that we must first examine the "primary receiver" of signs, that is, ourselves and our minds, and that only then can we place other subjects, especially animals, in the role of sign receivers.

6.   THE COMPOSITION OF MAN'S EXPERIENTIAL UNIVERSE SEEN AS A COMPOSITION OF SIGN PROCESSES

6.1.   Preliminary Note

The basic concept that life on the elementary level is sustained by cell subjects which, as autonomous units, transpose every impulse into subjective (private) signs—their ego-qualities—and which react only to these signs, requires investigation on two levels:

1. It requires the development of a new "anatomy" with which to clarify how higher forms of life with complex tasks are formed from the amalgamation of cell subjects and their elementary sign processes. This "anatomy" must "dissect" first the subjective Umwelt of the researcher, ascertaining how it is constructed from the elementary processes (the sign processes) of the cells and organs of his body.

2. It requires a description of how the "objective outer world" in which we observe ourselves and other living things develops from our subjective (private) universe—our Umwelt. This means, in other words, how the objective outer world is derived as an abstraction from our subjective universe. This problem can only be solved by an epistemological biology or a biological epistemology. This means biology and epistemology are joined together as one field of research.[8]

Only when this twofold problem has been solved is it possible to undertake the actual task of Umwelt research: To construct, from the knowledge gained about the structure of our human experiential universe, a model for the reconstruction of the experiential universes of other living things (their Umwelten).

The analysis of the human mind as a sign-receiver and the way it works in the construction of our experiential universe exhibits a structure or "anatomy" which is most impressive in its analogy to the structure of language: Just as language has signs of different integrational levels (phonemes, words, sentences, etc.), so the analysis of our experiential universe brings to light different levels, on each of which sign processes of varying complexity may be studied. On each of these levels the signs also reveal surprising analogies to the signs in human language.

6.2.   The Elementary Processes of Signs

Two classes of sign processes belong to the elementary level: the "organizing signs" and the "content signs." Both are conveyed from specific sensory cells as receptors.

The organizing signs, which will be considered first, may be described as the ego-qualities of cells, found either as tactile cells in the skin on the surface of our body or in the eye as specific perceptive cells in the retina. They respond to every stimulus with *local signs*, which we perceive as "positions" in our subjective universe. An organizing framework is thereby formed through a mosaic of positions.

When two tactile cells in the skin or perceptive cells in the retina are stimulated successively in such a way that the "ego-quality" of the first cell is diminishing while that of the second is increasing, then a new sign is created: The *directional sign* which connects two positions through a movement. Local signs and directional signs can only produce a two-dimensional surface of positions. Only through the active intervention of muscular activity which mobilizes the surface of the skin (primarily of the hands and arms) with its tactile cells, or which effects a change in the curvature of the optical lense, is a shift toward depth, and thereby into the third dimension, brought about.

It is still necessary, therefore, to be informed about the voluntary impulses which account for muscular activity. The signs responsible for this feedback are the *effector signs*, which are produced in the intention of muscular activity— that is, before the movement has even begun. What we are dealing with here is the feedback (to the periphery of the receptor) of the nerve-action current, which Erich von Holst and Horst Mittelstaedt (1950), on the basis of their neurophysiological test results, described as the re-afference principle. The effector signs are responsible not only for the third dimension of space, but also for the ability to distinguish between our own movements and the movements of other things. The significance of this type of feedback in the construction of a central control system, which forms the basis for such phenomena as the will, consciousness, and ego-formation, is noted here only in passing. Their significance for general semiotics, however, cannot be overestimated.

Within the scope of the Umwelt-theory a different aspect of the effector signs is emphasized, namely the significance of the apriority of space. These signs, resulting from the feedback of the intention of will, function independently of external influence (1973:38). This fact explains the ability of the mind to develop a concept of space which lends stability and order to our experiential universe without the aid of external experience. Space is hereby revealed as a "major component in our sensory organization and, as such, is a true law of nature, having both subjective and objective validity" (1973:39)

The same is true of time, whose elementary sign manifests itself as a "moment." However, in contrast to the elementary signs that form space, no success has as yet been achieved in the search for specific cell subjects that would act as mediators. Moments are therefore conceived of as signs of the synthetic, serially phased functioning of the mind, and apperception is regarded as a life process (1973:70).

Local signs, directional signs, and effector signs, together with time signs are the constituents of time and space in our experiential universe. As they impart to this universe the framework into which all other signs are set in the form of content, they are called *organizing signs*. These signs are the "organizers of the world" (1973: 111).

The *signs of content*, color, sound, smell, etc., which we will now consider, may also be classified as specific ego-qualities of certain cell-subjects. In the higher forms of life these take shape as the receptors in the sensory organs (eyes, ears, nose, etc.).

Within the framework of the complex organization of the human body, the sensory cells are linked, by nerves, to specific areas of the brain. Thus their ego-qualities depend on the functioning of a chain of coding and decoding processes in successively activated cell subjects. However, the cell subjects in the periphery of the sensory organs not only stand at the beginning of these processes, they themselves also initiate them through their own subjective reactions to stimuli. It is therefore, correct to assume that they are the elementary components of our sensory organization and that their ego-qualities are the elementary sign processes.

6.3. The Codes of the Elementary Sign Processes

We will now turn our attention to the analogies between the laws inherent in linguistics and those on the level of elementary signs. On this level, three aspects can already be clearly noticed, which are surprisingly similar to the aspects that Charles Morris identified in signs. In my opinion it is of particular interest to general semiotics that two researchers who, without knowledge of each other, developed a concept of the sign from totally different starting points, with altogether different objectives, and working in completely different fields, have discovered similar inherent laws.

Charles Morris (1938) distinguished between the syntactic, the semantic, and the pragmatic aspects of signs. These three aspects can also be found in Uexküll's elementary sign processes:

1. *The syntactic aspect*, which refers to the relationship of signs to one another, is revealed in the fact that all elementary signs exhibit a highly remarkable system of affinity (1973: 13). There is, for example, a system of affinity in the scale of color quality that assures that each color has a definite relationship to other colors. This system of affinity may be graphically illustrated as a hexagon or a chromatic circle. The system of affinity for sound may be illustrated by tonal scales, the one for odor by aroma scales. This same principle applies to heat, degrees of hardness, taste, etc.

These systems of affinity—and this is what makes them so fascinating—are always perceived unconsciously whenever a single sign appears. When we perceive the color red we always "see" that it is not green, yellow, or blue, but in an organizational relationship to all colors not at the moment visible. We also see the intensity of a red color on the invisible scale which grades from pale pink to the most intense red. The same applies to sound: In each individual tone heard, the complete scale of all other tones and the gradations of their intensity resonate as it were silently. This same principle applies to the perception of heat, odor, touch, and taste.

When we perceive a single sign, therefore, we are unconsciously perceiving the complete organizational system of all signs that belong to that particular system. This fact implies (in linguistic terminology) that the discursive sequence of individual signs (seen, in speaking, as the chronological order of words) is always embedded in the syntagmatic background of the system and its structure, or shows that the form (*Gestalt*) of the system, only synoptically comprehensible, is yet what determines, though unconsciously, the sequential process of the signs. Just as the game of chess (to use Saussure's example), which is only comprehensible as a system of abstract rules and relationships synoptically, governs every move, in the discursive sequence of an actual game, so, analogously, the abstract systems of the individual sensory spheres, with their organizational relationships, have the power to create in the discursive sequence of our concrete perception colors, odors, as well as the signs of touch and taste. To this creative power, which Saussure describes in language as *langue*, Uexküll applies the term *plan* in the field of biology. Each individual sign is only part of the hidden wholeness or systematic arrangement of a sign system comparable to the tip of an iceberg which projects above the surface of the sea (Hawkes, 1977).[12]

2. The *semantic aspect* of these laws, or this systematic arrangement, which reveal themselves in the organizational relationships, can be observed in the ability of the system to define itself and its elements, in an independent and, as it were, completely arbitrary manner. Each color—with respect to its quality, that is, its semantic meaning (of red, yellow, green, or blue)—is defined only on the basis of its relationship to the integrated system of the color chart. The same applies to all other sensory signs: tones, where quality of meaning is determined by the tonal scale; heat, where the quality of meaning is determined by the temperature scale; etc.

Perceived unconsciously and simultaneously with each individual sign, this systematic arrangement of all signs belonging to the same category (their structure of meaning) has an interesting consequence for the organizing signs: Through each local sign corresponding to a touch of the skin or the stimulation of a point on the retina, we "know" where to localize it in the space that surrounds us and of which our body is a part; we know, that is, whether it is above or beneath, to the right or to the left, ahead or behind. This means nothing less than the fact that the active plan or code, *space*, is constantly present in our mind as the semantic system of local signs. The structure of this space is not deduced from any concrete experience: it is *a priori* (1973:38f.). The same potential organization which we cannot escape—however hard we try—dwells in our mind as *time*. Time is the semantic system of the moment signs which are always arranged on a scale where a "present" is located in between a past and a future.

Semantic systems for the content signs, and semantic systems for the organizing signs with their law-governed structures, are abstract patterns. However, they produce the concrete signs which become meaningful only as elements of their semantic system, that is, only through the semantic system are the syntactic organizational relationships to other signs set up. Signs reach beyond themselves and refer to something which they themselves do not possess. On the level of the elementary sign processes this is in fact the system which makes organizational relationships between signs possible.

The self-contained, self-sufficient, self-defining character of the semantic systems of biological elementary signs, their as it were "inward" only, but not "outward" embedment, is the prerequisite for their capacity to be combined with the signs of other systems on a more complex level.

3. No less remarkable is the *pragmatic aspect* of signs in the Umwelt-theory. This aspect implies two different perspectives: The first refers to the distinction Uexküll makes between *perceptual sign* (Merkzeichen) and "*perceptual cue*" (Merkmal). Each perceptual cue (or "characteristic feature") is a perceptual sign that is "transposed to the outside." In other words, whereas the perceptual sign is received as an ego-quality of a sensory cell within the subject, the perceptual cue lies outside in the space of the external world (see also object).

> This is an indication that all perceptual signs, no matter what quality, always appear in the shape of an order or impulse . . . When I say the sky is blue, then I do so because the perceptual signs, which I have transposed to the outside, give the order to the most distant level: "Be blue!" . . . While constructing our world the sensations of the mind become the properties of things, or, as one can also put it, the subjective qualities form the objective world. Replacing sensation or subjective quality with perceptual sign, one can say that the perceptual signs of our attention turn into perceptual cues of the world." (1973:102)

For the local signs, which we receive on the surface of our body through our skin or through the retina, this aspect of impulse or command means "Be outside" at this particular point of space, which as a command has in this way been transposed to the outside! The expression "transposed to the outside," which we regularly encounter in Uexküll's works, only becomes plausible in the light of this pragmatic aspect of local signs. Or in other words, the quality, *outside*, can only develop when the local sign (which appears as ego-quality of the sensory cells in the skin or retina) is transposed to the position which, as perceptual cue, fulfills the command that it be localized in space.

The second perspective answers the question which from an epistemological standpoint is of central importance, namely how we derive the image of an objective world, with its physical features, from our subjective universe and, at the same time, what this world, on which our scientific observation is based, means to us and our experiential universe. Here we have to take into consideration the general system and its structure of relationships in which all organizing signs are related to one another and to our effector signs. Thus we can see that our experiential space, which is composed of a tactile space (of the local signs of the skin), a visual space (the mosaic of loci on the retina), and an operational space, reflects the basic pattern for all programs which connect our sensory perception with the possibilities of active motor intervention. From a biological

perspective, force, matter, and causality are only the general formulas for the
possible dispositions of the varied, innumerable, visual and tactile loci existing
within the space of our experimental universe to the possible muscular movements
under the control of effector and directional signs.

> Each colored area of our visual field, whatever kind it may be, is an obstacle, which
> can be near or far. They all awaken the same sensation, namely that of an obstacle,
> similar to a resistance which a hand encounters in touching an object. This is what
> gives them their material character, which generally speaking signifies nothing other
> than a real obstacle. Thus we describe as material all things that prove their reality
> by acting as obstacles. (1973:61)

> Force (*Kraft*) is originally nothing but a sensation linked with the movement of our
> muscles. This muscular sensation is spontaneously inferred to be the cause of the
> movement of our limbs, and then the cause of movements in general . . . *By reduction*
> *of the material processes in space to local and directional signs, the subjective nature*
> *of these phenomena as well has been proven beyond doubt, and thus the position of*
> *the so-called natural sciences within the field of biology has been clearly marked.*
> (1973:64–66; emphasis by T.v.U.)

This means nothing else but the fact that, through consistent abstraction
from all content signs and perceptual content cues the natural sciences construct
a representation of the world which is composed of organizing signs only. This
is the solution to the second problem described above. The significance of this
abstraction of an "objective" image of the world as the parameter for a cooperation
between various human subjects and thus for the development of a human culture
is evident (see also neutral object [*Gegenstand*]).

6.4. The Complex Levels or the Combinatorics of Sign
Processes

The linkage of sign processes to all cell subjects (as their ego-qualities)
has the advantage of making plain the parallels between complex signs and the
complex structure of the sensory organs in higher forms of life. Even the combination of organizing signs with content signs, and *a fortiori* the reciprocal
relation of local signs to effector signs in our subjective universe (a relation upon
which, as we have seen, our concept of an objective external world is based)
depend on complex nervous connections between receptive cell subjects and
control mechanisms in a central nervous system. This raises the question as to
how the complex signs have developed, which as objects and processes constitute
our experiential universe and which in all surrounding-worlds of higher living
forms have a directive function no less vital than that of navigational aids for
the sailor. What does the bond look like, that links the elementary organizing
and content signs with the sharply outlined objects and processes, "which we
see everywhere around us and whose unity we do not doubt" (1973:116)?

If we observe our mind when it is actively constructing and recognizing
the objects and processes in our environment, we will find that we do not just

resort to static memory images. Instead, the process of image formation is itself repeated, and the sequence of impulses for our muscular movements (e.g. when feeling the outline of an object with our hands or looking at some writing with our eyes) is thereby compared with programs of impulse sequences which are stored in our memory. Following Kant, Uexküll calls these programs *schemata*.

"Our whole memory—like the fly of a theater with its pieces of scenery—is filled with schemata which from time to time appear on the stage of consciousness . . ." (1973:121).

The private character of signs, which we have already emphasized with reference to the elementary sign processes (the perception of a color, a sound, a taste is just as strictly a subjective, private experience as the perception of a pain), applies just as strictly to the complex signs which we construct by means of programs or schemata. The table, the house, the tree which I perceive are also part of my experiential universe and are not identical with the table, the house, or the tree in the subjective universe of another person. "Unfortunately, we have no access to anyone else's stage of consciousness, as nothing could be more enlightening than to see the world through someone else's schemata. However, one thing should not be forgotten: When we see other people walking around us, they are walking on our stage while we do so on theirs. These stages are never identical, and in most cases are even entirely different. And we cannot expect to play the same part on someone else's stage as on our own" (1973:121f.).

At this point let me make a few explanatory remarks to suggest some connecting lines that lead from Jakob von Uexküll's Umwelt-theory to a human biology. A schema is a strictly private program for the formation of complex signs (neutral objects, etc.) in our subjective universe. Language produces intersubjectively valid signs, namely words (signs for the signs of the schemata). Thus language not only makes it possible to intersubjectively exchange information on the object-forming processes which take place in our experiential universes; it also makes it possible for all who hear the word to activate the same processes of formation. However, Uexküll's qualifying statement is still true: The schemata which we have formed during our life are intersubjectively identical only in the most general outlines.

On the complex level as well, signs can be analyzed under syntactic, semantic, and pragmatic aspects. In so doing, it becomes clear that the abstract systems which we "simultaneously perceive" as synchronic structures in the background of each complex sign are completely different from those on the level of elementary sign processes. On the complex level it is these systems which are the units of biological operations. The Umwelt-theory describes them as *circles* (Kreise) and distinguishes a food circle, an enemy circle, a circle of sexual partners, and a circle of the medium.

In each of these circles a *syntactic organization* ensures that the signs which appear in chronological order correspond to the catch words of the respective operation. Thus each newly occurring sign—according to the inherent logic of the operation—takes up where the preceeding process left off and prepares for the following one. The operation in the prey circle, for example, starts with the optical sign of the prey spotted; this is followed by tactile signs when seizing the prey, which are followed in turn by signs of taste when the prey is devoured. Thus the prey "has" optical, tactile, and taste qualities.

The *semantic organization* now ensures that each sign emphasizes a common purpose which distinguishes one circle (e.g. as food circle) from other circles (e.g. the enemy circle). Thus the same neutral object—as a meaning-carrier—can mean "feed" within the food circle, "danger" within the enemy circle, and "obstacle" within the medium circle. In this way it changes its meaning from circle to circle, that is, it transforms each time into a different object within the surrounding-world of the living being under observation.

In the *pragmatic organization* signs become operational instructions. They tell the subject (like navigational aids to the sailor) what to do.

7. THE SUBJECTIVE UNIVERSE OF THE OBSERVER AS THE KEY TO THE SELF-WORLD OF THE ANIMAL UNDER OBSERVATION

7.1. Neutral Object and Meaning-Carrier

As mentioned above, Jakob von Uexküll devoted himself to two tasks:

1. First, to analyze the subjective universe of the human observer. Apart from an "anatomy" of this subjective universe this also includes the solution to the question of how the representation of an objective external world, in which man observes himself and other subjects, is derived from his subjective universe.
2. Second, to place other subjects, *viz.*, animals, in the role of sign receiver.

I have shown how Uexküll resolved the first problem. Before I try to describe his resolution of the second, I would like to outline how his resolution of the first problem affects his approach to the second one.

The analysis of the manner in which the human mind functions as "primary receiver" shows how our surrounding-world (*Umwelt*) is composed of signs received by the cells which together comprise our receivers, the sensory organs. From this directly perceived subjective universe our intellect derives an objective external world which we assume to be the common stage upon which we and other subjects perform. In reality, however, it is a representation of the world which we, disregarding all content signs, have constructed from the organizing signs to which our subjective Umwelt owes its spatial and temporal arrangements.

The importance of this conclusion lies in the fact that the observer cannot perceive other subjects in their surrounding-worlds, but only within his own. They appear to his mind according to the organization of space and time that governs the human surrounding-world. This would not change even if we were to describe our observations in the terms that physics has developed to refer to the objects and processes of an objective, external world. When the observer wants to shift viewpoints and place other subjects (animals) in the role of the human sign receiver, he has to realize that there are objects in his world which never appear in the surrounding-worlds of animals. Chief among those things which do not occur in animal self-worlds are neutral objects because animals never approach their environment as neutral observers.

"Since no animal ever takes the role of an observer, one can maintain that an animal never builds up a relation to a 'neutral object' " (1970:108)

No neutral objects exist in animal behavior, only objects on which they are dependent as a result of biological needs (e.g. hunger) and which disappear from their surrounding-world as soon as the need has passed. Neutral objects have constancy, and we can maintain a certain distance from them. Objects of animal surrounding-worlds have neither constancy nor distance for their animal subjects. A dog that chases a hare is compelled to do so as long as the hare remains in its visual or olfactory field. As soon as it has disappeared, it has stopped being an object in the surrounding-world of the dog.

The human observer, therefore, who wants to place an animal in the role of sign receiver, must transpose the neutral objects which he sees spread out around the animal into objects of the animal surrounding-world. To this end he must realize that as soon as a subject builds up a relationship with them these neutral objects become meaning-carriers whose meaning bears the stamp of the subject.

"Each component of an animate or inanimate neutral object, as soon as this component appears in the role of a meaning-carrier on the life-stage of an animal subject, is brought into connection with what may be called a complement in the body of the subject, which serves as a meaning-utilizer." (1970:111)

The transformation of a neutral object of the human subjective universe into a meaning-carrier that takes on the meaning determined by the animal under observation is the decisive step. Only those who have learnt to share this step in a systematic manner are entitled to call themselves Umwelt-researchers.

This takes us to the core of the method developed by Uexküll: The transformation of a neutral object which the scientist can measure, weigh, separate, and alter according to the laws of physics into a meaning-carrier whose meaning is determined by the animal subject and is transformed by it into a sign in its sign system: This sign refers to a meaning-utilizer in the organism of the animal, just as within our subjective universe the sign *light* (as a meaning-carrier) refers to our eyes (as meaning-utilizers) or the sign *tone* (as a meaning-carrier) refers to our ears (as meaning-utilizers).

Thus it can be reduced to the formula: neutral object →meaning-carrier + meaning (= reference to the meaning−utilizer) = sign. This formula, as Uexküll stresses, is more important for biology than the formula of causality: cause →

effect = cause → new effect. Whereas the formula mentioned first governs the subjective universes of all living organisms, the second one applies only to the neutral objects of the human subjective universe and the "objective" representation of the world which is derived from it.

However, looked at from the latter perspective, the formula of causality is also of significance for the biologist: With the neutral object which he registers in the environment of the animal, the observer as it were holds the "handle" of a non-human sign in his hand, which projects from the surrounding-world (to him invisible) of the animal under observation into the surrounding-world of the observer. By way of dexterous manipulation of this handle he can alter the non-human sign 'attached' to it, and in this manner experimentally investigate the meaning the sign has in the animal's surrounding-world. In an early work of 1905, Uexküll is already comparing the objects of the natural scientist that have significance in the surrounding-worlds of animals to keys, and the animals to music boxes that can be wound up and set in motion by means of these keys.

7.2.   The Meaning-Carrier as Connecting Link between Heterogeneous Sign Systems

The term *meaning-carrier* requires two further explanatory remarks:
1. The meaning-carrier falls, as a sort of chimera or Janus-faced structure, on the border that divides two different sign systems. In each of them it "carries" a different meaning. Thus, metaphorically speaking, it links two different meanings and becomes a connecting link between heterogeneous sign systems. In each of them it represents a sign that is unknown in the other. Thus in our example, the meaning carrier in the surrounding-world of the human observer had the meaning of a physical object, which relates it, as a sign, to other physical objects and to the physicist as meaning-utilizer. This meaning does not exist in the surrounding-world of the animal under observation. Here the meaning-carrier takes on a completely different meaning, for example that of an obstacle which as a sign) refers to the motor organs of the animal (as the meaning-utilizer) or that of a prey that (as a sign) is meaningful to the raptorial organs of the hunting animal. Thus the meaning-carrier is transformed into a sign pertaining to a biological sign system whose meanings are not part of the surrounding-world of the human observer but have to be deduced from the animal behavior under observation.

2. Meaning-carriers do not necessarily have to "project" as physical objects from the animal self-world (invisible to the observer) into that of the human observer. Thus, for example, sounds an animal hears or produces can take on the meaning of an alluring melody or a cry of fear in the surrounding-world of a human observer, although they may have a completely different meaning in the animal's subjective-world. As sounds, they have in both subjective-worlds the meaning of acoustic signs which belong to an acoustic sign system. The

code of these sign systems, however, are very different. Sounds are not physical processes, and yet they fulfill the function of meaning-carriers that link meanings from different sign systems. (T.v. Uexküll, 1979).

Sounds can of course also be related to the sign system of the physicists. Here they can be measured as vibrations of the air and be related to vibrations of different frequencies. If, however, vibrations of air find their way to a subject with ears, they are transformed into meaning-carriers which link sign systems separated by semantic borders: They link the meaning of physical signs (vibrations of air) with the meaning of biological signs (tones).

As connecting links of heterogeneous sign systems, meaning-carriers can string together chains of different signs or give rise to intricately designed, net-like or hierarchically arranged structures which exceed semantic boundaries of many sign systems. Their formation, however, requires a link of meaning or transformation at each boundary.

It is always astonishing to see how effortlessly such complex structures as these chains are formed in nature, taking into consideration the fact that all signs we receive must previously be translated into the signs which our nervous system transports in the form of action currents. The nerve action currents are transformed into sounds or colors and these into words or images, which in turn are translated into even more complex signs.

These observations show the outstanding significance of the formula Uexküll has developed in order to gain access, as a biologist, to the animal worlds from which we are excluded.

7.3. The Meaning Rule as the Rule of Correspondence between Point and Counterpoint, or as the Rule of Systems Formation

The formula of sign = meaning-carrier + meaning (and meaning = reference to the meaning-utilizer) not only applies intra-individually, within the organism, to sign systems of cells, tissues, and organs, as well as to the relationship between the sign system of the organism and its surrounding-world; it also applies inter-individually, to sign systems of such different organisms as plants and animals. Thus, as it is expressed in the theory of meaning (1970:136) "the meaning rule" serves as "[. . .the] link between two elementary rules."[13]

In the terminology of Bertalanffy's systems theory (1968) we would say that the formula for signs, which Uexküll refers to as *meaning rule*, describes the structure of systems and that it is therefore valid within a system, but also valid between systems, once these have been joined together in a suprasystem. Thus, with this formula it is possible to research the composition of sign systems which govern the society of plants and animals in a biotope or in a biocenosis.

In the theory of meaning (1970:111f.) this is illustrated by an example that shows what different meanings the stem of a flower (as meaning-carrier) takes on in the subjective worlds of a girl, an ant, a cicada, and a cow. In the girl's subjective world the flower stem has the meaning of a handle for an ornament that the girl pins on her bodice. In this context the meaning refers to the girl's hand as the meaning-utilizer. In the self-world of the ant, the meaning-carrier *flower stem*, with its rough surface, refers to the legs of the ant which (as the meaning-utilizers) use the stem as their footpath, etc.

In order to illustrate the formula of sign = sign carrier + meaning (the meaning rule) as clearly as possible, Uexküll refers back to a term in music theory, which describes the way two tones complement each other as *point* and *counterpoint*. Plessner (1976) speaks of a *law of correlations*: "According to the principle which Uexküll once formulated in this manner, one must conclude that where there is a foot, there is also a path, where there is a mouth, there is also food, where there is a weapon, there is also an enemy . . ."

The comprehensive meaning structure of the contrapuntal correlation describes the structure of signs (*aliquid stat pro aliquo*[9]). This correlation is convertible, so that the organism of a living being and its surrounding-world are complementary to one another, which means that the surrounding-world as a sign refers to the organism of the living being just as the organism as a sign refers to its surrounding-world.[14]

Thus the formula of the contrapuntal correlation of meaning-carrier and meaning in a sign becomes significant for Uexküll as the instrument of a biology which sees the development of a theory of the composition of nature as its task (1970:140). In this theory of composition the properties of our surrounding-world and our sensory organs are also composed for each other. Thus, for example, one can say that our eyes (as *meaning-utilizers*) are "complementary" to the light-emitting sun, just as the sun (as meaning-carrier) refers to our sight-giving eyes. To Goethe's saying:

> Were our eyes not like the sun,
> Never could they see it

one must therefore add:

> Were the sun not like our eye,
> It could not shine in any sky. (1970:158)

8. THE FUNCTIONAL CIRCLE AS A SPECIAL CASE OF THE CONTRAPUNTAL CORRELATION

The general validity of the initially proposed linear formula for signs involves a problem in the task Uexküll wants to complete, namely to place other subjects (animals) in the role of the human sign receiver. This difficulty is made clear in his reference to a fundamental difference between plants and animals:

Animals possess surrounding-worlds, plants, however, only *dwelling envelopes* (1970:114).

This distinction implies that the meaning-utilizers of plants and animals differ in an essential point: In plants the utilization (of the meaning-carrier) is centrally executed by one and the same organ, whereas in animals this task is shared by two different organs with different functions. In the latter case a perceptor organ (receptor) and an operational organ (effector) must cooperate for the meaning-carrier to be utilized.

Thus, for example, the birch leaf is able by means of its chlorophyll to ensure the utilization of the meaning-carrier *solar energy*, or by means of its form, which is like a flag, it can use the meaning of the meaning-carrier *wind* (1970:119). In animals this centralized process is separated into receptor and effector components. Thus even so apparently simple a reflex as the blink of an eyelid requires, when a foreign body is approaching, the cooperation of receptor and effector functions in order to enable the animal to utilize the meaning for the eye (*foreign*) of the meaning-carrier *foreign body* (1970:115).

For this reason, the simple formula of the contrapuntal relationship of signs does not suffice to transform neutral objects of the surrounding-world of the human observer into objects of the surrounding-world of an animal under observation. It was necessary therefore to modify this formula in such a way as to enable it to describe the different functions of the perceptor organ and the effector organ as well as their cooperation. With this aim in view Uexküll developed the formula of the *functional circle*, which anticipates by twenty years the mathematical formulation of the feedback principle by Norbert Wiener (1943).

To this end it was necessary to specially redefine two terms for sign theory, which had regularly led to misinterpretations due to their psychological connotations: The terms *perception* (Merken) and *operation* (Wirken). F. Brock (1949:173), a longstanding collaborator of Uexküll's, describes the problem that was to be solved by this definition as follows:

> The non-expert is only too willingly inclined to describe "operational" and "perceptual" processes as conscious and voluntary operations. Unfortunately, we have no access at all to the inner life of other creatures. . . . Even human beings consciously perceive only a small fraction of all biological processes. If, for example, we put a drop of acetic acid of a particular concentration on our tongue, we will perceive the taste of something sour; and if we put a drop with the same concentration on the sphincter of the stomach it will contract, but there is no sensation of taste. Looked at from a biological point of view, the tongue as well as the pylorus "perceive" something, but only in the first case do we experience the perceptual cue consciously.

"Looked at from a biological perspective" refers to a process which has to be described in terminology that is indifferent to the opposition conscious/unconscious. "Perception" in this terminology denotes the first phase of a process of meaning-utilization which has to be supplemented by a second phase in which an operation confirms what has been "perceived." In this respect operation has just as little to do with the psychological phenomenon of a voluntary act as perception with that of conscious awareness.

With this distinction that the sign process undergoes as life proceeds from vegetative to animal forms, the first stages of a genealogy of the development of signs become apparent. Consciousness and volition, or conscious perception and conscious transmission of signs, can be described on this foundation as further differentiations of the vital sign process (T.v. Uexküll, 1980:81f.).

The basic model for those further differentiations is the functional circle (Figure 1). It describes how (in sign processes) the process of meaning-utilization differentiates into perception and operation and how both cooperate as partial functions. It shows how the subject as meaning-utilizer and the object as meaning-carrier are linked in a unified whole, a system (or complex sign).

"Metaphorically speaking, each animal subject grasps its object with two jaws of a pair of pincers—a perceptual jaw and an operational jaw. With the first jaw it imparts to the object a perceptual cue (*Merkmal*), and with the second an operational cue (*Wirkmal*). Thus particular properties of the object become perceptual cue carriers and others become operational cue carriers. Since all properties of an object are linked together through the structure of the object, the properties represented by the operational cue are forced to exert through the entire object their influence on the properties which carry the perceptual cue and also to modify the perceptual cue itself. This process is best described by the words: *The operational cue extinguishes the perceptual cue*". (1970:11)

In Figure 1, the meaning-utilizer has differentiated into a perceptor organ and an effector organ and the meaning carrier into a perceptual cue carrier and an operational cue carrier. Since this model applies to all sign processes taking their course on the stage of animal life, that is, to anthroposemiotic as well as to zoosemiotic ones, it becomes possible by this means to solve the problem of placing animals in the position of the human sign receiver and to transpose neutral objects from the surrounding-world of the human observer into objects of the surrounding-world of the animal under observation. To this end the observer

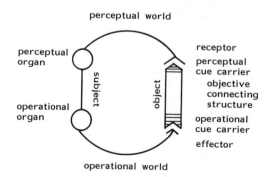

Figure 1. The functional circle.

has to analyze the receptors and effectors of the animal. Then he can ascertain which signs the animal can receive and which of them it can transmit. This knowledge puts him in a position to translate the neutral object, which he registers in his human surrounding-world and which appears in the model of the functional circle as an "objective connecting structure," into an object of the animal's surrounding-world, by putting the features and operations characteristic of the animal in place of human ones.

9. ESSENTIALS OF JAKOB VON UEXKÜLL'S THEORY OF SIGNS

After this attempt to sketch Uexküll's theory of signs, I want to describe some of its essentials in more detail. This will bring out certain contrasts and clarify similarities and differences between this and other theories of the sign.

9.1. Meaning as a Process of Meaning-Utilization

In the simple formula of sign = meaning-carrier + meaning and meaning = reference to the meaning-utilizer, "meaning" has the central function of bracketing heterogeneous elements into a whole (the sign). For Uexküll one of these heterogeneous elements (the meaning-utilizer) is an organ, that is, part of the organism of a living subject. Thus the formula, meaning = link between carrier and utilizer, takes on the nature of a dynamic process. Signs are realized as sign processes.

The formula or model of the functional circle makes it evident that this process does not exhaust itself in the linear coupling of links in a chain, but rather that it has a circular form: meaning-carrier and meaning-utilizer become elements of a "force field" within which they are driven apart and linked together again.

When a meaning-utilizer in the organism of a living being "harpoons" with the link-forming meaning some neutral object from its environment as a meaning-carrier, a fight or game between two unlike partners begins, one of which plays the part and the other the corresponding counterpart (point and counterpoint). Thus meaning turns out to be a "drama," which deals with meaning-utilization. Thus the metaphor of the "anatomy" of a surrounding-world takes on a deeper meaning; for now we see invisible tentacles coming out of the cells and organs of human and animal bodies, searching for meaning-carriers in the environment— in order to then connect them with the cells or organs. These "tentacles" extend the anatomy of the organism into its surrounding-world.

In this way, signs suddenly come alive. We can follow them in the interplay between the organism of a living being and the meaning-carriers in its environment. Here we can "see" how in the dramas between organizing signs and content signs neutral processes of the external world are received as meaning-carriers by the sensitive cells of our sensory organs, and are utilized as sensible stimuli. We can also see how physical vibrations of the air are taken up by our ears and become involved in the interplay between the tympanic membrane and the acoustic apparatus of the inner ear, in which sound originates. We "see" the same interplay between photons and the retinal cells of the eye. Again a little drama takes place which produces the sign "light" from parts and counterparts.

We can then see the plots of the dramas becoming more complex, but here too the part of the meaning-carrier always corresponds to its counterpart meaning-utilizer, and we see how the script of the action (the schema) again varies the subject matter "meaning-utilization." The work of the organism (as meaning-utilizer), Uexküll wrote elsewhere (1935), always corresponds to the complementary function of the object (as meaning-carrier). Thus, for example, a chair is only defined by its complementary function to the operation of our body, namely sitting: It has a "sitting quality."

The formula of the functional circle thus describes the basic structure of the dramas which take place between the human and animal organisms and the objects of their surrounding-worlds. These dramas consist principally of two acts: In the first act a neutral object from the environment is "harpooned" as a meaning-carrier by a perceiving organ or a perceiving cell, in the second act it is modified by the effector organ (as meaning-utilizer) in such a way that it disappears again from the surrounding-world. "The operational cue extinguishes the perceptual cue." Thus the condition has been created for the emergence of the next sign in the chronological sequence of the discussion which the living being holds with its objects.

This basic structure of the sign process even applies to the simple formula that only at first glance describes a linear process. When the sign relationship is established between a vegetable organ as meaning-utilizer and a neutral object or process of the environment as meaning-carrier, the formula of sign = meaning-carrier + meaning (meaning = dependence on the meaning-utilizer) only describes the first act of the "drama" of meaning-utilization that follows. Here, too, the second act leads to the transformation of the meaning-carrier and shows that beginning and end of the drama are related to one another in a circle. When, as in the abovementioned example, the chlorophyll of the birch leaf (as meaning-utilizer) "harpoons" solar energy (as meaning-carrier), a process is started in the course of which the meaning utilization again and again absorbs solar energy within organic substances, that is, the meaning-utilizer, here too, constantly extinguishes its meaning-carrier and tends to make the sign disappear.

9.2. The Sign Process as the Opposition of Self and Non-Self

For Uexküll the code that governs the life of the cell and ensures that it respond with its "ego-quality" to all influences from outside (1970:116) is the elementary sign. Or in other words: The most elementary sign process is the opposition of self (ego-quality) and non-self (non-ego-quality = external influence). The cell (as the meaning-utilizer) thus transforms every neutral influence into a meaning-carrier.

Life takes place, on every level, as variation and differentiation of these elementary sign processes, or to put this another way, each sign is a variation and differentiation of the opposition and linkage of self and non-self. This applies to the relationship between a plant and its dwelling envelope as well as to the relationship between an animal and its surrounding-world. The relation between hunter and prey, male and female, medium and medium user is in each case a variation of the basic melody, fundamental plan, or elementary code: self/non-self.

Thus one can already see that for Uexküll signs have a triadic structure. They consist of or develop from meaning-utilizer, meaning-carrier, and the code that defines the meaning and links both of them together. In the functional circle as the formula for sign processes on the stage of animal life there are the elements subject, object, and biological need that (as hunger, enemy, prey, medium, or sex) defines the functional circle.

A model for the opposition of self and non-self appears when one starts from the idea that in the functional circle effector organ (right through the subject) stimulates its own perceptual organ. "Self" can then be interpreted as self-stimulation and "non-self" as the variation of this self-stimulation through external influences. For the subject, which affirms its self through self-examination, these influences become non-self (T.v.Uexküll 1978).

9.3. The Problem of the Inseparability of Observer and Observation

The epistemologically fundamental problem, namely that all knowledge and every science is dependent on the nature of human cognition, is of central importance in the field of semiotics, and is also relevant when dealing with the question of the priority of language.[15] Uexkuell concerned himself with the problem of language only casually. He was convinced that everything the observer can observe and all conclusions he can draw from these observations can only be perceived within the boundaries of his human experience; and human experience can only occur within the human surrounding-world.

Therefore it is absolutely essential to analyze first the structure, the anatomy, of the human surrounding-world before turning to an examination of the neutral objects which one encounters in this surrounding-world. Uexküll confined himself to deducing our human representation of an objective external world from the biological reality of our surrounding-world by further adapting Kant's initiative to the field of biology.

However, he did not examine the question as to what language "does" to a primarily biological human surrounding-world, what part it plays in constructing the representation of a world of physical reality. What nevertheless allows the question of the significance of language for man to be raised in a new way is Uexküll's concept of a gradual differentiation of the biological sign processes first from a vegetative to an animal stage, and next from the simple forms of life which Uexküll studied in the lower animals he described as "realms of reflexes" (1980) to the complex ones which make use of a central nervous system.

10. CONCLUDING OBSERVATIONS: ATTEMPT AT A COMPARISON OF UEXKÜLL'S, PEIRCE'S, SAUSSURE'S, AND MORRIS' THEORIES OF SIGNS

In conclusion, I want to present some distinctions between biological and linguistic sign processes and try to relate them to the differences between Uexküll's, Peirce's, and Saussure's theories of signs and to make note of certain connections with Morris' theory of signs.

Biological sign systems differ from languages especially in two points:

1. The former are based on codes that are characteristic of the species and mainly innate. Thus one can describe them as "natural codes." The latter are based on culture-specific codes that have to be learnt and handed down from generation to generation, in short, on "cultural codes."[7]

2. The schema for sign transmission differs in the two cases: It is dialogical in languages; a listener (receiver) receives signs from a speaker (transmitter). Both use the same culture-specific code. In biological sign processes the scheme is based on monologue. In the functional circle, the model for this scheme, the functions of receiving and transmitting are brought together within the subject. With the receptors the subject has the function of a receiver, with its effectors the function of a transmitter. This is added by the physical or chemical source of stimulation—in the form of the external world—as a kind of "additional transmitter" which, however, as an "objective connecting structure" semantically remains outside the sign process. Its function is confined to modifying the signs which the subject as transmitter sends out to its own receptors (T.v.Uexkuell 1978) and in the course of which the fundamental process occurs in which a self (as the meaning-utilizer) is complemented by a non-self (as the meaning-carrier).

The attempt to compare some of Uexküll's fundamental ideas to the corresponding concepts in Peirce's and Saussure's theories reveals some remarkable differences. Many of these can be attributed to the different types of problems which the three semioticians occupied themselves with. For Uexküll, who studies biological sign processes, the question of the relationship between the human observer and the biological subject under observation is of prime importance. For both he has to consider the development of signs in which hierarchic integration is of significance as well, as can be observed in the field of biology even between processes in the sensory organs (receptors) and those in the central nervous system (the perceptual organ). Another essential problem, which he has solved through the model of a circular process, is the relationship between sign and behavior (perception and operation).

These aspects are of little importance to sign-theories which take as their objects human language as well as the logical structure of reality. Since, however, language and thinking have a biological foundation and biological components, the influence of the latter must be traceable in its former.

An essential difference between the three theories of signs is the following: Peirce's theory of signs is triadic, Saussure's is dyadic, and Uexküll's is conceived as a cyclic process.

It appears to me that the relation between Peirce's triadic and Uexküll's cyclic model becomes obvious if the former is conceived of as a synchronic system, the latter as a model for the discursive stream of sign processes.

Another interesting insight is revealed by a comparison of Uexküll's theory of signs to that of Saussure. According to Saussure the function of a sign can be interpreted as the opposition and connection of two elements from two different classes, of which one element represents the *signifiant*, the other the *signifié*. Uexküll adds a second opposition: The system (or the class) of signs of the human observer, in opposition to the system (or the class) of signs of the organism under observation. All conclusions which respect to signs, as well as to the receiver (receptor) and the transmitter (effector) of the organism under observation, necessarily bear the mark of the human observer.

As to the sign system of the human observer, its space, consisting of our local and directional signs, as well as its system of physical relations, are of particular importance, once they reflect the relationships between our sensory and (voluntary) motor capacities. In Uexküll's terminology physical objects are meaning-carriers whose meaning refers to the motor behavior of man (as the meaning-utilizer). The physical relations serve the human observer as a coordinate system in which he can ascertain and describe the relations of the organism under observation to its environment (to the surrounding-world of the human observer and its neutral objects). Therefore, the signs which he relates to the organism under observation as its perceptual signs are always taken from the observer's own repertoire of signs. But on the basis of the knowledge of the organization of the receptors and effectors of the organism under observation he can select those signs from this repertoire to which the living being under observation corresponds in its behavior, and then combine them with objects of the surrounding-world of the organism according to their significance for its vital activities.

Thus the neutral object of the observer represents a third element that is added as part of the semiotic chain to the *signifiant* and the *signifié* of Saussure's model and establishes the relationship between the human observer and the organism under observation. This third element represents the physical quality of the neutral object, which, as meaning-carrier, then establishes the connection between the physical sign system of the observer and the biological one of the organism under observation. Looked at from this aspect one can better understand why signs seem to have not only a dual structure (meaning-carrier + meaning), but so often also a dualistic structure of "material" sign-carrier and "immaterial" meaning.

The comparison of Uexküll's concept with Morris' theory exhibits some other possibilities of mutual complementarity:

Within the framework of Uexküll's model of the functional circle, perceptual and operational sign, and perceptual (characteristic feature) and operational cue, respectively, refer to one another as *signifiant* and *signifié*. Both receive their complementary meaning reference (as meaning-carrier and meaning-utilizer) from the biological "tinge" of the functional circle (as the circle of food, enemy, sex, etc.), that is, the "tinge" of the functional circle corresponds to the interpreting conscious mind. Each step of an action, and the action as a whole, follows the schema of the functional circle: Only when the perceptual cue has been extingushed by the complementary operational cue can a new perceptual cue initiate the next step of the action or finish the action.

Morris' theory (and that of George H. Mead as well) fails to consider the division of an action into perceptual and operational steps, and hence misses the circular principle of negative feedback. This is exactly what characterizes the enterprise of pragmatism. Instead, in Morris' model action as a whole is divided into phases of orientation, operation, and satisfaction, the signs of which refer to one another and which likewise have a common meaning reference (interpretants) in the form of the "impulse," which in the field of biology largely corresponds to the "tinge" of Uexküll's functional circle.

At this point it would be useful to combine both concepts under the aspect of a "double structure." The functional circles, which describe the individual steps of an action according to the theory of signs, could then be interpreted as the elementary level, whose elements are combined by the "impulses" to form the three phases of a higher-level action.

As the result of this comparative analysis the following statements can be made:

1. There is no alternative among the concepts of signs just analyzed, in the sense of one being more accurate or better than the other. They rather tend to complement one another. Each of them seems to emphasize a different aspect in a more comprehensive context.

2. The future task of general semiotics is to study and delineate this comprehensive context. Its objective—to use Uexküll's words—can be described as a theory of the composition of nature which also encompassses man and his sign systems.

3. The contours of this future task become clearer if one differentiates four continents in the universe of sign systems according to the meaning-utilizers to be found there:

   a. A continent of intracellular sign systems, in which cell organelles function as meaning-utilizers; the fundamental system appears to be the genetic code;

b. A continent of cellular and intercellular sign systems, which corresponds to the *endosemiotic* area, in Sebeok's terminology (1976). It includes the communication systems of unicellular organisms and cell assemblies (plants) at various levels of organization. Here it is finally the cells that are the meaning-utilizers.

c. A third continent can be seen in those sign systems in which organisms (animals) appear as the meaning-utilizers of meaning-carriers in their environment. Sebeok's *zoosemiotic* area (1976) would form a subcontinent here.

d. Finally, a fourth continent is indicated by those sign systems in which social groups rather than individual organisms can be identified as meaning-utilizers. The prototype of this system would be human language. Jakob von Uexküll's field of research was confined to the second and third of these continents, but his initiative reveals its fruitfulness in reaching beyond the boundaries of his own field of research.

NOTES

1. The question as to the founders of ethology is too complicated to be dealt with in this context. See J. Jaynes, *Animal Behaviour*, 17 (1969), 601–606 among others.

2. Jakob von Uexkuell and Ernst Cassirer were friends; whether and to what extent he came into contact with Peirce and his philosophical concepts must remain an open question. It is, however, not very likely, since Cassirer saw mainly the aspect of natural science in Uexküll's concept of biology, and not that of a sign theory. See also note 3.

3. This essential fact was clearly recognized by Cassirer, who writes: "Biology, according to Uexküll, is a natural science which has to be developed by the usual empirical methods—the methods of observation and experimentation. Biological thought on the other hand, does not belong to the same type as physical or chemical thought. Uexküll is a resolute . . . defender of the principle of the autonomy of life. Life is an ultimate and selfdependent reality. It cannot be described or explained in terms of physics or chemistry." E. Cassirer, *An Essay On Man*, Yale University Press 1944.

4. The history of its development shows that in German mysticism the concept of *Gemüt* still referred to the whole inner world of man. Later a differentiation developed that resulted in dividing this inner world into its component parts and the term was more and more set in contrast to those areas it had previously encompassed, for example to the term *spirit*.(Geist) *Gemüt* was confined to the field of emotions and value-perception. In this form it was introduced into the German terminology of psychiatry and psychopathology. Following K. Schneider we speak of the "gemuetloser Psychopath" meaning an "abnormal personality" which is characterized by a lack of sympathy, shame, remorse, sense of honor, and conscience. Thus the term obtains a completely different meaning from the way it was used by Kant and Uexküll. In Kant's *Kritik der Reinen Vernunft*, Gemüt is defined as the essence and origin of the transcendental capacity of knowledge, as "die gegebenen Vorstellungen zusammensetzende und die Einheit der empirischen Apprehension bewirkende Vermögen (animus)" (*Historisches Wörterbuch der Philosophie*, Bd. III, 1974, 259–267). Uexküll understands by *Gemüt* the synthetic function of apperception which combines the signs to form larger entities. It constructs the surrounding-world of the living being in its spatial and chronological organization and fills it with objects

made up of organizing signs and content signs, and which are linked together by schemata (*Theoretische Biologie*, 1973, pp. 11, 13, 117, etc.).

The concept of *Gemüt* has not been adopted by psychology and psychoanalysis, due to its numerous and often not very precise connotations. It is in just this context, however, that it would be useful to look for the links that exist, for example, between the concepts of emotional disturbance, imagination, and above all the ego and its functions on the one hand, and Uexküll's concept of *Gemüt* on the other. In this connection, H. Hartmann's definitions are of particular interest. He distinguished between defensive and synthetic functions and placed at the center of his observations a conflict-free zone of the ego. There are to be found here some concepts of great interest for genetic semiotics, which is concerned with the question of the formation of consciousness and consciousness of self.

5. In his essay "Die Zahl als Reiz" Number as Stimulus, Uexküll examines how numbers can attain the meaning of signs in the surrounding-world of animals, and how they differ from the numbers used by man. *Tierseele. Zeitschrift für vergleichende Seelenkunde*, 1 [1913/14], 336–367; reprint 1980.

6. In a letter to Heinrich Junker of Berlin (in the collection "Autographs" of the Deutsche Staatsbibliothek, East Berlin) Uexküll writes:

"I am convinced that you know much more about language than I do, which is evident especially in your fine paper on Wilhelm von Humboldt.

"Language interests me mainly as a means of communication between man and animals, and as a means of communication between animals themselves. Besides sequences of movement, sequences of sounds, the knowledge of which is innate, serve as a means of communication as well. Pheasant chicks can be raised by turkey hens, but not by ordinary hens, because pheasants understand the call and warning-cry of turkeys and answer them with appropriate behavior, but they give no heed to the ordinary hen's calling and warning. The turkey-language must be a dialect of the pheasant's language, whereas the language of ordinary hens belongs to an entirely different family of languages.

"Many animals are capable of using special sounds or sequences of sounds as secondary perceptual cues—Pavlov was able to demonstrate that dogs that were accustomed to listening to a special ringing of a bell before being fed started the secretion of saliva after this sign alone. Pavlov called this a 'conditioned reflex.' You can also utter the word 'meat,' instead of ringing a bell. Nevertheless, it is not possible to conclude from this observation that the dog understands the word "meat."

"A different approach was used in the experiment Dr. Sarris performed in the Institue for Umwelt-Research. A dog was trained to sit on a special chair after the command 'Chair! ' Then the chair was removed and the command repeated. Now the dog took its place on every object a dog could sit on. This observation can be expressed as follows: special objects have a 'sitting-quality' for a dog. [More information on this can be found in 'A Stroll through the Worlds of Animals and Men' by Uexkuell and Kriszat (English version in J. v. Uexküll, 1957), and in E. G. Sarris, "The Umwelt of a Dog," in *Die Welt im Fortschritt*, Verlag Herbig, series 1, book 3.]

"For a dog the word 'chair' does not have the meaning of a definite object but of a performance: to sit. This seems fundamental for language as a means of communication, between men as well. The spoken word, i.e., a definite sequence of sounds as a carrier of meaning, relates to a definite performance and not to a definite object.

"Of the questions you asked me I especially took up those which are of personal interest to me. Linguistics itself is rather remote from my area, but I am convinced that you have set out on the right path by making it into a biological science.

Sincerely yours,
J. v. Uexküll

7. It is open to speculation whether all language rules are acquired by learning or whether some are innate.

8. For Uexküll the question of how inanimate nature can be interpreted on the basis of life is posed, not however the reverse, how life can be interpreted from the perspective of inanimate nature. Since for man as a living being "the inanimate" exists only on the basis of its differentiation from the animate and its relationship to the latter—only against the background of life—he can never take the inanimate or anorganic as a first point of departure which, as such, he knows nothing about.

    Sebeok remarks in this connection: "In other words, the critical feature of living entities and of machines programmed by humans, is *semiosis*." (personal communication).

9. Sebeok's comment as to this point: "This is the doctrine of *aliquid stat pro aliquo*, or what Jakobson recently dubbed *renvoi*." (personal communication)

10. *Atom* here is used in its original sense of "that which is indivisible"—which indeed, like the physical atom, can be dissected into elements, but as a system represents a unity that can be dissected only at the expense of its destruction.

11. This comment probably applies only to the unmusical semiotician. E. Leech (1978) considers music to be an even better paradigm than language, because in music metaphor (paradigmatic association, harmony) and metonymy (syntagmatic chain, melody) are permanently effective together. He says: The prototype of a general message-bearing system is not the line of type, but the performance of an orchestra where harmony and melody work in combination. His quotation of Lévi-Strauss sounds like an illustration of Uexküll's plan: "The myth and the musical work thus appear to be the conductors of an orchestra whose audience is the silent musicians."

12. The permanent presence of unconscious units of perception that ensure organization and relation 'beyond' the conscious perception of the succession of single impressions, which has been postulated here, appears at first glance to be just as unlogical as unlikely. We hardly have a concrete understanding of "unconscious perception." In the last few years however, characteristics of the human brain were discovered which support the assumption, initially considered to be improbable.

    It has been known for a long time that the two hemispheres of the human cerebrum have different functions. However, as both are connected with many millions of neurons, which ensure an intensive cooperation, until recently but little was known about most of these functions. Since there have been a number of patients who—due to life-threatening epileptic fits—underwent a new method of operation, the severance of all connections between the two hemispheres, further details have broadened our knowledge. It was found that the functions of the left hemisphere, in which the center of speech is localized for all right-handed persons, are almost completely intact after the operation. The patients can write, solve arithmetic problems, speak, and think just as before the operation. But they can no longer perceive image-like overall impressions and gestalt-like relations, and the right hand that is controlled by the left hemisphere is now incapable of expressing such relations. The right hemisphere, however, which is incapable of producing any acts of speech and thinking whatsoever, can do this, and the left hand controlled by it can structure these impressions even after the operation. But it is now unable to perform precision work, as the right can do even after the operation. Thus, it is assumed that the abilities of thinking in images and configurations, chronological arrangement, and comprehension of general pattern relations are localized in the right hemisphere. This also includes the musicality, which is affected by the operation as well. Apart from the capacity for speech, those for abstract analogies, chronological analysis, perception of details, and mathematical abilities seem to be localized in the left hemisphere. In healthy persons each of the two hemispheres appears to contribute its specific share in close cooperation with the other concerning the processing of information that arrives: The left hemisphere makes possible the perception of details, the analysis of the successiveness of impressions, and the ability to consciously reflect on it. The right hemisphere permanently accompanies this conscious perception against a background of unified and organization-producing structures and relations which, however, are beyond any conscious experience, as the right hemisphere possesses no capacity for speech.

An interesting hypothesis starts from the assumption that a different kind of consciousness
is localized in the right hemisphere, whose existence, however, remains hidden due to the lack
of speech ability. There has even been speculation as to whether this "speechless and thus
unconscious consciousness" could be similar to animals, which are also speechless (Eccles,
1974).

13. Here a—or *the* fundamental—thesis of every theory of signs is formulated, namely that signs
represent a unity or wholeness which consists of heterogeneous elements. This fundamental
thesis can also be described as identity within difference or as a dialectic unity of opposing
elements (Baer, 1983). In Uexküll's terminology this fundamental thesis means that each very
sign represents a plan, a scheme, or a code according to which a meaning rule links together
heterogeneous elements (as meaning-carriers and meaning-utilizers) in an overall unity.

In this way the vision of an infinite hierarchy is formed, in which the meaning rule (of
the plan, scheme, or code) of a sign constantly links the meaning rules (plans, schemes, or
codes) of signs that now become elements of the overall unity of the new sign. In the terminology
of systems theory, one speaks of systems which are integrated as subsystems into suprasystems.

14. Baer very clearly illustrated this aspect in his chapter on Thomas A. Sebeok's theory of signs
and brought out the connections to René Thoms' theory of catastrophes.

15. Cf. the chapter on Thomas A. Sebeok's theory of signs, below.

REFERENCES

Baer, E. (1983). *Medical Semiotics: The State of the Art*. Bloomington, Indiana University Press.
Bertalanffy, L. von (1968). *General Systems Theory*. New York: G. Braziller.
Brock, F. (1949). "Ordnungsgesetzlichkeit in der Biologie." *Universitas*, 4, 171–176.
Cassirer, E. (1944). *An Essay on Man*. New Haven: Yale University Press, p. 23.
Eccles, J. C. (1977). "Hirn und Bewußtsein." In K. Popper & J. C. Eccles, *The Self and its Brain*.
New York: Springer.
Hartmann, H. (1949). "Comments on the Psychoanalytic Theory of the Ego." *The Psychoanalytic
Study of the Child, 5,* 74–96.
Hawkes, T. (1977). *Structuralism and Semiotics*. Berkeley and Los Angeles: University of California
Press, p. 21.
Holst, E. von, & Mittelstaedt, H. (1950). Das Reafferenzprinzip. *die Naturwissenschaften*, 37, 469–
476.
Hünemörder, C. (1979). *"Jacob von Uexküll (1864–1944) und sein Hamburger Institut für Umwelt-
forschung"* In *Festschrift zum 90. Geburtstag von Hans Schimank. Disciplinae Novae. Zur
Entstehung neuer Denk- und Arbeitsrichtungen in der Naturwissenschaft*. Veröffentlichung
der Joachim-Jungius-Gesellschaft der Wissenschaften Hamburg, No. 36. Göttingen: Van-
denhoeck & Ruprecht, pp. 105–125.
Jaynes, J. (1969). *Animal Behaviour, 17,* 601–606.
Leach, E. (1978). *Kultur und Kommunikation*. Frankfurt a. M.: Suhrkamp.
Morris, C. W. (1972). *Foundation of the Theory of Signs*. Chicago: University of Chicago Press.
Müller, J. P. (1840). *Handbuch der Physiologie des Menschen*, Vol. II. Coblenz, p. 254.
Plessner, H. (1976). *Die Frage nach der Conditio Humana*. Frankfurt a. M.: Suhrkamp, p. 47.
Sebeok, T. A. (1976). *Studies in Semiotics*. Lisse: De Ridder.
Sebeok, T. A. (1979). *The Sign and Its Masters*. Austin: University of Texas Press, 187.
Uexküll, J. von (1902). "Psychologie und Biologie in ihrer Stellung zur Tierseele." *Ergebnisse der
Physiologie*, 1, 212–233.
Uexküll, J. von (1905). *Leitfaden in das Studium der experimentellen Biologie der Wassertiere*.
Wiesbaden.

Uexküll, J. von (1931). *Der Organismus und die Umwelt*. Rpt. Berlin: Propyläen 1980.

Uexküll, J. von (1935). Der Kampf um den Himmel. *Die Neue Rundschau*, 46, 367.

Uexküll, J. von (1947). *Der Sinn des Lebens*. Godesberg, Rpt. Stuttgart. Klett 1977.

Uexküll, J. von (1970a). *Streifzüge durch die Umwelten von Tieren und Menschen*. Rpt. Frankfurt a. M.: Fischer (first edition 1934).

Uexküll, J. von (1970b). *Die Bedeutungslehre*. Rpt. Frankfurt a. M.: Fischer (first ed., 1940).

Uexküll, J. von (1973). *Theoretische Biologie*. Rpt. of second edition of 1928, Frankfurt a. M.: Suhrkamp.

Uexküll, J. von (1980). *Kompositionslehre der Natur—Biologie als undogmatische Naturwissenschaft, Ausgewählte Schriften*. Ed. by T. von Uexkuell. Berlin: Propyläen.

Uexküll, T. von (1978). "Autopoietisches oder autokinetisches System? In P. M. Hejl et al. (Eds.), *Wahrnehmung und Kommunikation*. Frankfurt a. M.: Peter Lang, p. 141.

Uexküll, T. von (Ed.) (1979). *Lehrbuch der Psychosomatischen Medizin*. München: Urban & Schwarzenberg, pp. 68, 100f.

Uexküll, T. von (Ed.) (1980). *Jakob von Uexkuell, Kompositionslehre der Natur—Biologie als undogmatische Naturwissenschaft. Ausgewählte Schriften*. Berlin: Propyläen.

Wiener, N. (1963). *Kybernetik*. Düsseldorf: Econ.

CHAPTER 8

Thomas A. Sebeok's Doctrine of Signs

EUGEN BAER

Semiosis must be recognized as a pervasive fact of nature as well as of culture. In such matters, then, I declare myself not only a Peircean but a (René) Thomist. (Sebeok, 1979a: 64)

1. SEBEOK'S CAREER AND THEORETICAL POINT OF DEPARTURE

This being a very personal reckoning, I would like to seize this occasion to publicly avow my good fortune at having first encountered semiotic notions in a University of Chicago seminar of Morris' in the early 1940s—precisely midway, that is, between his *Foundations of the Theory of Signs* (1938) and *Signs, Language, and Behavior* (1946). I have thus had the singular, and very likely unique, privilege of having studied both with Morris and, not long afterwards, Jakobson, the two having cross-pollinated in the intervening years. (Sebeok, 1976: 155)

Thomas A. Sebeok was born in Budapest in 1920, and arrived in the United States in 1937, where he first studied at the University of Chicago (B.A. 1941), with Charles Morris as his most important professor. He then attended Princeton University (M.A. 1943; Ph.D. 1945), where Roman Jakobson in particular, from his base in New York, exercised a great influence on him. Since 1943, Sebeok has taught linguistics, anthropology, and semiotics at Indiana University in Bloomington, where he also directs the Research Center for Language and Semiotic Studies. In 1975 he was president of the Linguistic Society of America. From 1976 to 1980 he was Executive Director of the Semiotic Society of America, whose founding and rapid growth can largely be attributed to his initiative and expertise, and in 1984 he served as its president.

EUGEN BAER • Department of Philosophy, Hobart and William Smith Colleges, Geneva, New York.

Sebeok is the author and editor of many books, whose themes converge at the crossroads of linguistics, semiotics, anthropology, and ethology. Among his principal works are *Contributions to the Doctrine of Signs* (1976), *The Sign & Its Masters* (1979), and *The Play of Musement* (1981). Since 1969 he has been Editor-in-Chief of the journal *Semiotica*, of which 55 volumes have been published to date (1985). In addition, he is the editor of numerous series of books in linguistics and semiotics, including *Current Trends in Linguistics* (1963–76, 13 volumes plus an index volume), *Approaches to Semiotics* (1968–), *Studies in Semiotics* (1975–78), *Advances in Semiotics* (1974–). *Studies in Contemporary Semiotics* (1979–), and *The Newberry Series in Nonverbal Behavior* (1979–1985).

The point of departure for Sebeok's doctrine of signs is found in biology. He has in this respect a self-affirmed intellectual affinity with Peirce, who on the basis of logic developed for the theory of signs a starting point that reduced the "logic of the universe," the "logic of life," and the "logic of language" to the common denominator of universal semiotic relations. In a similar vein, Sebeok situates communication systems as they extend throughout the entire biological spectrum, from cell to animal to man, within the framework of the systematic interplay of signs. In its broadest dimension, this interplay is to be understood as a convergence of genetics and linguistics (Sebeok, 1976: 69):

> The terminology of genetics is replete with expressions borrowed from linguistics and from the theory of communication, as was recently pointed out by Jakobson (1974), who also emphasized the salient similarities and equally important differences between the respective structures and functions of the genetic and verbal codes. These, of course, urgently need further elucidation and precision. Yet it is amply clear even now that the genetic code must be regarded as the most fundamental of all semiotic networks and therefore as the prototype for all other signaling systems used by animals, including man. From this point of view, molecules that are quantum systems, acting as stable physical information carriers, zoosemiotic systems, and, finally, cultural systems, comprehending language, constitute a natural sequel of stages of ever more complex energy levels in a single universal evolution. It is possible, therefore, to describe language as well as living systems from a unified cybernetic standpoint. While this is perhaps no more than a useful analogy at present, hopefully providing insight if not yet new information, a mutual appreciation of genetics, animal communication studies, and linguistics may lead to a full understanding of the dynamics of semiosis, and this may, in the last analysis, turn out to be no less than the definition of life.

Such a broad—i.e., biologically rooted—semiotics as Sebeok advocates in this passage functions as an echo of the anthropic cosmological principle (Barrow and Silk, 1980). According to this principle, the conditions of the macrophysical universe originally were determined so as later to bring about human life on earth, a situation whose result is presumably to render the human observer an indispensable part of the macrophysical world. Sebeok formulates the homologous relation between the genetic code and language in similar fashion, namely, as a variation on the theme of prefiguration. According to Sebeok, all semiosis, in its infinite variety, takes place on our planet within the bounds of two universal sign systems. The first and foundational system is constituted by the genetic code, which, as it seems, exhibits the same structure in all organisms on earth. The other, crowning sign system is the verbal code of natural language, which likewise exhibits a more or less common structure among all peoples of the earth. In between these two systems life in its multifarious variations runs its course—variations which all turn out to be on the single theme "semiosis," for semiosis is in Sebeok's view the criterion and principle of organization for all life.

The minimum structure of semiosis is the triadic sign relation as formulated by Peirce. In accordance with this structure, organism and *Umwelt* [to use Uexküll's term for the environment as it is structured perceptually by an organism according to its organization and biological needs/translator] stand in a relation of mutual reference and hence in a reciprocal sign relation. An organism functions as a sign-vehicle of its Umwelt; that is, we can conclude from the structure of the organism to that of its Umwelt. Conversely, the Umwelt functions as sign-vehicle of the organism which corresponds to it; analysis of the Umwelt enables us to infer the structure of the organism. Thus organism and Umwelt stand in a reversible relation where each serves interchangeably as sign-vehicle and as object of the sign. This relation is made possible on the basis of a meaning-plan (Uexküll, 1940: 43) encompassing the organism and its Umwelt, which functions as the third element necessary for semiosis (namely, as code) and establishes the meaning link between the sign-vehicle and its object.

The meaning-plan precedes the individual organism ontogenetically, such that succeeding generations of living beings are seen as progressive interpretive chains of the meaning-plan. The meaning-plan itself undergoes changes throughout the course of this progression, albeit such changes are recognizable only over relatively long periods of time. Sebeok sees the groundwork of semiotics as resting in the process of biological reproduction, to the extent that reproduction brings to light that a sign completes itself only through replication in another sign. Living beings are signs that reproduce themselves; they are complex forms that through ongoing procreation interpret an Umwelt which emerges through the same process, and, conversely, are interpreted by the Umwelt and thus acquire their specific being.

By comprehending semiosis in this way, Sebeok consciously places semiotics upon the foundations of information and communication theory, much as do Bentele and Bystřina (1978) in the German-speaking world. The upshot of this is that he speaks of sign processes wherever information is transferred, and this is already the case with the simplest monerans. Semiosis, considered as the exchange of information, encompasses the entire domain of that which we commonly designate as "life," keeping in mind with Sherrington (1963) that "life," although a quite useful concept, is not a precise one. What we conventionally call "life" is perhaps best characterized as an integrated form of organization in

which one system of energy, in an ordered process of exchange with another
system of energy that surrounds it, is capable of maintaining itself as at once
an independent (closed) system and a dependent (open) one, in other words, as
simultaneously self and nonself. The link between these two conditions is established by the concept of code, as Sebeok remarks (1976: 2):

> Messages may be emitted and/or received either by inorganic objects, such as machines,
> or by organic substances, for instance, animals, including man, or by some of their
> component parts (e.g., ribonucleic acid, mRNA, that serves as an information-bearing
> tape "read" by particles, called ribosomes, that travel along it, carrying amino acid
> sequence information [Ičas, 1969: 8]); one may also speak of information, for instance,
> in cardiovascular functioning, where messages are conveyed from peripheral vessels
> to the brain, relayed thence to the heart and back to the brain [Adey, 1967: 21]. The
> interaction of organic beings with inorganic things (such as communication between
> a man and a computer) can also be treated as a semiotic problem.

We have here one of the broadest understandings of semiotics possible.
Sebeok sees himself as developing further the semiotic tradition established by
Peirce's pioneering work. His own historical point of departure goes back much
further, though, and, significantly, can be found in ancient medicine. Semiotics
was originally equivalent to medical symptomatology. Just as the natural sciences
have their origin in medicine (Buchanan, 1938: 44), so too are the deepest roots
of semiotics, which Sebeok maintains is gradually coming to reveal itself as the
general organon of all fields of knowledge, to be found in the "semeiology" of
the Hippocratic tradition.

2. HISTORICAL SKETCH OF THE SEMIOTIC TRADITION

> The term *semiotic*, confined in earliest usage to medical concerns with the sensible
> indications of changes in the condition of the human body, that is, symptomatology,
> later came to be used by the Stoics with a broader meaning and seems to have been
> introduced into English philosophical discourse by John Locke, in Chapter XXI of
> his *Essay Concerning Humane Understanding* (1690).
>
> ——Sebeok, 1976: 63——

Although Sebeok legitimately maintains that a comprehensive history of
semiotics "is yet to be written" (1976: 4 n. 8, 55), he nonetheless offers a series
of brief outlines (e.g., 1976: 3–26, 59f., 150–156, 181–185) that reveal a certain
systematic perspective. The most significant of his historical sketches may well
be the "semiotic tripod" of three foundational semiotic traditions, which he
formulates as follows (1976: 181):

> In our semiotic Pantheon, the name of Saussure stands engraved as the emblem
> for the linguistic affinities and extensions of the hierarchically superordinate field,
> while that of Peirce, "the heir of the whole historical philosophical analysis of signs"

> (Morris, 1971: 337), and now manifestly the benchmark for all contemporary delib-
> erations, epitomizes its manifold filiation with the profoundest strata of human wis-
> dom. The third, admittedly uneven leg upon which semiotics rests, very likely the
> most deeply rooted, is medicine, the revered ancestral figure surely being Hippocrates
> (c. 460–c. 377 B.C.), "der Vater und Meister aller Semiotik." (Kleinpaul, 1972: 103)

According to Sebeok, the first doctrine of signs was developed in medicine, no doubt at least partly for the reason that in the archaic social environment, the offices of physician, priest, and patriarch were united in a single individual, a union which corresponded on the objective side to a consubstantiality of medicine, religion, and way of life. Comparative ethnology offers many examples of such reciprocal relations between medicine and myth, medical diagnosis and divine revelation. So it was also entirely natural that in some cultures inferences were made about the symptomatology of the cosmos on the basis of that of the body and vice versa. The Pre-Socratics of Asia Minor and the Chinese Taoists (to cite two parallel examples) understood the body and the cosmos as a functional unity in their doctrine of the rhythmic harmony of the elements (in Asia Minor four, in China five). This concept of unity was further developed by the Stoics and the alchemists in terms of a homologous relation between macrocosmos and microcosmos. Sebeok brings to our attention, again in this area, the pioneering work accomplished by such physicians as Sextus Empiricus and Galen (Sebeok, 1976: 125–126):

> Symptomatology, or semeiology [cf. Sebeok, 1976: 53f.], eventually developed into
> a branch of medicine with a specialized threefold preoccupation with diagnostics,
> focusing on the here and now, and its twin temporal projections into the anamnestic
> past and the prognostic future (or as Galen [A.D. 130–? 200] used to teach, "Semeiot-
> ice in tres partes dirimitur, in praeteritorum cognitionem, in praesentium inspectionem
> et futurorum providentiam").

Locke, too, who in 1690 reintroduced the term "semiotic," this time into epistemology, was originally a physician. For the most part, though, maintains Sebeok, physicians have failed to recognize the semiotic foundations of their art. It has only been in most recent times—principally as a result of von Bertalanffy's (1950) application to biology of systematic philosophical thought (Kant, 1781; Hegel, 1807)—that a renewal of medicine as a science of communication has been ascertainable, emerging out of psychoanalysis and psychiatry. Representatives in the United States include particularly the Palo Alto Group (D. D. Jackson, J. Haley, J. Weakland, J. Ruesch, G. Bateson, P. Watzlawick) and Harley C. Shands (1970). In the German-speaking world, particular mention should be made of Viktor von Weizsäcker (1947) and Thure von Uexküll (1979c; reviewed in Baer, 1981).

Of all contemporary semioticians, none has alluded more than Sebeok to the medical origin of the doctrine of signs or done more to promote publications in the area of medical semiotics (Shands 1970, 1977; Ruesch 1972; Scheflen 1973; Baer 1975; Staiano 1979). The *Lehrbuch der Psychosomatischen Medizin*, edited by Thure von Uexküll, stands as a classic example of what Sebeok has striven toward for many years in a broader anthropological and ethological—i.e., intercultural and biological—framework.

The second pillar of Sebeok's semiotic triad is philosophy, which emerged among the Pre-Socratics out of the native soil of medicine and which the Sophists emancipated as a distinct discipline. The semiotic heritage passes from Heraclitus, who roots semiotics in the Delphic oracle and situates the quest for the self in a cosmic meaning plan (Romeo 1979), through Socrates, Plato, and Aristotle, to its first explicit development of terminology in the Stoics. It proceeds through Plotinus and Augustine to the "scientia sermocinalis" of the Middle Ages (grammar, logic, and rhetoric). John Poinsot (1589–1644), also known under the name John of St. Thomas, provides, with his *Tractatus de Signis* (1632; cf. Powell as cited in Deely 1985: 470), the transition to Leibniz and the British Empiricists. The interest that Leibniz showed in syntactic structures and his attempt to establish a universal sign system (*characteristica universalis*) were further developed by logicians such as Boole, Carnap, Frege, Gomperz, Husserl, Lambert, Peano, Russell, Tarski, and Whitehead. The British empiricists (Francis Bacon, Bentham, Berkeley, Hobbes, Hume, Locke) occupied themselves more with the semantic dimension. Between these two movements is situated the transcendental philosophy introduced by Kant, which Hegel transformed into a dialectical science whose profound semiotic dimensions have yet to be investigated. Peirce, who in one place characterized his philosophy as "resuscitat[ing] Hegel, though in a strange costume" (c.1892: 1.42), stands, in the final analysis, as "the real founder and first systematic investigator of modern semiotic" (Sebeok, 1976: 5). He united the syntactic and semantic dimensions in singular fashion and is thus viewed by Sebeok as the principal representative of the philosophical pillar of the semiotic triad.

The third pillar in the metaphorical triad is linguistics, as reshaped and opened up by Saussure (Sebeok 1976: 11–12):

> In contrast to Peirce—who was heir to the entire tradition of philosophical analysis of signs—Saussure's point of departure and constant center of attention was language: for him, the notion of the sign was primarily a linguistic fact, that somehow expanded to encompass the other processes of human, in particular social, signaling behavior. As for Locke before him, and for many scholars after him—for instance, Bloomfield, who asserted that "Linguistics is the chief contributor to semiotic" (1939: 55), or Weinreich, who called natural human language "the semiotic phenomenon par excellence" (1968: 164)—for Saussure language occupied pride of place among all semiotic systems.

Saussure recognized that a general theory of signs (*sémiologie*) was indispensable for the interpretation of natural languages. For this reason he sought to compare language with other human sign systems. In contrast to Peirce, though, he viewed the linguistic model as providing the common pattern for all semiotics. For Sebeok, the role of language is of great importance, but he sees the predominance of the linguistic model in semiotic research as constricting the general theory of signs at the expense of zoosemiotics. From the point of view of the glottocentric Saussurean tradition, maintains Sebeok, it is difficult to see semiosis as a biological as well as a human social process. There exists on this account a tension between the Locke-Peirce-Morris pattern on the one hand and Saussurean pattern on the other. Still, this tension need not have crippling consequences for semiotics, but can have beneficial, complementary effects, as is evidenced in the work of Roman Jakobson. "It is precisely in the writings of Jakobson," states Sebeok (1976: 152), "that the two principal modern semiotic traditions—what I referred to elsewhere (ibid.: Ch. 2) as the 'Locke-Peirce-Morris pattern' and the 'Saussure pattern'—have creatively coalesced."

We will nonetheless see the tension between Saussure and Peirce resurface in another form in Section 6, below, in our discussion of Sebeok's encounters with Roland Barthes and René Thom. The opposition between the two starting points, which can be roughly characterized as "linguistic" versus "biological," is too important to Sebeok for him to try to resolve it in some kind of facile synthesis. What is at stake for Sebeok in this tension is nothing less than that entire area of semiotics which he has become famous for naming and researching— namely, zoosemiotics.

3. ANTHROPOSEMIOTICS AND ZOOSEMIOTICS

> Man's total communicative repertoire consists of two sorts of sign systems: the anthroposemiotic, that is, those that are exclusively human, and the zoosemiotic, that is, those that can be shown to be the end-products of evolutionary series. The two are often confused, but it is important to distinguish the purely anthroposemiotic systems, found solely in man, from his zoosemiotic . . . systems, which man shares with at least some ancestral species.
>
> ——Sebeok, 1976: 65——

Sebeok introduced the term "zoosemiotics" in 1963 (Sebeok, 1963: 465–466) to refer to the intersection of the doctrine of signs and ethology. Zoosemiotics is a branch of biosemiotics, but it is not restricted to the communicative behavior of animals, as is often falsely supposed today. On the contrary, it has as its subject matter those aspects of human communication and information processes which we share with other animals. Two concepts stand above all others at its center: ritualization and morphology.

The term "ritualization" was coined by Julian Huxley in 1914 to characterize the so-called "penguin dance" that takes place during the courtship ceremony of the great crested grebe. It designates the ordering and channeling—the "semiotization"—of genetically informed behavior. Sebeok designates ritualization as "the semiosis of *gene-dependency*" (1979a: 29), and distinguishes it from three other kinds of semiosis (Figure 1).

	I.	2.
A. SYNCHRONIC	*Ego-Dependency* Signification Structure "Being"	*Interdependency* Communication Function "Behaving"
B. DIACHRONIC	*Alter-dependency* Infancy, senescence, incapacitation Learned codes	*Gene-dependency* Ritualization Hereditary codes
	"Becoming"	
	3.	4.

Figure 1. Four varieties of semiosis. From Sebeok, 1979a: 30.

Of course, these four varieties of semiosis cannot actually be divided so neatly. On the synchronic level, the ego-dependency of signs represents their organization and structure. This is the object of structural analysis of signs, while the aspect of interdependency is investigated by means of functional analysis and in the communication sciences. On the diachronic level, genetically mediated sign structures (e.g., the genetic code) are distinguished from socially mediated structures (e.g., traffic codes). But the entire scheme must be comprehended in terms of the interaction of all its elements, such as takes place, for example, when a child learns its native language. According to Sebeok, semiotic research is still in its infancy and has first to learn its own native language, namely, the general theory or doctrine of signs. The neglect of such a common "language" has had as its consequence that none of the several million biological meaning-plans that exist on our planet and fall under the rubric of ritualization has been adquately investigated. In Sebeok's own words (1976: 87):

> As for the pious goal of a perfect ethogram, unfortunately this still remains just that, for, despite the fact that the literature of animal behavior is now enormous, and still rapidly ramifying, none of the several millions of codes still in use is entirely understood by man. This is true even of the best researched code, namely, the one that regulates the remarkable communication system evolved in *Apis mellifera*, the honeybee. While the fact that these bees perform intricate movements—their famous 'dances'—in directing hive-mates to a source of food supply, or to new quarters, has been widely reported and is now a familiar story, it is less well known that these insects transmit information by acoustic means as well. Investigators in several laboratories, working independently of one another, have been attempting to complete an account of this facet of the apiarian ethogram, in spite of the prejudgment of some major scholars that the ancient ideas of acoustic communication among the bees "belong in the realm of fantasy." Communication by sounds does occur in bees, and it is probably even more elaborate and significant than has been anticipated. As K. von Frisch himself once remarked, "the life of bees is like a magic well. The more you

draw from it, the more there is to draw." The same is undoubtedly true of the life of all the other speechless creatures, while our knowledge of their communicative capacities and means remains even more rudimentary.

The general biological morphology developed by René Thom (1974) with the aid of mathematical topology stands alongside ritualized behavior and is even more fundamental. I will address this in more detail in Section 6, below. Suffice it to say here that for Sebeok the biological generation of forms, or morphogenesis, is the sign function *par excellence*, in precisely the sense of the structurally and functionally reciprocal relation between an organ or organism and its functional correlate, or Umwelt, discussed in Section 1, above.

Sebeok contrasts anthroposemiotics on the one hand with zoo- and biosemiotics on the other. As distinguished from biosemiotics, which deals with the sign systems of all living beings, anthroposemiotics analyzes only those sign systems which are exclusively human. The principal constituent of this branch of semiotics is language, considered not only in its verbal aspect but also in its alternate acoustic and visual forms, such as are used by persons with disabilities of sight, hearing, and speech. All other alternate forms of linguistic communication—for example, monastic sign languages (Barakat, 1975), the sign languages of certain peoples in Australia and the Americas (Umiker-Sebeok and Sebeok, 1978), Morse code and similar transmission codes—belong to anthroposemiotics as well. To anthroposemiotics, too, belongs the concept of secondary modeling systems that is found among Soviet semioticians (the so-called Moscow-Tartu school). Such systems are implicitly contained in art, science, literature, religion, politics, and so forth, as common models of the world, and can ultimately be traced back to natural languages—or, as Wittgenstein would say (1958), to "language games"—as the primary modeling system (Winner and Winner, 1976). All secondary modeling systems, therefore, are anthroposemiotic.

According to Sebeok, the threshold between zoosemiotics and anthroposemiotics is not abrupt. There is, rather, a border region of sign systems which have traditionally been designated as anthroposemiotic but whose prefigurements are present in animals (Sebeok, 1979c; reprinted in Sebeok, 1981: 210–259). For example, we have today the field of ornithomusicology (Szöke, 1963). It is possible that bird melodies phylogenetically influenced the emergence of the first human music. In addition to music, there are other nonverbal forms of art that can be considered as zoosemiotic prefigurements of anthroposemiotic phenomena, such as the nonrepresentational painting of apes and the colorful ornamentation of certain birds' nests. For this reason Sebeok suggests as a general heuristic rule (1979a: 40; 1979c) that all sign systems which are not obviously dependent on language (e.g., kinaesthetic, musical, artistic, and architectonic signs) be considered as zoosemiotic systems as long as the contrary is not proven.

Language and its alternate forms indeed appear to be the only anthroposemiotic systems. Even in language, though, Sebeok finds a structural principle that links it with the biological infrastructure of the genetic code (1976: 86–87):

The code underlying any system of animal communication differs crucially from any language insofar as the former is simply tantamount to the total repertoire of messages at the disposal of the species, whereas a true language is always imbued by the structural principle that linguists have called 'double articulation' or 'duality of patterning', involving a rule governed device for constructing a potentially infinite array of larger units (e.g., sentences, in the so-called natural languages) out of a finite, indeed, very small and stable assembly of smaller ones (viz., the uniformly binary distinctive features). This enormously powerful and productive hierarchic arrangement—obviously recognized by Darwin in his keen observation that "The lower animals differ from man solely in his almost infinitely larger power of associating together the most diversified sounds and ideas . . ."—seems to have emerged but twice in terrestrial evolution, both times with stupendous consequences: the same structural principle informs the genetic code (the Beadles' 'language of life') and the verbal code (our own faculty of language). It has, however, so far, not been identified in any other animal communication system studied (including, incidentally, that of captive chimpanzees in the Western United States, who have recently enjoyed publicity of the sort previously accorded only to bottle-nosed dolphins, those fading stars of fact and fiction of yesteryear). It is therefore scientifically inaccurate, as well as, even metaphorically, highly misleading, to speak of a 'language' of animals.

Such a unique structural analogy justifies, in Sebeok's view, the need for a comparative semiotics, which has as its object, in addition to the multitude of human sign systems, the signaling behavior of the other two million or so existing animal species. Sebeok himself offers the best evidence of how fruitful such a zoosemiotically informed point of departure can be for the general enterprise of semiotic classification.

4. CONTRIBUTIONS TO THE CLASSIFICATION OF SIGNS AND SIGN SYSTEMS

The outlines of a semiotics that eschews anthropocentrism, coupled with an ethology that shuns parochialism, can already be envisaged. It seems likely that a full-fledged synthesis will be achieved before long, offering both a new paradigm and a methodology for the comparative analysis of semiosis in its full diversity, ranging from the two vast linked polymer languages at one end of the scale to the thousands of natural languages at the other, with a host of singular information coding and transmission devices, inside and outside the body of every organism, in between. Semiosis, independent of form or substance, is thus seen as a universal, criterial property of animate existence.

——Sebeok, 1976: 93——

It is clear that from the standpoint of Sebeok's comparative semiotics, signs cannot be classified on the basis of the traditional division, dating from Aristotle, between linguistic and nonlinguistic sign users. Sebeok's biological foundation makes possible a view of the scope of semiotics in which linguistic (i.e., anthroposemiotic) signs occupy a relatively small place, as is shown in one of his diagrams (Figure 2).

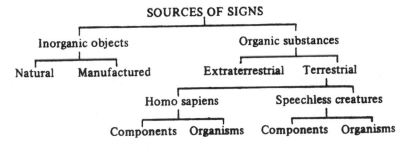

Figure 2. Classification of signs according to source. From Sebeok, 1976: 27.

This model is limited to systems whose components are all living, and is set up from the point of view of sources of signs, or sign producers—that is, from the side of input, where the encoding of the information exchange begins. The scheme is greatly simplified, but it immediately becomes more complex when we introduce the same model on the side of the sign receiver, i.e., on the other side of the feedback chain of a communicative situation. Thus arises a second point of view for purposes of classification, namely that of the interaction between senders and receivers. With animal senders and receivers, sign interaction takes place either within a single species (intraspecifically) or among members of two or more species (interspecifically), one of which may also be man or a machine (cf. Hediger, 1967). Those message exchanges which are species-specific to man can be further divided into the intrapersonal, for which only one participant is needed (here we have the phenomenon of inner speech or internal dialogue), the interpersonal (e.g., a dialogue that requires a Thou in addition to an I), and the pluripersonal (in the oral tradition of the Eskimos, for example, "the myth-teller speaks as many-to-many, not as person-to-person" [Carpenter, 1960; quoted in Sebeok, 1976: 28]). The semiotic paradigm, maintains Sebeok (ibid.), is in the position to bring under a common denominator a wealth of disciplines and viewpoints that have otherwise not been seen as related:

> A human message may be directed at a machine, or at a personified supernatural, as in an incantation or a prayer addressed to a deity (Sebeok, 1962a); communication with ancestral spirits is prevalent and commonplace in many cultures, for example, in New Guinea (Eilers, 1967: 34–36). Vice versa, animates may receive signs from the environment—cf. the phenomenon of echolocation (Griffin, 1968),—or fancy receiving them, "as in some of the epigrams of Callimachus and of his imitators, the stone is thought of as carrying on a brief dialogue with the passerby" (Hadas, 1954: 50–51), or again from the location of stars and planets, the length and intersection of lines in the hand, the entrails of sheep, the position of dregs in a teacup—in brief, by those pseudo-semiotic divinatory techniques that are known variously as augury, astrology, palmistry, haruspication, and the like (Kleinpaul, 1888: Ch. III; Kahn, 1967: 92).

A third factor in sign classification is that of the media of transmission, or *channels*, which link together sender and receiver, input and output. Sebeok

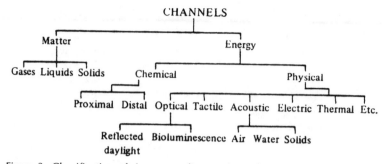

Figure 3. Classification of signs according to channels. From Sebeok, 1976: 30.

(1976: 30) has drawn up a simplified diagram of the classification of signs according to their channels (Figure 3).

We can immediately grasp the breadth of Sebeok's semiotic perspective if we extract a single element from Figure 3 and further subdivide it. Sebeok has already done this (1979a: 48) for the class of acoustic signs (Figure 4).

Sebeok's fundamental tendency to extend the scope of semiotics to the broad and largely unresearched area of zoosemiotics is again manifest in a fourth point of view from which he suggests signs can be classified, namely, the point of view of the distinction between signs produced by the body alone (organismal) and those produced with the aid of tools (artifactual). Both animal and human sign systems can be thus divided. Sebeok shows, often masterfully (see, for example, Sebeok, 1979c), the great variety and richness of sign systems among animals. In a 1971 article (published in Sebeok 1976: 1–45), he describes the use of semiotic tools in the animal kingdom (ibid.: 30–31):

> The use of both ready-made objects and shaped artifacts as tools is known to occur variously throughout the animal world, ranging from moths and spiders through birds, otters, and primates. Chimpanzees of the Gombe Stream Reserve, for instance, build nests, fold selected leaves to facilitate drinking or to wipe their body, use sticks, twigs, and grasses to get termites, ants, or honey, and use them, as well, as olfactory

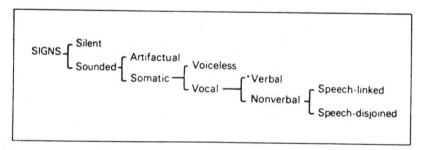

Figure 4. Subclassification of acoustic signs. Categories marked by asterisks are assumed to be purely anthroposemiotic. From Sebeok, 1979a: 48.

probes; they also use stones to break nuts, and employ both sticks and stones in agonistic displays (van Lawick-Goodall, 1968). The instrumental behavior of these chimpanzees exemplifies a twofold function of tool using in animals and man: a (presumably) primary amplifying function, and a (presumably) secondary semiotic function . . . The instrumental—as opposed to the merely somatic—production of animal signs sometimes takes exceedingly bizarre forms, as in those "wonderful arena birds called bower birds, with their houses and ornamented gardens and their courtship displays that replace plumage with glittering natural jewelry" (Gilliard, 1963).

Perhaps Sebeok's greatest contribution to the doctrine of signs consists in his systematic application of fundamental semiotic concepts to the animal world. Since 1971 he has tirelessly dedicated himself to demonstrating how signals, symptoms, and syndromes, icons, indices, symbols, and names are found not only in the human domain, but also in those of other animals. Out of this large body of research, I wish simply to select Sebeok's three basic notions of icon, index, and symbol presenting first Sebeok's definition, then briefly summarizing some of his explanatory remarks. The literature relevant to this subject can be found in Sebeok, 1968, 1972, 1976, 1979a, 1979b, and 1979c.

4.1. Icon

"A sign is said to be iconic when there is a topological similarity between a signifier and its denotata" (Sebeok, 1976: 43).

The hind end of an aphid's abdomen can signify to a worker an the head of another ant (Figure 5). Aphids are small insects that are "milked" by ants; that is, the ants vibrate their antennae on the aphids' backs, and this stimulates the aphids to secrete drops of honeydew that the ants consume. This most interesting relation appears to be rooted in a similarity between the hind end of the aphid and the front end of the ant, a similarity that remains completely mystifying to the human observer. According to Sebeok, we are dealing here with an effigy, a subtype of icon. Alluding to Uexküll's terminology (1920), he calls the likeness produced by the aphid's hind end an "iconic releasing

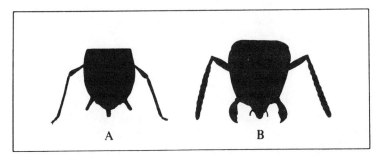

Figure 5. Aphid and ant. A. Icon. B. Object. From Sebeok, 1979a: 13.

(*auslösendes*) schema" (Sebeok 1979a: 14) which "sparks off the ant's chain of behavior pattern" (ibid.).

This reduces ethological and semiotic analyses to a common denominator. It must, however, be noted that the iconicity Sebeok establishes for the animal— in contrast to us as observers—stands ground only when the ant's receptors (e.g., eyes, antennae, pheromonal senses of smell) are comprehended as encoding the aphid's hind end much as our own visual perception would. Jakob von Uexküll (1940), let us recall, endeavored throughout his entire life to draw attention to the fallacy of conceiving animal modes of perception in terms of our own.

4.2. Index

"A sign is said to be indexic insofar as its signifier is contiguous with its signified, or is a sample of it" (Sebeok 1976: 43).

In the family *Picoidea*, species *Indicator indicator*, there is a small group of wax-eating birds, the well-known honey-guides (Sebeok 1979a: 14–18). These birds follow certain mammals, including the honey badger, the baboon, and man, to nests of wild bees. This is a genuine case of symbiosis between two very different species. The bird can find beehives, often on almost inaccessible branches, but cannot open them. The above-mentioned mammals cannot easily find well-hidden hives, but have no problem in opening them. Each species assists the other in a genuine interspecific partnership. For example, the bird will approach African natives (sometimes the natives use signals to call the bird) and will chirp until they follow it. Although the seesawing flight of the bird, with its white tail feathers widely spread, is striking in itself, the honey-guide "indicates" largely with the aid of a repeated chain of chirruping sounds that abate only when its goal is reached—that is, when the bird sees or hears flying, buzzing bees. It is well worth noting that the bird does not depend at all upon wax for its sustenance. From this it can be concluded that other factors besides mere chance mutation and natural selection must have played a role in the formation of this indexical meaning-plan. What kind of factors these might have been still remains unknown. Moreover, this phylogenetic problem is underscored and intensified by an ontogenetic puzzle. The honey-guide is a brood parasite, and thus the question arises as to how it learns its indicating behavior, since the "stepparents" that raise it have nothing to do with the matter.

4.3. Symbol

"A sign without either similarity or contiguity—but only with a conventional link between its signifier and its denotata, and with an intensional class for its designatum is called a symbol" (Sebeok 1976: 43).

The so-called balloon fly, a member of the carnivorous family Empidiae, offers the female of its species during courtship a captured insect as a "wedding present" (Sebeok 1979a: 18). As copulation takes place, the female sucks peaceably on the captured insect. Immediately following copulation, the female drops the present, and if she is still hungry she eats her now useless partner. In the species *Hilara sartor*, discovered by Osten-Sacken, the male offers the female an empty balloon. Instead of a wedding present, there is only a gift package with nothing inside. According to Sebeok (ibid.: 19), we are faced here with "the realization of the American dream"—"all packaging, no content." The female is so preoccupied with opening the package that the male can copulate in peace and preserve his well-being. The empty balloon is evidently a case of a completely arbitrary sign. The "discovery" of this symbol saves the life of the male balloon fly.

With respect to his three "biosemiotic fables" illustrating uses of icons, indices, and symbols among animals, Sebeok often insists, as does Peirce (1902: 2.303), that the icon/index/symbol distinction is not a trichotomy of mutually exclusive significative features. Rather, each of these aspects can be found in the same sign, and a given sign is legitimately, albeit indeterminately, labeled according to its predominant aspect (Sebeok 1976: 121).

5. ENDOSEMIOTICS AND EXOSEMIOTICS: THE SEMIOTIC SELF

[Life is] only a sign's way of making another sign.

——*Sebeok, 1979a: xiii*——

Sebeok has in common with the Romantics not simply their admiration of the magnificient systematic arrangement of nature. He also shares their interest in the polarity of self and non-self and their formulation of this polarity in terms of correlative mirror images. There is, however, this difference: Sebeok extends the mirror relation to the entire biological order and formulates it afresh semiotically. In this way, Jakob von Uexküll's extension of Kant's system to the animal world links up with the dialectical logic of Novalis and Hegel, a linkage embodied in his conceptual pair, endosemiosis/exosemiosis.

To understand this polarity, it is necessary to begin with Novalis' and Hegel's formulations and their transformations in Sebeok's work. According to Novalis (1901: 239), an ego is an ego only "insofar as it is a non-ego" ("insofern es ein Nicht-Ich ist"). Hegel explains this by maintaining that the non-ego is a *translation* (*meta-phora, trans-latio*) of the ego which is realized through the actions of the ego (Hegel, 1807: 239–240): . . . action simply translates an initially implicit being into a being that is made explicit. . . . Accordingly, an individual cannot know what he [really] is until he has made himself a reality through action." (German original, p. 227: "Das Tun ist nämlich nur reines Übersetzen aus der Form des noch nicht dargestellten in die des dargestellten

Seins. . . . das Individuum kann daher nicht wissen, was *es ist*, eh es sich durch das Tun zur Wirklichkeit gebracht hat." [Hegel, 1973: 227]) Here the Umwelt is seen as a representation of or in contrast to the Innenwelt (inner world). The transition from this to Sebeok is simply a matter of terminology. For him, the Innenwelt is semiotically tied to the Umwelt; the outer and the inner are so related "that the minimal information derivable from inner sources comes to be a reliable index of the external situation" (Shands, 1976: 303). Sebeok designates as "endosemiotic" those sign processes which take place internally to an organism and "exosemiotic" those which involve the organism along with its environment. An extensive code governs the translation of endosemiosis into exosemiosis and vice versa. The boundaries between the interconnected worlds of the ego and the non-ego obey a most interesting biological regulatory rhythm, which varies from the virtually complete effacement of the boundaries in sleep to a state of highly pointed intensity when the organism is warding off enemies.

Endosemiotics and exosemiotics have as their object these regulatory processes, which, taking them together, Sebeok also terms "the semiotic self" (1979a: 263–267). This "self" is provided with a casing, as it were, of an immune system on the one hand and a system of anxiety signals on the other, systems which complement one another. Sebeok sees them as memory systems, the immune system for the most part inherited biologically and the system of anxiety signals mostly learned. Both "internalize" the organ or organism itself; that is, they secure the preservation of the above mentioned boundaries of ego and non-ego in accordance with an encompassing code. In this way, both regulate the oscillating balance between endo- and exosemiosis and hence must be viewed as communication systems with complex semiotic functions that can have a devastating effect on the self if they respond incorrectly to information. The immune system must have appeared early on in evolution. As information processes increased in semiotic complexity, the system of interpretive anxiety signals developed as a supplementary sign system in order to sustain reproduction, particularly among mammals.

Since Sebeok believes that life developed on our planet from a single primordial pattern, he sees the self, as did Schopenhauer before him, as an improvised variation on the theme of life, and consequently as a diacritical sign that is endowed with the astonishing ability to reproduce specific differences as variations of the same phenomenon.

6.   SEBEOK'S "THOMISM"

I regard the semiotic intimations of the French polymath René Thom as pure nuggets of gold, in the aggregate containing the sole contemporary pointers toward the elevation of our doctrine to the status of a theory or a science.

——Sebeok, 1979a: viii——

Sebeok's *Contributions to the Doctrine of Signs* (1976) is for the most part devoted to surveying semiotics and to examining its terminology. In *The Sign and Its Masters* (1979a), which appeared three years later, he demonstrates in noteworthy fashion the holistic power of general semiotics as the "instrument of the sciences" (Morris, 1971: 17), in continuity with Aristotle's and Bacon's concept of an organon. The French mathematician René Thom receives much admiration from Sebeok on this account (Sebeok, 1976: 156):

> Movement towards the definition of semiotic thinking in the biological and anthropological framework of a theory of evolution represents . . . at least in my view, the only genuinely novel and significantly holistic trend in the 20th century development in this field; by far the greatest forward steps in this direction have come from the awesome imagination of the French topologist, René Thom . . . .

Signs, the object of semiotics, are for Sebeok the material from which we and the world are made. If in Heidegger's (1959) and Wittgenstein's (1945–1949) opinions our experience of the world is linguistically mediated and we are thereby constantly surrounded by language even (and indeed precisely) when language is the object of study, for Sebeok (following Peirce) this is true of all signs and not merely of language. We move in signs as bodies move in space and time, we think and feel in signs, and we ourselves, along with our analyses of signs, are produced by signs: "omne symbolum de symbolo" (Peirce, c.1895: 2.302). It is hardly surprising that Sebeok views semiotics as possessing a special holistic power since the thinker, the act of thinking, and what is thought all belong to the category of sign: "in principio erat signum" (Romao, 1976).

For Sebeok, as for Peirce, the distinctive feature of the sign is the so-called "thirdness" that connects the sign vehicle with its object. The physicist George Gamow, who liked to tell stories about Hungarian aristocrats, begins his book *One, Two, Three . . . Infinity* (1959) with "a story about two Hungarian aristocrats who decided to play a game in which the one who calls the largest number wins.

> 'Well,' said one of them, 'you name your number first.'
> After a few minutes of hard mental work the second aristocrat finally named the largest number he could think of.
> 'Three,' he said.
> Now it was the turn of the first one to do the thinking, but after a quarter of an hour he finally gave up.
> 'You've won,' he agreed. (Gamow, 1959: 15.)

This story, as practically all stories about Hungarian aristocrats and Budapest boulevardiers, can give us important clues about intricate matters, in our case about the distinctive features of the sign. Much like Hegel, who in the opening pages of his *Phenomenology* (1807) shows that the infinity of thinking is reached once one realizes that opposites implicate one another reciprocally in a third element, so Peirce developed the category of thirdness as the distinctive semiotic category or, in a sense, as the largest semiotic number (c.1890: 1.363).

The third "bridges over the chasm" (ibid.: 1.359) of sign-vehicle and denotatum, of signifier and signified, of yes and no, presence and absence, agent and patient, ego and non-ego, finite and infinite, life and death. It is "the process which leads from first to last" (ibid.: 1.361), hence essentially mediation, interpretation, a kind of meso-scene. In its most elementary archetypal form, the sign of thirdness is a bridge that breaks and holds open the cleft between sign vehicle and denotatum, and at the same time, paradoxically, overcomes it. It is therefore best represented as a transformational loop which contains a twist at which, much like the "jump" of a Moebius strip (Lacan, 1966), inner becomes outer and vice versa. It is precisely such loops that Thom has termed "catastrophes," i.e., archetypal forms representing continuity within discontinuity, schematic signs which model the shapes and transformations of all forms of life, from organisms and organs to economic growth and inflation. The paradigm case of such a catastrophic loop, and the one on which Sebeok bases his thesis of the biological foundation of semiotics, is the organism-environment mutual feedback loop (Uexküll's *Wechselwirkung*). For Thom, as for Peirce, an organism should be seen as an interpretant sign of its environment and vice versa, the environment as interpretation of the organism. Basic to this mirroring is Lotman's axiom (1971: 96) that "at the basis of every exchange lies the contradictory formula 'equivalent but different,'" which puts the main topos of philosophic discourse, namely, that identity paradoxically involves difference (Heidegger, 1957), in the center of semiotic studies. This is quite appropriate, because a sign is not only a presence of an absence but also a continuous whole composed of discontinuous 'jumps' or alterities, whose simplest geometrical figure is the figure/ground dialectic (Figure 6), in which one figure refers to another as the condition of its possibility.

We seem to need simple geometric illustrations of complicated semiotic issues not only because, as the Greeks had it, "God is always a geometer," but also because, as Piaget (1971) has convincingly shown, the sensorimotor schema occupies a central place in all knowledge and behavior. Thom's appeal for Sebeok

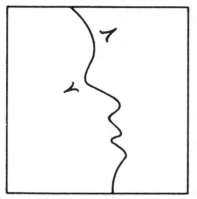

Figure 6. Figure-ground dialectic. From Ehren-zweig, 1967: 23.

can be partially explained by the fact that he construes the elementary biological production of forms geometrically and formulates it semiotically. States Sebeok (1979a: xii), "Thom's new contributions become so immensely valuable, elevating, however hesitantly, the problem area out of its customary metaphysical trappings into the realm of geometry: 'Voir l'identité en principe formateur et la différence en principe informateur, voilà ce qu'on gagne à géométriser la signification, en première approximation' (Thom, *Morphogenèse et imaginaire*, p. 132)."

Thom's ingenious application of topology to the realm of semiotics is particularly indebted, as Thom himself affirms, to Jakob von Uexküll's theory of meaning (*Bedeutungslehre*). Sebeok deserves credit, as Uexküll's elder son Thure puts it (1979: 39), for having "discovered J. von Uexküll's contribution to a general semiotic theory" ("erst Sebeok hat J. von Uexküll's Beitrag für eine allgemeine Semiotik entdeckt"). For Sebeok (1979a: 12), Uexküll "not only foreshadows one of the basic tenets of cybernetics, but also makes plain and richly exemplifies what I already cited as Peirce's canonical principle of semiotics [1906: 5.448 n.1], 'that all this universe is perfused with signs . . .' " Sebeok sees his commitment to view "semiosis as *the* criterial attribute of life" as strengthened by Uexküll's theory of meaning. He sees in Thom's catastrophe theory an attempt to capture this attribute in a theory of analogies, whose aim is to specify "a list of archetypal topological structures (catastrophes) together with rules for combining them (syntax) that could formally model all the static and dynamic morphologies of the natural world" (Sebeok 1978: 25).

Since Thom's theory is so important to Sebeok's perspective, let us outline briefly one of Thom's simplest analogies, namely, his schema of the *grip morphology* (Figure 7). Thom speculates that the grip morphology originated in a kind of *Ur-Zeichen*, an original mark (e.g., a point, a line, a circle) called an "attractor" (Figure 8). If the attractor enters into competition with itself, or, in Aristotelian terms, "contemplates itself," a "re-production" emerges whose structure Thom captures in the so-called *Bifurcation catastrophe* (Figure 9). The bifurcation catastrophe is paradigmatic for doubling processes such as reproduction, repetition, identity, and translation. If a third attractor inserts itself into the bifurcation or is captured by it, we have a *grip archetype* (Figure 10).

The force of Thom's mathematical geometrization of such elementary morphologies as the grip resides in its analogical applicability to various levels of morphogenesis, from the growth of organisms to the growth of thoughts. The organism, for example, "grips" its object as between the jaws of a pair of pliers, i.e., between receptor and effector signs (Thure von Uexküll 1979a: 46). We see the same grip form in bone structures (knee, elbow, hand), then again in maps of action (gripping, grasping, embracing), in tool structures (pliers, scissors, cranes), in interiorized sensorimotor maps (i.e., schemata) of grasping things, and finally, by way of semiotic extension, in conceptual thought ("concept" from Latin *capere*: to capture), as is manifest in linguistic expressions such

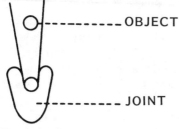

Figure 1. The grip morphology. From   Figure 8. The attractor.
Thom, 1975: 306.

as "grasping a thought," "the gripping power of an idea," etc. Even Sebeok's foundational model for semiotics is indebted in this sense to the grip archetype, since, as already mentioned in Section 1 above (cf. Sebeok 1979a: Ch. 3) he views the field of semiotic research as bounded by the genetic code on one side and language on the other. If one looks at the grip archetype in its wider functional application—for example, in the functional loop of predator and prey—one is struck by the profoundly semiotic nature of this relationship because of the paradoxical simultaneous identity and difference of subject and object. For, as Thom points out (1975: 299), the hungry predator *is* the prey, is consubstantial with it—i.e. (ibid.), ". . . the mind of the predator is dominated by the image of its prey. In some sense, the nervous system is an organ that allows an animal to be something other than itself, an *organ of alienation*. As soon as the external prey is perceived and recognized by the predator, it becomes itself again, and it jumps from the surface corresponding to the prey to its own surface in an instantaneous *cogito*."

Semiotic formulations such as these, in which the subject–object relation is seen as a mirror-image relation—or, in what may be an even more appropriate characterization, as an echo phenomenon (Thure von Uexküll, 1979c: 78)— enable us to speak of a new paradigm for the theory of the sciences which is

Figure 9. The bifurcation catastrophe.   Figure 10. The grip archetype.

rooted in semiotics (Thure von Uexküll, 1979b) such that life and its phenomenology are seen as meaning leaps whose elementary structures are outlined
in Thom's catastrophes. Sebeok therefore envisages, under the "umbrella" of
Thom's imposing catastrophe theory, the outline of a "biologically informed
sign-science" and a "semiotically sensitive life-science" (1979a: 34). And while
he seems to be reasonably optimistic about the effects of such a powerful synthetic
theory, Thom himself remains, like the oracle of Delphi (whose insights into
semiosis he believes he has reformulated after 2500 years), typically ambiguous
about its future impact (1977: 621):

> Catastrophe theory favors a dialectical, Heraclitean, vision of the universe, of a world
> which is the continuous theatre of the strife between "logoi," between archetypes . . .
> It will perhaps have the same fate as psychoanalysis. There is no doubt that the
> essentials of Freud's discoveries in psychology are true. But the knowledge itself of
> these facts has had only few practical results (notably for the cure of mental disturb-
> ances). Just as the hero of the Iliad could oppose the will of a god such as Poseidon
> only by invoking the power of an opposed deity such as Athena, we too can restrain
> the action of an archetype only by opposing to it an antagonistic archetype in an
> ambiguous strife whose results must remain uncertain. The very reasons which allow
> us to extend our possibilities of action in a certain case condemn us to impotence in
> others. One can perhaps show the ineluctable character of certain catastrophes such
> as disease and death. The knowledge will not necessarily be any more a promise of
> success or survival; it could quite as well be the certainty of our failure, of our end.

7. FORMS OF LIFE AND FORMS OF LANGUAGE

Willst du ins Innere der Physik dringen, so lass dich einweihen in die Mysterien der
Poesie.

——Friedrich Schlegel, 1799: 266 (Idee 99)——

Poetry is indeed something divine. It is at once the centre and circumference of
knowledge; it is that which comprehends all science, and that to which all science
must be referred.

——Percy Bysshe Shelley, 1821: 32 ——

It is clear from what has been said above that Sebeok semiotically extends
Aristotle's definition of man as *zóon lógon échon*—the living being that possesses
the *logos*—to life and living things as a whole. Thus "logos" is not taken in the
narrow sense of "language," but as sign, as a schema or blueprint that combines
organism and environment into an Umwelt in Uexküll's sense. But the question
is thereby once again raised of the predominance of the linguistic model in
semiotics, a controversial question in East (in the Moscow-Tartu school, for
example) and West alike. Sebeok's zoosemiotics has of course done an enormous
amount to put the verbal model in its place (for verbal sign systems). In this
connection, his polemic against the French semiotician Roland Barthes constitutes an important element of his semiotic system.

Sebeok sees in Barthes' claim that "il n'y a de sense que nommé" the same arrogance that he detects in Protagoras' dictum from Plato's *Theaetetus* that man (*anthropos*) is the measure (*metron*) of all things. It is important here, however, to insist that zoosemiotics is linguistically mediated. Zoosemiotics has in common with all other sciences that it is a human symbolic construction in Peirce's sense (1868: 5.283):

> ". . . whenever we think we have present to the consciousness some feeling, image, conception, or other representation, which serves as a sign. But it follows from our own existence (which is proved by the occurrence of ignorance and error) that everything which is present to us is a phenomenal manifestation of ourselves."

Thus the autobiographical aspect of knowledge—collective as well as personal—is brought to light. Our experience of the world, which is fundamentally mediated by language, is in effect an appearance of our own form of life (*Lebensform*). The human *Lebensform*—that is, *Lebensform* considered from the point of view of anthroposemiotics—is language, and language is always a form of life (see Baer, 1980).

A comparison between Thom and Holton (1973) is instructive here. Thom compares his method of attributing "all morphogenesis to conflict, a struggle between two or more attractors" (1975: 323) to that of the pre-Socratics Anaximander and Heraclitus, who "used a vocabulary with human and social origins (conflict, injustice, etc.) to explain the appearance of the physical world." He justifies this unavoidable anthropomorphism "by the following fundamentally valid intuition: the dynamical situations governing the evolution of natural phenomena are basically the same as those governing the evolution of man and societies" (ibid.). But he sees the warrant for this in geometrical archetypes, not in the symbolic constructions of language. According to Thom (ibid.), the geometrical archetypes are common to all life forms, including language: "when we geometrize also the words 'information,' 'message,' and 'plan,' as our models are trying to do, any objection to the use of these terms is removed."

When contrasted with Thom's position, that of Holton (1973) yields a diametrically opposed but nonetheless complementary picture of the relation between forms of life and forms of language. Holton points out that the associated production of nuclear particles, visible in bubble-chamber photographs (i.e., as some kind of geometrical form), is described by nuclear physicists in terms of life-cycle stories: particles "encounter" other particles, "interact" with them; they "attract" or "repel" one another, rather as do people; they "experience" forces, are "captured" or "escape." They "live" and "decay." Observes Holton (1973: 106–107), ". . .as in Babylon and Greece, where family relationships were projected into the very naming of constellations in the sky above, the nuclear physicist projects human relationships into his equipment and data."

Holton's point is that geometric forms, too, are linguistically mediated in order to make sense. This is Barthes' point, too. On the other hand, it must be stressed that there has to be something to be mediated, and that is precisely

Thom's complementary thesis: language exists in relation to elementary morphogenetic archetypes. The entire controversy can be summarized dialectically as follows: the theme finds in the schema its "Sitz im Leben," and vice versa. The most profound dimension of this thesis of the linguistic mediation of the world is arrived at when language is no longer adequate to our experience, that is, in situations where language founders or is out of place, rendering us mute. In the context of negation, whose logic is best developed by Hegel (1807) and Freud (1925), silence is the linguistic phenomenon *par excellence*. It becomes a sign of that which, for some reason, I "cannot *say* (yet, anymore)," and which for precisely this reason I affirm as language-related in the deepest sense. In this instance silence becomes a sign that the root of language is not to be found in language, but, as Hegel showed in singular fashion, must necessarily pass over (be carried over, *meta-pherein*, *trans-ferre*) into its opposite.

The moment one intuits that all taxonomies involved in our descriptions of the world are directly or indirectly connected with language, then it is only appropriate for us to reverse the dialectical relation and investigate the nonlinguistic (understood even now as a linguistic construction) on its own terms, in its own territory. Considered from Sebeok's biological vantage point, this territory is thoroughly semiotic. The thesis of the linguistic mediation of the world does not entail acceptance of the position that the linguistic model should dominate semiotic analysis. On the contrary, in order to show the mutual containment of verbal and nonverbal sign systems, the models and rules for their analysis must be generated in a way which is internal to each system at hand. Sebeok is therefore justified in maintaining (1979a: 158) that "the analysis of aboriginal sign languages, like that of visual sign systems in general, has been plagued by language-dominated concepts and methods." He himself has published, together with Jean Umiker-Sebeok, more than 2500 pages on this subject (Sebeok & Umiker-Sebeok, 1976; Umiker-Sebeok & Sebeok, 1978). An additional volume on monastic sign languages was published by Plenum in 1986. Sebeok shows very well how the reciprocal preconditions of anthroposemiotics and zoosemiotics presuppose, like Thom's catastrophes, an interplay of autonomy and correlative heteronomy. This is precisely one of the main points of Saussure's *Cours de linguistique generale*, where he writes (1906–1912: 168–169): "La langue étant ce qu'elle est, de quelque côté on l'aborde, on n'y trouvera rien de simple; partout et toujours ce même équilibre complexe de termes qui se conditionnent réciproquement."

8. TOTEM AND TABOO

"I can't explain *myself*, I'm afraid, sir," said Alice [to the caterpillar], "because I'm not myself, you see . . ."

——Carroll, 1886: 49–50——

There is a delightful story, reported by Gamow (1959: 15 n.), about a group of Hungarian aristocrats who "lost their way hiking in the Alps. One of them, it is said, took out a map and after studying it for a long time, exclaimed: 'Now I know where we are.' 'Where?' asked the others. 'See that big mountain over there? We are right on top of it.' "

One could hardly state more eloquently the displacement and transfer which takes place in semiosis. Peirce's notion of infinite semiosis, in which an interpretant gets its meaning not from itself but from something which it is not, i.e., from another interpretant, and so on *ad infinitum* (1902: 2.303), makes it clear that all signification is transfer or *renvoi* from self to other, a leap that forges two heterogeneous elements into a unity. A sign is always a functional unity of self and other and is therefore internally meta-phorical (transferred, carried over), since its meaning is in each case imported (imputed) from that which it is not. This principle is equally true of zoosemiotics as a whole, and it can be demonstrated by observing it at work within one of the most ancient systems of signification with which we are familiar, namely totemism. Two relatively recent masterpieces on this topic can serve as major inspirations, Freud's *Totem und Tabu* (1913) and Lévi-Strauss' *La pensée sauvage* (1962).

Freud describes the Oedipal interdict of self-containment or self-union (of child and mother) and emphasizes the necessity, for the child, of finding identity by becoming the other. This other—in the Oedipus archetype, the father—is, however, also not a guarantor of absolute self-containment or of complete authority, a fact which is symbolized for Freud by the killing of the father. The murder of the father triggers a chain of substitutes (often totemic animals) which, in principle, is infinite and structurally resembles Peirce's infinite semiosis. We can summarize Freud's major thesis by the paradoxical semiotic formula that *Selbsterkenntnis ist Fremderkenntnis*, self-knowledge is knowledge of the other, self-reference is always reference to another.

A similar approach to totemism is taken by Lévi-Strauss, who views mythical systems as based on the mutual containment of nature and culture. The phenomenology of myth resides in homological morphologies (1962: 123): "le systeème mythique et les représentations qu'il met en oeuvre servent donc à établir des rapports d'homologie entre les conditions naturelles et les conditions sociales."

The homologous structure linking anthroposemiotics with zoosemiotics exhibits two kinds of anthropomorphisms that are often confused with one another. The first and unavoidable kind is constituted by the linguistic mediation of the world. The world is identical with the models we form of it; there is no world outside and independent of our various descriptions of it. But those who identify and criticize various "degrees" of anthropomorphism presuppose precisely such an independent and meaningful world, since they designate a so-called "objective world" as the measure of their hierarchy. To posit such a measure is erroneous, however, since the world we deal with is a linguistically mediated one, one that is meaningful or meaningless only in the framework of such mediation. There are no "degrees" of this first kind of anthropomorphism. All descriptions of the world are equally *human* descriptions.

There is a second kind of anthropomorphism, however, which can legitimately be expunged and to whose obliteration Sebeok's zoosemiotics contributes a good deal. This consists in the failure to recognize in linguistic mediation the fact that all reality is relative to the subject, the term "subject" being understood by Sebeok as applicable to all organisms. Many of Sebeok's studies constitute fundamental continuations of Uexküll's project of Umwelt research, in that they carry the classification of signs over into the animal kingdom and exhibit their species-specific applications in concrete functional circles, and they subject communicative channels and the interaction between sender and receiver to a fresh semiotic investigation.

An example of such indispensable research is Sebeok's analysis of the famous horse "Clever Hans," which proves that the ability to count was falsely attributed to a receiver (i.e., the horse), whereas the counting response was actually cued by a human sender (Figure 11). In addition, Sebeok has shown that similar misinterpretations of the true semiotic state of affairs take place in cases where it is claimed that animals have learned a natural language. Making use of the Clever Hans phenomenon, he argues that the situation in the human-animal dyad is actually one of transmission by imitation, whereby the animal perceives and responds to human nonverbal signs such as muscular movements. The human, however, mistakenly interprets these responses as answers to verbal signs. The Clever Hans phenomenon thereupon becomes for Sebeok the paradigm case of the mirror effect in communication in general, where the sender receives his own message back from the receiver in distorted (translated) fashion (cf. Lacan, 1966). This is especially true of the parent–child dyad but is also generally applicable to the subject–object and organism–Umwelt dyads. It is characteristic of Sebeok's biological orientation that, for him, the animal (namely the horse Clever Hans) is the prototype of the traditional body–soul or nature–culture problem, and not the human being. The central question of semiotics remains

Figure 11. Blondie and Clever Daisy. (Reprinted with permission of King Features Syndicate, Inc.)

for Sebeok that of how endosemiosis becomes exosemiosis and vice versa, or, in other words, the question of the translation of Innenwelt into Umwelt and conversely.

With this, it becomes clear why Sebeok shows such a lively interest in medical semiotics (cf. Sebeok, 1984). Medicine has always grappled with the link between soma and psyche as an existential question of life and death, and it now appears to have found in semiotics an integral form of language, as has been programmatically outlined by Thure von Uexküll and W. Wesiack (Thure von Uexküll 1979c: 48):

> Semiotics can acquire particular significance for medicine, and especially for psychosomatic medicine, by aiding us in overcoming the dichotomy between soma and psyche and the threat of disintegration into various technical jargons (physiological, psychological, and sociological). The fundamental distinction between (subjective) complaints and (objective) diagnoses will become irrelevant when analyzed within the framework of information theory.

9. SEMIOTICS IN TRANSITION

> A monk asked Chao-Chou, "Does a dog have the nature of Awakening?" "No," said the Master. Another time, another monk asked him, "Does a dog have the nature of Awakening?" Chao-Chou replied: "Yes."
>
> ——Thich Nhat Hanh, 1974: 59——

Sebeok begins his book *The Sign and Its Masters* with a story from his native Budapest (1979a: vii):

> When two Budapest boulevardiers meet, one of them may confront the other with the first half of a familiar wry political two-liner: "This is a transitional year." The other party is then most likely to rejoin, less with a peal of laughter than a rueful sigh: "Yes, it is decidedly worse than last year, but sure to be better than the next."

Sebeok's work marks a transition of semiotics from a one-sided subjection to the linguistic model to a biologically oriented investigation into the Umwelt. This transition is given its best expression in an analysis, co-authored by Sebeok and Erica Brady (1979a: 168–179) of the Croesus story in Herodotus' *Histories*. The Croesus myth plays a role for Sebeok similar to that which the Oedipus myth played for Freud. In it we can find a symbol of the shift in emphasis from anthroposemiotics to zoo- and biosemiotics. The highest degree of consolidation of this symbol is found in the two sons of Croesus. One of the sons has a name (Atys), is eloquent, and has a special gift of interpretation. The other has no name and is deaf and mute (without *phōnē*). In a reversal of fate, the speechless and nameless son begins to speak, and as a consequence of this he saves his father's life. The other, rhetorically gifted son is delivered to the anonymous silence of the grave as a result of his talent. This unexpected reversal is predicted by the oracle at Delphi. Its priestess, Pythia, is made to state that the oracle understands especially him who is "without speech" (*ou phoneúontos*).

Sebeok may very well find this stirring tale so interesting because he recognizes in it his own history and destiny. After all, his zoosemiotics points the way toward the semiotic analysis of that which lacks speech but which seems, nonetheless, to contain the true richness and the true enigma of semiotics.

NOTES

1. "Die Semiotik kann für die Medizin—insbesondere für die psychosomatische Medizin—dadurch besondere Bedeutung gewinnen, das sie uns hilft, die Dichotomie in Soma und Psyche und den drohenden Zerfall in verschiedene Sprachsysteme (physiologische, psychologische und soziologische) zu überwinden. Der grundsätzliche Unterschied zwischen (subjektiven) Klagen und (objektiven) Befunden wird bei informationstheoretischer Analyse irrelevant."

REFERENCES

Adey, W. R. (1967). "Historical Review." In: Diane M. Ramsey, ed., *Information and Control Processes in Living Systems* (pp. 20–22). New York: New York Academy of Sciences.

Baer, E. (1975). *Semiotic Approaches to Psychotherapy*. Bloomington: Indiana University Press.

Baer, E. (1980). "How do reflexive systems communicate?" In: T. A. Sebeok, ed., *Semiotic Systems and Their Functions*. Bloomington: Indiana University Press.

Baer, E. (1981). "Medical Semiotics: A New Paradigm." *Semiotica, 37*, 165–191. (Essay review of T. von Uexküll, 1979c.)

Baer, E. (1983). *Medical Semiotics: The State of the Art*. Unpublished ms.

Barakat, R. A. (1975). *The Cistercian Sign Language: A Study in Non-verbal Communication*. Kalamazoo, Michigan: Cistercian Publications.

Barrow, J. D., & Silk, J. (1980). "The Structure of the Early Universe." *Scientific American, 242*, 118–129.

Bentele, G., & Byst̆rina, J. (1978). *Semiotik*. Stuttgart: Kohlhammer.

Bertalanffy, L. von. (1950). "An Outline of General Systems Theory." *British Journal for the Philosophy of Science, 1*, 139–164.

Bloomfield, L. (1939). "Linguistic Aspects of Science." *International Encyclopedia of Unified Science*, 1 (4).

Buchanan, S. (1938). *The Doctrine of Signatures*. London: Kegan Paul.

Carpenter, E. S. (1960). *Eskimo*. Toronto: University of Toronto Press.

Carroll, L. (1886). *Alice's Adventures Under Ground*. New York: Dover, 1965.

Deely, J. N. (1974). "The Two Approaches to Language: Philosophical and Historical Reflections on the Point of Departure of Jean Poinsot's Semiotic." *The Thomist*, 38, 856–907.

Deely, J. N. (1985). "Editorial Afterword" to Poinsot (1632), q.v., pp. 394–514.

Ehrenzweig, A. (1967). *The Hidden Order of Art*. Berkeley: University of California Press.

Eilers, F.-J. (1967). *Zur Publizistik schriftloser Kulturen in Nordost-Guinea*. St. Augustin: Steiger.

Freud, S. (1913). *Totem und Tabu*. Vienna: Heller.

Freud, S. (1925). "Verneinung." In *Studienausgabe*, Bd. 3. Frankfurt a. M.: S. Fischer, 1975.

Friedmann, H. (1955). "The Honey-Guides." *U.S. National Museum Bulletin, 208*. Washington: Smithsonian.

Galen (c.150–200). *Opera omnia*. Ed. C. G. Kühn. Hildesheim: Georg Olms, 1965.

Gamow, G. (1959). *One, Two, Three . . . Infinity*. New York: Mentor.

Gilliard, E. T. (1963). "The Evolution of Bowerbirds." *Scientific American*, 209, 38–46.

Griffin, D. R. (1968). "Echolocation and its Relevance to Communication Behavior." In: Sebeok, 1968 (q.v.): 154–164.

Hadas, M. (1954). *Ancilla to Classical Reading*. New York: Columbia University Press.

Hediger, H. (1967). "Verstehens- und Verständigungsmöglichkeiten zwischen Mensch und Tier." *Schweizerische Zeitschrift für Psychologie und ihre Anwendungen*, 26, 234–255.

Hediger, H. (1973). "Ein verrätischer Vogel." *Tages-Anzeiger-Magazin*, 23, 24–31.

Hegel, G. W. F. (1807). *Phänomenologie des Geistes*. Frankfurt am Main: Ullstein, 1973. (English trans. by A. V. Miller, *Hegel's Phenomenology of Spirit*. Oxford: Oxford University Press, 1977.)

Heidegger, M. (1957). *Identität und Differenz*. Pfullingen: Neske.

Heidegger, M. (1959). *On the Way to Language*. Trans. Peter D. Hertz. New York: Harper & Row, 1971.

Holton, G. (1973). *Thematic Origins of Scientific Thought*. Cambridge: Harvard University Press.

Ičas, M. (1969). *The Biological Code*. Amsterdam: North-Holland.

Jakobson, R. (1974). *Main Trends in the Science of Language*. New York: Harper & Row.

Kahn, D. (1967). *The Codebreakers*. New York: Macmillan.

Kant, I. (1781). *Kritik der reinen Vernunft*. Darmstadt: Wissenschaftliche Buchgesellschaft, 1956.

Kleinpaul, R. (1888). *Sprache ohne Worte*. The Hague: Mouton, 1972.

Lacan, J. (1966). *Ecrits*. Paris, Editions du Seuil.

Lawick-Goodall, J. van (1968). *The Behavior of Free-Living Chimpanzees in the Gombe Stream Reserve* (= *Animal Behaviour Monographs*, 1, part 3).

Lévi-Strauss, C. (1962). *La Pensée sauvage*. Paris: Plon.

Locke, J. (1690). *An Essay Concerning Humane Understanding*. London: Bassett.

Lotman, J. (1972). Primary and Secondary Communication-Modeling Systems. In: D. P. Lucid, ed., *Soviet Semiotics*. Baltimore: Johns Hopkins University Press.

Morris, C. W. (1938). *Foundations of the Theory of Signs*. Chicago: University of Chicago Press.

Morris, C. W. (1946). *Signs, Language, and Behavior*. Englewood Cliffs, N.J.: Prentice-Hall.

Morris, C. W. (1971). *Writings on the General Theory of Signs*. The Hague: Mouton.

Novalis. (1901). *Sämtliche Werke*, Bd. 4. Leipzig: Eugen Diederichs.

Peirce, C. S. (1868). "Some Consequences of Four Incapacities." In: Charles Hartshorne & Paul Weiss (eds., vols. 1–6), Arthur W. Burks (ed., vols. 7–8), *The Collected Papers of Charles Sanders Peirce* (pars. 5.264–317). Cambridge: Harvard University Press. All references to the *Collected Papers* (CP) are according to the standard format of volume number followed by a period and paragraph number. Chronology for CP entries is based on Burks' bibliography in Volume 8 of this collection, pp. 249–321.

Peirce, C. S. (c.1890). "A Guess at the Riddle." CP 1.354–368, 373–375, 379–416.

Peirce, C. S. (c.1892). "Hegelism. Two Passages on Hegel from Separate Fragments." CP 1.40 and 1.41–42.

Peirce, C. S. (c.1895). Fragment, probably from Ch. 2 of a draft of Peirce's *Grand Logic*. CP 2.297–302.

Peirce, C. S. (1902). Sign. CP 2.303–304.

Peirce, C. S. (1906). Portions of *Basis of Pragmatism*. CP 1.573–574, 5.549–554 (continuing 1.574), 5.448 n. 1 (following somewhat after 5.554).

Piaget, J. (1971). *Biology and Knowledge*. Chicago: University of Chicago Press.

Poinsot, John. (1632). *Tractatus de Signis. The semiotic of John Poinsot*. Interpretive arrangement by John Deely in collaboration with Ralph Austin Powell. Berkeley: University of California Press, 1985.

Romeo, L. (1976). "Heraclitus and the Foundations of Semiotics." *Versus*, 15, 73–90.

Ruesch, J. (1972). *Semiotic Approaches to Human Relations*. The Hague: Mouton.

Saussure, F. de. (1906–1911). *Cours de linguistique générale*. Paris, Payot, 1971.

Scheflen, A. (1973). *Communicational Structure: Analysis of a Psychotherapy Transaction*. Bloomington: Indiana University Press.

Schlegel, F. von. (1799). "Ideen." In H. Eichner (Ed.), *Charakteristiken und Kritiken*, Vol. 2 of the *Kritische Friedrich-Schlegel-Ausgabe* (pp. 256–272). Munich: Schöningh.

Sebeok, T. A. (1962). "The Texture of a Cheremis Incantation." *Mémoires de la Société Finno-Ougrienne*, 125, 523–527.

Sebeok, T. A. (1963). "Communication among Social Bees; Porpoises and Sonar; Man and Dolphin." Review article. *Language*, 39, 448–66.

Sebeok, T. A., ed. (1968) *Animal Communication. Techniques of Study and Results of Research*. Bloomington: Indiana University Press.

Sebeok, T. A. (1972). *Perspectives in Zoosemiotics*. The Hague: Mouton.

Sebeok, T. A. (1976). *Contributions to the Doctrine of Signs*. Bloomington: Indiana University, and Lisse: The Peter de Ridder Press.

Sebeok, T. A. (1979a). *The Sign & its Masters*. Austin: University of Texas Press.

Sebeok, T. A. (1979b). "Semiotics." *Explorer's Journal*, September, 132–135.

Sebeok, T. A. (1979c). "Prefigurements of Art." *Semiotica, 27, 1/3*, 3–73. Reprinted in Sebeok (1981), q.v.: 210–259,

Sebeok, T. A. (1981). *The Play of Musement*. Bloomington: Indiana University Press.

Sebeok, T. A. (1984). "Symptom." In James E. Copeland, ed., *New Directions in Linguistics and Semiotics* (pp. 211–230). Houston: Rice University Press.

Sebeok, T. A. (1986). *I Think I Am a Verb*. New York: Plenum.

Sebeok, T. A. & Umiker-Sebeok, D. J., eds. (1976). *Speech Surrogates: Drum and Whistle Systems*. The Hague: Mouton.

Shands, H. C. (1970). *Semiotic Approaches to Psychiatry*. The Hague: Mouton.

Shands, H. C. (1976). "Malinowski's Mirror: Emily Dickinson as Narcissus." *Contemporary Psychoanalysis*, 12, 300–334.

Shelley, P. B. (1821). "A Defense of Poetry." In R. H. Shepherd, ed., *The Prose Works of Percy Bysshe Shelley*, vol. 2 (pp. 1–38). London: Chatto and Windus.

Sherrington, C. (1963). *Man on His Nature*. Cambridge: The University Press.

Staiano, K. V. (1979). "A Semiotic Definition of Illness." *Semiotica*, 28, (1/2), 107–125.

Szöke, P. (1963). "Ornitomuzikológia." *Magyar Tudomány*, 9, 592–607.

Thich Nhat Hanh (1974). *Zen Keys*. Garden City: Anchor.

Thom, R. (1974). *Modèles mathématiques de la morphogénèse: Receuil de textes sur la théorie des catastrophes et ses applications*. Paris: Inédit.

Thom, R. (1975). *Structural Stability and Morphogenesis*. Reading, Mass.: W. A. Benjamin.

Thom, R. (1977). La Théorie des catastrophes: État présent et perspective. In: E. C. Zeeman, ed., *Catastrophe Theory* (pp. 615–621, 633–638). Reading, Mass.: Addison-Wesley.

Uexküll, J. von. (1920). *Theoretische Biologie*. Frankfurt am Main: Suhrkamp, 1973.

Uexküll, J. von. (1934, 1940). *Streifzüge durch die Umwelten von Tieren und Menschen* (with illustrations by Georg Kriszat) and *Bedeutungslehre*. Frankfurt am Main: S. Fischer, 1970. (An English translation of *Bedeutungslehre* by Thure von Uexküll appeared as a Special Issue of *Semiotica* [42, No. 1, 1982] under the title *The theory of meaning*. Page references in this present essay are to this English translation.

Uexküll, T. von. (1979a). "Die Zeichenlehre J. von Uexkülls." *Zeitschrift für Semiotik*, I, No. 1, 37–47.

Uexküll, T. von. (1979b). "Die Umweltlehre Jakob von Uexkülls und die Wissenschaft von Menschen." Merkur, 33, No. 7, 621–635.

Uexküll, T. von, ed. (1979c). *Lehrbuch der Psychosomatischen Medizin*. Munich: Urban und Schwarzenberg.

Umiker-Sebeok, D. J., & Sebeok, T. A., eds. (1978). *Aboriginal Sign Languages of the Americas and Australia.* 2 vols. New York: Plenum.

Weinreich, U. (1968). "Semantics and Semiotics." *International Encyclopedia of the Social Sciences* 14, 164–169.

Weizsäcker, V. von. (1947). *Fälle und Probleme.* Stuttgart: Enke.

Whitehead, A. N. (1925). *Science and the Modern World.* New York: Macmillan.

Winner, I. P., & Winner, T. G. (1976). "The Semiotics of Cultural Texts." *Semiotica*, 18, 101–156.

Wittgenstein, L. (1945–1949). *Philosophische Untersuchungen/Philosophical Investigations.* German with facing English text trans. G. E. M. Anscombe. Oxford: Blackwell, 1958.

Glossary

abstractive relevance

Bühler's thesis that there is a simple and universal relation between the meaning and the material quality of the sign, which allows variations of this quality, for example, of the sound, so long as this variation moves within a universally definable domain: "The philosopher will say reflectively: with meaningful signs the case is such that the sensible thing, the perceptible something, *hic et nunc*, must enter into the semantic function without the fullness of its concrete properties. Rather, only this or that abstract moment can become relevant for its task of functioning as a sign. Put in a simple form: this is the principle of abstractive relevance" (Bühler, 1933:35).

act, action

Actions arise out of the continuum of BEHAVIOR and thereby they have a beginning and an end. They are structured with regard to the fulfillment of a goal. "According to Mead, if an impulse (as a disposition to a certain kind of action) is given, the resulting action has three phases: the *perceptual*, the *manipulatory*, and the *consummatory*. The organism must perceive the relevant features of the environment in which it is to act; it must behave toward these objects in a way relevant to the satisfaction of its impulse; and if all goes well, it then attains the phase of activity which is the consummation of the act. Since act and object are correlative in his account, Mead also speaks of the *distance* properties of the object, its *manipulatory* properties, and its *consummatory* properties" (Morris, *Writings on the General Theory of Signs*, pp. 403–404).

actant analysis

The goal of actant analysis is to describe the STRUCTURE of actants in a semiotic relationship, e.g., in a narration. Above all, actants, seen formally, are organisms or things which take part in a process. In semiotic literature the concept replaces that of "person." Algirdas J. Greimas distinguishes between the actants of COMMUNICATION and of narration. Actants of communication are the narrator and the receiver of the narration. Actants of narration are subject and object, sender and receiver with roles in the narration (e.g., hero, enemy, assistant, etc.).

action situation, primary. See ACT, ACTION

actualization. See DEAUTOMATIZATION

alienation

An artistic means which should aim at the DEAUTOMATIZATION of the public's habits of seeing and hearing. It consists of a departure from the fleeting norms which concern the material, syntactic and semantic aspect of the work of art. Psychologically, this means a deviation from the public's expectations and thus a FRUSTRATION of these expectations.

ambiguity

Ambiguity is one of the most important results of poetry and art in general. It is attained through overlapping of the principles of SIMILARITY and CONTIGUITY. "In poetry, where similarity is superinduced upon contiguity, any METONYMY is slightly metaphoric and any METAPHOR has a metonymic tint. Ambiguity is an intrinsic, inalienable character of any self-focused message, briefly, a corollary feature of poetry. . . . The supremacy of the poetic function over the referential function does not obliterate the reference but makes it ambiguous" (Jakobson, *S.W.* III, 1981:42).

anthropomorphism

Property of all human conceptions; in the OBJECT they reflect the human organism and its life form as functional correlate. At least two types of anthropomorphic concepts can be distinguished: one type which belongs to the essence of all human knowledge, an insight which, for example, is stressed in J. von Uexküll's UMWELT theory; the other type which is based on the insufficient difference between the receptors of the observer and of the observed animal.

anthroposemiotics

Theory and investigation of SEMIOSIS which belongs exclusively to man. On the one hand, it concerns language as model-forming system and, on the other hand, nonlinguistic model-forming systems. "Anthroposemiotic systems are again of two types: first, language, plus those for which language provides an indispensable integrating base; and second, those for which language is merely—and perhaps mistakenly— thought to provide an infrastructure, or at least an analytical model to be approximately copied" (Sebeok, *Contributions to the Doctrine of Signs,* p. 65).

antonymy

Antonymy designates a relationship of the OPPOSITION of two signs on the CONTENT PLANE. There is a distinction between polar antonyms which permit no intermediate stages (e.g., married/single) and gradated antonyms (warm/cold; lukewarm). In the logical relationship between antonyms, as seen here, there are contradictory antonyms (married/single), opposite antonyms (to/from), and reciprocal antonyms (buy/sell).

aphasia (= speech defect)

According to Jakobson, two principal types of speech defects can be distinguished. The one type manifests itself in the (more or less advanced) inability to SELECT words. It concerns the PARADIGMATIC axis of language and is manifested as a disturbance of associations, i.e., of SIMILARITIES in the meaning of a word in connection with DECOD- ING, i.e., with understanding. The other type of speech defect manifests itself in the inability to COMBINE words. It concerns the SYNTAGMATIC axis of language and is expressed as a disorder of CONTIGUITY, i.e., the ability to form contexts, i.e., to code.

appeal
Appeal is, in Bühler's ORGANON MODEL, that third language function which defines
the meaning elements of the sign that possess validity only in relation to the receiver
of the sign. This function is enlarged through the REPRESENTATIONAL and the EXPRES-
SION- or expressive functions: "It is the third function only in our enumeration; for *in
natura rerum*, it is in the exchange of signs in the human and animal domains,
specifically with respect to the *behavior* of the receiver, that the appeal becomes
accessible to the researcher first of all and in the most exact manner" (Bühler, 1934:31).

arbitrary, arbitrariness (French *arbitraire*)
According to Saussure, a SIGN represents an arbitrary bond between SIGNIFIER and
SIGNIFIED: "First principle: the sign is arbitrary" (Saussure, *Course in General Lin-
guistics*, p. 167).

argument (for Peirce)
Third member of the sign in the interpretant aspect; it is understood as the sign of a
legitimate relationship; it represents an object in its character as sign, e.g., as element
of a system of signs; it can only be a symbol in the object aspect and only a LEGISIGN
in the GROUND (= the ten main SIGNCLASSES); it includes a DICISIGN or a sentence
as its premise, whereby the premise is regarded as a connected sentence and therewith
as a uniform premise of the conclusion which is necessary to the completion of the
argument; hence it is necessarily true. "An Argument is a Sign which for its Interpretant, is a Sign of law . . . a Sign which is understood to represent its Object in its
character as Sign" (Peirce, *CP* 2.252).

autonomous (sign systems)
Sign systems are called autonomous when they do not serve as parallels of or substitutes
for other sign systems. For example, a natural language is an autonomous sign system,
while the alphabet, which serves as parallel of the spoken language in the visual
channel, is not autonomous.

autonomy
The property of all organisms, previously of single cells, to determine the reciprocal
actions with the environment itself on the basis of their SPECIFIC ENERGY. "An arbitrary
inorganic body, whether it forms an unconnected mass of single parts or is an excellent
machine with a richly connected ground plan, behaves completely differently with the
external world than any organism or any organ which consists of living cells because
every living cell is an autonym and not a heteronym" (J. von Uexküll, 1931:208).

basic number
A basic number is a (conceived) collection of objects which is defined according to
a definite POINT OF VIEW and is divided into NUMBERS, i.e., CLASSES.

behavior
Everything which can alter within an organism during the course of time. "This term
is presupposed by semiotic and not defined within it. Roughly speaking, behavior
consists of the sequences of responses (actions of muscles and glands) by which an
organism seeks goal-objects that satisfy its needs. Behavior is therefore "purposive"
and is to be distinguished from response as such and from the even wider class of
reactions" (Morris, *Writings on the General Theory of Signs*, p. 360).

binary, binarism

A structure is binary when a relation of OPPOSITION exists between two ELEMENTS in a system. In addition to Saussure, the Prague phonologists, particularly, developed the process of binary opposition. Influenced by INFORMATION THEORY and the associated development of electronic grid plans which function on the basis of binary arithmetic, Jakobson introduced the principle of binarism as a general heuristic method for the analysis of SEMIOTIC STRUCTURE hierarchies.

biosemiotics

Theory and investigation of SEMIOSIS as it is considered in Sebeok's broadest statement as criterion, i.e., as definition of life. "It seems likely that a full-fledged synthesis will be achieved before long, offering both a new paradigm and a methodology for the comparative analysis of semiosis in its full diversity, ranging from the two vast linked polymer languages at one end of the scale to the thousands of natural languages at the other, with a host of singular information coding and transmission devices, inside and outside the body of every organism, in between. Semiosis, independent of form or substance, is thus seen as a universal, criterial property of animate existence" (Sebeok, *Contributions to the Doctrine of Signs*, p. 93).

catastrophe

An expression coined by René Thom (1975) and taken over by Sebeok, which brings elementary morphologies to representation in mathematical (topological) form, in so far as they have the property of SIGNS. Catastrophes bring the elements of continuity and discontinuity between SUBJECT and OBJECT to a common denominator which finds its analogous use on different planes of morphogenesis (somatic, psychic). "Catastrophe Theory is—quite likely—the first coherent attempt (since Aristotelian logic) to give a theory on *analogy*. When narrow-minded scientists object to Catastrophe Theory that it gives no more than analogies, or metaphors, they do not realise that they are stating the proper aim of Catastrophe Theory, which is to classify all possible types of analogous situations" (Thom, 1977:637).

characterizing sign (cf. compare SYMBOL)

"A characterizing sign characterizes that which it can denote. Such a sign may do this by exhibiting in itself the properties an object must have to be denoted by it, and in this case the characterizing sign is an *icon*; if this is not so, the characterizing sign may be called a *symbol*" (Morris, *Writings on the General Theory of Signs*, p. 37).

class (cf. NUMBER)

A class is an abstract collection of objects which, on the basis of one or more DISTINGUISHING FEATURES, stands in OPPOSITION to one or more other classes in a BASIC NUMBER of objects.

classes of signs

Combination classes of signs (sign classification); Peirce arrived at ten fundamental classes of signs (so-called principal sign classes) through the triadic combination of the trichotomic underlying three sign aspects. If, instead of only six, fully ten trichotomies are assumed (according to the differentiation in two object aspects and three interpretants), fully 66 sign classes are formed instead of 28 sign classes (including the ten principal sign classes) (compare *CP* 2.255–264/8.341). The triadic relation of signs is, according to its original form, constructed only out of legisign, symbol, and argument (up to the tenth principal sign class: argumentative-symbolic legisign). All remaining classes represent diminutions of this form. The formation of sign classes presupposes that the universal categories are well ordered; it is continually advanced from the highest to the lowest signs.

classification
Classification is the cognitive process of the distribution of objects of a BASIC NUMBER to CLASSES (NUMBERS). A classification process which is always undertaken according to a definite POINT OF VIEW has, as a result, a CLASSIFICATION SYSTEM.

Clever Hans phenomenon
Sebeok's paradigm for the error of attributing properties to the receiver (counting ability to the horse Hans) which are actually attributed to the sender (unintentional small movements of the human observing Hans). According to Sebeok, it is a question of a mirror- or echo-effect which is active in all communicative situations and which illustrates the self-reflecting relationship between organism and environment, SUBJECT and OBJECT.

code (1) (= Sign System; cf. MESSAGE, LANGUAGE)
Saussure employed the word *code* previous to using the concept of LINGUISTIC PATTERN (see also SPEECH). "Speech . . . is an individual act of the will and the intelligence, in which one must distinguish: (1) the combinations through which the speaker uses the code provided by the language in order to express his own thought, and (2) the psycho-physical mechanism which enables him to externalize these combinations." (Saussure, *Course in General Linguistics*, p. 14). With the terminology of INFORMATION THEORY Jakobson brought the OPPOSITION, code/MESSAGE into recognition in linguistics and semiotics. The opposition nearly corresponds to the Saussurean opposition, linguistic pattern/speech: The code is the system which underlies every single realized message. Jakobson uses the concept, however, at the same time also in the sense of "signal repertoire," which was taken over from information theory, when he designates as well the merely differentiating units of language (PHONEMES) as components of a "phonological code." For semiotics the use of the term *code* certainly ought to remain restricted to SIGNS, hence units of SIGNIFIERS and SIGNIFIEDS. Accordingly, a code always presents itself as a "list" of correlations of certain signifiers. Under this definition the concept is applicable far beyond the scope of LINGUISTICS and is also applicable to ZOOSEMIOTICS and BIOSEMIOTICS (e.g., genetic code). There is still a broader definition of code in which this term also describes systems of rules according to which signs are combined (COMBINATION). Different codes would therefore match different rule points. Such a use of the term appears, however, too broad since it depreciates the concepts of the SYNTAGM and the SYNTAX without obvious advantages. Codes are often composed out of SUBCODES, which play an important role by their change.

code (2)
Code is also understood as an integrated organization-form through which an energy system surrounding it can simultaneously maintain itself as both an independent (closed) *and* dependent (open) system, and can therefore be at one and the same time both

self and non-self. So it is, for example, attributed to the code as a comprehensive methodology that, as Alfred N. Whitehead precisely formulated it: "An electron within a living body is different from an electron outside it, by reason of the plan of the body" (Whitehead, 1967:79).

J. von Uexküll does not employ the concept *code*, using instead the terms *melody*, RULE, PLAN.

combination

Combination is one of two basic semiotic (and artistic) operations and it concerns (in contrast to CHOICE, e.g., selection) the syntagmatic aspect of language, e.g., of a SIGN SYSTEM. Combination is an operation which is based on the outer CONTIGUITY of elements of different paradigms, i.e., on their linkage, vicinity (e.g., distance), sub-ordination, and coordination in a context. Every combination creates a context. This operation therefore implies the CONTEXT-sensitivity of language or of sign systems.

communication (semiology of communication). Cf. THEORY OF COMMUNICATION

Communication is the production of a social relation through INDICES which are produced expressly in order for the sender to influence the receiver. The one side of these indices is the realization of a SIGNIFIER through a SIGNAL, the other, the MESSAGE, which is brought to realization by the class of influence which the sender wishes to exert on the receiver. The message realizes the SIGNIFIED belonging to the signifier. Although signals are produced in order to transmit messages, it is a question of semiology of communication in connection with the semiotic analysis of the meaning process. When produced indices in a meaning process do not arise for the purpose of communication, then it is a question of SIGNIFICATION.

commutation, commutation test

The commutation test is an operation for the establishment of a relation between SIGNIFIER and SIGNIFIED. If one element of the signifier (e.g., a sound) is exchanged for another, the signified changes as well. Similarly, the signifier changes when a change is undertaken with respect to the signified. The commutation test therefore makes possible the discovery of discrete units on the planes of EXPRESSION and CON-TENT. Through the commutation test the concepts of PHONEME and of RELEVANT DISTINGUISHING FEATURES could be worked out in the Prague PHONOLOGY.

competence

The concept of competence was introduced into linguistics by Noam Chomsky and it describes the (innate) ability of man to speak (and to understand) a natural LANGUAGE. The concept represents a psychologizing of the Saussurian concept of LINGUISTIC PATTERN. Its OPPOSITION is PERFORMANCE.

componential analysis

Componential analysis serves in SEMIOTICS to describe the components of a meaning on the basis of RELEVANT and DISTINGUISHING FEATURES. It therefore makes use of the same means which are used in phonology (on the signifier plane) with regard to the planes of the SIGNIFIEDS. Originally, it started from the investigation of limited systems such as, e.g., the system of relationship. In such a system, for example, relevant distinguishing characteristics are: related by blood/connected by marriage, laterally related/vertically related, closely related/distantly related, etc.

comsign

" . . . a sign that has the same signification to the organism that produces it that it has to other organisms." (Morris, *Writings on the General Theory of Signs,* p. 360; compare also Morris, 1964:59f. = 1975;274ff.) Comsigns are modality-neutral and interpersonal. They appear as *comsignals* or *comsymbols*.

concept. See MEANING, SIGNIFIED

connotation, connotative (cf. SIGNIFICATION)

Objects, e.g., MESSAGES, must be doubly CLASSIFIED at any given time in order to be realized. First, they must be set down over against all objects or messages which the producer or sender could have realized in place of a given object or a given message. When it has been determined in the first classification *what* should be realized (DENO-TATION), it is determined in a second classification process *how* the selected function, e.g., the exerting influence (= message) should be realized (= connotation). The semiology of connotation is concerned with the meaning phenomena which are con-nected with the manner of realizations (e.g., STYLE).

connotative sign

Signing (i.e., "double-articulated") structure with which GLOSSEMATICS draws EXTER-NAL ("pragmatic") factors into the denotative sign. The denotative sign is the "expres-sion" of the connotative sign.

consummatory phase. See ACT, ACTION

consummatory property. See ACT, ACTION

content (in the sense of GLOSSEMATICS)

Content is the meaning side of signs *(signifié),* in which a distinction is made between content form and content substance. Opposed to EXPRESSION.

content plane. See CONTENT, SIGNIFIED

content signs (cf. ORGANIZING SIGNS)

According to J. von Uexküll, signs of content are the ego-qualities of the different sensory organs—optic, acoustic, tactile, etc. *(Semiotica* 42–1 (1982), 87).

context

A context is the resulting linkage, vicinity (e.g., distance), subordination, and coor-dination of signs through COMBINATION. A context can result either through linear union or through bundling in time and/or space. The elements of a context stand in the relationship of CONTIGUITY to one another. They form a SYNTAGM.

context sensitivity (cf. CONTEXT)

Since SIGNS are grouped by COMBINATION in contexts, their meaning is determined not only through their SIGNIFIED, but often also through their contiguity with other signs, i.e., through their context. To the extent that a SIGN SYSTEM is constantly changeable through its context, it is called context sensitive. The production of context sensitivity concerns the relation of adjacent signs and sign users (SENDER and RECEIVER). It is therefore a question of PRAGMATICS in particular. Natural languages are considered as context sensitive to a particular extent. This aspect is especially stressed by PRAG-MALINGUISTICS (in part, at the cost of other aspects).

contiguity (cf. CONTEXT)
Contiguity is, according to Jakobson, the principle of a comprehensive COMBINATION of units which lie outside the latter's SIMILARITY-NUMBER. Contiguity can be given in time or in space through LINEAR UNION, as in the case of language and writing. It can, though, also result in the form of a temporal or spatial bunching of unities. Through the contiguity of elements a CONTEXT arises. INDEXICAL connections between signifier and signified are based on contiguity of the same.

continuous (sign systems)
In contrast to discontinuous (DISCRETE) sign complexes, in which the elements are separable, like words and letters for example, there are also sign complexes in which the signs indeed model but are scarcely separable from one another, such as the single objects on the surface area of a painting, for example. Such sign complexes can be called *continuous,* because they blend into one another.

deautomatization (= actualization)
Deautomatization is a POETIC function which is intended to prevent the automatization of the public's habits of seeing and hearing. It occurs, furthermore, through the violation of received norms on all levels of artistic SEMIOSIS. "It is poetry which protects us against automatization, against the rust which threatens our formulation of love and hate, of revolt and reconciliation, of faith and negation" (Jakobson, *Questions de poétique,* p. 113).

degenerate signs
Process or state of the weakening derivation of one sign from another. Central to understanding this is the definition of symbol as "genuine" sign. Thus the INDEX is characterized as a weakly degenerate and the ICON as a strongly degenerate sign in the object aspect. "Of these three genera of representamens, the Icon is the Qualitatively degenerate, the Index the Reactionally degenerate, while the Symbol is the relatively genuine genus" (Peirce, *CP* 5.73). Degenerations occur in the other aspects as well. The method of combination of all sign relations into sign classes is determined according to degeneration (compare Peirce, *CP* 2.265). At the basis is the theory of categories according to which the idea of "thirdness" is the highest point, while both of the other ideas represent gradual decreases of that idea (= categorical and semiotic loss of meaning).

denotative sign (for Hjelmslev)
A sign without regard for connotative, EXTERNAL factors.

denotation, denotative (in Luis J. Prieto)
Under denotation, in the broader sense, is understood the CLASSIFICATION PROCESS through which a subject determines which object or which message should be realized in contrast to other objects or messages. This classification process is distinguished from a broader one in which the subject determines the manner in which the object determined in the first classification or the selected message should be realized. The second classification process is CONNOTATIVE in relation to the first.

denotatum

In the primary ACTION SITUATION, according to George W. Mead, an impulse-satisfying object which has performance properties and towards which a perceptual stimulus points. "When what is referred to actually exists as referred to, the object of reference is a *denotatum* . . . A DESIGNATUM is not a thing, but a kind of object or class of objects—and a class may have many members, or one member, or no members. The denotata are the members of the class." (Morris, *Writings on the General Theory of Signs*). " . . .anything that would permit the completion of the response-sequences to which an interpreter is disposed because of a SIGN. (Morris, *Writings on the General Theory of Signs*, p. 361).

designated (cf. MEANING, DENOTATUM, DESIGNATUM, SIGNIFIED)

The designated, in the Saussurean tradition, is identical with MEANING, e.g., the SIGNIFIED.

designating (= designation). See SIGNIFIER

designatum (cf. SIGNIFIED)

In the primary ACTION SITUATION, according to Mead, the designatum is the number of consummatory properties towards which a perceptual stimulus points. "The designatum of a sign is the kind of object which the sign applies to, i.e., the objects with the properties which the interpreter takes account of through the presence of the sign vehicle. And the taking-account-of may occur without there actually being objects or situations with the characteristics taken account of (Morris, *Writings on the General Theory of Signs*, p. 20). "My earlier monograph did not adequately differentiate between signification and denotation, since it included the latter in the former. The present terminology avoids this by limiting 'signifies' to significatum; thus a sign denotes a denotatum but does not signify it" (Morris, *Writings on the General Theory of Signs*, p. 169).

diachrony, diachronic

Saussure coined the concept of diachrony, in contrast to SYNCHRONY, in order to grasp the transformation of the system of a language over time. "The multiplicity of signs . . . precludes . . . any attempt to study simultaneously relations in time and relations within the system. That is why we must distinguish two branches of linguistics. The terms available are not all equally appropriate to indicate the distinction in question. 'History' and 'historical linguistics' cannot be used, for the ideas associated with them are too vague. Just as political history includes the description of periods as well as the narration of events, it might be supposed by describing a sequence of states of a language one was studying the language along the temporal axis. But in order to do that, it would be necessary to consider separately the factors of transition involved in passing from one linguistic state to the next. The terms *evolution* and *evolutionary linguistics* are more exact, and we shall make frequent use of these terms. By contrast, one may speak of the science of linguistic *states*, or *static linguistics*. But in order to mark this contrast more effectively . . . we shall speak for preference of *synchronic* linguistics and *diachronic* linguistics" (Saussure, *Course in General Linguistics*, p. 81).

dicent sign (dicisign)

Second member of a sign in the interpretant aspect; a sign which urges the consciousness to decision and to action and which, logically characterized, is capable of assertion
and is either true or false. "A *Dicent Sign* is a Sign, which, for its Interpretant, is a
Sign of actual existence. It cannot, therefore, be an Icon, which affords no ground
for an interpretation of it as referring to actual existence. A Dicisign necessarily
involves, as a part of it, a Rheme, to describe the fact which it is interpreted as
indicating. But this is a peculiar kind of Rheme; and while it is essential to the Dicisign,
it by no means constitutes it" (Peirce, *CP* 2.251).

difference

For the semiological tradition since Saussure, the difference between two (or more)
objects/forms the foundation for the VALUE of a sign in a sign system, its "sense"
(French *sens*). Certainly a difference can be recognized only on the basis of similarity
(and vice-versa). The perceiving subject assigns an object or Sign on the basis of
RELEVANT DISTINGUISHING FEATURES of a CLASS (NUMBER), whose COMPLEMENT (COM-
PLEMENTARY NUMBER) contains all different objects. "Just as the conceptual part of
linguistic value is determined solely by relations and differences with other signs in
the language, so the same is true of its material part. The sound of a word is not in
itself important, but the phonetic contrasts which allow us to distinguish that word
from any other. That is what carries the meaning. . . . Everything we have said so
far comes down to this. *In the language itself, there are only differences.* Even more
important than that is the fact that, although in general a difference presupposes positive
terms between which the difference holds, in a language there are only differences,
and no positive terms. Whether we take the signification or the signal, the language
includes neither ideas nor sounds existing prior to the linguistic system, but only
conceptual and phonetic differences arising out of that system" (Saussure, *Course in
General Linguistics*, pp. 116 and 118).

dimensions of sign use

"A SIGN is used with respect to some goal if it is produced by an INTERPRETER as a
means of attaining that goal; a sign that is used is thus a means-object. Four main
uses of signs are distinguished: the *informative, valuative, incitive,* and *systemic.*"
(Morris, 1946:356) "Signs may be used to inform someone of the properties of objects
or situations, or to induce in someone preferential behavior toward some objects or
situations, or to incite a specific course of action, or to organize the dispositions to
behavior produced by other signs. There is no necessary selection of such uses in
terms of the kinds of signification which signs have. But, in general, designative signs
are used informatively, appraisive signs are used valuatively, prescriptive signs are
used incitively, and formative signs are used systematically" (Morris, *Writings on the
General Theory of Signs,* p. 413). Dimensions of sign use are distinguished from
sign dimensions (SEMIOTICS), DIMENSIONS OF SIGNIFICATION and DIMENSIONS OF
VALUE.

dimensions of value

"Since the life process depends on the selection or rejection of certain objects or
situations, preferential behavior (positive or negative) is a basic phenomenon of life.
I have proposed that axiology (as the study of 'value') be considered as the study of

preferential behavior." (Morris, 1964:17 = 1975:219f.) *"Dependence, Dominance and Detachment . . . are primary 'dimensions of value'. . . . They are primary in the sense that they correspond to, or are involved in, the three basic phases of ACTION. In the perceptual stage of the act, the detachment dimension of value is involved. . . . In the manipulatory stage of the act, the dominance dimension of value is involved. . . . In the consummatory stage of the act, the dependence dimension of value is involved"* (Morris, 1964:21f. = 1975:226).

directional signs
According to J. von Uexküll, a directional sign is a sensation that arises when two receptor cells in the skin or in the retina of the eye are stimulated one after the other in such a way that the EGO-QUALITY of the first fades in strength while that of the second cell becomes stronger (*Semiotica* 42–1 (1982), 83). Three pairs are distinguished, which correspond to the three levels of direction in space: right/left, over/under, before/behind. These three levels of direction, also called "coordinate system," owe their existence to the three canals of the inner ear.

directional step
Projected DIRECTIONAL SIGN. The smallest power of movement. The directional step joins three adjacent LOCI (J. von Uexküll, 1973:84).

discrete (= discontinuous)
Among semiotic objects there are those which are separable from one another, such as, for example, words and letters; these are called discrete, i.e. discontinuous unities. They are distinguished from continuous objects which are modulated, like surfaces of a painting from which discontinuous units can scarcely be detached.

distinguishing feature
Objects can be attached to different CLASSES on the basis of the presence (or absence) of certain features on which a (CLASSIFICATION) SYSTEM is based. Since there are infinitely many distinguishing features between objects, the RELEVANT distinguishing features are determined by the POINT OF VIEW according to which the classification is undertaken. The concept of relevant distinguishing features served initially to differentiate phonemes (Prague phonology), was then generalized for all areas of semiotics, and has above all proven to be the most important tool in the COMPONENTIAL ANALYSIS of semantics.

double articulation (arrangement)
According to Hjelmslev, a structural property of (linguistic) signs whose material side ("expression") is formed differently from the meaning side ("content"). Generally (e.g., for Sebeok), double articulation is also called "duality of patterning." By this is understood a type of morphogenesis by which, in principle, infinitely many larger units of meaning can be produced out of a relatively small number of minimal units which are meaningless (e.g., the letters of writing or the phonemes of speaking as the smallest meaning-differentiating [diacritical], but not meaning-carrying, linguistic units, or morphemes as the smallest meaning-carrying linguistic units within a linguistic CODE). Only the smallest, diacritical units are considered "second" articulation, the meaning-carrying units, "first" articulation.

dwelling

Since plants possess neither a nervous system nor specialized PERCEPTUAL or EFFECTOR ORGANS, they do not construct any UMWELTS, but select from their ENVIRONMENT only the MEANING-CARRIERS for the cells of their surfaces and with these build their *dwelling-sheath*. "The plant does not possess any special umwelt organs but is immersed directly in its dwelling sheath" (J. von Uexküll, 1970:114). "It [the plant] is only surrounded by a dwelling which consists of meaning factors" (J. von Uexküll, 1970:117).

dynamical interpretant

A dynamical interpretant is the actual effect which emanates from the sign, the reaction which a sign calls forth. The dynamical interpretant is that which is experienced in every act of interpretation and is distinct from every other interpretational act; it is therefore a singular, actual occurrence. Its modes run in a trichotomous division: (1) sympathetic, (2) offensive, (3) usual. The relation of the sign to the dynamical interpretant can be: (1) suggestive, (2) imperative, (3) indicative. The direct interpretant which proceeds it and the final or logical interpretant which follows it are distinguished from the dynamical interpretant (cf. Peirce, *CP* 8.314/8.369f.).

dynamical or real object

The dynamical object is the object itself, independent of any representation, which nevertheless enables and causes the sign to determine its representation. While the question is the Direct object in connection with the object which is represented by the sign, the question is the dynamical or real object in connection to the object which the sign proves. Its modes run in a trichotomous division: (1) abstract, (2) concrete, (3) collective. The relation of the sign to the dynamical or real object breaks down into the trichotomy ICON, INDEX, and SYMBOL (cf. Peirce, *CP* 8.314/8.366f.).

effector

The EFFECTOR ORGAN with which a SUBJECT acts upon its objects and supplies them with an OPERATIONAL CUE through the giving of appropriate changes. Effectors are coordinated with the MEDIUM in such a way that their construction indicates the medium in which the animal lives (fin/water, wing/air). "The first look teaches us whether we have an air- or land- or water-animal in front of us. The fins, the wings and the feet carry, unambiguously, the stamp of what they are meant for" (J. von Uexküll, 1903:20).

effector cue

For J. von Uexküll, the effector cue is a part of the OPERATIONAL world of the subject, a SIGN for the changes which the EFFECTOR evokes in the OBJECT through which the PER-CEPTUAL CUE is extinguished. Thereby, the effector cue establishes the completion of the functional circle and concludes the action or the pace of action (see FUNCTIONAL CIRCLE).

effector organ

According to J. von Uexküll, an effector organ is a part of the nervous system in which the IMPULSES for the activation of the EFFECTORS are coordinated. The effector organ is, for its part, brought about through INDUCTION from the activity of the PERCEPTUAL ORGAN.

ego-quality

Specific quality of every SUBJECT, originally of the single cell. Expression of its SPECIFIC ENERGY, which can be observed in the nerve cell as stimulant wave, in the muscle cell as shortening, in the sense cell as sensation. "A living cell possesses its own ego-quality" (J. von Uexküll, 1980:326f.)

element
The components of a SYSTEM are called its *elements*. In number theory a BASE NUMBER consists of NUMBERS, which in turn comprise elements.

endosemiotics
Theory and investigation of endosemiosis, i.e., the sign system within the organism insofar as this can be considered a relatively closed and independent system. Endo-semiotic systems are synonymous in their totality with J. von Uexküll's *inner life* or the SUBJECT, and thus are necessarily related to exosemiotic systems on the basis of a comprehensive CODE (EXOSEMIOTIC) (= J. von Uexküll's UMWELT or totality of the OBJECT).

environment
In connection with J. von Uexküll, environment is understood as the UMWELT of the observer which he sees spread out around the observed subject and from which he has, through abstraction in his imagination, erected the concept of an objective world (see also NEUTRAL OBJECT, OBJECT, and MEANING-CARRIER).

exosemiotics
Theory and investigation of exosemiosis, i.e., of sign systems outside of the organism which are nevertheless joined with its (the organism's) endosemiotic systems (ENDO-SEMIOTICS) on the basis of a comprehensive code. For Sebeok, much of the ambiguity of the meaning-link involved in endosemiosis and exosemiosis is expressed paradig-matically in the CLEVER HANS PHENOMENON.

expression (in Bühler)
Expression, in Bühler's ORGANON MODEL, is that language function that represents those meaning elements of linguistic signs that stand in relation to the properties of the speaker. In every linguistic sign this function is enlarged through REPRESENTATION and APPEAL, so that a functional totality results, from which no partial function, expression included, can be eliminated: "For a residue of expression also remains even in the chalk marks which the logician or mathematician draws on the board. It is therefore necessary first to betake ourselves to the lyric poet in order to discover the expression function as such; but admittedly in the case of the lyric poet the exploitation of this function will be richer" (Bühler, 1934:32).

expression (in the sense of GLOSSEMATICS)
The material side of signs, in which a distinction is made between expression form and expression substance, opposed to CONTENT.

expression plane. See EXPRESSION, SIGNIFIER

extensional semantics (cf. SEMANTICS)
According to Rudolf Carnap's *Introduction to Symbolic Logic*, the extension of a one-syllable predicate is defined as the CLASS of single objects which possess the property which the predicate designates. The characteristic itself is called the INTENSION of the predicate. The extension of the one-syllable predicate "book" is the class of books,

the extension of "blue" is the class of all blue objects. Since SEMANTICS (according to Morris) covers the connection of SIGNS and MEANING to the neutral object, *extensional semantics* (according to some authors) examines the number of objects in keeping with a certain meaning (e.g., "seating accommodation"), or (according to other authors) the number of sign meanings that appears in those of the same meaning constituent (e.g., "above). According to Jakobson, extensional semantics investigates the pragmatically bound, contextual aspect of the meaning of signs related to use, while INTENSIONAL SEMANTICS for a subject investigates the invariable, general aspect of the meanings of signs.

external

Sociological, psychological, historical, and other factors in connection with scientific description of LANGUAGE which has nothing to do with its treatment as an IMMANENT SYSTEM. The distinction between external and immanent linguistics goes back to Saussure.

extrinsic (cf. arbitrary)

For Eric Buyssens (1943, 1970), all SIGNS are conventional, in contrast to Saussure, and he proposes to substitute for the arbitrary relation between SIGNIFIER and SIGNIFIED in Saussure, the concept of extrinsic connection. "All signs are therefore conventional in the sense that the individuals are agreed to use them such as they are. On the other hand, the concepts *arbitrary* and *motivated* badly describe the acts in question. . . . The selection of the term INTRINSIC for the so-called motivated signs brings with it the term *extrinsic* for the so-called arbitrary signs. Here, as a rule, the link between signifier and signified is unknown; only historians can eventually retrieve the source of this connection" (Buyssens, 1970:64).

factor of nature

Ordered factor based on immaterial relations (MEANING, IMPULSE, PLAN, RULE, MELODY, but also SPECIFIC ENERGY, SUBJECT), "which compels the physical/chemical processes to follow particular paths." (J. von Uexküll, 1980:149).

final or logical interpretant

The final or logical interpretant is the effect which the sign would evoke in every consciousness if conditions permitted the sign to develop its full effect; it is the interpretive outcome which every interpreter is determined to reach when the sign is considered adequate; it is that interpretant towards which the actually occurring interpretation tends. The nature of the final or logical interpretant is (1) saturation (producing enjoyment), (2) practical (producing action), (3) pragmatic (producing self-control). The relation of the sign to the final or logical interpretant breaks down into the trichotomy: seme, pheme, deloma, for instance, which means: RHEME, DICISIGN and ARGUMENT (cf. Peirce, *CP* 8.314/8.369).

form

In GLOSSEMATICS, the constantly regarded structural principle, as opposed to its substantial manifestations.

frustrated expectation

Among the artistic and POETIC operations which were worked out by the Russian

Formalists and the Prague Structuralists, the most important was that of DEAUTO-
MATIZATION (e.g., ACTUALIZATION) of the MESSAGE. A means through which deautomatization can be reached is (artistic) ALIENATION. Psychologically, alienation means
a divergence from the expectations of the receiver of the artistic message. The result
for the receiver is a frustrated expectation.

functional circle

The cyclic connection between parts of the ENVIRONMENT of a living being with its
PERCEPTUAL ORGANS and EFFECTOR ORGANS. A methodological tool for the reconstruction of foreign UMWELTS. "Graphically speaking, every animal subject seizes hold of
its object with a pair of tongs—a perceptual and an operational tong. With the one
tong it gives the object a perceptual cue and with the other an operational cue. In this
way certain characteristics of the object become perceptual cue carriers and others
operational cue carriers. Since all characteristics of an object are connected with one
another through the construction of an object, the characteristics concerned with the
operational cue must exert throughout an influence on the characteristics bearing the
perceptual cue by means of the object and also act on changing themselves. Briefly,
this is best expressed thus: *the operational cue extinguishes the perceptual cue.*" (J.
von Uexküll, 1970:10f.)

functions of language

Jakobson's model of the six functions of language proceeds from the indispensable
components of the communication process, which include the sender, the message,
the receiver, the context (on which the MESSAGE is based), the contact between sender
and receiver, and the CODE which underlies the message. The functions of language
are derived from the attitude, i.e., the emphasis given to the individual components
of the communication process. The emphasis of one individual component is never
brought to realization; rather, differential hierarchical arrangements of the functions
result which can be designated according to the dominant function. When emphasis
is placed on the sender, the emotive function of self-expression dominates; when it
is on the receiver, language is revealed in its persuasive and entreating function. When
the accent is put on the context with which the message deals, language reveals itself
in its referential function. The phatic function of language presents itself in all expressions which serve the function of maintaining contact between sender and receiver
("Do you understand me?"). If the emphasis is focused on the message itself, the
POETIC function of language comes into play. The METALINGUISTIC function assures
that sender and receiver use the same code. The concept of functions of language,
which Jakobson first considered only for linguistics and poetics can also be transferred
to non-linguistic sign systems.

gesture (in Morris)

Stimulus which releases in the RECIPIENT a later phase of its ACTION, while it points
towards a later phase of action in the SENDER. A gesture which releases a later phase
of its action in the sender as well, while it points towards a later phase in the action
of the receiver, is a *signifying* gesture. Other gestures are *non-signifying*.

Glossematics

School of European structural linguistics founded by the Danish linguist Hjelmslev as an extension of Saussure, *Glossematics* conceives of language (*langue*) as pure form.

heteronomy, heteronym (compare SYNONYMY)

Heteronymy denotes a relation of IDENTITY, on the CONTENT PLANE, between two signs from different CODES. Foreign words are heteronyms.

icon

First member of the sign in the object aspect; it describes its object, i.e., it has at least a feature in common with its object; it denotes the quality of its object. "An *Icon* is a sign which refers to the Object that it denotes merely by virtue of characters of its own, and which it possesses, just the same, whether any such Object actually exists or not. It is true that unless there really is such an Object, the Icon does not act as a sign; but this has nothing to do with its character as a sign. Anything whatever, be it quality, existent individual, or law, is an Icon of anything, in so far as it is like that thing and used as a sign of it" (Peirce, *CP* 2.247).

According to Morris, an icon is a CHARACTERIZING SIGN. Sebeok speaks of an iconic SIGN, when a topological similarity exists between designating and designated. "There are many instances of iconicity in animal discourse . . . involving virtually all of the available channels, e.g., chemical, auditory, or visual. The iconic function of a chemical sign is well illustrated by the alarm substance of the ant *Pogonomyrmex badius:* if the danger to the colony is momentary, the signal—a quantum of released pheromone—quickly fades, and leaves the bulk of the colony undisturbed; conversely, if it persists, the substance spreads, involving an ever increasing number of workers. The sign is iconic inasmuch as it varies in analogous proportion to the waxing or waning of the danger stimuli" (Sebeok, *Contributions to the Doctrine of Signs*, pp. 130–131).

identity

The identity of an object is determined by its distribution in a CLASS within a CLAS- SIFICATION SYSTEM. Since this distribution must come about on the basis of RELEVANT DISTINGUISHING Features, an object maintains its identity only as a member of an (abstract) class in a classification system which was laid down from a definite Point of View. Saussure expresses this, referring to linguistic objects, in this way: "There are different types of identity. . . . No linguistic act exists outside of some relation of identity. But the relation of identity depends on the POINT OF VIEW that one decides to adopt; thus there is no trace of linguistic acts outside of a definite point of view which presides over distinctions" (Saussure, *SM*:43).

idiomorphic (particular form)

" . . . systems capable of building propositions are to be distinguished from all other semiotic types practiced in human society. In contradistinction to such propositional systems, which include language and variform superstructures upon language, all other systems may be labeled idiomorphic, since their makeup is relatively independent of linguistic structure, though the rise and use of these systems imply the presence of language" (Jakobson, *S.W.* II, 1971:706).

immanent (in the sense of GLOSSEMATICS)

Elimination of external (sociological, psychological, historical, etc.) and substantial (material consciousness, etc.) factors in connection with the scientific description of language.

immediate interpretant

According to Peirce, the Immediate Interpretant is the interpretant which appears in the correct understanding of the sign, i.e., in that which is called the meaning of the sign. It is based on the condition that every sign possesses its own particular interpretability before it has any interpreter; it is an abstraction which exists in a possibility. Its modes run in a trichotomic division: (1) hypothetical, (2) categorical, (3) relative. Two further interpretants are distinguished from that: the DYNAMIC and the FINAL or logical interpretant (cf. Peirce, *CP* 8.314/8.369f.).

impulse

Imperative character of the MEANING of a SIGN, e.g., of a report. The impulse does not underlie the rule of causality but rather rules, such as a PLAN, a melody or a CODE, which determine the context of signs. "The coming forward of impulses obeys another law like the notes of a melody" (*Semiotica* 42–1 (1982), 84). Through the combination (for the human observer) of the material sign-carrier with the immaterial meaning, causality and systematizing are linked in the interpretation of biological processes. "The impulse . . . releases a process. . . . While physicists and physiologists have developed purely material concepts for these releasing factors and arranged them into the causal chain, we must attribute to impulses an immaterial character which, on the one hand, enables them to begin new causal chains but, on the other hand, places their growing power under the control of a systematic rule. As analogy to this, the occurrence of tones in a song according to the constraint of the melody may be drawn upon" (J. von Uexküll, 1973:220).

index (cf. CHARACTERIZING SIGN)

Second member of the sign in the object aspect; it stands in real, causal and direct relation to its object, points to it directly or indicates it. "An *Index* is a sign which refers to the Object that it denotes by virtue of being really affected by that Object. It cannot, therefore, be a Qualisign, because qualities are whatever they are independently of anything else. In so far as the Index is affected by the Object it necessarily has some Quality in common with the Object, and it is in respect to these that it refers to the Object. It does, therefore, involve a sort of Icon, although an Icon of a peculiar kind; and it is not the mere resemblance of its Object, even in these respects which makes it a sign, but it is the actual modification of it by the Object" (Peirce, *CP* 2.248). "In general, an indexical sign designates what it directs attention to. An indexical sign does not characterize what it denotes (except to indicate roughly the space-time co-ordinates) and need not be similar to what it denotes" (Morris, *Writings on the General Theory of Signs*, p. 37).

The *Index* as a special class of signs does not appear in the work of Saussure himself. Certainly, however, Jean Piaget (1936) at very early stage already added to this concept of the classification of representation in signs and symbols that was taken over from Saussure. He understands the term as referring to signs of the objects themselves that are linked to the presence of objects as they are given immediately after their birth in passive and then in active perception.

In contrast to this, the child later develops the ability to represent absent neutral objects by means of SYMBOLS and SIGNS.

Eric Buyssens (1943, 1970) employs the concept of index in order to characterize interpretable circumstances which are not realized for the purpose of communication. "It is possible to affect others without knowing it: a friend's manner of speaking can suggest to us that he is troubled; the pronunciation of an unfamiliar person can reveal to us that he is a foreigner; an epileptic's behavior fills us with pity. In such cases we are dealing with indices; we become aware of something, we identify it, we interpret it, but no communication takes place" (Buyssens, 1970:12).

For Luis J. Prieto (1966, 1968), every sign is an index; he distinguishes between artistic indices which were expressly produced for the purpose of supplying an indication = SIGNALS, and indices which indeed convey information but were not artistically produced for this purpose (e.g., animal tracks, fingerprints, etc.). By this means a subdivision of SEMIOLOGY into semiology of COMMUNICATION, on the one hand, and of SIGNIFICATION, or CONNOTATION, on the other hand (Prieto, 1975a, 1975b).

Sebeok speaks of an indexical SIGN when its signifier is adjacent to (contiguous with) the signified, or when such a case is presented. "The term *contiguous* is not to be interpreted literally in this definition as necessarily meaning 'adjoining' or 'adjacent': thus the Polaris may be considered an index of the North celestial pole to any earthling, in spite of the immense distances involved" (Sebeok, *Contributions to the Doctrine of Signs*, p. 131). The principle of CONTIGUITY as the main feature of the index contrasts with that of similarity as the main feature of the ICON.

index field

According to Bühler, the index field of language is unequivocally determined by means of the systematic associative connection of all deictically applied expressions with the position of the speaker in the intuitively accessible domain indicated by the words "I, here, now" (origin of the index field). Although different for every person, as "model of linguistic exchange" the index field exists of necessity along with a second field, the SYMBOL FIELD: " . . . all deictic linguistic expressions belong together for the reason that their meaning is fulfilled and given precision from case to case . . . What is "here" or "there" shifts with the position of the speaker in exactly the same way as "I" or "you" shifts with the exchange of role of the sender or the receiver . . . " (Bühler, 1934:80).

induction

With the concept of induction, which Hans Spemann introduced for the release of development steps, J. von Uexküll describes the successive operation of different PLANES and SUBJECTS, as well as of the cell and organ subjects within the organism. In acts of experience newly acquired inductions are found. Induction is, for example, " . . . the bringing about of an operational plan through a perceptual plan" (J. von Uexküll, 1980:331).

information theory (= news theory)

Information theory is a mathematical theory which describes the statistical regularities of the transfer of information (not in the everyday sense of language). The information content of a MESSAGE is measured while the average probability of the existence of the SIGNAL of a fixed repertoire, which is contained in the message, is assessed by

the frequency of its actual realization in the message. If one understands these probabilities as BINARY selection steps, the result is, for instance with equal probability of
the existence of two signals for the selection of one of the two signals an information
of 1, with four signals 3, with eight signals 4, etc., measured as a number of selections
and designated as "bit" (binary digits). The corresponding mathematical reformulation
of the increase of information by binary selection of an increasing number of equally
probable signals occurs through the determination of the second power of the corresponding number or, similarly, of the dual logarithm ($\log_2$). Claude E. Shannon (*A
Mathematical Theory of Communication,* 1948, together with W. Weaver) and Norbert
Wiener (*Cybernetics,* 1948), above all, are regarded as the originators of information
theory. Since the transfer of information is only conceivable with regard to dynamic
systems, information theory can also be considered as a branch of cybernetics.

instrument, instrumental
According to the generalization developed by Luis J. Prieto (1973, 1975a), and stemming from the sign concept of Saussure, an instrument is a SEMIOTIC STRUCTURE
which, analogous to the construction of the SIGN, is formed out of SIGNIFIER and
SIGNIFIED, out of OPERANT and UTILITY. This generalization, according to which a
sign represents a specially occurring type of instrument in COMMUNICATION or SIG
NIFICATION, is justified in the conception of language signs and of signs in general as
"artistic products," as Adolf G. Noreen (1888) previously presented it so explicitly.

intensional semantics (cf. EXTENSIONAL SEMANTICS, SEMANTICS)
According to Rudolf Carnap's *Introduction to Symbolic Logic,* a one-syllable predicate
denotes a quality. The one-syllable predicate "book" denotes the quality of "bookness,"
"blue," the color quality of certain objects. These qualities are designated as the
intension of their predicates. The intension of a sentence is the statement (proposition)
which this sentence contains. Since SEMANTICS (according to Morris) covers the connection of signs and meaning to the object, intensional semantics investigates the
qualities, i.e., the manner, according to which (universal) invariables of meaning are
constructed. So Jakobson writes with regard to Russian grammar: "In analyzing cases
or some other morphological category we face two distinct and interconnected questions: the morphological INVARIANT, "intension," general meaning of any case
within the given declensional system must be distinguished from the contextual,
syntactically and/or lexically conditioned variants, "extension," actual application of
the case in question" (Jakobson, *S.W.* II, 1971:179).

intention, intentional
The concept of intention designates a willful and conscious action. It is often referred
to in order to distinguish the act of COMMUNICATION from that of SIGNIFICATION.
According to Rulon S. Wells, "intending" and "willing" are both expressed in standard
speech by "to mean." "When communication using language-signs occurs, the speaker
wills to emit something that will be taken as a sign by the hearer . . . the speaker
means something that is taken as meaningful by the hearer. According to the scholastic
language reintroduced by Brentano into modern philosophy, when the hearer takes
something, x, as a sign of something, y, he intends y, and y is called the intentional
object of x. This technical sense of 'intend' is easily distinguished from the more
familiar sense in which for example someone intends to keep a promise and in which

'intention' means the same as 'intent' and 'intentional' means the same as 'deliberate, on purpose.' The familiar and the technically philosophical sense of the verb 'intend' and derivatives are easily distinguished, but in semiosis par excellence there is a certain necessary connection between them: the speaker intends in the familiar sense, and the hearer intends in the philosophical sense: the speaker intends that the hearer shall intend such and such. When the communication is nonlinguistic, there are ana- logues to speaker and hearer: in plastic art, artist and spectator (observer, esthete); in music, musician (split into composer and performer) and audience" (Wells, 1977:12).

interlingual translation. See INTERPRETATION

Interpretant

For Peirce, the Interpretant is the third correlate of the triadic sign relation; the Interpretant is the interpreting consciousness of the interpreter; in the interpretant aspect the sign acquires its own meaning; the interpretant is the field of operation of the explanation of a sign through other signs; since the interpretant establishes the meanings first of all, it is considered a necessary condition for the production of the sign, as sign designating value.

According to George H. Mead and Morris, the interpretant is in the primary ACTION SITUATION, the arrangement of the acting through the use of the impulse-satisfying object to eliminate the action impulse (Morris, 1938:4 = 1975:21; see SIGN PROCESS). " . . . disposition in an interpreter to respond because of a sign, by response-sequence of some behavior-family" (Morris, *Writings on the General Theory of Signs,* p. 363); Morris, 1964:2 = 1975:2; see SIGN PROCESS.)

In the Saussurian tradition there is indeed no concept of the interpretant. But the first draft of one exists in the PERSPECTIVE of the subject established chain of classi- fications as equivalent. According to this first draft, the POINT OF VIEW from which the conception of a subject is undertaken is the interpretant. Since every point of view is established through a wider point of view, a chain of viewpoints is yielded which represents an equivalent to the Peircean concept of SEMIOSIS.

interpretation (= translation)

According to Jakobson, there are three types of interpretation of a verbal sign: "It may be translated into other signs of the same language, into another language, or into another, nonverbal system of symbols. These three kinds of translation are to be differently labeled: (1) intralingual translation or *rewording* is an interpretation of verbal signs by means of other signs of the same language; (2) interlingual translation or *translation proper* is an interpretation of verbal signs by means of some other language; (3) intersemiotic translation or *transmutation* is an interpretation of verbal signs by means of nonverbal sign systems" (Jakobson, *S.W.* II, 1971:261). Translation is therefore for Jakobson the essence of SEMIOSIS.

interpreter

"The agents of a SIGN PROCESS are the interpreters" (Morris, *Writings on the General Theory of Signs,* p. 19). " . . . organism for which something is a sign" (Morris, *Writings on the General Theory of Signs,* p. 363). For Morris, the interpreter is a comprehensive concept for the SIGN PRODUCERS and the SIGN RECEIVERS of a COMSIGN.

intersemiotic transmutation (= intersemiotic translation). See INTERPRETATION

interval scale

The interval scale represents a measuring- or scale-level which is realized when the ELEMENTS of a NUMBER outside of the common property, on the basis of which they are considered among this number, can be arranged in equal intervals so that they are proportional to one another, as is the case for example with length. There are interval scales with a conventional and those with a "true" zero. Thermometers have a conventional and scales a true zero. The operations which an interval scale permits can be rendered through the signs $=$, $\neq$, $<$, $>$, $+$, $-$, $:$, x. The interval scale represents the highest measuring level in comparison to the ORDINAL SCALE and the NOMINAL SCALE because it permits the most operations.

intralingual translation. See INTERPRETATION

intrinsic

For Eric Buyssens (1943, 1970), all signals are conventional, in contrast to Saussure. Because the concepts ARBITRARY and MOTIVATED describe the circumstances badly, Buyssens proposes instead the concepts EXTRINSIC and *intrinsic* as the connection between SIGNIFIER and SIGNIFIED. "In the case of the so-called motivated signs, the auditory or visual signifier has a property which in a narrower or broader sense recalls the signified; one can then say that this connection between signifier and signified is inherent in the nature of the signifier, that it is an intrinsic connection" (Buyssens, 1970:64).

isomorphism, isomorphous

The formal identity of two or more STRUCTURES is known as *isomorphism*.

language. See LINGUISTIC PATTERN (cf. CODE)

legisign

Third member of the sign in the ground; a legitimately used sign which maintains its identity in every realization. "A *Legisign* is a law that is a Sign. This law is usually established by men. Every conventional sign is a legisign (but not conversely). It is not a single object, but a general type which, it has been agreed, shall be significant. Every legisign signifies through an instance of its application, which may be termed a *Replica* of it" (Peirce, CP 2.246).

linear, linearity

For Saussure, the first property of (linguistic) signs was the ARBITRARINESS of the connection of SIGNIFIER and SIGNIFIED, the second their linearity. "The linguistic signal, being auditory in nature, has a temporal aspect, and hence certain temporal characteristics: (a) it occupies a certain temporal space, and (b) this space is measured in just one dimension: it is a line. . . . Unlike visual signs (e.g., ships' flags) which can exploit more than one dimension simultaneously, auditory signals have available to them only the linearity of time. The elements of such signals are presented one after another: they form a chain" (Saussure, *Course in General Linguistics*, pp. 69–70). The SYNTAGMATIC of linguistic signs in speech and writing is therefore linear, in contrast to other forms of syntagmatic.

language (German, *Sprache*; cf. CODE)

In the Saussurean tradition, *linguistic pattern* designates a SIGN SYSTEM that is analyzed purely SYNCHRONICALLY. The concept stands in opposition to "speech" (= Speech Activity), which is understood as the realization of linguistic elements and rules advanced in a sign system. "Linguistic structure is no less real than speech, and no less amenable to study. Linguistic signs, although essentially psychological, are not abstractions. The associations, ratified by collective agreement, which go to make up the language are realities localised in the brain. . . . The utterance of a word, however small, involves an infinite number of muscular movements extremely difficult to examine and to represent. In linguistic structure, on the contrary, there is only the sound pattern, and this can be represented by one constant visual image. For if one leaves out of account that multitude of movements required to actualise it in speech, each sound pattern . . . is only the sum of a limited number of elements or speech sounds, and these can then be represented by a corresponding number of symbols in writing. Our ability to identify elements of linguistic structure in this way is what makes it possible for dictionaries and grammars to give us a faithful representation of a language. A language is a repository of sound patterns, and writing is their tangible form. . . . A language is a system of signs expressing ideas, and hence comparable to writing, the deaf-and-dumb alphabet, symbolic rites, forms of politeness, military signals, and so on. It is simply the most important of such systems" (Saussure, *Course in General Linguistics,* p. 15).

In glossematics, *linguistic pattern* is understood only as language envisioned as abstract object (system, structure) by structural linguistics.

linguistics (General Linguistics)

According to Saussure, linguistics is a part of SEMIOLOGY: "Linguistics is only one branch of this general science. The laws which semiology will discover will be laws applicable in linguistics, and linguistics will thus be assigned to a clearly defined place in the field of human knowledge. It is for the psychologist to determine the exact place of semiology. The linguist's task is to define what makes languages a special type of system within the totality of semiological facts" (Saussure, *Course in General Linguistics,* p. 16).

local signs

Sensations of LOCUS that are received by special cells of the skin and the retina as the ego-quality of these cells (*Semiotica* 42–1 (1982), 84).

locus (place, locality)

Smallest element of space = projected LOCAL SIGN (spatial power of resolution). "A place in the UMWELT corresponds to every element of sight (the retina of the eye), since it has turned out that a local sign belongs to every element of the eye" (J. von Uexküll, 1970:23).

manipulatory phase ACT, ACTION

manipulatory property. See ACT, ACTION

material

A semiotic analysis of objects and signs occurs on various levels. The object or sign is produced out of the material level. In linguistics, for example, the material aspect exists in the articulation of sounds by means of the vocal organs. With the help of segmented sound material the contents of ideas (MEANINGS) are differentiated. On the plane of MORPHOLOGY the manner in which material is structured in order to fulfill its function (i.e., the differentiation of meaning) is analyzed.

meaning SIGNIFIED

meaning (for Saussure = CONCEPT, SIGNIFIED; cf. SENSE)
The meaning of an object, according to the Saussurean tradition, is the signified, i.e., the concept with which the signifier, i.e., the receiving sound pattern (or seeing, tone, touch symbol, etc.) is connected. Meaning, as a concept which is bound as signified with a signifier to a sign, is distinguished from VALUE of a sign, which is determined by the contrast with other signs of a system. Thus the content of a word sign, according to Saussure, is "determined in the final analysis not by what it contains but by what exists outside it. As an element in a system, the word has not only a meaning but also—above all—a value. And that is something quite different " (Saussure, *Course in General Linguistics*, p. 114). The meaning of a sign is produced through OPPOSITION to the meanings of other symbols in a system of meanings.

meaning (for J. von Uexküll)
Meaning is a property which an element has by virtue of its function in a system, or that it acquires with it. Every arbitrary part of the environment gains a meaning as soon as it transfers the role of a MEANING-CARRIER to the life-stage of a SUBJECT, because it now occurs as an element in the system SUBJECT–OBJECT or organism–ENVIRONMENT. The meaning joins the elements with one another. "Every component as soon as it appears in the role of a meaning-carrier on the life-stage of an animal subject, putting into relation what we can call a 'complement' in the body of the subject, becomes something that serves as meaning-utilizer" (J. von Uexküll, 1970:111). "Meaning is the guiding star that biology must follow (*Semiotica*, 42–1 [1982], 84) and not the poor rule of causality which is incapable of seeing further than one step forwards or backwards, but to which the important relations remain completely concealed" (J. von Uexküll, 1970:127).

meaning-carrier
According to J. von Uexküll, the component of the ENVIRONMENT which is of biological meaning for the organism. The subject imprints the organism's meaning on it. "The stone lies in the objective observer's hand as a neutral object, but it is transformed into a meaning-carrier as soon as it enters into a relationship with a subject" (*Semiotica* 42–1 [1982], 27).

meaning rule
According to J. von Uexküll, the *meaning rule* matches the CODE which joins the MEANING-CARRIER and the MEANING-UTILIZER in a SIGN.

meaning-utilizer
Every component in the organism of a living being which enters into a meaning relation with a MEANING-CARRIER. Together with this it forms a SIGN corresponding to the actual MEANING-RULE.

medium

The part of the environment of an organism that is coordinated in complementary correlation (CONTRAPUNTALLY) to its organs of movement (foot/ground, fin/water, wing/air, etc.). 'In every case, the effector organs for running, jumping, climbing, fluttering, flying, or soaring are formed contrapuntally t the properties of the respective medium" (J. von Uexküll, 1970:142).

message (cf. CODE, SPEECH)

Jakobson formulated the concept of *message,* stemming from information theory, in OPPOSITION to the concept CODE, in order to express what Saussure meant by SPEECH. "There is a direct help that linguistics is in line to receive from mathematics at this moment, especially from the so-called 'information theory' or theory of communication. The fundamental dichotomous notions of linguistics, particularly singled out by F. de Saussure, A. Gardiner, and E. Sapir and called *langue* and *parole* in France, 'linguistic pattern' and 'speech' in America, now receive a much clearer, simpler, logically less ambiguous, and operationally more productive formulation, when matched with the corresponding concepts of communication theory, namely with 'code' and 'message' " (Jakobson, *S.W.* II, 1971:224).

A message is the "sense" (French, *sens*) of signals. The sense of signals is a determined influence which the sender wishes to exert on the receiver. The two main types of influence are information and injunction (= determination). "That which a SIGNAL brings to the receiver as an intentionally created Index is then the property of a determined class of influence which the sender tries to exert on it through the production of the signal in a determined CLASS. The influence which the sender wishes to exert on the receiver through the production of the signal is none other than that which is called the *sense* of the signal. One could just as well designate this influence as the *message* which the *signal* transmits" (Prieto, 1975a:24). A message is thus a concretizing of a determined abstract class on the plane of the SIGNIFIED, just as a signal is the realization of a class on the plane of the SIGNIFIER.

metalanguage, metalinguistic

The concept *metalanguage* was introduced by the logicians of the Viennese School in order to distinguish language which is spoken about from that which is used for this purpose. Hjelmslev carried over this distinction to semiotics, since he distinguished between CONNOTATIVE semiotics, or SEMIOLOGIES as objects, and scientific, or non-scientific metasemiotics, which treat these objects. A metasemiotics is scientific when its object is a scientific semiotics (e.g., mathematics). A metasemiotics is unscientific when its object is an unscientific semiotics. The general, customary concept of SEMIOTICS or of SEMIOLOGY is thereby congruent with Hjelmslev's definition of unscientific metasemiotics. Jakobson attributed a special metalinguistic function in his model to the LINGUISTIC functions of language, in addition to others.

metaphor, metaphorical

A metaphor is based on the SELECTION of a new SIGN as substitute for an old one on the basis of SIMILARITY. It originates, therefore, out of the similarity number of signs which is given in a PARADIGM. According to Jakobson, lyric poetry is based predominately on metaphorical elements, while epic poetry is, rather, METONYMIC. Surrealism, Romanticism and Symbolism are predominately metaphorical artistic directions.

metasemiology (in the sense of GLOSSEMATICS)
Scientific sign structure whose content is semiology, but which is particularly occupied with the substances of signs which are excluded from semiology.

metasemiotics (= metasemiology). See METALANGUAGE

metonymy, metonymic
A metonymy is based on the substitution of one sign for another on the basis of its content CONTIGUITY. Such a contiguity may, for instance, be based on a causal relation or on the relation of a part to the whole (*pars pro toto*). According to Jakobson, epic poetry is based on the principle of metonymy while in the lyric the METAPHORICAL element dominates. Realism and Cubism are predominantly metonymic artistic directions.

mind
According to J. von Uexküll, the mind is our primary receptor of SIGNS. "Since the activity of our mind is the only part of nature which is known to us directly, its rules are the only ones which rightly can be given the name natural laws." (J. von Uexküll, 1973:40)

modi significandi (modes of signifying, dimensions of signification)
". . . a differentiation of signs in terms of the most general kinds of SIGNIFICATA. Five modes of signifying are distinguished (*identificative, designative, appraisive, prescriptive,* and *formative*), and signs signifying in these modes are called respectively *identifiors, designators, appraisors, prescriptors,* and *formators* (Morris, *Writings on the General Theory of Signs,* p. 364). "It is widely recognized that signs . . . differ greatly in the kind of SIGNIFICATION they have. . . . My suggestion is that signification is tridimensional, and that these three dimensions are explicable in terms of three phases or aspects of ACTION. I shall follow George H. Mead's analysis of an act. . . . A sign is *designative* insofar as it signifies *observable* properties of the environment or of the actor, it is *appraisive* insofar as it signifies the consummatory properties of some object or situation, and it is *prescriptive* insofar is it signifies how the object or situation is to be reacted to so as to satisfy the governing impulse. In these terms, usually 'black' is primarily designative, 'good' is primarily appraisive, and 'ought' is primarily prescriptive" (Morris, *Writings on the General Theory of Signs,* pp. 403–404).

moment
Fundamental sign of temporal perception. With reference to Karl Ernst von Baer, it is defined as measurement for the shortest unit of time (temporal power of disintegration). " . . . every span of time which an organism uses in order to receive external impressions as simultaneous perceptual cues" (J. von Uexküll, 1980:198).

morphology
For 19th-century linguistics, grammar consisted of morphology and syntax. Morphology was occupied with the parts of language which had the dimension of words, syntax with the combination of words into larger units such as sentences.

motivation, motivated (versus unmotivated)
According to Saussure, a SYMBOL represents a "natural" (= motivated) connection between SIGNIFIER and SIGNIFIED. "For it is characteristic of symbols that they are

never entirely arbitrary. They are not empty configurations. They show at least a vestige of natural connexion between the signal and its signification" (Saussure, *Course in General Linguistics,* p. 68).

nature

Systematically ordered and complete structure of all UMWELTS whose meaning is sought in its overlapping composition. ". . . it is a systematic, complete structure which is understood as being in continuous systematic transformation and renewal" (J. von Uexküll, 1980:204).

neutral object (German, GEGENSTAND)

According to J. von Uexküll, a neutral object is clearly distinguished from an OBJECT. Neutral objects represent constructions of human understanding as independent and, consequently, meaningless objects and exist only in our conceptual world. Generally, relations (and meanings) which, objects can have for physicists and chemists, are defined as the "objective properties" of those objects. The formation of neutral objects assumes the ability to abstract, which is first acquired with language. This ability makes possible the production of relations which do not directly serve biological needs and, with this, "observation." "Because no animal ever plays the role of an observer, one may assert that they never enter into relationships with neutral objects" (J. von Uexküll 1970:108).

nominal, nominal scale

The concept NOMINAL designates a measure- or scale-level which is realized when the ELEMENTS of a NUMBER outside the general property, on the basis of which they are considered in this number, exclude one another, as is the case, for instance, with shades. The operations which a nominal scale allows can be reproduced through the signs = and ≠. The nominal scale represents, in contrast to the ORDINAL SCALE and the INTERVAL SCALE, the simplest measure level because it permits the fewest operations.

number (cf. CLASS)

Numbers are components of a BASIC NUMBER in which they stand in OPPOSITION to one another on the basis of RELEVANT DISTINGUISHING FEATURES. They consist of the objects assigned to them as their ELEMENTS.

object

The part of the FUNCTIONAL CIRCLE which is seized by the RECEPTORS and EFFECTORS of the SUBJECT, as in the case of a pair of tongs. Objects consist of PERCEPTUAL CUES and EFFECTOR CUES which are connected with one another by an OBJECTIVE CONNECTING STRUCTURE. There are objects in contrast to NEUTRAL OBJECTS, that are only as elements of subjective UMWELTS. "The perceptual signs of a group of perceptual cells unite outside of the perceptual organ, indeed, outside of the animal body in units which become properties of the objects lying outside of the animal-subject. Exactly the same thing occurs in the perceptual organ." (J. von Uexküll, 1970:10) The object is a functional correlate of the SUBJECT, as it is represented in J. von Uexküll's functional circle. Sebeok sees in René Thom's CATASTROPHES the best scientific formulation of the reciprocal transformation of SUBJECT and object. The object is, accordingly, a type of replication of the subject through which the subject first properly (re)produces itself as SIGN.

objective connecting structure
Connection between the perceptual carrier and the effector carrier of the object which does not enter the UMWELT itself (but rather part of the ENVIRONMENT of the living organism, i.e., it remains the umwelt of the human observer), but "this objective connecting structure of the object is also constantly taken into the construction of the animal subject, although no effect at all can emanate from the objective connecting structure of the object to the structure of the subject." (J. von Uexküll, 1980:275f.)

operant (cf. INSTRUMENT)
Operant is, according to Luis J. Prieto (1973, 1975a), the abstract class of variants of a TOOL with the same UTILITY. The SIGNIFIER is, as an abstract class of variants of SIGNALS with the same SIGNIFIED, a special case of operant. A TOOL is the realization of an operant, just as a SIGNAL is the realization of a signifier. The relation of operant and utility is asymmetrical: while the same utility always corresponds to the operant of an instrument, different operants can match one and the same utility, i.e., the same utility can play a role in different instruments.

operate, operation
In J. von Uexküll's sense, an operation is an activity of the combined cells in the EFFECTOR (muscle cells, cells of the appendage structures: claws, teeth, feathers, fins, etc.).

operation
An operation is, according to Luis J. Prieto (1973, 1975a), the concretization of a definite abstract CLASS of UTILITY. An operation can also be designated as instrumental action. An operation is connected with a TOOL which the realization of an OPERANT represents.

operation signs (impulse-to-action signs)
In J. von Uexküll's sense of the word, an operation sign is the subjective sensation of the return message of the IMPULSES which the EFFECTOR Organ sends to the EFFECTORS: Information concerning the innervation which we send to our muscles before the muscle answers this innervation with a contraction (see also REAFFERENCE PRINCIPLE).

operational world
Sum of the EFFECTOR CUES in the UMWELT of the subject; complementary part of the PERCEPTUAL WORLD. What the subject "effects becomes its operational world" (J. von Uexküll, 1970:4).

opposition (= contrast)
In the Saussurean tradition, the concept is based on an operation which defines a relation between two ELEMENTS in a SYSTEM or a PARADIGM. "The moment we compare one sign with another as positive combinations, the term *difference* should be dropped. . . . It is a term which is suitable only for comparisons between sound patterns (e.g., *père* vs. *mère*), or between ideas (e.g., 'father' vs. 'mother'). Two signs, each comprising a signification and a signal, are not different from each other, but only distinct. They are simply in *opposition* to each other . . . What is usually

called a 'grammatical fact' corresponds in the final analysis to our definition of a unit. For there is always an opposition of terms involved. What is special is that the opposition happens to be particularly important, e.g. German plural formations of the type *Nacht* vs. *Nächte*. . . . Each of the items which contrast grammatically . . . is itself the product of the operation of oppositions within the system. In isolation, *Nacht* and *Nächte* are nothing: the opposition between them is everything" (Saussure, *Course in General Linguistics*, pp. 119–120).

opposition structure

All CLASSES of a BASIC NUMBER which on the basis of RELEVANT DISTINGUISHING FEATURES of the objects associated with them, and standing in OPPOSITION to one another, form an opposition structure.

ordinal, ordinal scale

The concept *nominal* designates a measure- or scale level which is realized when the ELEMENTS of a NUMBER outside of the general property, on the basis of which they are considered in this number, can be arranged hierarchically, as is the case with different degrees of brightness of the same shade, or with degrees of hardness of objects. An ordinal hardness scale can, for instance, be produced through the rubbing together of objects, whereby the softer of the two objects receives scratch marks from the harder one. The operations which an ordinal scale permits can be rendered through the signs $=$, $\neq$, $<$, $>$. The ordinal scale represents in comparison to the nominal scale a higher, and, in comparison to the INTERVAL SCALE, a lower, measure level.

organizing signs

Sensations of the qualities of space and time. They are the receptacles for the CONTENT SIGNS which, together with the organizing signs, form the UMWELT. The organizing signs become "moments, loci, directional steps . . . which are the builders of the world." (J. von Uexküll, 1973:111)

organon model

Bühler's tripartite model of the sign functions of language which are defined as operating among the phonic substrate of the sign, the sender, the receiver, and the objects and states of affairs whereby the "concrete sound phenonmenon" always and simultaneously displays the functional relations to the three "foundations of the relations" (sender, receiver, objects and states of affairs): "It is a *symbol* by reason of being correlated with objects and states of affairs, *symptom* (index) by reason of its dependence on the sender, whose interiority it expresses, and *signal* by reason of its appeal to the hearer, whose outer behavior it directs just like other traffic signs" (Bühler, 1934:28).

ostensive signs (cf. SIGNS)

According to Jakobson, signs which must be produced by some part of the human body, whether directly or through the medium of special instruments, are distinguished from a semiotic presentation of ready objects. This semiotic presentation is called *ostension*. "This use of things as signs . . . may be illustrated by the exhibition and compositional arrangement of synecdochic samples of shop goods in show windows or by the METAPHORIC choice of floral tributes, e.g. a bunch of red roses as a sign of love. A particular kind of ostension is the theatric show with men as SIGNANTIA (actors) of men as SIGNATA (personae)" (Jakobson, *S.W.* II, 1971:702).

pansemiotic
Jakobson distinguishes between the transfer of linguistic MESSAGES (field of linguistic research) and the mere transfer of messages (field of semiotic research which includes linguistics). There can be general properties of linguistic messages with one or several types of nonlinguistic messages (e.g., the LINEARITY of language and music). Such properties are semiotic in nature. Properties which are common to all (including linguistic) messages would be pansemiotic in nature (e.g., the construction of signs out of SIGNIFIER and SIGNIFIED).

paradigm, paradigmatic (= associative opposition)
A paradigm is a class (e.g., NUMBER) of elements which could take the same place in a SYNTAGM. Such elements are determined through the so-called COMMUTATION TEST. Elements so determined stand to one another in a relation of OPPOSITION which can be attributed to RELEVANT DISTINGUISHING FEATURES. Saussure compared the paradigmatic opposition to columns of different styles which could take the same place in a building: " . . . if the column is Doric, it will evoke mental comparison with the other architectural orders . . . which are not in this instance spatially co-present. This relation is associative" (Saussure, *Course in General Linguistics,* p. 122).

perception
Reactions of receptor cells of the sense organs which correspond to their SPECIFIC ENERGY. Perceptual signs are organized in the PERCEPTUAL ORGAN of the nervous system into definite SCHEMES, and projected as PERCEPTUAL CUES (of Objects). They form in their totality the PERCEPTUAL WORLD, which is coordinated with the OPERATIONAL WORLD; both together constitute the UMWELT of the organism.

perceptual cue
Part of the PERCEPTUAL WORLD of the SUBJECT; projected PERCEPTUAL SIGNS; releasing property of the OBJECT (signal stimulus, key stimulus, release). "If one puts the perceptual sign in place of the feeling or subjective quality, it can be said that the perceptual signs of our attention become the perceptual cues of our world" (J. von Uexküll, 1973:103).

perceptual organ
The perceptual organ is, according to J. von Uexküll, the part of the nervous system that orders the PERCEPTUAL SIGNS into PERCEPTUAL CUES and projects them as properties of OBJECTS into the UMWELT of the organism. The perceptual organ INDUCES the PERCEPTUAL ORGAN to activate the EFFECTORS.

perceptual phase. See ACTION

perceptual property. See ACTION

perceptual signs
According to J. von Uexküll, perceptual signs are elementary sensations of the Receptor. ORGANIZING SIGNS or CONTENT SIGNS correspond to the individuality of the receptor.

perceptual world

Sum of the PERCEPTUAL CUES with which an organism designates the properties of his UMWELT. In the human being it corresponds to the observable world which he, as observer, sees round about the observed animal. "Everything which a subject perceives becomes his perceptual world" (J. von Uexküll, 1970:4).

performance

The concept of performance was introduced into linguistics by Noam Chomsky and it describes the individual realization (as language and understanding) of (innate) linguistic COMPETENCE. The concept of performance represents a psychologizing of the Saussurian concept of Speech and it stands in OPPOSITION to COMPETENCE (≈ LANGUAGE)

perspective. See POINT OF VIEW

phoneme

A phoneme is a linguistic sound classification which does not divide into any further subclasses but can, for its part, be built up into superordered classes of sounds (e.g., syllables). Every phoneme is defined by the presence, or absence, respectively, of a limited number of PHONOLOGICAL DISTINGUISHING FEATURES. "The speech sound is an aggregate of auditory impressions and articulatory movements, comprising what is heard and what is spoken, one delimiting the other. It is thus a complex unit, with a foot in each camp. . . . After analysing a considerable number of sound sequences from a variety of languages, the linguist is able to recognise and classify the units involved. It emerges that, if we leave out of consideration those minutiae which do not affect auditory discrimination, the number of sound types is limited" (Saussure, *Course in General Linguistics,* p. 41).

phonology

Phonology is a discipline of linguistics which analyzes the linguistic sounds of natural languages. Moreover, phonology determines the sounds out of which entire utterances of a language are constructed, and it puts these sounds together on the basis of RELEVANT DISTINGUISHING FEATURES into a SYSTEM. Phonology was developed in the 1920s in connection with Saussure, above all by N. S. Trubetzkoy and Jakobson in connection with the Prague linguistic circle.

plan

According to J. von Uexküll, a plan is the immaterial law which governs the relations of the elements within every unity, as a melody governs the unity of the song, or a CODE the unity of a sign system. The plan in this way controls the IMPULSES as well.

poetics, poetic

This designation, stemming from Aristotle, for the theory of poetic art (and other arts) was taken up again by the Prague Structuralists, above all by Jakobson, in order to designate the semiotic aesthetics developed out of Russian Formalism and the Prague School. Semiotic aesthetics is based on, among other things, the observation that the aesthetic MESSAGE is the result of an attitude which concentrates on the structure of the message itself, whereby other functions of the same message (e.g., the reference to circumstances) become incidental. The arrangement of the structure of the message results from a succession of aesthetic operations, among which ALIENATION plays an important role. It serves DEAUTOMATIZATION. AMBIGUITY is one of the most important results of poetic operations. It is attained through the overlapping of the principles of Similarity and CONTIGUITY. "The poetic function projects the principle of equivalence from the axis of SELECTION into the axis of COMBINATION. Equivalence is promoted to the constitutive device of the sequence. In poetry one syllable is equalized with any other syllable of the same sequence; word stress is assumed to equal word stress, as unstress equals unstress . . ." (Jakobson, *S.W.* III, 1981:42).

point of view (= perspective)
A CLASSIFICATION of objects according to RELEVANT DISTINGUISHING FEATURES can only be undertaken according to a definite point of view (from a definite perspective). This point of view is determined, as a rule, through a human practice. Human sounds, for example, can be classified according to many points of view. The hearer classifies ("understands") the sounds of the speaker from the point of view of the practice of human communication through language. The IDENTITY of an object depends, therefore, on the point of view from which the object is classified.

practice. See ACT, INSTRUMENT
In semiotics, the practice of communication, that is SPEECH ACTIVITY, e.g., the transmission of MESSAGES, is distinguished from other human practices, from INSTRUMENTAL actions. The practice of communication forms only a section of the whole human practice which, in turn, is differentiated through different historical and social conditions.

pragmalinguistics
According to Morris, the semiotic discipline of pragmatics deals with the relationship between signs and users of signs. Pramalinguistics is therefore a restriction and application of pragmatics to the relation between linguistic signs and their users. Pragmalinguistics particularly works out the influence of the use of signs and the accompanying circumstances on communication and interpretation and stands in a true contrast to STRUCTURALISM in which language is understood as independent from its use as SYSTEM.

pragmatics
Pragmatics "may be the relation of SIGNS to INTERPRETERS. This relation will be called the *pragmatical dimension* of SEMIOSIS, symbolized by 'D_p', and the study of this dimension will be named *pragmatics*." (Morris, *Writings on the General Theory of Signs,* pp. 21–22) " . . . that branch of SEMIOTIC which studies the origin, the uses, and the effects of signs. It is distinguished from SEMANTICS and SYNTACTICS" (Morris, *Writings on the General Theory of Signs,* p. 365). Also compare Morris, 1964:44f. = 1975:256f.

pragmatism, pragmaticism
Philosophical theory established by Peirce. Its most striking characteristic is its acknowledgement of an inseparable connection between rational knowledge and rational purpose; centerpiece of this theory is semiotics whose scientific-theoretical place is located in the "logic" of the third "normative science." "Phenomenology" (also: "phaneroscopy") leads the "normative sciences" ("aesthetics," "ethics," "logic"), the second part of the "architectonic," his pragmatic, e.g., pragmaticist philosophy. The task of

this first part is to discover and to determine the fundamental modes (UNIVERSAL CATEGORIES) in the description of "phenomena;" the third part and crowning conclusion forms a "metaphysics" (constructed in "tychism," "agapism," "synechism") of a universally real character: It ought to bring the world, independent of natural sciences and the arts, to representation.

Pragma is the Greek expression for object, thing, fact, deed, act, action. Peirce's distinction of the terms borrowed from Kant (compare KrdrV A824–B852), "practical" and "pragmatic"; " . . . as far apart as the two poles, the former belonging in a region of thought where no mind of the experimentalist type can ever make sure of solid ground under his feet, the latter expressing relation to some definite human purpose" (Peirce, *CP* 5.412). "Pragmatism is the principle that every theoretical judgment expressible in a sentence in the indicative mood is a confused form of thought whose only meaning, if it has any, lies in its tendency to enforce a corresponding practical maxim expressible as a conditional sentence having its apodosis in the imperative mood" (Peirce, *CP* 5.18). Compare formulation of the pragmatic maxims *CP* 5.402.

presupposition (German, *Voraussetzung*)
This concept plays a role in logic and linguistics. It designates a relation between two or more objects or signs (e.g., concepts, assertions). The term is, however, also applied to both the act of presupposition and the object of the presupposition (the presupposed). In semiotics this concept is significant, especially in PRAGMATICS, since in the relation of signs and users of signs certain signs often presuppose other signs which therefore are either released from the sender or, from another quarter, are disclosed by the receiver out of the communication situation, i.e., must be presupposed.

qualisign
First member of the sign in the ground; the physical, visible appearance of that which is interpreted in the sign. "A *Qualisign* is a quality which is a Sign. It cannot actually act as a sign until it is embodied; but the embodiment has nothing to do with its character as a sign" (Peirce, *CP* 2.244).

reafference-principle
A recalling of an IMPULSE for the activation of the EFFECTORS on the RECEPTORS, identified by Erich von Holst and Horst Mittelstaedt in 1950 (that is, after the death of J. von Uexküll), on the basis of neurophysiological investigations.

reality
The question in cognitive theory as to the discernibility of reality has only indirect relations to semiotics. It is discussed there under the concept of REFERENTS, e.g., of the OBJECT ASPECT. At the same time, the different schools take various positions. The more philosophical or scientific schools of semiotics, respectively, give the question of the recognizability of reality a certain importance and resolve it in various ways (compare Peirce, J. von Uexküll). The earlier linguistic beginnings of semiotics confine themselves to the question of recognizability and to the function of signs and regard the cognitive-theoretical questions as irrelevant for semiotics.

receiver (sign recipient; cf. INTERPRETER)
Organism for which a BEHAVIOR is a SIGN.

receptor

As sense organ it answers all effects upon a SUBJECT corresponding to the SPECIFIC ENERGY of the perceptual cells out of which the receptor is erected. It thereby changes parts of the ENVIRONMENT into UMWELT. "The selecting activity of the receptors, which are the gates for the stimuli, plays the leading role" (J. von Uexküll, 1970:61).

redundance (cf. INFORMATION THEORY)

In INFORMATION THEORY, the information content of a MESSAGE is measured, while the average probabilities of the occurrence of SIGNALS of a constant realization in the message are estimated. These probabilities are understood as BINARY steps of selection and the information content can be measured accordingly as the number of necessary steps of selection in "bits" (binary digits). As the average probability of the realization of signals, information is always understood as only a fraction, i.e., as a value less than 1. Redundance is the equivalent of the information contents of a message which is mathematically determined while the information content is subtracted from 1. If the information content means a gauge of "surprise" with which the scarcity of the realization of signals is measured, so does redundance mean a gauge for the opposite of surprise, i.e., the repetition of signals.

relevant, relevance

For the CLASSIFICATION of objects there are DISTINGUISHING FEATURES which, from a certain point of view, are relevant (that is, pertinent) for their relation to different CLASSES. Beyond that there are infinitely many distinguishing features between objects which are not relevant from a certain point of view. The concept of relevance was first introduced by the phonologists of the Prague School along with the distinction between PHONEMES as CLASSES of sounds and such sound variants which are not relevant for the difference between phonemes. Relevance is valid, though, beyond the field of phonology and has proven especially important for SEMANTICS.

representation, representational function

According to Bühler's organon model of language the representation of objects and states of affairs is the most important function of language, which is delimited through the other two functions, that of APPEAL and of EXPRESSION. The representational function distinguishes human language from animal sign systems, which only exercise appeal- [appellative] and expression- [expressive] functions. "The following has as its appropriate goal to delimit the indiscucible *dominance* of the representational function. It is not true that everything for which a sound is a medial phenomenon, a mediator between speaker and hearer, is touched upon by means of the concept 'the things' or through the more adequate defining terms 'objects and states of affairs.' Rather the other position has to be maintained as true: in the structure of the speech situation the sender as effector of the act of speaking, the sender as *subject* of the speech-action, as well as the receiver as appealed to, the receiver as *addressee* of the speech action, have their own proper positions" (Bühler, 1934:30f).

rheme

First member of the sign in the interpretant aspect; a supplemental individual sign which, logically interpreted, is neither true nor false. "A *Rheme* is a Sign which, for its Interpretant, is a Sign of qualitative Possibility, that is, is understood as representing such and such a kind of possible Object. Any Rheme, perhaps, will afford some information; but it is not interpreted as doing so" (Peirce, *CP* 2.250).

rule

According to J. von Uexküll, a rule is an immaterial relative unity = CODE, melody, PLAN to which IMPULSES (SIGNS) are subordinated (see also FACTORS OF NATURE).

selection

Selection is one of two semiotic (and artistic) basic operations and, according to Jakobson, it concerns the PARADIGMATIC aspect of language, e.g., of a SIGN SYSTEM. "A selection between alternatives implies the possibility of substituting one for the other, equivalent to the former in one respect and different from it in another. Actually, selection and substitution are two faces of the same operation" (Jakobson, *S.W.* II, 1971:243). Selection is an operation which is based on the Similarity of elements within a PARADIGM. This selection operation stands in OPPOSITION to the operation of COMBINATION.

semiology, semiological

The expression coined by Saussure for the science of signs. "It is therefore possible to conceive of a science *which studies the role of signs as a part of social life.* It would form part of social psychology, and hence of general psychology. We shall call it *semiology* (from the Greek *semeion,* 'sign'). It would investigate the nature of signs and the laws governing them" (Saussure, *Course in General Linguistics,* p. 15). The concept semiology is already attributed to Saussure in the book which appeared in 1901, *New Classification of the Sciences. Philosophical Study* by Adrien Naville (Dean of the faculty for literature and social sciences at the University of Geneva). Before Saussure, the Swedish linguist Adolf G. Noreen coined the expression "semiology." In GLOSSEMATICS, semiology is a scientific sign structure (metasign) whose "content" (and indeed whose form) exists out of signs.

semiose, semiosis

For Peirce, the triadic relationship of sign members implies a process, the so-called sign process, the semiose. "All dynamical action, or action of brute force, physical or psychical, either takes place between two subjects . . . or at any rate is a resultant of such actions between pairs. But by 'semiosis' I mean, on the contrary, an action, or influence, which is, or involves, a cooperation of *three* subjects, such as a sign, its object, and its interpretant, this tri-relative influence not being in any way resolvable into actions between pairs. Σημειωσιν in Greek of the Roman period, as early as Cicero's time, if I remember rightly, meant the action of almost any kind of sign; and my definition confers on anything that so acts the title of a 'sign' " (Peirce, *CP* 5.484).

According to Peirce, semiose is a continuous sign process that is based on the INTERPRETATION of one sign through another. Jakobson described this process as translation. " . . . the meaning of any linguistic sign is its translation into some further, alternative sign, especially a sign 'in which it is more fully developed,' as Peirce, the deepest inquirer into the essence of signs, insistently stated" (Jakobson, *S.W.* II, 1971:261). Also, semiose is understood in BIOSEMIOTICS as a transfer of SIGNS, e.g., an INTERPRETATION through which signs are replicated and further developed. Examples of such dynamic reproductions extend, for Sebeok, from the genetic CODE through all stages of transmission of information up to human speech, action and thought. The replication of a thought into another thought which translates or interprets the first is, accordingly, analogous with the biological reproduction of the type or of the functional reproduction of the SUBJECT in the OBJECT. A mathematical system of such analogies is developed in René Thom's theory of CATASTROPHES.

semiotic structure (cf. STRUCTURE)

If structure is understood as the NUMBER of relations between the ELEMENTS of a system, a semiotic structure is the number of all relations between SIGNIFIERS and SIGNIFIEDS in a SIGN SYSTEM. A semiotic structure consists of two structures of opposition: of the plane of the signifier on which the signifiers stand in a relation of OPPOSITION to one another, and of the plane of the signified, on which the signifieds stand in a relation to one another.

semiotic theory of cognition

There can be no "reality" independent of thought; a reality for which there are no sign representations is no reality for the human being. Peirce replies to the question of the reality of the mind: "The mind is a sign developing according to the law of inference" (Peirce, *CP* 5.313).

semiotics (semiotic, semeiotic, doctrine of signs)

Greek: *semeiotiké; semeion* = sign. The theory of the signs in general, not only the special semiotics of linguistics, aesthetics, design theory, medicine, zoology. "Logic, in its general sense, is, as I believe I have shown, only another name for *semiotic* (σημεειωτική), the quasi-necessary, or formal, doctrine of signs" (Peirce, *CP* 2.227).

Three scientific branches of semiotics logically result from the introduction of the sign as a triadic relation concerning ground, object, and interpretant: grammatica speculativa, proper or critical logic, and pure rhetoric (compare Peirce, *CP* 2.229).

For Morris, semiotics means semiotic, theory of signs. " . . . linguistic signs sustain three types of relations (to other signs of the language, to objects that are signified, to persons by whom they are used and understood) which define three dimensions of meaning. These dimensions in turn are objects of investigation by SYNTACTICS, SEMANTICS, and PRAGMATICS, semiotic being the general science which includes all of these and their interrelations" (Morris 1937:4). Compare Morris 1938:6ff. = 1972:23ff. "Semiotic, then, is not concerned with the study of a particular kind of object, but with ordinary objects in so far (and only in so far) as they participate in semiosis" (Morris, *Writings on the General Theory of Signs,* p. 20). "The science of signs. Its main subdivisions are SEMANTICS, SYNTACTICS, and PRAGMATICS. Each of these, and so semiotic as a whole, can be *pure, descriptive,* or *applied.* Pure semiotic elaborates a language to talk about signs, descriptive semiotic studies actual signs, and applied semiotic utilizes knowledge about signs for the accomplishment of various purposes" (Morris, *Writings on the General Theory of Signs,* p. 366). Also compare Morris, 1964:1 = 1975:199.

sender

Organism whose BEHAVIOR is a SIGN for another organism.

sense (cf. MEANING)

The distinction between sense and MEANING stems from the philosopher Gottlob Frege

(*On Sense and Reference,* Zsch. f. Philosophy and Philosophical Criticism, 1892). For Frege, the sign has a sense (i.e., an INTERPRETANT; for instance, a signified) and a meaning (i.e., a REFERENT; for instance, an OBJECT ASPECT). In the Saussurian tradition of semiotics the object aspect is therefore ignored because it has the function of SIGNS for its subject. For this tradition Frege's distinction is therefore superfluous. For the Peircean tradition of semiotics the object aspect emerges chiefly in the distinction of ICON, INDEX and SYMBOL. However, the Peircean meaning is rather a question of SEMIOSE, i.e., of the INTERPRETATION of a sign through another sign.

shifters (cf. INDEX, CONTEXT)

According to Jakobson, Message (M) and the one definite message underlying CODE (C) function in a double manner: They can simultaneously be used and be brought into relation one after another. " . . . a message may refer to the code or to another message, and on the other hand, the general meaning of a code unit may imply a reference (*renvoi*) to the code or to the message." (Jakobson, *S.W.* II, 1971:132) For Jakobson, two circular relations (M→M, C→C) and two overlapping relations (M→C, C→M) result from this assumption. The shifters belong to the overlapping relation type: C→M: "Any linguistic code contains a particular class of grammatical units which Jespersen labeled *shifters*: the general meaning of a shifter cannot be defined without a reference to the message. . . . According to Peirce, a symbol . . . is associated with the represented object by a conventional rule, while an index (e.g., the act of pointing) is in existential relation with the object it represents. Shifters combine both functions and belong therefore to the class of *indexical symbols*. . . . The peculiarity of the personal pronoun and other shifters was often believed to consist in the lack of a single, constant, general meaning. . . . For this alleged multiplicity of contextual meanings, shifters in contradistinction to symbols were treated as mere indices (Bühler). Every shifter, however, possesses its own general meaning. Thus *I* means the addresser (and *you*, the addressee) of the message to which it belongs . . . In fact, shifters are distinguished from all other constituents of the linguistic code solely by their compulsory reference to the given message" Jakobson, *S.W.* II, 1971:132).

sign (representamen)

According to Peirce, a sign is something that is determined by an object and at the same time determines an idea in a consciousness. It therefore has a triadic relation to its object and to its interpretant; it *mediates* between an object and a subject, e.g., it *represents* an object to a subject. Something is therefore then a sign when it produces a ground, an object aspect, and an interpretant aspect, i.e., is understood as a trichotomous, ordered relation. "A sign is something which stands to somebody for something in some respect or capacity" (Peirce, *CP* 2.228/2.303). "To exemplify what is meant, the dyadic relations of logical *breadth* and *depth,* often called denotation and connotation, have played a great part in logical discussion, but these take their origin in the triadic relation between a sign, its object, and its interpretant sign" (Peirce, *CP* 3.608). Sign is, in the primary ACTION SITUATION, according to George H. Mead, a perceptual stimulus which points to an impulse-satisfying neutral object. "The most effective characterization of a sign is the following: *S* is the sign of *D* for *I* to the degree that *I* takes account of *D* in virtue of the presence of *S*." (Morris, *Writings on the General Theory of Signs,* p. 19). For Morris, a sign is "roughly: something that directs behavior with respect to something that is not at the moment a stimulus. More accurately: If A is a preparatory-stimulus that, in the absence of stimulus-objects initiating response-sequences of a certain behavior-family, causes in some organism a disposition to respond by response-sequences of this behavior-family, then A is a sign. Anything that meets these conditions is a sign; it is left undecided whether there are signs that do not meet these conditions." (Morris, *Writings on the General Theory of Signs*, p. 366) Morris 1946:2 = 1975:200: see SIGN PROCESS. For Saussure, sign is not used as an inclusive concept for different types of relations between SIGNIFIER and SIGNIFIED, but as the class of ARBITRARY relations. This is in contrast to the class of motivated relations which Saussure calls SYMBOL. "The link between signal and signification is arbitrary. Since we are treating a sign as the combination in which a signal is associated with a signification, we can express this more simply as: *the linguistic sign is arbitrary*. . . . when semiology is established one of the questions that must be asked is whether modes of expression which rely upon signs that are entirely natural (mime, for example) fall within the province of semiology. If they do, the main object of study in semiology will none the less be the class of systems based upon the arbitrary nature of the sign. . . . The word arbitrary . . . must not be taken to imply that a signal depends on the free choice of the speaker.. . . The term implies simply that the signal is *unmotivated*: that is to say arbitrary in relation to its signification, with which it has no natural connexion to reality." (Saussure, *Course in General* Linguistics, pp. 67–69) Originally, Saussure had employed the concepts "conventional symbol," e.g., "independent symbol, instead of sign (Saussure *SM*: 45). He was also later not satisfied with the concept sign because he suspected that this would easily be confused with the mere signifier side of the sign (compare *CLG*: 133). In the "notes item" (N 15.1–19, see particularly 3310.11) he established, for example, the advantages of the concept sem (French *sème*) vis-à-vis that of sign (French *signe*), compare also *SM*: 51.

Jean Piaget (1932, 1945) took up the Saussurian version of the concept of sign, along with the suspected shift to the signifier side, and he defended it in the face of the Peircean terminology (Piaget 1968).

In the sense of Hjelmslev's GLOSSEMATICS, signs are "doubly articulated," interpretable items, i.e., dimensions, which have "expression" (*signifiant*) and "content" (*signifié*), always with different forms (expression form and content form) between which a mutual dependence exists (sign function). In J. von Uexküll's sense, signs originate as sign processes when a MEANING CARRIER enters into a relation with a MEANING UTILIZER. This process is represented with help of the FUNCTIONAL CIRCLE as a cyclic occurrence in which each element points to the other. Signs have a triadic structure, in so far as the meanings of signs which a SUBJECT receives are imprinted by the need that controls the actual functional circle (nourishment, enemy, sex, medium). Signs are subjective events; they indeed signify events in the environment, e.g., talking signs or writing signs signify objects in the environment of the talking or writing person: they express that, but only that, which the designated phenomenon means for the subject receiving the sign. They do not make statements of any sort concerning an objective physical reality independent from the subject. "Helmholtz explained . . . the qualities for signs of an external occurrence which elapses parallels with the change of qualities. This external occurrence remains, though, forever unknown to us. With his famous 'trust and act' as the wisdom of final conclusion, he correctly explained the bankruptcy of physiological psychology." (J. von Uexküll, 1973:8) Signs belong to specific sign systems (e.g., colors to the system of the circle of color) and must be translated into other sign systems. "The stimuli are altogether translated into a language of nervous signs." (*Semiotica* 42–1 (1982) 86) For Sebeok, an item then becomes a sign when it maintains MEANING for a SUBJECT and thereby becomes an OBJECT. This always occurs within a CODE which establishes the connection between the SIGNIFIER and the SIGNIFIED. "A sign, then, by all accounts—from Stoic philosophy to contemporary thinking—is conceived of as constituted of two indispensable halves, one sensible, the other intelligible: the *signifier*, a perceptible impact on at least one of the sense organs of the interpreter; and the content *signified*" (Sebeok, *Contributions to the Doctrine of Signs*, p. 37).

sign in relation to its object (object aspect)

Second correlate of the triadic sign relation for Peirce. The relation of the sign to its object presupposes that the sign itself is introduced as ground (possesses a "ground"). In a sign's relation to its object, the object is designated; the designation of an object constitutes its meaning (in the interpretant aspect). The sign in its relation to its object is divided into a trichotomy: ICON, INDEX and SYMBOL.

sign in itself (ground)

First correlate of the triadic sign relation for Peirce: something becomes a sign by this means: first of all it is explained as pure, sensory ground (then as regards the object and finally as regards the interpretant); the means of the sign constitutes the sign object (which for its part constitutes the sign interpretant). The ground is divided into the trichotomy of QUALI-, SIN- and LEGISIGN.

sign process (semiosis; cf. SEMIOSE)

"Semiosis is accordingly a mediated-taking-account-of. The mediators are *sign vehicles*; the takings-account-of are *interpretants*; the agents of the process are *interpreters*; what is taken account of are *designata*. . . . It should be clear that the terms 'sign', 'designatum', 'interpretant' and 'interpreter' involve one another, since they are simply ways of referring to aspects of the process of semiosis" (Morris, *Writings on the General Theory of Signs*, p. 19). " . . . a process in which something is a sign to some organism" (Morris, 1946:353f. = 1973:421)." " . . . a five-term relation—v,w,x,y,z,—in which v sets up in w the disposition to react in a certain kind of way, x, to a certain kind of object, y (not then acting as a stimulus), under certain conditions, z. The v's, in the cases where this relation obtains, are *signs*, the w's are *interpreters*, the x's are *interpretants*, the y's are *significations*, and the z's are the *contexts* in which the signs occur" (Morris, *Writings on the General Theory of Signs*, pp. 401–402).

sign producer

A SENDER which, at the same time, is RECIPIENT of its own SIGN (cf. GESTURE).

sign recipient. See RECEIVER

sign system (= Code; cf. SIGN, SYSTEM)

When a system generally designates a NUMBER of ELEMENTS together with the number of relations of the elements among themselves, a sign system is thus a number of SIGNS, i.e., unities out of SIGNIFIERS and SIGNIFIEDS and their relations with each other through which the signs first receive their VALUE. A sign can be considered SYNCHRONIC, i.e., as a static simultaneous number of signs, or DIACHRONIC, i.e., with regard to the development phase. For Saussure, language was one among many sign systems.

sign use

"A SIGN S will be said to be *used* with respect to purpose y of an organism z if y is some goal of z and if z produces a sign which serves as a means to the attainment of y." (Morris 1946:92f. = 1973:179) "If→PRAGMATICS is concerned with the origin, uses, and effects of signs, then to speak of the "use" of a sign presupposes that it already has a signification. Hence in this framework 'signification' and 'use' are distinguished" (Morris, *Writings on the General Theory of Signs,* p. 403).

signal

Stimulus that releases a later phase of ACTION in the recipient while pointing to the properties of realization of an impulse-satisfying object. " . . . a SIGN that is not a symbol, that is, not produced by its interpreter and not a substitute for some other sign with which it is synonymous" (Morris, *Writings on the General Theory of Signs,* p. 366). According to Luis J. Prieto (1966), a signal is the realization of one of the objects of the abstract CLASS of a signifier with the express purpose of establishing COMMUNICATION.

signans/signatum (= SIGNIFIER/SIGNIFIED).

Jakobson, going back to the scholastics, frequently employs the Latin designations signans/signatum instead of the expressions signifier/signified proposed by Saussure. " . . . the essential property of any sign in general, and of any linguistic sign in particular, is its twofold character: every linguistic unit is bipartite and involves two aspects—one sensible and the other intelligible—or, in other words, both a *signans* (Saussure's *signifiant*) and a *signatum* (*signifié*). These two constituents of any linguistic sign (and of any sign in general) necessarily presuppose and require each other" (Jakobson, *S.W.* II, 1971:103).

signifiant (French, SIGNIFIER)

signification (compare CONNOTATION)

Indices (INDEX) which are not produced expressly with the purpose of transmitting an indication which, though, nevertheless possess MEANING for an INTERPRETANT, belong to the sphere (of SEMIOLOGY) of signification. In the semiology of signification the processes of meaning are dealt with which, for example, comprise natural SIGNS (e.g., animal prints); on the other hand, how a MESSAGE is realized (CONNOTATION), the question of STYLE (e.g., also of dialect) belongs to the sphere of the semiology of signification. Since there can be no realization of messages or objects without a certain manner, i.e., without style, the semiology of signification is in part identical with the semiology of CONNOTATION.

significatum

In the primary ACTION SITUATION, according to George H. Mead, the number of properties of fulfillment to which a perceptual stimulus points. "Conditions such that whatever meets these conditions is a denotatum of a given sign" (Morris, *Writings on the General Theory of Signs,* p. 366). For Saussure, a liniguistic sign was the unity of sound pattern and concept. He proposed to substitute the expression "concept" with signified: "We propose to keep the term *sign* to designate the whole, but to replace *concept* and *sound pattern* respectively by *signification* and *signal*" (Saussure, *Course in General Linguistics*, p. 67). That Saussure did not see the concept of signified limited to linguistic signs results indirectly from the fact that he expressly mentions visual SIGNIFIERS. In general, a signified is the abstract class of messages, e.g., meanings which can be transmitted into certain CODES, such as LANGUAGE, for example, through signals of different signifiers. One and the same specified can then, therefore, be assembled in different signs with different signifiers, i.e., one and the same meaning can be "expressed" through different signs (compare DESIGNATION, CONCEPT, MEANING).

signifié (French, SIGNIFIED)

signifier
Saussure called the sound pattern which, together with concept, forms a linguistic SIGN, the signifier: "We propose to keep the term *sign* to designate the whole, but to replace *concept* and *sound pattern* respectively by *signification* and *signal*" (Saussure, *Course in General Linguistics*, p. 67; Harris trans.). That Saussure saw the concept of the signifier not limited to language issues from the following remark: "Unlike visual signals (e.g. ships' flags) which can exploit more than one dimension simultaneously, auditory signals have available to them only the linearity of time . . ." (Saussure, *Course in General Linguistics*, p. 70). In general, a signifier is the abstract class of variants of SIGNALS with the same SIGNIFIED and as such is a special case of OPERANT. The relation of signifier and signified is in certain CODES, e.g., language, assymetrical: while the same signified always corresponds to the signifier of a sign, one and the same signified can correspond to different signifiers, i.e., the same MEANING can be "expressed" through different signs.

similarity
According to Jakobson, similarity is not only the principle that a sign makes an ICON in its relation between SIGNIFIER and SIGNIFIED. Similarity, in all of its forms, from the approach to identity (as with SYNONYMS) to the relation of ANTONYMS, from resemblance to analogy, from METALANGUAGE to Metaphor, from equivalence to contrast, from translating to translation, is the criterion of a similarity NUMBER which the operation of SELECTION makes possible. An important type of similarity number is the PARADIGM.

sinsign
Second member of the sign in the ground; the solitary, original state or form of that which is interpreted as the sign. "A *Sinsign* (where the syllable 'sin' is taken as meaning 'being only once,' as in *single, simple*, Latin *semel*, etc. is an actual existent thing or event which is a sign. It can only be so through its qualities; so that it involves a qualisign, or rather, several qualisigns. But these qualisigns are of a peculiar kind and only form a sign through being actually embodied" (Peirce, *CP* 2.245).

sound pattern (cf. SIGNIFIER)
The perceived sound pattern which, together with a CONCEPT, forms a linguistic SIGN.

sound substance (cf. SUBSTANCE)

Saussure considers the SIGN, as a unity of SIGNIFIER (SOUND PATTERN) and SIGNIFIED (CONCEPT), to be a form and not a substance: "Linguistics, then, operates along this margin, where sound and thought meet. *The contact between them gives rise to a form, not a substance*" (Saussure, *Course in General Linguistics*, p. 111). Hjelmselv made this concept more precise by dividing not only the CONTENT but also the EXPRESSION Plane into FORM and (formed) SUBSTANCE. The concept of substance is not identical with the material base, though, for Hjelmslev. Therefore the sound substance is understood as a variable manifestation of forms, e.g., speech and music, which were imprinted by the unformed material of the sound.

speaking

Speech Activity Speech

specific energy

Concept coined by Johannes Müller (German physiologist, 1801–1858, teacher of Hermann von Helmholtz) for the characteristic reaction to arbitrary impulses for every living unity; also designated as totality or life energy. Basis of the AUTONOMY of living creatures.

speech (= Speech Activity; cf. SPEAKING)

For Saussure, the term *speech* ("*parole*"), in contrast to Linguistic Pattern ("*langue*" = language as SYSTEM), refers to the process or the activity of speech through which the signs and rules deposited in the language system are realized. "The study of language thus comprises two parts. The essential part takes for its object the language itself, which is social in its essence and independent of the individual. This is a purely psychological study. The subsidiary part takes as its object of study the individual part of language, which means speech, including phonation. This is a psychophysical study. These two objects of study are doubtless closely linked and each presupposes the other. A language is necessary in order that speech should be intelligible and produce all its effects. But speech also is necessary in order that a language may be established. Historically, speech always takes precedence. How would we ever come to associate an idea with a verbal sound pattern, if we did not first of all grasp this association in an act of speech? Furthermore, it is by listening to others that we learn our native language. . . . Finally, it is speech which causes a language to evolve. The impressions received from listening to others modify our own linguistic habits. Thus there is an interdependence between the language itself and speech. The former is at the same time the instrument and the product of the latter" (Saussure, *Course in General Linguistics*, p. 19).

stimulus

Influence of the ENVIRONMENT on the RECEPTORS; corresponds to the MEANING CARRIER which must be associated with a certain part in the organism as MEANING UTILIZER so that it can be answered as stimulus. "Every component of an organic or inorganic object (or reaction) becomes, as soon as it appears in the role of a meaning carrier on the stage of life in an animal subject with, let us say, a 'complement' connected to the body of the subject, that which serves as meaning utilizer" (J. von Uexküll 1970:111).

structuralism

The concept of structuralism is often used in order to designate the structural linguistics proceeding from Saussure. It is a question of the concept of language as semiotic STRUCTURE which is based on structures of opposition. This concept of structuralism must be distinguished from that which designates an analysis of human scientific problems oriented toward structural linguistics, such as that which has been pursued in France since 1960. This second type of structuralism, in particular, led therefore to problematic results because its supporters frequently found no distinction between COMMUNICATION and SIGNIFICATION.

structure

The NUMBER of relations between the ELEMENTS of a SYSTEM (and the number of all ISOMORPHIC TRANSFORMATIONS of these relations) is called the structure of the system.

style (compare CONNOTATION)

Style designates, in contrast to the judgement concerning it (which object or which message should be realized as opposed to other objects or messages), a decision regarding the manner in which an object or a message should be realized. The latter decision is inevitable if the former has occurred (but not vice-versa): There is no realization without "style." But the question of style cannot be asked without a judgement first being passed concerning which object or message should be realized. This first decision is DENOTATIVE, while style is a question of CONNOTATION.

subcode (= special code; compare CODE)

Codes are often erected out of relatively independent subcodes. "Language is a SYSTEM of systems, an overall code which comprises various subcodes. These diverse linguistic styles do not form a random, mechanical accumulation, but a legitimate hierarchy of special codes." (Jakobson, *S.W.* II, 1971:275) In LINGUISTICS dialects, for example, are considered as subcodes. A subcode, generally and semiotically, is the result of a STYLE, i.e., a CONNOTATIVE function. This function plays a decisive role in the constant change and renewal of a code. "The variety of functional, mutually convertible subcodes requires a careful and consistent structural analysis. Such an analysis makes possible a synchronic study of the phonemic and grammatical changes in progress, which initially present a necessary coexistence of the older and newer form in two related subcodes. . . . On the other hand, the inquiry into the system of subcodes encompasses the various forms of interdialectal and even interlingual code switching and thus establishes an intimate bond between the description of an individual or local dialect and the vast horizons of linguistic geography" (Jakobson, *S.W.* II, 1971:283).

subject

Center of an UMWELT which the subject, as a receiver of signs, erects out of the received signs that are interpreted according to a species-specific CODE. On the level of plant life the subject is the center of a DWELLING-envelope. In the terminology of UMWELT theory, the subject is a factor of nature which biology, as understood by J. von Uexküll, separates from positivistic physiology since cells are already AUTONOMOUS subjects. "The subject is the new factor of nature which Biology introduces in Natural Science" (*Semiotica* 1982).

For Sebeok, the subject is the self as SIGN, i.e., as a relatively stable variation of the theme SEMIOSE. The relative stability is maintained by the genetic CODE and the

IMMUNE system informed by it in a dynamic way. In the case of such organisms, especially vertebrate animals, the system of the anxiety signal appears for that purpose as complementary maintenance system of self. "There are at least two apprehensions of the Self: (a) *immunologic,* or biochemical, with semiotic overtones; and (b) semiotic, or social, with biological anchoring. . . . Communicational errors occur in both processes, and may have devastating effects upon the Self" (Sebeok 1979b:267).

substance
In GLOSSEMATICS, the variable or neutrally conceived manifestation of the form as opposed to the form.

symbol
For Peirce, the third member of the sign in the object aspect; a sign which neither delineates nor indicates its object but is composed independently of the object; it represents the object voluntarily and thus underlies the usage. Since it is indebted to free composition it is considered as "genuine" sign (compare DEGENERATE SIGNS). "A *Symbol* is a sign which refers to the Object that it denotes by virtue of a law, usually an association of general ideas, which operates to cause the Symbol to be interpreted as referring to that Object. It is thus a general type or law, that is a Legisign. As such it acts through a Replica. Not only is it general itself, but the Object to which it refers is of a general nature." (Peirce, *CP* 2.249) For the universality of the sign as symbol compare UNIVERSAL CATEGORIES (the sign as categorical "third").

For Morris, a symbol is a CHARACTERIZING SIGN, but also "a SIGN that is produced by its Interpreter and that acts as a substitute for some other sign with which it is synonymous; all signs not symbols are signals" (Morris, *Writings on the General Theory of Signs,* p. 367).

For Saussure, the concept symbol is employed in contrast to the concept→Sign. While the sign represents an ARBITRARY connection between SIGNIFIER and SIGNIFIED, this connection in symbol is MOTIVATED. "The word *symbol* is sometimes used to designate the linguistic sign, or more exactly that part of the linguistic sign which we are calling the signal. This use of the word *symbol* is awkward, for reasons connected with our first principle. For it is characteristic of symbols that they are never entirely arbitrary. They are not empty configurations. They show at least a vestige of natural connexion between the signal and its signification. For instance, our symbol of justice, the scales, could hardly be replaced by a chariot" (Saussure, *Course in General Linguistics,* p. 68).

Jean Piaget (1932, 1945) took up the Saussurian version of the concept of symbol in connection with the Freudian concept (also compare Piaget 1968). In Hjelmslev's GLOSSEMATICS a symbol is an interpretable neutral object to which a substance of content, but none from the form of expression (as distinguished from a form of content), can certainly be attached; it is consequently not "double-structured" and hence not a "sign" in the sense of glossematics: "interpretable non-semiotic entities" (Hjelmslev 1943/63: 114).

For Sebeok, a symbol is a SIGN which simply points to a conventional relation between designating and designated and which occupies an INTENSIONAL class for its designatum. "For our present purposes, an intensionally defined class is one defined by the use of a propositional function; the denotata of the designation are defined in terms of properties shared by all, and only by, the members of that class (whether these properties are known or not . . ." (Sebeok, *Contributions to the Doctrine of Signs*, p. 134). For Sebeok, the capacity to symbolize is consequently based on the power to form intensional class concepts, i.e., universals. Although the human being is designated as *animal symbolicum,* according to Sebeok, the animal kingdom is a complete symbol system. "The fondly cherished mythic characterization of man, adhered to by E. Cassirer's epigones and many others, as a unique *animal symbolicum* can be sustained only if the definition of 'symbol' is impermissibly ensnared with the concept of natural language, which G. G. Simpson quite aptly characterized as 'the most diagnostic single trait of man.' By every other definition—invoking the principle of arbitrariness, the idea of a conventional link between signifier and its denotata, Peirce's 'imputed character', or the notion of an intensional class for the designatum— animals demonstrably employ symbols." (Sebeok, *Contributions to the Doctrine of Signs*, p. 89). In a very broad application of the concept of symbol Sebeok sees, finally, the organism as organ of symbolization in agreement with the motto: "Life is a sign's way of making another sign." Since Sebeok's definition for "symbol" in this sense finds application to the sign as a criteriological property of life, in life as SEMIOSE it is finally a question of symbolic constructions through which the SUBJECT and OBJECT are joined in a first impoverished and then genetically written CODE.

symbol field

For Bühler the concept of the symbol field denotes the framework constituted by the semantic, syntactic, and environing context of a sentence (or of some other linguistic or non-linguistic sign) that determines the meaning of a sign as a representational device. The symbol field presupposes the INDEX FIELD: "The linguistic *symbol field* in the structurally articulated language work furnishes a second class of means, collected under the name of *context,* for facilitating construal or understanding; situation and context, therefore, are, roughly put, the two sources from which in every case the precise interpretation of linguistic utterances is nourished" (Bühler, 1934:149).

synchrony, synchronic

The concept synchrony was proposed by Saussure in contrast to DIACHRONY in order to characterize the simultaneous existence of a number of linguistic data which constitute a state of LANGUAGE as SYSTEM. "Everything is synchronic which relates to the static aspect of our science, and diachronic everything which concerns evolution. Likewise *synchrony* and *diachrony* will designate respectively a linguistic state and a phase of evolution" (Saussure, *Course in General Linguistics,* p. 81).

synonym, synonymy

Synonymy designates a relation of IDENTITY of two signs on the CONTENT plane. It can be determined through a Commutation Test: When, for instance, a word in a Context can be substituted by another without the MEANING of the context changing, so are both words synonyms in so far as they belong to the same language. Synonyms are therefore SEMANTICALLY similar words of the same CODE. If semantically similar words belong to different codes, then they are designated as HETERONYMS.

syntactic structure (cf. SYNTAX, STRUCTURE)

The SIGNIFIERS of different sign systems can only be put into COMBINATION according to rules which are combined in a syntax for every one of these sign systems. The number of all regular relations which the signifiers of a sign system can enter into with one another forms the syntactic structure of this sign system. The different possibilities of combination of this syntactic structure have, in turn, SEMANTIC implications.

syntactics

"Since most SIGNS are clearly related to other signs, since many apparent cases of isolated signs prove on analysis not to be such, and since all signs are potentially if not actually related to other signs, it is well to make a third dimension of semiosis co-ordinate with the other two which have been mentioned. This third dimension will be called the *syntactical dimension of semiosis,* symbolized by 'D_{syn}', and the study of this dimension will be named *syntactics*" (Morris, *Writings on the General Theory of Signs,* p. 22). " . . . that branch of Semiotic that studies the way in which signs of various classes are combined to form compound signs. It abstracts from the signification of the signs it studies and from their uses and effects; hence, it is distinguished from SEMANTICS and PRAGMATICS" (Morris, *Writings on the General Theory of Signs,* p. 367). The syntactics of a natural language contain its syntax as a section.

syntagm, syntagmatic

A syntagm consists of a combination (e.g., composition) of elements in a sequence (e.g., language) or on a plane surface, e.g., in space. Its combination results on the basis of a selection. The elements of a syntagm always stand in a mutual relationship of dependence. Every syntagm finds, for its part, a place in a superposed unity. A syntagmatic analysis is then concluded when a unity is no longer divisible into subordinated syntagms. This unity is then an element of a PARADIGM. Saussure compared the syntagmatic linear combination of language with the vertical structure of a building. "Considered from these two points of view, a linguistic unit may be compared to a single part of a building, e.g., a column. A column is related in a certain way to the architrave it supports. This disposition involving two units co-present in space, is comparable to a syntagmatic relation" (Saussure, *Course in General Linguistics,* p. 122).

syntax, syntactic

In semiotics (as in linguistics) syntax and SEMANTICS form the components of grammar. There is a distinction between formal syntax, which can be developed out of purely formal elements without reference to semantics, and conceptual syntax in which syntactic relations themselves possess meaning.

system

System is designated (in system theory) as a GROUP of ELEMENTS together with the group of relations between these elements.

theory of communication

The modern communication science developed in connection with INFORMATION THEORY. Yet problems of COMMUNICATION must be separated from those of information. "It is a question here of the first order regarding the differentiation of two classes of signs—of Indices and Symbols, as Peirce calls them. Indices, such as the physicist of the external world gathers, are not convertible, and he transforms these nature-given indices into a particular system of scientific symbols. In linguistics [and in communication science in general, M. K.], the situation is entirely different. Symbols exist directly in the Language [and in the general sign system, M. K.]. Instead of the scholar who extracts certain indices from the external world and reconstructs them in symbols, an exchange of symbols takes place between the parties concerned with the communication. The role of sender and receiver is interchangeable here. For that reason, the task of linguistics [and of communication science in general, M. K.] is also entirely different. We simply seek to translate this code which is given objectively in the community of speech into a METALANGUAGE. Symbols are for the natural scientist a scientific tool, while for the linguist they are above all the true objects of his research (Jakobson, *S.W.* II, 1971:276). Jakobson regarded linguistics as part of a general communication science: "Three integrated sciences encompass each other and present three gradually increasing degrees of generality: (1) Study in communication of verbal messages = linguistics; (2) study in communication of any messages = semiotic (communication of verbal messages implied); (3) study in communication = social anthropology jointly with economics (communication of messages implied)" (Jakobson, *S.W.* II, 1971:666).

tool (French, *utile*)

A tool, according to Luis J. Prieto, is the realization of one of the assigned objects of the abstract CLASS of an OPERANT which serves the purpose of accomplishing an OPERATION.

transformation

Generally, the operation of transformation refers to the correlation (i.e., the production of a relation) between two or more semiotic objects. Such transformations can be produced between semiotic objects (e.g., different texts) or within such an object. In the latter case, one distinguishes between transformations on the level of depth structures (horizontal) and those which can be determined between depth and surface structures (vertical). V. J. Propp's rules concerning the relations between Russian fairy tales offer an example for transformations between texts. Vertical transformations result, for example, between the active and passive form of the same sentence in the generative grammar of Noam Chomsky.

trichotomy of signs

Classification of every correlate of the triadic relation of signs into three members: the trichotomy QUALI-, SIN-, and LEGISIGN belongs to the ground; the trichotomy ICON, INDEX and SYMBOL belongs to the object aspect; the trichotomy RHEME, DICISIGN and ARGUMENT belongs to the interpretant aspect (compare Peirce, *CP* 2.43). With the help of trichotomies a classification of signs is reached (cf. Classes of signs). "The three trichotomies of sign result together in dividing signs into *ten classes of signs* . . . " (Peirce, *CP* 2.54). The trichotomies are established with the table of categories (see UNIVERSAL CATEGORIES)

umwelt, umwelts (subjective universe, phenomenal world, self-world)

The umwelt of a SUBJECT is the part of the ENVIRONMENT of a subject that it "selects" with its species-specific sense organs according to its organization and its biological needs (hunger, locomotion, sexual instinct, etc. corresponding to the FUNCTIONAL circles) and equipped with its subjective PERCEPTUAL and EFFECTOR CUES (*Semiotica*

42–1 (1982), 87). "Every subject is the constructor of its Umwelt" (J. von Uexküll 1980:335).

universal categories

According to Peirce, universal categories are the categories of "firstness," "second-ness," and "thirdness," whereby "firstness" is understood as of a one digit, "second-ness" as of a two digit and "thirdness" as of a three digit relation. The relational interpretation of categories demonstrates that there must be at least three relations different from one another, but that all other plural relations can be traced back to these three (= categorical totality and irreducibility) (cf. *CP* 1.54ff./1.568f.). "First-ness is the mode of being of that which is such as it is, positively and without reference to anything else. Secondness is the mode of being of that which such as it is, with respect to a second but regardless of any third. Thirdness is the mode of being of that which is such as it is, in bringing a second and third into relation to each other. I call these three ideas the cenopythagorean categories" (Peirce, *CP* 8.328).

utility (cf. INSTRUMENT)

Utility is, according to Luis J. Prieto (1973, 1975a), an abstract class of definite OPERATIONS which can be performed through (different) tools. The SIGNIFIED is, as an abstract class of definite MEANINGS, e.g., MESSAGES which can be transferred through (different) signals, a special case of utility. One and the same utility can be constructed with different OPERANTS by different INSTRUMENTS, while this same utility always corresponds to an operant in a definite instrument. Therefore the relationship of utility and operant is asymmetrical.

value (French, *valeur*)

Value designates, for Saussure, the "place value" of an object in a (CLASSIFICATION) SYSTEM. The membership of an object in a CLASS, which is determined through classification on the basis of RELEVANT DISTINGUISHING FEATURES, constitutes the IDEN-TITY of this object. The difference between value and MEANING exists in the fact that a SIGN, on the one hand, is determined through its place value in a system and on the other hand, possesses its meaning in the form of a concept (signified) which is linked with the signifier in the unity of the sign: "On the one hand, the concept appears to be just the counterpart of a sound pattern, as one constituent part of a linguistic sign. On the other hand, this linguistic sign itself, as the link uniting the two constituent elements, likewise has counterparts. These are the other signs in the language" (Saus-sure, *Course in General Linguistics,* p. 113).

vaudeville

Originally (15th century), vaudeville was a designation for satirical songs from the Norman region Vaux-de-Vire. Later the word become a general one for folk songs and couplets (18th century). Finally, an entire genre was given the name: a half-musical farce which was considered as forerunner of the comic opera in France. According to Eco, the silent film resembles vaudeville, the talking film resembles opera.

Young Grammarians

General linguistics was, for a long time, defined by the question of the historical source relations of languages with each other. Relationships between older and younger languages were described through sound shifts and meaning changes. Primitive languages were reconstructed in a similar way. The origin of such historical changes was understood as organic growth, e.g., deterioration. In the 1870s a group of, at that time, young linguists attacked this interpretation. These so-called young grammarians postulated the existence of phonetic laws which had to be observed also directly in living languages and which represented the source of all linguistic changes. The positivist view of SPEECH ACTIVITY left open the question of LANGUAGE as a whole. Saussure, in contrast to the young grammarians, devoted himself particularly to this question.

zoosemiotics

According to Sebeok, zoosemiotics is the theory and investigation of that part of BIOSEMIOTICS which the human and animal communication and information systems hold in common. The concept of ritualization and that of morphology (see CATAS-TROPHE), above all, belong to it. " . . . the connection first made explicit in 1963, summed up by yet another coinage, *zoosemiotics,* intended as a mediating concept for reconciling these two seemingly antithetical spheres of discourse, ethology and semiotics: the former, anchored in the realm of Nature, embracing the totality of the multifarious phenomena of animal behavior . . . the second, rooted in the matrix of Culture, traditionally held by many to comprise exclusively man's signifying competence" (Sebeok, 1979:82). Since the kingdom of the animal planes of meaning is still to a great extent unresearched, Sebeok proposes a heuristic tactic: to consider all semiotic systems as zoosemiotic until the converse can be proven.

REFERENCES

Jakobson, Roman. "Qu'est-ce que la poésie?" In Jakobson, Roman. *Questions de Poétique.* Paris: Editions du Seuil, 1973, pp. 113–126.
Jakobson, Roman. *Selected Writings,* III. The Hague: Mouton, 1981.
Morris, Charles. *Signification and Significance.* Cambridge, Mass: MIT Press, 1964.
Morris, Charles. *Writings on the General Theory of Signs.* The Hague: Mouton, 1971.
Prieto, Luis. *Pertinence et Pratique.* Paris: Les Editions Minuit, 1975.
Saussure, Ferdinand de. *Course in General Linguistics.* Trans. and annot. by Roy Harris. Eds. Charles Bally and Albert Sechehaye. London: Gerald Duckworth, 1983.
Sebeok, Thomas. *Contributions to the Doctrine of Signs.* Bloomington, IN: Indiana University Publications, 1976.
Semiotica 42-1 (1982); Glossary by Thure von Uexküll, pp. 83–87.
von Uexküll, Jakob. *Streifzüge durch die Umwelten von Tieren und Menschen.* Frankfurt: Fischer Verlag, 1970.
Wells, Rulon. "Criteria for Semiosis." In Sebeok, Thomas A. *Perfusion of Signs.* Bloomington, IN: Indiana University Press, 1977.

Author Index

259

Subject Index